Dr Russell Rees

CCEA A2
PARTITION OF IRELAND 1900-25

COLOURPOINT
EDUCATIONAL

© Dr Russell Rees and Colourpoint Creative Ltd, 2022

Print ISBN: 978 1 78073 200 8
eBook ISBN: 978 1 78073 350 0

This text is a revised edition of *Ireland 1900–25*, R Rees, Colourpoint, 2008.

First Edition
Second Impression 2024

Layout and design: April Sky Design
Printed by GPS Colour Graphics Ltd, Belfast

All rights reserved. No part of this publication may be reproduced, stored in a retrieval system or transmitted in any form or by any means, electronic, mechanical, photocopying, scanning, recording or otherwise, without the prior written permission of the copyright owners and publisher of this book.

Colourpoint Educational
An imprint of Colourpoint Creative Ltd
Colourpoint House
Jubilee Business Park
21 Jubilee Road
Newtownards
County Down
Northern Ireland
BT23 4YH

Tel: 028 9182 0505
E-mail: sales@colourpoint.co.uk
Web site: www.colourpointeducational.com

Russell Rees completed a doctoral thesis in Irish History at the University of Ulster in 1986. He spent the next 30 years teaching History at Omagh Academy. Among the books he has written are *Ireland 1900–25* (2008), *Ireland Under the Union 1800–1900* (2018), both of which were published by Colourpoint, and *Labour and the Northern Ireland Problem 1945–51: The Missed Opportunity* (2009).

This book has been written to help students preparing for the A2 History specification from CCEA. While Colourpoint Educational and the authors have taken every care in its production, we are not able to guarantee that the book is completely error-free. Additionally, while the book has been written to closely match the CCEA specification, it is the responsibility of each candidate to satisfy themselves that they have fully met the requirements of the CCEA specification prior to sitting an exam set by that body. For this reason, and because specifications change with time, we strongly advise every candidate to avail of a qualified teacher and to check the contents of the most recent specification for themselves prior to the exam. Colourpoint Creative Ltd therefore cannot be held responsible for any errors or omissions in this book or any consequences thereof.

For my father, Bob Rees

Contents

Chapter 1	**Ireland 1900–1910**	**1**
	Introduction	1
	Ireland 1900–1910	4
	The state of Irish Nationalism	5
	The state of Irish Unionism	23
	The Irish Question in British Politics	37
	Conclusion	46
	Historiography	48
Chapter 2	**The Ulster Crisis, 1911–14**	**57**
	Motives and methods	57
	The Third Home Rule Bill	65
	Ulster resistance	71
	The search for a solution	76
	The crisis deepens	86
	Conclusion	96
	Historiography	97
Chapter 3	**The Path to Separation, 1914–18**	**109**
	Ireland and World War 1	109
	The causes of the rising	117
	Insurrection	126
	Executions and martial law	132
	The 1916 Lloyd George negotiations	136
	Sinn Féin gains momentum	142
	The Irish Convention	149
	Sinn Féin triumphant	153
	Conclusion	159
	Historiography	161

Chapter 4	**The Emergence of the Irish Free State, 1919–25**	**172**
	The War of Independence	173
	1920 – year of terror	182
	Towards the truce	194
	The Anglo-Irish Treaty	203
	The negotiations	212
	Reaction to the Treaty in Britain and Ireland	221
	The Civil War and its aftermath	227
	Conventions and conflict	231
	State-building	248
	Conclusion	254
	Historiography	257
Chapter 5	**Northern Ireland and its Problems, 1920–25**	**272**
	The road to partition	272
	The Government of Ireland Act	278
	The challenges facing the Northern Ireland government, 1921–25	284
	Conclusion	299
	Historiography	302
Conclusion		**310**
Index		**314**
	Index of People	314
	Index of Historians	318
	General Index	320

Acknowledgements

I have incurred a number of debts in writing this book. The staff of Colourpoint Books have been supportive and patient in bringing the project to a successful conclusion. My editor, Deirdre O'Neill, proved to be thorough and painstaking in completing her work. My indexer, Jane Rogers, completed her work in a timely fashion. My greatest debt at Colourpoint is to Dr Wesley Johnston, one of the company's managing directors, with whom I have worked for many years.

For a very long period I have been inspired by the work of four eminent historians. Dr Eamon Phoenix remains the foremost authority on northern Nationalism and I have enjoyed many occasions listening to his take on events surrounding partition. Professor Paul Bew has been supportive in the past and his historical insights distinguish him as one of Ireland's leading historians over the past four decades. Professor Alvin Jackson is a brilliant writer whose understanding of Irish Unionism sets him apart from others working in the field of modern Irish history. I would also like to record my thanks to the late Professor Tony Hepburn, who supervised my doctoral thesis and collaborated in my earlier publications.

I am indebted to Dr Claire Allen and Dr Gordon Rees who took the time to read early drafts of some of the content. Mr. Wilbert McIlmoyle generously gave of his time to work on some of the maps and images used in the book.

Finally, my greatest debt is to Jean, my wife, who typed the entire manuscript. Without her love and support over more than 40 years none of this would be possible.

Russell Rees
October 2022

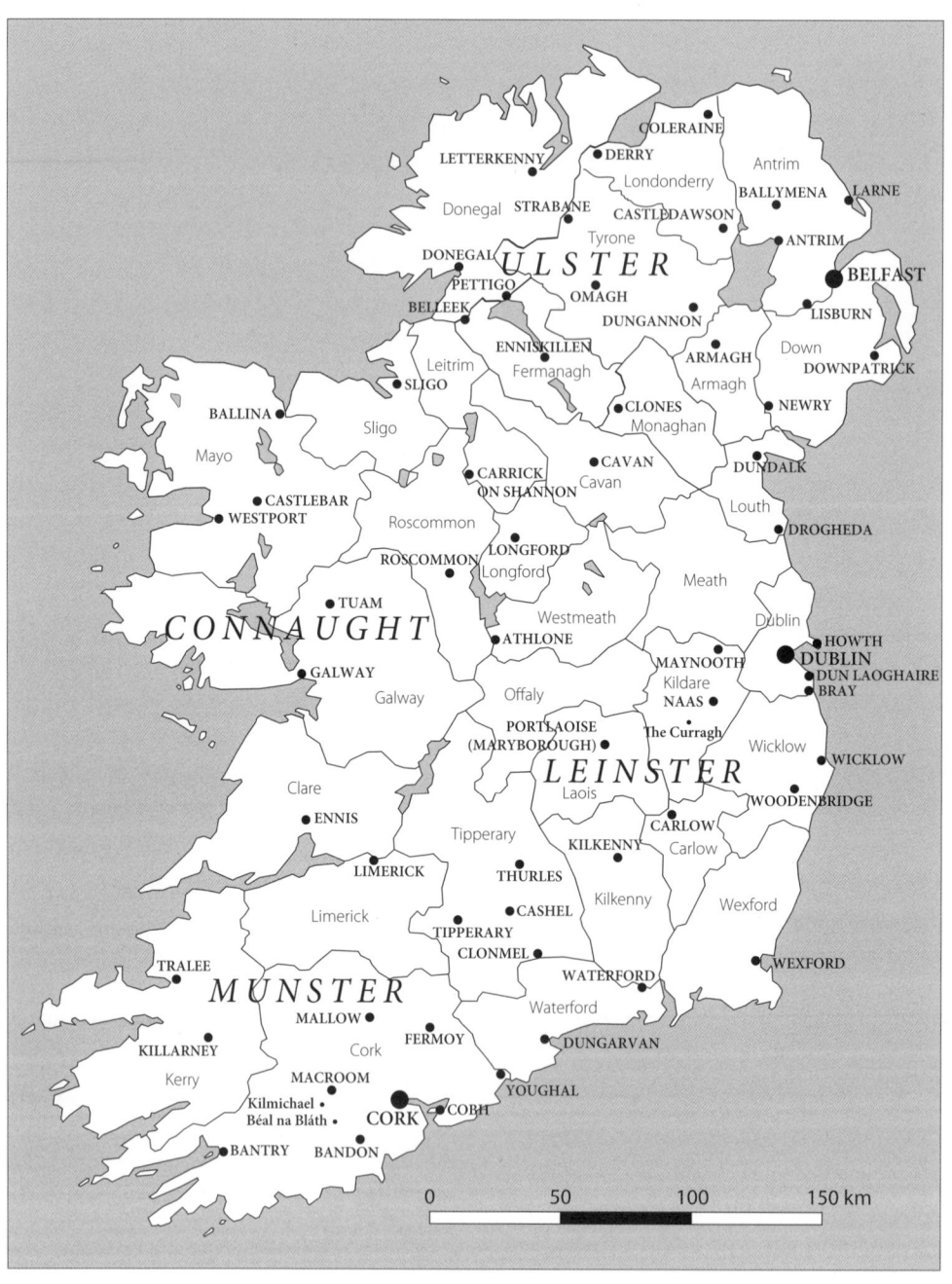

Ireland

Chapter 1
Ireland 1900–1910

Introduction

On 17 December 1885, William Ewart Gladstone, the great reforming Liberal leader, made an announcement to the press in which he declared that he was ready to accept Home Rule for Ireland. This bombshell forced the Irish question to the top of the political agenda at Westminster. Gladstone's conversion was viewed as a personal triumph for Charles Stewart Parnell, the Irish Nationalist leader, who had directed the campaign for Home Rule in Ireland and at Westminster. Under Parnell's leadership, the Nationalists had built a united, disciplined political force in the House of Commons, that was supported in Ireland by the massed ranks of the tenant farming class. Parnell had also taken time to cultivate support among Irish communities living in England and Scotland. Gladstone had been a close observer of this development. Following the 1885 general election, Parnell's Irish Parliamentary Party (IPP) held the balance of power with its 86 seats. This gave the IPP the power to make or break a government, another development that caught Gladstone's attention. Parnell had also grasped the importance of balancing the type of militant rhetoric and action required to mobilise support in Ireland with the more moderate and subtle approach necessary to influence public opinion in Britain. This was a tactic that was subsequently copied by the Unionist leader, Sir Edward Carson, in the period immediately before World War I.

The Liberal Party's support for Irish Home Rule was countered by the Conservative Party's determined defence of the Union. Thus, around the turn of the century, the Irish question emerged as one of the great issues dividing the two main parties at Westminster. The Liberals' endorsement of Home Rule coincided with the formation of the Irish Unionist Party. Its electoral strength rested primarily in Ulster, where it was closely linked in these early years to the Orange Order, the Church of Ireland and the former Irish Tory Party. These Unionists believed that Ireland's present and future prosperity depended on the maintenance of the Union.

Electoral reform in 1884–5 provided the backdrop for the emergence of more modern and representative Unionist and Nationalist parties. Parnell had risen to prominence as one of a handful of "obstructionist" Nationalist MPs who incurred the wrath of fellow MPs by holding up parliamentary business. The objective was to force the House of Commons to consider Irish Home Rule. This raised his profile in Ireland, but it was his involvement in agrarian agitation that elevated Parnell to the leadership of the IPP.

In late 1879, Parnell accepted an invitation to become president of the Land League, the radical agrarian body that fronted the campaign for peasant proprietorship. With generous financial support from the Irish diaspora, particularly in the United States, the organisation spread quickly across the country from its County Mayo base. While its network of branches failed to extend into North-East Ulster, the Land League proved very successful in forcing rent reductions and restricting evictions in many parts of the country. The institution of landlordism was effectively undermined by the movement's actions, as successive Westminster governments responded to the agitation by paving the way for the tenant farmers to become owners of their holdings. Indeed, such was the intensity of this agrarian struggle that it was commonly known as the Land War, as the forces of the state found themselves battling with the Land League for control over much of rural Ireland. While the Land League withheld official backing for the violence that was increasingly deployed to enforce the movement's wishes, the level of agrarian crime threatened to overwhelm the civil authority. The agitation was brought to a close by a combination of government concessions and Parnell's decision to adopt a new strategy in 1882. Yet the 1879–82 campaign marked only the first phase of a prolonged period of agrarian strife that would recur intermittently until the early years of the twentieth century.

The Land League had mobilised the tenant farming class in the struggle against Irish landlordism, and Parnell recognised that this development could have a significant bearing on the campaign for Irish Home Rule. In effect, the land and the national questions overlapped. Under his leadership, the social and economic objectives of the Land League were harnessed to the political demand for Home Rule. In mid-1882, Parnell took the necessary steps to wind down the agrarian agitation to focus on the demand for Home Rule, a campaign that would be pursued by exclusively constitutional means. The Land League was replaced by the Irish National League, a body that was more political in character. While it expanded upon the work begun by the Land League, the Irish National League was a much more centralised organisation that was firmly under Parnell's control. It quickly swallowed the Land League's structures and soon had branches all over the country. The National League was at the forefront of the campaign for self-government, highlighting the mantra that only an Irish parliament could resolve Irish problems. It was also active at local level, where the selection of parliamentary candidates became one of its primary functions. The efforts of the National League ensured that the demand for Home Rule dominated the political discourse in Ireland, while Parnell's stature as leader of the IPP, together with his carefully crafted ambiguous rhetoric, attracted a broad range of Nationalist support. Gladstone was confident that he could deal with Parnell, and he introduced his first Home Rule Bill in 1886. However, the Liberal prime minister failed to gain the unanimous approval of his own backbenchers, and the bill was rejected on its second reading in the House of Commons. A second attempt to pass a Home Rule Bill followed in 1893, and it secured a majority in the Commons before being overwhelmingly defeated in the House of Lords. The ageing Liberal leader subsequently resigned. Although Gladstone had failed to deliver Home Rule, an informal alliance had been established with Parnell and his successors, which meant that the issue was likely to be revisited by the Liberals at some point in the future.

Following the defeat of the first Home Rule Bill, Parnell largely withdrew from public life. The primary reason for this was that he had previously begun a relationship with Katherine O'Shea, the wife of an Irish Nationalist MP. Consequently, Parnell spent much of his time in England living with Mrs O'Shea. The liaison was hidden from the public, but this changed dramatically in December 1889, when Parnell was named as co-respondent in divorce proceedings initiated by Mrs O'Shea's husband, Captain William O'Shea. The negative publicity surrounding the divorce case destroyed Parnell's career, and he lost the leadership following a vote by his Irish MPs in December 1890. Parnell did not yield without a fight, and a minority of the party remained fiercely loyal to the deposed leader. Within a year, however, and less than four months after his marriage to Katherine, Parnell died at the age of 45 following an exhausting by-election campaign in Ireland. The subsequent Parnellite split sapped much of the IPP's energy during the 1890s, a period that was dominated by bitter divisions over party strategy. There were also predictable accusations of betrayal made against those who had ousted Parnell. In spite of the stigma around divorce in the late Victorian era, Parnell's reputation did not suffer after his death. While his achievements were highlighted, his failures were largely ignored. In truth, Parnell's refusal to endorse the Plan of Campaign that ran from 1886–90 distanced him from senior figures in the IPP. The Plan was yet another phase of the agrarian struggle that had been prompted by a sharp fall in agricultural prices. Individual landlords were targeted in the south and west of the country, but the Plan failed to repeat the success of the Land League as Parnell remained aloof from the agitation. By this stage Home Rule was Parnell's clear priority, and he believed that violence in rural Ireland only damaged his cause in Britain.

Parnell's distant and autocratic style of leadership had created tension in the IPP's senior ranks. When he died, a power struggle ensued in which John Dillon, William O'Brien, Tim Healy and John Redmond played prominent roles. Personality clashes and serious disagreements over policy sustained the rancour and internal strife until the party was reunited in 1900. By then the United Irish League, the latest radical agrarian movement, had created the right circumstances for reunification, but the IPP struggled to recapture the dynamism of the early Parnellite years. Moreover, the experience of the bitter infighting during the 1890s would cast a shadow over the reunited party in the early part of the twentieth century. The internal wrangling had also weakened the party's influence on Dublin Corporation. The 1880s had witnessed a Parnellite takeover of the Corporation, but it was not immune from the acrimony of the 1890s. Later, the extension of the local government franchise in 1898 created a platform for opponents of constitutional Nationalism on the Corporation. At the national level, meanwhile, the IPP retained its association with the land issue, as the struggle for peasant proprietorship reached its climax.

At the opposite end of the political spectrum, Irish Unionism, which had emerged as a response to the Home Rule threat, would place the defence of landlord rights at the heart of its programme. These Irish Unionists emphasised their religious and cultural connections with the people of Great Britain. They were also eager to highlight their place in the British Empire, which they identified as a progressive group of nations that promoted liberty and progress. Unionism, however, was even more prone to division than Nationalism. Regional, denominational and class tensions were never far from the surface. Yet, when Home Rule threatened, these differences were set aside as Unionists quickly and effectively closed ranks to defend the constitutional status quo.

Ireland 1900–1910

In the first decade of the twentieth century, Ireland experienced major social change, as the process by which land was transferred from the landlords to the tenants was rapidly accelerated. This largely resolved the land question that had dominated Irish politics in the second half of the nineteenth century. The land struggle had provided the battleground for Nationalism, which emerged as a powerful force in the guise of the Irish Party, or Irish Parliamentary Party (IPP), towards the close of the century. Charles Stewart Parnell, its enigmatic leader, had used the land question to mobilise support for his Home Rule campaign. This, in turn, provoked a response from opponents of Irish Nationalism who viewed Home Rule as a threat to the long-term stability of the Union between Ireland and Great Britain. More specifically, Unionist leaders also claimed that their social, economic, political and religious status would be threatened under a Home Rule parliament. Both Irish Unionism and Nationalism faced internal challenges in the first decade of the new century. While each looked to one of the two major parties at Westminster to promote their interests, these relationships were often strained. It had been William Ewart Gladstone's adoption of Home Rule in the mid-1880s that had created a new faultline in British politics. Gladstone introduced two Home Rule Bills in 1886 and 1893, but neither could secure parliamentary approval. Thereafter, the Liberals and Conservatives clashed on Irish policy, a division which became one of the main features of British politics up to 1914.

The state of Irish Nationalism

The royal visits to Ireland in 1900 and 1903 created considerable excitement, as a significant body of Irish citizens eagerly demonstrated their loyalty to the Crown. Queen Victoria's largely private visit in April 1900 generated real interest, with thousands lining the streets of Dublin to welcome the ageing monarch. The more formal engagements associated with the visit of her successor, King Edward VII, in July 1903 were met with rousing scenes as Dubliners prepared to greet the new king. Yet these visits also highlighted deepening divisions within Irish Nationalism. Queen Victoria's visit had been approved by prominent figures in the IPP, particularly those who were members of Dublin Corporation. This sparked an angry response from a vocal group of more strident Nationalists who claimed that the real purpose of Queen Victoria's visit was to stimulate army recruitment for the ongoing conflict in South Africa, the Boer War. These advanced Nationalists went on to form Cumann na nGaedheal in September 1900. They widened their criticism to attack the broad principles underpinning constitutional Nationalism. These dissident Nationalists rarely missed an opportunity to castigate the IPP for its alleged feebleness and ineffectiveness. A particular target was the IPP's new leader, John Redmond, whose sincere Irish patriotism was sometimes obscured by his instinctive sympathy for British imperialism.

The IPP's chief tormentors at the turn of the century were the prolific Dublin journalist, Arthur Griffith, and the English-born political activist, Maud Gonne. Griffith concentrated his fire on pseudo-Nationalists, particularly those who rushed to climb on the royalist bandwagon, while Gonne courted publicity by engaging in a number of dramatic protests against the IPP. One of these ended in mayhem, as she challenged local Nationalist leaders about their attitude to Edward VII's forthcoming visit during a rally at the Rotunda in Dublin. Griffith's propaganda, meanwhile, outlined a separatist alternative to what he regarded as the party's limited objective of Home Rule. Starting from the premise that the

John Edward Redmond (1856–1918).   *Arthur Griffith (1871–1922).*

IPP did not reflect the real aspirations of the Irish electorate, Griffith charted a more radical course for Irish Nationalism that would destroy, rather than reform, the Union. His sympathy for the abandoned Parnell, whose power had been partly based on the activities of extra-parliamentary agitators, was another personal justification for his scathing treatment of the self-serving elite that monopolised control in the IPP. Yet, while he had flirted with Fenianism, Griffith rejected the need for violence to achieve Irish freedom. Instead, he advocated the withdrawal of Irish MPs from Westminster as part of a broad strategy of non-cooperation with the British state. This, he argued, would force Britain to accept, as Austria had done with Hungary in 1867, an arrangement whereby Ireland became an autonomous nation, sharing only the paraphernalia of the monarchy with Britain. Griffith claimed that such freedom would also spark a dramatic upturn in the Irish economy, as protective tariffs could be used to establish new domestic industries. These fundamental principles of abstentionism and economic Nationalism would become the central planks in the political programme of Sinn Féin, the movement that Griffith would establish in 1905.

Before this, however, Griffith launched a journalistic offensive on the IPP and its allies who had refused to condemn the 1903 royal visit. The government had hoped that King Edward VII's visit to Ireland would herald a fresh dawn in Anglo-Irish relations. The English press had portrayed the new king as a modernising influence on the monarchy. He was also reputed to be more in touch with his subjects and, not surprisingly, more popular than his austere mother. His visit took place against the backdrop of the Wyndham Act, a major piece of legislation that was closely identified with George Wyndham, who served as chief secretary for Ireland from 1900 to 1905. Wyndham was a young progressive Tory politician whose sympathy for Irish Nationalism steered him towards the 1903 Land Conference report. This was the result of a conference between representatives of both the landlords and the tenant farmers, and Wyndham included some of the report's key recommendations in the Land Bill which he introduced on 25 March 1903. The bill's generous financial provisions ensured that tenants would pay less in annual mortgage repayments than they currently paid in rents. The Wyndham Act formed the basis of a comprehensive land settlement that would transform Irish society by making huge numbers of tenant farmers owner-occupiers. The chief secretary had persuaded the Treasury to loosen the purse strings by suggesting that a successful Land Act would, over time, allow the authorities to recoup their outlay through savings on security expenditure, as coercion was likely to be phased out. The 1903 Land Bill, which became law in August, was the centrepiece in the Tory government's policy of conciliation. Wyndham recognised that a golden opportunity now existed for opening a new door in Anglo-Irish relations and hoped that the new king's July visit might prove useful in setting the tone for such a transformation.

There was considerable anticipation in Dublin on the eve of the king's visit. Naturally, Unionists were excited by the prospect of a royal visit, but even the Nationalist *Freeman's Journal* acknowledged that Edward VII was a "friendly sovereign". Of course, officials at Dublin Castle took great care to emphasise the positive aspects of the visit, and a tour of Dublin's slums was added to the itinerary. This allowed the king to voice his concerns about the welfare of the city's poorest citizens. However, the visit also spurred radical Nationalists into action. Again, Griffith took the lead by attacking the IPP, particularly its high-profile Dublin mayor, Timothy Harrington, for its ambivalence on the impending royal visit. Indeed, such was the impact of Griffith's propaganda assault that the Corporation abandoned its plans for the presentation of a loyal address to welcome the new monarch. Clearly, King Edward VII's visit in July 1903 had given advanced Nationalists a new focus, which they seized upon to rally opposition to conventional Nationalism. To coordinate their attacks, these militants formed the National Council, and Griffith made the running in his attempt to frustrate and embarrass the IPP in relation to the visit. Demanding full independence for Ireland, Griffith and his colleagues intensified their criticism of the party, which was condemned for its betrayal of the Nationalist masses. The National Council would continue to function after the king's visit, and at its annual convention in 1905 it was renamed Sinn Féin. The royal visits of 1900 and 1903 had enabled Griffith and like-minded advanced Nationalists to question the integrity of the IPP. While Nationalist members of Dublin Corporation were his primary target, Griffith was increasingly vocal in his criticism of the party's failure to achieve any of its goals at Westminster. Although the National Council was essentially a Dublin organisation that would struggle to pose a viable electoral challenge to the IPP, it did, nevertheless, attract support for its separatist agenda. Indeed, the normally phlegmatic Redmond conceded that these radical Nationalists were proving a thorn in the party's side. In early April 1903, he confided to his colleague, William O'Brien, that he was very concerned about the potential consequences of the forthcoming royal visit.

While most Irish Parliamentary Party MPs probably hoped that Home Rule might pave the way for full independence, Redmond never shared this aspiration. Self-government was Redmond's goal, and he dismissed separation as neither achievable nor desirable. Indeed, recrimination and division had been a marked feature of constitutional Nationalism since the demise of Parnell. The formal reunification of the party in early 1900 papered over, rather than removed, some of the more serious differences. Ideologically, Parnellites and anti-Parnellites were at odds on the role of the party at Westminster. John Dillon, the leading anti-Parnellite, insisted that Home Rule could only be achieved by continuing to foster close relations with the Liberals. The Parnellites, on the other hand, argued that success would ultimately depend on the party's ability to retain its independence. Only by doing so, they claimed, could MPs exert maximum pressure on a Liberal government to deliver Home Rule.

There was also a serious divergence of opinion within the majority anti-Parnellite faction. Dillon essentially advocated Parnellism without Parnell.

John Dillon (1851–1927), photographed in September 1888.

He was a firm believer in both the Liberal alliance and the need for powerful central control of the party's organisation. He warned that only a united and disciplined party directed by a determined leadership could hope to become an effective political force both in Ireland and at Westminster. Meanwhile, Parnell's nemesis, Tim Healy, sought to curb central authority in the party, replacing it with a loose structure in which local constituency branches would exercise much more control. Such a development would have taken Nationalism in a more conservative direction by giving greater power to the Catholic Church, particularly in the selection of candidates for parliamentary seats. Dillon and Healy vied with each other for control of the party for much of the 1890s. It was the former who emerged as the dominant force, even though Healy's influence was never extinguished.

This prolonged period of faction fighting sapped much of the energy of constitutional Nationalism and did lasting damage. The endless squabbling and personal invective also undermined the status and authority of Irish MPs in the eyes of the electorate. Voters became disenchanted and disillusioned, as Redmondites, Dillonites and Healyites attacked each other with a viciousness that was altogether absent when they criticised either their Unionist opponents or the British government. The clashes between Dillon and Healy were particularly bitter, and the contempt and suspicion that these two Nationalist leaders reserved for each other would continue throughout their political careers. Clearly, Parnell still cast a long shadow over the party. Dillon's aim had been to remodel the party on Parnellite lines, but what was absent was a Parnell figure to give it an effective voice both inside and outside parliament. Party organisation was crumbling in many constituencies, and the Tory victory in the 1895 general election eliminated any immediate prospect of Home Rule. Indeed, the Conservative government's policy of constructive Unionism only appeared to add to the IPP's difficulties. While Redmond and Healy welcomed the benefits to the Irish economy, Dillon was much more reticent, believing that the Tories could well succeed in their objective of "killing Home Rule with kindness". This was a recurring concern in Dillon's relationship with a succession of Westminster administrations, as he insisted that the IPP must not be sidetracked from its primary objective of Home Rule. Of course, a successful outcome for such a strategy depended on the continued support for Home Rule by a Liberal Party that no longer had Gladstone at its helm.

There were other senior Nationalist figures who had strong claims to lead the IPP. Thomas Sexton, the MP for North Kerry until his resignation in 1896, was the party's financial expert and a very accomplished debater. From 1892 he chaired the board that controlled the *Freeman's Journal*, the principal Nationalist newspaper, but Sexton was reluctant to press his leadership claims. The combative

Timothy Charles Harrington, who represented Dublin Harbour from 1885 and later became Lord Mayor of Dublin, was a firm advocate of national unity. Unswervingly loyal to Parnell, Harrington was the Irish National League's key strategist, and he had been the driving force behind the Plan of Campaign, the party's response to a new wave of tenant distress in the late 1880s. Another major figure was Harrington's associate in the execution of the Plan, William O'Brien. The volatile O'Brien was a brilliant journalist who possessed considerable political skills, but his personality was better tuned to the role of a militant agrarian campaigner. In fact, O'Brien lost patience with the party because of the internal bickering, and he resigned his parliamentary seat in 1895. He subsequently moved to a remote part of County Mayo, but was soon drawn out of retirement by the re-emergence of the land question in the western province of Connacht in the late 1890s.

O'Brien was spurred into action by the plight of the poorest farmers in Connacht, which he witnessed at first hand. The potato continued to provide the main source of food for many of these smallholders, but the crop was badly hit in 1896 and 1897. The ensuing rural crisis led to the creation of a new movement of agrarian protest. O'Brien played the key role in the formation of the United Irish League (UIL), which was launched following a public meeting in Westport in January 1898. The new organisation made clear from the outset that its primary aim was the establishment of peasant proprietorship, but O'Brien insisted that the UIL would target not the landlords but the graziers. Connacht was an overwhelmingly rural province where prosperous graziers rented large tracts of land, usually more than 400 acres, though a significant number of these "ranches" were in excess of 1,000 acres. The ranches were scattered among a swathe of smallholdings where tillage farming based on the potato crop was widely practised. While this juxtaposition was not exclusive to the western province, the coexistence of barely viable smallholdings, together with large commercial grazing ranches, was a particularly common feature across Mayo, Galway and Roscommon. Not surprisingly, rural anger stoked by the consecutive poor harvests of 1896 and 1897 was directed at the graziers. The fact that such individuals were frequently townsmen who employed stockmen to look after their cattle herds only added to the class tension that was present in rural Ireland during this period. Auctioneers, solicitors, doctors and, especially, publicans were among the middle-class dwellers in the small western towns who had the necessary capital to stock these ranches. Against this background, the revival of the Land League mantra, 'the land for the people', stirred the smallholders of the west, as the UIL demanded the break-up of the large grazing ranches.

While O'Brien's immediate priority was agrarian, he was anxious that the UIL should acquire a political dimension that could provide a basis for the reunification of the IPP. Indeed, it was quickly apparent that the agrarian campaign could attract support from different Nationalist factions, a development that O'Brien had anticipated. While clear divisions persisted at national level, a consequence in part of the ongoing personal bitterness among Nationalist leaders, O'Brien's focus on the obvious rural distress encouraged a new spirit of unity at local level. This cohesion generated the momentum that was central to the process of reunification. By the end of 1898, a total of 94 UIL branches had been established in Mayo. In the early months of the following year, the movement spread quickly across Connacht, and branches were being formed in the provinces of Munster and Leinster before the close of 1899. As the UIL extended its reach beyond Connacht, it was clear that the new organisation had acquired a sharper political edge. Two further factors strengthened this political dimension. The outbreak of the Boer War in October 1899 pulled Nationalist leaders together to condemn British policy in South Africa. All shades of Nationalist opinion instinctively sympathised with the Boers in their struggle against the Empire, and early successes against complacent British forces were welcomed by Irish Nationalists. Secondly, the efforts made by the Westminster administration to frustrate the impact of the UIL emphasised the movement's political character. The government quickly deployed a range of draconian measures to try to crush the agitation, which had resurrected the old strategy of passive resistance with the boycott at its centre. Yet, in bringing local leaders before the courts and by enforcing bans on public meetings, the authorities created the impression that they were engaged in a political struggle against the UIL.

O'Brien reacted to these developments with predictable defiance, and he used the recently acquired influence of the UIL to press the case for Nationalist unity. He insisted that the various factions within the IPP could not promote unity from within and that only an exterior movement with the necessary dynamism and organisational structure could hope to restore party unity. It was evident by the close of 1899 that the UIL had united grass-roots elements across much of the country and was in a strong position to lead a campaign for the restoration of a united IPP. The momentum established by the UIL soon prompted leading Nationalist figures to consider their positions, and Redmond was unanimously elected to the chairmanship of a reunited IPP in early February 1900. Dillon had been the last to move, but he was persuaded by O'Brien to support Redmond's candidature. This proved crucial in allowing the party to move forward. Redmond had led the minority Parnellite faction since Parnell's death in 1891 and, not surprisingly because of his experiences during the 1890s, became highly sensitive to the possibility of dissent within the reunited party. The fact that O'Brien, Dillon and Healy had returned to the fold appeared to strengthen the IPP's hand, but each of these notoriously difficult personalities was intent on exerting considerable influence over Redmond and the policies that the reunited movement would adopt. Unity, therefore, was by no means certain to endure. Healy was soon expelled from the party, while the volatile O'Brien resigned in late 1903 following a clash with Redmond over the direction of party policy. This left Redmond and Dillon at the top of the party, though they would be joined by others before the crisis over the third Home Rule Bill broke in 1912. While the two men never enjoyed a close personal relationship, together they formed an effective partnership with Redmond's formidable oratorical skills complementing Dillon's detailed knowledge both of parliamentary procedure and of grass-roots Nationalist opinion in Ireland.

With the reunification of the IPP, the United Irish League, which under O'Brien's direction sought to intensify land agitation in 1900, became the party's principal constituency organisation. It also assumed increased responsibility for party fundraising. With 1,000 branches in operation across the country by the summer of 1901, the UIL clearly had the capacity to undertake these roles. O'Brien's intention was that the UIL would be the conduit for grass-roots views, but the movement was quickly subsumed by the party, losing its independent voice in the process. Yet the UIL's success in sustaining the land agitation was one of the factors prompting the Westminster government to pass far-reaching land legislation in 1903. This would allow two-thirds of the country's farmers to become owners of their land by 1914. The details of this Land Bill had been worked out over the previous winter by the Land Conference, a working group comprising landlord and tenant representatives who had met to consider proposals that might formally resolve the land issue. Lord Dunraven was the key figure among the landlord representatives, while Redmond and O'Brien were two of the four delegates acting on behalf of the tenant farmers. This ensured that the IPP guarded its position of influence. For O'Brien, the experience of the Land Conference pointed the way to further progress in overcoming Ireland's many social and economic problems. Cooperation between the representatives of Unionism and Nationalism had, in O'Brien's view, produced concrete results. Therefore, he urged Redmond to embrace fully this new strategy of conciliation as the IPP turned to its other objectives. However, Redmond, who was acutely aware of the suspicion raised by the party's close cooperation with both a Tory chief secretary and representatives of southern Unionism, refused to be drawn.

The *Freeman's Journal* had already warned of the dangers that such a course might pose for Irish Nationalism, and this traditional view was reinforced by Dillon in a well-publicised speech in Swinford, County Mayo, on 25 August 1903. Dillon, who had refused to participate in the Land Conference, launched a scathing attack on O'Brien and warned of the pitfalls associated with the principle of conciliation. The "Swinford revolt", as the address quickly became known, warned that continued agitation, rather than conciliation, was the only route to success for Irish Nationalism. Clearly, the sceptical Dillon reflected broader Nationalist thinking, and Redmond declined to endorse O'Brien's radical approach. The result was that the impetuous O'Brien, who had coined the phrase "conference plus business" to capture the essence of his bold new strategy, resigned from the party in November 1903.

Dillon's stance was consistent with his long-term analysis of Anglo-Irish relations. He was suspicious of the motives of both liberal Unionism and a Tory government that, in his view, promoted the type of social and economic reforms that might undermine the case for Home Rule. Moreover, he repeatedly warned that the IPP must not be deflected from its ultimate goal. O'Brien's resignation, meanwhile, did not lead to his retirement from politics. He was re-elected unopposed as the MP for Cork City in August 1904 and reached an electoral arrangement with Redmond for the general election in January 1906. This ensured that O'Brien and a number of his associates in the Cork area were returned without facing a challenge from the IPP. In rejecting O'Brien's conciliatory vision, Redmond had held the IPP together, but the opportunity to develop a bold reform agenda based on cooperation between progressive landlordism and broader Nationalism had been lost. This was unfortunate, as Redmond possessed the necessary skills and outlook to engage in the kind of consensus politics advocated by O'Brien. However, the desire for unity pulled Redmond in a different direction. O'Brien continued to operate on the fringes of the party until the 1909 National Convention, when he and his supporters were subjected to particularly roughhouse tactics as the meeting ended in disorder. A fortnight later, following a private meeting in Cork on 25 February 1909, O'Brien launched the All-for-Ireland League (AFIL). While the new movement would seek "to obtain self-government for the Irish people in Irish affairs", O'Brien declared that the league would be built on "the broadest toleration of differences" and would emphasise the "scrupulous respect for the rights and feelings of our Protestant fellow-countrymen". A dismayed Redmond warned voters that electoral support for the new movement would lead to yet another catastrophic split in Nationalist ranks.

While O'Brien had clearly frustrated the mainstream Nationalist leadership, the AFIL did not emerge as a serious rival to the IPP. Indeed, in many ways, its existence helped to justify Redmond's emphasis on the importance of Nationalist unity. This focus was important at a time when the party was undergoing significant change. During the first decade of the twentieth century, an increasing number of UIL-backed candidates became MPs. Such men generally lacked the debating skills of their older, longer-serving parliamentary colleagues. The privately educated gentlemen of the party, like Redmond and Dillon, had the financial security to act as full-time politicians and felt very much at home in the exclusive Westminster club. Their newer colleagues, by contrast, tended to be drawn from the lower ranks of Ireland's middle class, meaning that they had to earn a living while parliament was in recess. Yet these new MPs were invariably loyal to the party leadership and the fact that they were usually selected by their local constituencies ensured that they enjoyed a good measure of popularity with the electorate. This was significant during a period when the leadership was becoming further detached from the party's rank and file. In addition, it was becoming increasingly clear that the supporters of the IPP were themselves being exposed to significant change. The Irish Parliamentary Party had been rooted in its tenant farmer base when it became the dominant political force in Ireland under Parnell. The social base was greatly reduced as tenant farmers took advantage of land purchase legislation to buy their own farms. Though less enthusiastic in their support for the IPP thereafter, these farmers retained their national identity, a factor that contributed to the effectiveness of the IPP in promoting its Home Rule message.

From his appointment in 1900, it was clear that the chief secretary, whose name was invariably linked to the 1903 Land Act, was determined to improve relations with Nationalist Ireland. George Wyndham sought to extend his predecessor Gerald Balfour's constructive Unionist agenda, and intended that his Land Act should become the centrepiece of an ambitious new reform programme. His goal was the final resolution of the Irish problem in a way that would strengthen the United Kingdom. This was the context behind Dillon's paranoia about the dangers that such a strategy would pose to the Irish quest for Home Rule. In spite of its extensive scope, however, the Wyndham Act offered little comfort either to the poorest small farmers or to the large group of landless labourers. Land hunger remained a powerful motive in many western counties, precipitating a new wave of agrarian agitation towards the close of 1906. This Ranch War, as the new campaign was described, targeted the graziers who dominated livestock farming across much of rural Ireland. The campaign was largely confined to the five counties of Roscommon, Galway, Clare, Meath and Westmeath. The initiative in the Ranch War was taken by the new MP for North Westmeath, Laurence Ginnell, a leading radical agrarian campaigner in the UIL. While the Ranch War saw the return of the boycott, the primary tactic of these rural militants was cattle-driving. This practice involved scattering large herds of grazing cattle off the land at night, allowing them to wander along country roads often many miles from their home farms. The wealthy graziers frequently paid over the odds to rent very large holdings, thus distorting the market, and they were a natural target for agrarian militants. These radical agrarians wanted the ranches to be divided up among the smallholders and labourers, a development that, it was assumed, would lead to a reduction in livestock farming and a return to arable production.

The Ranch War created a dilemma for the IPP. While a number of its MPs supported the campaign and displayed general sympathy for the rural poor, it was also true that many of the graziers were influential Nationalists. This made it difficult for the IPP, and even the UIL, to offer unequivocal support for the latest phase of the agrarian struggle. Redmond's position was particularly tricky. Hitherto, agrarian protest had been central to the party's success in mobilising the rural masses. Yet, in achieving many of its aims on the land issue, the party had inadvertently intensified social tensions in the Irish countryside. One consequence of land reform had seen the Irish grazier replace the English landlord as the target for the agrarian militants. While this led to obvious difficulties, Redmond recognised the impact of agrarian campaigning in strengthening the party's bonds with its grass-roots supporters. Accordingly, he added his voice to the call for compulsory purchase, omitted from the Wyndham Act and a key demand of those leading the Ranch War campaign. Redmond knew that his party risked accusations of hypocrisy by associating itself with attacks on the grazier interest that was so prominent in many Nationalist circles. On a wider level he was also aware that reports of serious disorder across midland and western counties could undermine support for the Home Rule cause in Britain. For Redmond, therefore, leadership of mainstream Irish Nationalism meant striking the right balance between rousing support among this traditional base in rural Ireland and courting sympathy for the cause of Irish devolution among British voters. Of course, the same dilemma had faced Parnell, but, in the first decade of the twentieth century, Redmond was denied the luxury of turning on the agrarian tap to galvanise his followers into action.

The Liberal government's 1909 Land Act eased some of Redmond's difficulties. The legislation finally conceded the principle of compulsory purchase, and its troublesome passage through the House of Lords added to the IPP's sense of achievement. When it became law in December 1909, the party and the UIL immediately distanced themselves from the cattle-driving campaign. Order was soon restored across those counties where such action had been most prevalent. Again, the IPP was quick to claim credit for Westminster's latest capitulation to pressure from Irish Nationalists. While significant grievances on the land issue remained, Redmond could point to the large-scale transfer of land to former tenant farmers that was well under way by 1910. At the same time, state aid to the poorest parts of the country had brought tangible economic benefits. Improvements in agriculture, communications and rural housing provided visible evidence of the IPP's success in redressing Nationalist grievances. Yet, in spite of this well-publicised record, the party had clearly lost some of its dynamism. A succession of land reforms had placated many of the most prominent elements in the UIL, leading to a loss of enthusiasm among individual members. Consequently, there was a steady decline in the number of active branches, which clearly weakened the party's organisational structure.

Progress on the land issue was not mirrored by progress towards the ultimate Nationalist goal of Home Rule. Yet some hope was raised by the actions of a group of progressive landlords led by Lord Dunraven who had continued to meet following the passage of the 1903 Land Act. Under discussion was a devolution scheme that would see the transfer of some powers from Westminster to a new representative council in Dublin. In an attempt to flesh out the detail of this idea, the landlords turned to Sir Antony MacDonnell, the under secretary at the Castle, who jumped at the chance to make his mark on Irish policy. Following a long and successful career in India, MacDonnell became Ireland's top civil servant in 1902. It was made clear to him by Wyndham, the chief secretary, that he would be given considerable latitude in developing policy change in Ireland. MacDonnell's brother served as the Irish Parliamentary Party MP for Queen's County (now County Laois) from 1892–1906. MacDonnell was broadly sympathetic to the Nationalist cause, which naturally rendered him a figure of suspicion for Irish Unionism. Emboldened by the success of the Land Conference, which had produced the 1903 Land Act, MacDonnell discussed the establishment of new legislative and financial councils with Lord Dunraven. The under secretary was the principal actor in drawing up this new devolution scheme which was unveiled to the public in September 1904. A political storm ensued as Irish Unionist MPs claimed that MacDonnell was endangering the Union and was being encouraged by Wyndham in following this course of action. The truth was somewhat different. MacDonnell's devolution proposals may have been significant, but they stopped well short of Home Rule, a fact that was conveniently ignored by Irish Unionists. Secondly, Wyndham's real transgression was to have been asleep at the wheel while MacDonnell pressed ahead with his devolution plans. In the end Unionists' persistence forced Wyndham's resignation, but they were outraged by the Conservative government's decision to allow MacDonnell to continue in his role at Dublin Castle.

Although the IPP was denied the halfway house that MacDonnell's plans appeared to offer, the furore over Wyndham's intentions had damaged a Tory government that was, in truth, running out of steam after a decade in power. Redmond and Dillon seized the opportunity to add to the government's discomfort by insisting that Wyndham was being sacrificed to appease diehard Unionist opposition. Balfour appeared to substantiate this allegation when, in March 1905, he replaced Wyndham with Walter Long, an outspoken critic of Irish Nationalism in all its forms. Later, in June, Balfour demonstrated his exasperation with Irish representatives at Westminster when he announced his intention to

Walter Long (1854–1924).

reduce substantially the number of Irish MPs in a redistribution of parliamentary seats. Such a challenge again played to Redmond's strengths as a parliamentarian. His extensive knowledge of House of Commons procedure forced Balfour to abandon his plans for the ending of Irish over-representation at Westminster. This victory for the IPP drew fulsome praise in the Nationalist press. Furthermore, the collapse of the devolution scheme confirmed to all IPP supporters that meaningful political change was unlikely to be delivered by a Tory government. When the crisis broke, Dillon had been particularly forceful in condemning the government's devolution scheme, viewing it as a vehicle for undermining Nationalism. Therefore, it was clear by the end of 1905, when the Tories lost power, that constructive Unionism depended ultimately on the engagement of an IPP that regarded such cooperation as extremely hazardous.

The return of a Liberal government at the beginning of 1906 was naturally welcomed by Irish Nationalists. However, it soon became clear that the new administration, led by Sir Henry Campbell-Bannerman, would not meet the IPP's expectations. From the outset the incoming chief secretary, James Bryce, a figure who did not endear himself to Irish Nationalists, indicated that only minor changes to the government of Ireland were being contemplated. This was not surprising as the Liberal government faced a host of domestic challenges, one of which was its relationship with the House of Lords. In January 1907 Bryce was replaced by Augustine Birrell, a more popular figure who acknowledged the importance of the Liberal–Nationalist alliance. MacDonnell, meanwhile, continued to develop his devolution plans. Such ideas should have appealed to a government that refused to provide any commitment on Home Rule but was anxious to placate Irish Nationalists. Moreover, the limited nature of the MacDonnell initiative carried the added advantage of being so innocuous that it might be approved by the House of Lords. Yet the Liberal cabinet was divided on the wisdom of introducing any scheme of Irish devolution. When Birrell eventually introduced his Irish Council Bill in May 1907, it received a cool response from the leadership of the IPP. The intention was to establish an Irish Council of 107 members, three-quarters of whom were to be elected, which would be granted more powers than had been envisaged in the previous devolution proposals. The bill was immediately denounced by the *Freeman's Journal,* and this was followed by further criticism in the provincial press and from Nationalist-controlled local government councils. A special UIL convention was held to pronounce on the scheme on 21 May, but the mood in Ireland made acceptance of the bill extremely problematic. There was some speculation that the IPP might approve the bill and then seek to amend it at the committee stage, but Redmond was unequivocal in his rejection of the measure when he addressed the 3,000 delegates who had assembled in Dublin for the convention. While he had been tempted by the Irish Council plan, Redmond, after considerable hesitation, judged that such a move was too risky. Once again, his primary concern was to maintain party unity, though the strong suspicion that he had been in favour of the bill must have damaged Redmond's authority.

While the leaders of the IPP argued that continued support for the Liberal government was their only option, there was evidence of growing disquiet with this strategy among both backbench MPs and rank-and-file supporters. Clearly, the Irish Council Bill debacle had contributed to this unease. A direct challenge to the party arrived with the resignation of Charles Dolan on 30 January 1908. Dolan, the MP for North Leitrim, had been at loggerheads with the party for many months. On his resignation he joined Sinn Féin and called on all Nationalist MPs to withdraw from Westminster. At the ensuing by-election, Dolan contested the seat for Sinn Féin. In what proved to be a feisty encounter, the IPP's candidate, F. E. Meehan, emerged victorious, winning close to 75 per cent of the total vote. While the Sinn Féin leader, Arthur Griffith, declared the result a moral victory, the reality was that the outgoing MP, who was genuinely popular in the constituency, had been soundly beaten by the official Nationalist candidate. The by-election outcome was naturally welcomed by Redmond and the leadership, but the events leading to Dolan's resignation confirmed an underlying feeling of frustration with the party's performance.

Redmond could, however, point to a significant success with the passage of the Irish Universities Bill in 1908. For many years the IPP had campaigned for what was in essence a Catholic university. While Trinity College was opened to Catholics in 1793, with all religious tests finally abolished in 1873, the Catholic bishops retained their fierce opposition to Catholic students enrolling in what they regarded as an episcopalian institution. Birrell had grasped the importance of the university question and was determined to redress this Nationalist grievance. Trinity's independent status was not touched, but the bill, which became law in the late summer of 1908, established the National University of Ireland,

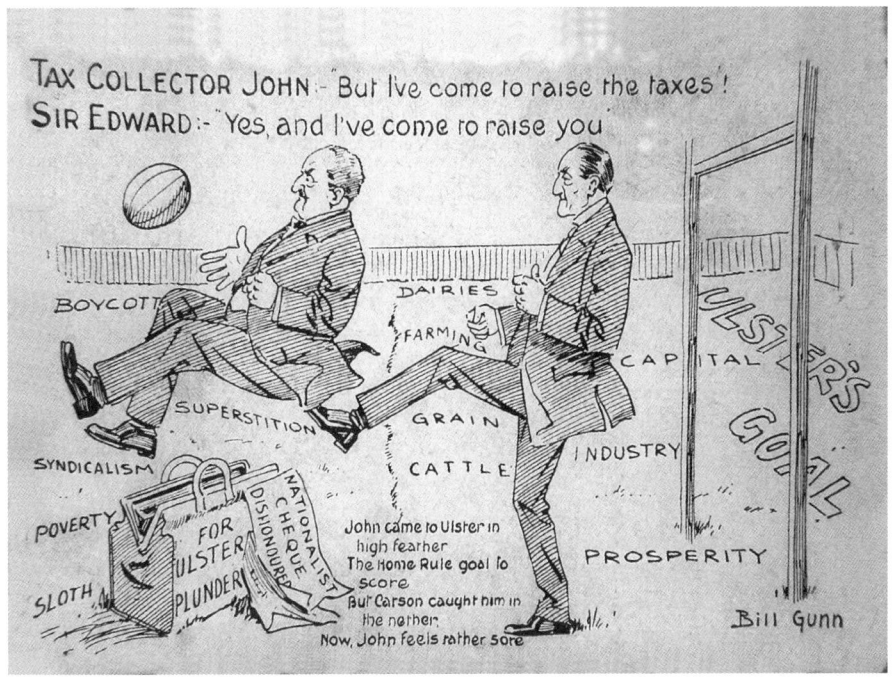

Ulster Unionist postcard Tax Collector John.

together with its constituent college, University College Dublin. Unionist MPs claimed that the changes would lead to unchecked clerical interference in higher education, but Birrell persevered and secured a comfortable majority for the new measure, allowing Redmond and Dillon to champion its benefits for Nationalist Ireland.

Despite its success in securing concessions on higher education, the IPP's suspicion of the Liberal administration soon resurfaced. This was brought into sharper focus when the government introduced its budget in late April 1909. The chancellor's proposals included new taxes to pay for vastly increased spending on defence and social services. From Ireland's standpoint the budget dealt a heavy blow to both its liquor trade and distilling industry. The fact that many publicans were prominent in the ranks of the IPP certainly added to the problems confronting Nationalist leaders. The budget caused a political storm in Britain, pitching the two main parties into a bitter struggle that would have significant consequences for Irish politics. While Redmond spoke in favour of the social changes that had the introduction of old-age pensions as its centrepiece, he had to acknowledge that the increased taxes imposed on the drink trade would damage Ireland's economic prosperity. The party voted against the budget on its second reading on 9 June, but then chose to examine each clause on its merits and vote accordingly during the committee stage. Rising criticism of the budget in Ireland created further problems for the IPP's leaders, but they were given a reprieve when the House of Lords vetoed the budget on 30 November 1909. This led to a general election in January 1910.

The election campaign in Ireland was marked by serious acrimony as O'Brien's AFIL candidates clashed with the IPP in eleven seats. Bitterness also dominated the North Louth contest, where Healy and Redmond engaged in personal recriminations. In the end the party lost eleven contests to independent Nationalists, with O'Brien's AFIL winning eight seats, six of which were in County Cork. Over most of the country, however, the IPP remained in control, taking 70 seats. When it became clear that the election had resulted in a hung parliament, the strength of the IPP ensured that it would hold the balance of power. In theory, this meant that it could either make or break a government, but the reality was that it would tie itself to the Liberals and their leader, H. H. Asquith. Prior to the election, Redmond had probably been hoping for a strong Liberal majority which would allow the government to deal decisively with the House of Lords before turning to the question of self-government for Ireland. Yet the result of the January 1910 election appeared to deal Redmond an even stronger hand. He was now catapulted into the front rank of Westminster politics. It seemed to his supporters in Ireland that the ultimate prize of Home Rule was now within touching distance. Redmond's adherence to the principle of the Liberal alliance was one of the key factors separating the IPP and the AFIL, which argued that Irish Nationalists should be independent of the two main parties at Westminster.

Herbert Henry Asquith (1852–1928).

Following the general election, Redmond participated in unofficial negotiations with the Liberal leadership. The budget was the Liberal government's priority, but Redmond made it clear that his party's support for the measure, which would be crucial in a hung parliament, was conditional on prompt government action to deal with the House of Lords. The significance of such a move was obvious to both supporters and opponents of Home Rule. The Irish leader was applying serious pressure on Asquith, a development that enraged the Tory press, but the unexpected death of the king in early May appeared to offer the prime minister an escape from Redmond's clutches. Asquith had been in regular contact with Edward VII, updating the sovereign on the government's options, one of which might involve a request for the creation of additional peers to overcome opposition to the government in the upper chamber. The prime minister was keen to shield the new king from the pressures of the constitutional crisis, and Redmond sensed that the government might seek to use these unprecedented circumstances to delay action on the Lords issue. The Irish leader knew that George V supported the idea of a conference between Liberal and Conservative representatives, which might produce some compromise formula that would be detrimental to Irish Nationalist interests. At the same time, Redmond was alive to the opportunity that the post-budget crisis had presented. He was determined that Asquith and the Liberals would not escape their commitment on Home Rule, which was the price of the IPP's support for the budget. To all observers of the constitutional crisis, it was clear that the question of Irish Home Rule loomed large in any discussion to curtail the powers of the House of Lords. The breakdown of the constitutional conference in November 1910 was widely anticipated, and all the parties made preparations for a fresh election.

Redmond, who had just returned from a triumphant American speaking tour, opened the campaign in Wexford on Sunday, 27 November by telling supporters, "Whatever happens in this election, Ireland stands to win." The focus was on the fate of the House of Lords, and the IPP leader confidently declared that the power of the upper chamber was broken. Two days later, Joe Devlin, the MP for West Belfast, told a packed Mansion House that with the destruction of the Lords, Home Rule would be inevitable. Voting was stretched out between 3 and 19 December, but a confident Redmond, speaking at a meeting in Rathmines on 8 December, insisted "with absolute certainty that the veto of the House of Lords was dead". The popular slogan "Kill the Veto" struck a chord with voters, while Redmond reminded

Joe Devlin (1871–1934).

the sceptics that his strategy, which had been savagely condemned by O'Brien and Healy, had brought Home Rule considerably closer. Indeed, when the final outcome was revealed, he stressed that the government now had "a clear and unequivocal mandate to settle the Irish question finally and with the least possible delay". With the two main parties tied on 272 seats, the Liberals were set to continue in government as they could count on the support of both the IPP and the smaller Labour Party. Redmond welcomed the formation of another hung parliament, and he hailed the result as "a great and unprecedented triumph for the progressive and democratic forces of Great Britain and Ireland". The IPP had been challenged in 21 constituencies by O'Brien's AFIL. This was significantly higher than the number of Nationalist–Unionist contests. The AFIL won a total of ten seats in December 1910, eight of which were in County Cork. This confirmed that Redmond's party was the dominant force in Nationalist Ireland, as the O'Brienites struggled to make any real impact outside their southern stronghold. Following a difficult opening, 1910 had proved to be a good year for the IPP.

Nevertheless, the very existence of the AFIL was a considerable source of irritation for Redmond. His experience of the factionalism and feuding within Irish Nationalism during the 1890s was a constant reminder of the importance of party unity. The 1892 general election had been a particularly bitter affair, and the party reunion in 1900 never fully healed the rancour and division of the post-Parnell years. Still, Redmond had seen off his Nationalist challengers, and, by the close of 1910, he was clearly highly regarded by his backbench MPs. His undoubted ability, oratorical skill, judgement, patience, dignity and calmness were qualities that were appreciated and acknowledged by his followers. Redmond was, of course, careful to reflect the fact that these Irish MPs had little interest, beyond Irish affairs, in wider parliamentary activity. However, he was clear that the ultimate objective of Home Rule could only be delivered through an alliance with the Liberals. Following the December 1910 general election, Redmond clearly felt vindicated in pursuing such a strategy. While the years following their landslide victory in 1906 were disappointing, with Redmond convinced that the Liberals were deliberately stalling on the Home Rule issue, the Irish leader knew that patience was essential. He never considered turning out the Liberals when the parliamentary arithmetic would have given him the option after January 1910. This greatly limited his power, a state of affairs that was more apparent to the Liberal leadership than to the IPP's supporters at home in Ireland.

Moreover, the party's organisational support structure had come under pressure during the decade. At the turn of the century, the UIL had established itself as a powerful political and agrarian movement, but its influence in both these spheres declined sharply. Enthusiasm among its tenant farmer base was sapped by the combination of a lack of discernible progress on the Home Rule question and the impact of popular Westminster land purchase legislation. Agrarian radicalism might still cause ripples, but Redmond was never as comfortable in dealing with such elements as his lieutenant, John Dillon. As the UIL became less significant, the Ancient Order of Hibernians (AOH) became more prominent. The movement had been established in New York in 1836 before slowly spreading across the Atlantic. It was an insignificant body in Ireland until 1900, when, under Devlin's inspiration, it began to attract new recruits in Belfast. By 1909 it had 60,000 members, but it never replicated the geographical spread of the UIL, being largely confined to the northern half of the country where it provided an effective challenge to political Unionism. The other notable feature of the early twentieth century was the growing interest in the revival of the Irish language. Nationalist MPs took little interest in this development, though Redmond was supportive, but its growth highlighted the existence of a significant body of Nationalists who had become unenthusiastic supporters of the IPP by the end of 1910.

The state of Irish Unionism

Unionism had emerged as an organised political movement in the mid-1880s, when Home Rule became a live political issue at Westminster. From the outset its supporters were adamant that the establishment of a devolved parliament in Dublin would eventually conclude with an unstoppable demand for full independence. For supporters of the Union in Ireland, Home Rule was viewed as a threat to their social standing, their economic status, their cultural identity and their religious freedom. In these early years the battle in Ireland over Home Rule could be seen as an extension of the broader landlord–tenant struggle, with the landed class the first to recognise the dangers posed by a Nationalist triumph on the Home Rule question. It was, of course, the landed gentry that had been targeted by the increasingly frequent bursts of agrarian agitation in the last quarter of the nineteenth century. By 1900, therefore, the defence of the Union was closely linked to the defence of Irish landlordism. Yet it was at precisely this moment that the economic and political influence of Irish landlordism appeared to be in terminal decline. Ironically, this was due in part to the land purchase legislation implemented by Conservative administrations. While this allowed frequently over-mortgaged Irish landlords to make a dignified exit, it also weakened the influence of some of the Union's core support. This was certainly the case in the three provinces outside Ulster where the landed gentry played the leading role in arguing the case against Home Rule. In Britain, meanwhile, support for the Union appeared rock solid among Conservatives who regarded any tampering with existing constitutional arrangements as a threat not only to the integrity of the United Kingdom but to the unity of the British Empire.

It was, of course, the parliamentary strength of Unionism, with the Conservative Party dominant, that saw off the Home Rule legislative challenges in 1886 and 1893, the former achieved through victory in the Commons and the latter in the safety net of the House of Lords. By this stage, Irish Unionist MPs had formed their own political party, and this was evidence of concern about the Conservative Party's long-term commitment to the Union cause. Led by Colonel Edward Saunderson, a County Cavan landlord who represented the North Armagh constituency in the House of Commons, the Irish Unionist Party (IUP) was dominated by Ulstermen, a reflection of the party's electoral appeal. In Ulster, Unionist candidates looked to their overwhelmingly Protestant voters in parliamentary elections, and the Orange Order played a key role in mobilising electoral support. Southern Unionists, meanwhile, struggled to make an electoral impact but had a powerful presence in the House of Lords. An overwhelming majority of Irish Unionist peers had links to the three southern provinces. Although there were obvious regional differences within Irish Unionism, the fear of Home Rule was sufficient to ensure that Unionists across the island acted in unison wherever there was any perceived threat to the Union. Saunderson's leadership promoted such unity. As a landlord he moved in Irish gentry circles, and his political instincts were those of an Irish Unionist.

However, it was more difficult for leaders of political Unionism to present a united front when the threat of Home Rule receded, as it did during the long period of Conservative rule from 1895 to 1906. Its strength in Ulster had been its ability to mobilise a broad class alliance in response to the challenge of Home Rule. This alliance comprised landlords, tenants, rural labourers and the business and professional classes in addition to skilled and unskilled urban workers. Claims that a Nationalist-dominated devolved parliament in Dublin would pose a serious risk to Protestant civil and religious liberty was the key to building such cross-class support in Ulster. Yet, once the Home Rule danger passed, the class tensions that were never far from the surface meant that cracks quickly developed in the Unionist facade. This was particularly true in rural Ulster, as the state of landlord–tenant relations became a major concern for the Unionist leadership. Denominational differences played some part as Church of Ireland landlords were sometimes accused of a lack of empathy by their largely Presbyterian tenants. However, the landlord–tenant divide in Ulster was widened by the actions of one Unionist MP who broke ranks with the party at the beginning of the twentieth century. T. W. Russell, MP for South Tyrone from 1886 to 1910, quickly acquired the reputation of a radical on the land question. During the winter of 1894–95, Russell had toured rural Ulster in an effort to mobilise Presbyterian tenant farmer support. He was demanding the acceleration of the land purchase process, an objective that was, in large part, achieved through the Conservative government's 1896 Land Act.

While his fellow Unionist MPs looked nervously at Russell's championing of the tenant farming class, his undoubted ability had caught the attention of two Conservative Party heavyweights, Arthur Balfour and Joseph Chamberlain, both of whom had taken a keen interest in Irish affairs. Russell was frequently asked to speak on behalf of Tory candidates in British by-elections, another feature that distinguished him from his more insular Unionist colleagues. Russell's progressive ideas reflected the "constructive Unionism" philosophy of a Conservative government that had land purchase at the core of its Irish policy. This would lead to his appointment as a junior minister in Lord Salisbury's government. While Russell's radicalism was partially constrained by government office, it was never extinguished. In November 1900 he was dismissed from the government following his declaration of support for compulsory land purchase, a radical demand that would have compelled landlords to sell their estates. Although Russell's sacking was welcomed by Saunderson and other leading landed figures in the Unionist movement, it freed the South Tyrone MP to challenge the party on the land question. Russell then resigned from his constituency party and formed the Ulster Farmers' and Labourers' Union and Compulsory Purchase Association in June 1901. This drew him into line with radical agrarians on the Nationalist side who were demanding a complete overhaul of the Irish land system. Russell's intention was to challenge Ulster Unionist candidates at the polls whenever the opportunity arose. On three occasions from February 1902 to March 1903 Russellite candidates fought by-elections in what had been safe Ulster Unionist seats, winning East Down and North Fermanagh and polling respectably in South Antrim. This rattled the dominant Unionist party, though support from Catholic tenant farmers had proved pivotal in tipping the balance in favour of the Russellites in both East Down and North Fermanagh.

Russell's impact was short-lived, as both seats were retaken by official Unionist Party candidates at the 1906 general election. Russell had misjudged the appeal of class-based politics in Ulster. The truth was that if the Home Rule threat re-emerged, as it did in muted form in 1904–5, class politics would be pushed to the margins. Russell had managed to retain his South Tyrone seat in 1906, and he was joined at Westminster by a fellow agrarian campaigner who had defeated the prominent Unionist, William Moore, in North Antrim. This was a constituency in which Presbyterian tenant farmers often took an independent stand. In the 1906 general election the victorious candidate, R. G. Glendinning, who stood as an Independent Unionist with Russellite backing, also received support from Thomas Sloan. He was another Unionist maverick who had distanced himself from the official party when he launched the Independent Orange Order in

June 1903. Sloan, a shipyard worker who had risen to prominence through his membership of the fiercely anti-Catholic Belfast Protestant Association, had become a savage critic of the Unionist Party, and of Saunderson in particular, for what he described as its failure to demonstrate sufficient zeal in safeguarding Protestant interests. Sloan had enough support in Belfast, especially in the Sandy Row area, to defeat the Unionist Party's candidate in the South Belfast by-election held in August 1902. While the Independent Orange Order was dwarfed by established Orangeism, it did make inroads in parts of South Belfast and North Antrim, a development that had worked to Glendinning's advantage in the 1906 election. However, Sloan's narrow brand of sectarian politics never threatened to do lasting damage to the Unionist Party in Ulster in the period up to 1914.

The lesson drawn by senior Unionist figures in the north from these events was that the party's dominance was only challenged during those periods when there was no prospect of Home Rule. Without this impending danger, Unionist politics was frequently characterised by apathy. While the party's MPs had a reasonable record of attendance at Westminster, it was clear that most of them, like their Nationalist counterparts, had little interest in wider United Kingdom affairs. Party discipline was never rigidly enforced, and the Irish Unionists often appeared as an incoherent group of individuals with the capacity to annoy their Conservative allies in government. Younger, more able MPs began to blame the ageing Saunderson for this state of affairs. In the early years of the twentieth century, he was essentially semi-retired and deaf to any suggestion that the party he had founded needed to change in order to halt this drift. The party's apparent inability to deal effectively with the challenges posed by Russell and Sloan only added to the sense of frustration felt by these younger men. Saunderson's political instincts had made the defence of landlord interests a primary concern, but landlord influence, though still powerful, had declined by the end of the nineteenth century. In Ulster a new group of younger men drawn from the professional middle classes had grown impatient with Saunderson and were determined to modernise the party. Led by William Moore, the MP for North Antrim since February 1899, and Charles Craig, who first entered parliament in February 1905, these younger MPs quickly attracted publicity through their attacks on the under secretary at Dublin Castle. Sir Antony MacDonnell's appointment as the top civil servant in Ireland in 1902 clearly did not meet with the approval of these more outspoken new MPs. MacDonnell was a Catholic and the brother of an Irish Parliamentary Party MP, and his reform agenda immediately raised suspicions among the Ulster Unionist MPs. It was also widely known that Wyndham, the Irish chief secretary, had given MacDonnell considerable latitude in the formulation of the government's Irish policy. This made both Wyndham and MacDonnell targets for angry Unionist MPs who were fiercely critical of what they saw as Westminster's readiness to appease Irish Nationalism. Wyndham, in turn, was often appalled by the sectarian politics associated with these Ulster Unionists.

Moore, Craig and other Ulster Unionists had expressed concern about the danger posed by O'Brien's conciliation strategy. The idea that progressive landlords, such as Dunraven, could work closely with moderate Nationalists to build consensus was anathema to those Ulster Unionists who viewed any tampering with the Union as a recipe for Home Rule. At the same time, these Ulster militants held Saunderson responsible both for the failure to distance the Unionist party sufficiently from the liberal landlords and for his ineffectiveness in challenging what the *Belfast News-Letter* described as the "anti-Unionist policy" of the government. This dissatisfaction led to the organisation of a conference in Belfast on 2 December 1904, at which delegates from across Ulster expressed their determination to resist any attempt by the government to introduce any devolution scheme in Ireland. While each speaker at the conference acknowledged that the current Balfour-led Conservative government was sound on the Constitution, it was clear that part of the reason for the growing concern among Unionist MPs was that they never completely trusted the Tory Party's commitment to the Union. Significantly, Saunderson was unable to be present at the conference due to ill health. One of the principal speakers at the Belfast YMCA hall was the prominent business and political figure, Thomas Sinclair, who had played a central role during the Ulster Unionist Convention in 1892. Sinclair told delegates that he had been "startled" to learn of Dunraven's thinking on devolution and warned that there was now an urgent requirement to inform opinion in Britain on Ulster Unionist feeling. Wyndham's "conciliatory administration" came under fire from a number of delegates who widened their criticism to denounce proposals for a new Catholic university. MacDonnell, in particular, was accused of "undermining the principles of Unionism", and Balfour was called upon to purge the Irish administration of all devolutionists.

One of Moore's declared aims in preparing for the Belfast conference was the intention to develop closer links between MPs and their constituents. Hence, many of the delegates attending the December meeting were selected by their constituency associations. This was an indication that these younger MPs wanted to modernise Unionism and strengthen its grass-roots base to create a more professional political party. This meant a move away from the landlord-influenced paternalism that had been a pronounced feature of early Unionism. J. B. Lonsdale, the MP for Mid-Armagh, had informed the delegates that it would be a "great advantage to have a strong Central Council able to declare the mind of the Loyalists of Ireland on every important question". Moore, in turn, was adamant that the new body should "represent the collective Unionist strength of the province". The Belfast conference would pave the way for the establishment of the Ulster

Unionist Council (UUC) on 3 March 1905. At this gathering Moore accused the Conservative government of following an "anti-Unionist agenda" before driving home his attack on the Wyndham–MacDonnell combination. He also vented his anger at sections of the press in Britain that had "sneered at and reviled the Ulster Unionist Party for the vigour and determination with which they have prosecuted the campaign against the Wyndham-MacDonnell secret compact". The campaign did lead to success. Three days later, on 6 March, Wyndham's resignation was announced, though MacDonnell, who had been accused by Moore of "acting as a politician", remained in post. The devolution affair had sparked a furious reaction from Ulster Unionists, but its most significant consequence was the establishment of the UUC. It was an exclusively Ulster body that confirmed the existence of a powerful regional element within Irish Unionism. Moore and his colleagues had become increasingly frustrated by Saunderson's laissez-faire attitude and by Unionism's failure to silence independent Unionist voices such as Russell and Sloan. Previously, Ulster's business and professional classes had been content to allow the landlords to lead Irish Unionism, but the creation of the UUC signalled an end to this situation. The new body would reflect grass-roots opinion and enable an emerging, more militant bourgeois leadership to place Ulster's, particularly Belfast's, interests at the heart of its campaign to defend the Union.

Balfour aimed to soothe Unionist nerves with the choice of Walter Long to succeed Wyndham as chief secretary. Long had a reputation as a staunch defender of the Union, and his instinctive sympathy for Irish landlordism ensured that the strict enforcement of law and order throughout the country would be prioritised. Naturally, this focus on a firm security policy was welcomed by Irish Unionists, but Long rejected Ulster Unionist demands to have MacDonnell removed from the Irish administration. Although he informed the cabinet that the under secretary had been given too much latitude by his predecessor, Long insisted that sacking MacDonnell "would cause profound dissatisfaction in many quarters". Long's refusal to dismiss MacDonnell angered Unionist MPs who were determined to keep the spotlight on the under secretary. When Long resisted further pressure, the Ulster MPs met at Westminster on 6 April, announcing that they would refuse to pledge their support to the Irish administration while MacDonnell remained in Dublin Castle. Yet the new chief secretary was determined to win their confidence. Significantly, Long chose Belfast for his first public speech in his new role, speaking to a gathering of leading Ulster Unionist figures on 20 April. His host, Lord Londonderry, had prepared the ground by informing the audience, "So long as Mr Long held the office of chief secretary … the Irish government would be conducted on lines consistent, both in letter and spirit, with Unionist principles and with Unionist interests." In his address Long told those present, and this included the Unionist MPs, that his principal objective was to secure the Union. At the same time, he emphasised that there would be major changes in the way that Dublin Castle operated under his direction. Long declared that it was the duty of any chief secretary "not to do anything ... nor countenance anything on the part of those who served under him which would tend to weaken the foundations on which the Union rested". The new chief secretary went on to confirm that there would be a much greater focus on the maintenance of law and order across Ireland under his leadership, adding that the law would be applied "fairly and impartially".

Indeed, Long was anxious to appear impartial in governing Ireland. He made regular tours of the country, meeting local representatives and taking a genuine interest in their concerns. One such tour took him to the west of the country where he reviewed the work of the Congested Districts Board and offered government assistance for local projects. The trip to the west in September 1905 included a well-publicised visit to Achill Island. Yet for all his rhetoric about governing Ireland fairly, Long barely concealed the fact that he made extensive use of his patronage powers to strengthen Unionist influence. Furthermore, when advice was required, the chief secretary preferred not to consult his officials in Dublin Castle but to liaise with leading Unionists, particularly Saunderson. In the month following his Belfast visit, Long spoke to an audience of 200 leading southern Unionists at an event organised by the Irish Unionist Alliance (IUA) in Dublin's Gresham Hotel. Once again, he presented an impassioned defence of the Union, claiming that it was vital both to the stability of the Empire and for prosperity for Ireland. He also played to his audience by highlighting the importance of strict enforcement of the law, particularly in relation to the defence of property. However, most of his speech was taken up with a denunciation of Dunraven and his support for conciliation. Clearly, Long was intent on rebuilding Unionist trust in the Conservative government, and he achieved some progress in this regard during his nine-month stint in office.

The 1906 general election was a traumatic experience for the Tory Party. It had gone into the election split over the issue of tariff reform, and Balfour's refusal to relinquish the leadership of the party in the wake of a humiliating reverse ensured that the bitter internal feuding would continue. The situation alarmed Long, who felt that the defence of the Union should be the party's priority. The Liberal victory had put Home Rule back on the agenda, and Long knew from his many contacts in Ireland that Unionist confidence in the Tory Party had been significantly damaged during its last two years in office. By 1906, moreover, Long had a further reason for seeking absolute clarification on the Conservative Party's Irish policy. In the recent general election, Long had lost his South Bristol seat, but he immediately secured the Unionist nomination for the South Dublin

County seat, which he won with a majority of more than 1,300 votes. Apart from Trinity College, which returned two safe Unionist seats, South Dublin County was the only Unionist success outside Ulster. In total the Unionists won twenty seats, though three of these MPs were classified as Independent Unionists: Russell retained South Tyrone, Glendinning defeated Moore in a straight fight in North Antrim, and John Gordon took South Derry. The latter was described as a Liberal Unionist, but he would soon join the mainstream Unionist ranks. Indeed, the outcome of the 1906 election confirmed that Moore and his colleagues had been successful in galvanising Ulster Unionism following the devolution crisis.

The fact that MacDonnell remained at the head of the civil service in Dublin Castle added to Unionist apprehension about the immediate future. Long was now aware that many Unionist MPs suspected Balfour of promoting the recent devolution plan. This made the former chief secretary's task of cementing links between British Conservatism and Irish Unionism more difficult. His bold response to this situation was to demand the publication of all documents relevant to MacDonnell's appointment as under secretary in 1902. All involved knew that MacDonnell had been given considerable freedom in formulating Irish policy, but such a request would determine whether this had been the result of a personal arrangement with Wyndham or an agreement made at the behest of the government. Long's unexpected move drew him into conflict with an angry Balfour, who refused to release the material. What followed was a series of bitter exchanges between the two, with Wyndham and MacDonnell joining in the correspondence on Balfour's side. Long quickly widened his attack by accusing the Wyndham-led administration of presiding over a hopelessly ineffective security policy, but it was his comments on devolution that attracted most attention. Balfour's reaction revealed that he viewed Long as a puppet who was being manipulated by the Irish Unionists, but it was clear from the correspondence that the former premier was being too dismissive of Unionist fears. One result of this reopening of the devolution affair was that Long's influence in Irish Unionist circles soared. The other was that those Conservatives who took a keen interest in Irish affairs now viewed Long as the Tory Party's Irish expert. Long had first raised the devolution affair in a speech to the annual meeting of the IUA in Dublin on 29 August 1906. As the principal speaker, Long was careful to emphasise his Unionist credentials as he highlighted the danger to the Empire posed by Home Rule. Significantly, he then declared that recent press speculation suggesting that Unionists were softening their stance on Home Rule was wholly inaccurate. The clear message was that, going forward, Unionists would view any tampering with the Union as the start of the slippery slope to Home Rule.

Clearly, Long had impressed his Unionist colleagues. It was, therefore, no surprise when he was installed as chairman of the Irish Unionist Party following

Saunderson's death in October 1906. This "English squire", as he was often described in the press, now intensified his efforts to educate British opinion on the Irish question. In January 1907 Long launched the Union Defence League, an essentially British Unionist organisation that was responsible for disseminating anti-Home Rule propaganda in Britain. Long himself undertook a number of speaking engagements across England, attempting to stimulate interest in Irish affairs among Conservative supporters. Speaking in Leeds on 14 March, Long returned to the theme of the danger that Irish Home Rule would mean for the stability of the British Empire. For Long, apathy among Conservative voters who could not see beyond the tariff reform controversy was his greatest challenge at a time when he knew that MacDonnell, now with the cover of a Liberal government, was working on a variation of his earlier devolution scheme. In January 1907 Long had warned Ulster Unionists of the Liberal government's plan to introduce Home Rule by "instalment", claiming that such a strategy was part of a plan for "hoodwinking the British people". However, the withdrawal of the Irish Council Bill removed any immediate danger, leaving Long with the difficult task of trying to highlight the future threat posed by a Westminster government that would be tempted to alter the constitutional status quo.

In addition to promoting closer links between British and Irish Unionists, Long was equally anxious to encourage greater unity among Unionists in Ireland. Interestingly, during his address to the IUA the previous August, Long admitted, "I know little of Ulster", but he rejected immediately the notion that Ulster might be treated separately in any future Home Rule settlement. Clearly, he was uncomfortable with the idea that Unionists in the north had the ability to protect their own interests. Long used his position as the head of Unionism's two principal organisations to press for greater Unionist unity. In January 1907 he was elected chairman of the UUC, having already been selected as chairman of the IUA. Speaking at the annual meeting of the UUC on 30 January, Long recorded the determination of Ulster Unionists to oppose any alteration of the present constitutional link, adding that such a stance was crucial for imperial unity. Two days later, in an address at the Reform Club in Belfast, he paid tribute to his Ulster Unionist hosts, describing them as "a resolute minority representing … the wealth, the intelligence, the commercial activity of the land" who were intent on defending their liberties. While Long carefully tailored his arguments for his respective northern and southern followers, he pursued his strategy of seeking greater unity between the regional groups. In December 1907 he succeeded, with strong southern Unionist backing, in establishing the Joint Committee of Unionist Associations. This new body drew its membership from both the IUA and UUC and alternated its meetings between Dublin and Belfast, but it never fully functioned as Long had intended. Ulster Unionists increasingly highlighted their separate identity, a trend that had been strengthened by the formation of the UUC. The one area in which there was effective cooperation was in propaganda work on the mainland. Both Ulster and southern Unionists were frequent visitors to Britain where they were prominent figures in support of Tory candidates in by-elections. To this end, an avalanche of propaganda material setting out the Unionist case was distributed across Britain, with marginal seats identified for particular attention.

While Long struggled to turn Irish Unionism into a cohesive force, he did make some headway in developing British Unionism by attracting support for the Unionist cause among Tory voters on the mainland. Following the collapse of the Irish Council Bill, Long turned his attention to the deteriorating security situation in Ireland, as the Ranch War caused unrest in a number of counties in the west and midlands. In a letter to *The Times* in November 1907, he attacked Birrell for his inability to deal with cattle-driving. Claiming that order in the countryside could be restored in a few weeks by resolute action, Long accused the government of trying to appease Irish Nationalism. Over the next year he continued to highlight the breakdown of law and order in the country, arguing that the government had been "cowardly" in its response to boycotting. Yet, apart from these sporadic interventions, Long struggled to give Irish Unionism a voice as the decade drew to a close. For much of 1908 Long suffered from ill-health, which meant that he was unable to attend the annual meeting of the UUC. His absence did not please leading Ulster Unionists. During 1909 he spent several months holidaying in South Africa and Rhodesia as he sought to recuperate, but he had already begun to consider his own position as he mapped out his political future. Long's natural instincts meant that the defence of the Union would always remain his guiding star, but by 1909 the political agenda at Westminster was dominated by Lloyd George's radical budget proposals. These prompted hysteria among many Conservatives, particularly those associated with the landed class. Long was a natural spokesman for these angry squires, and he became President of the Budget Protest League on his return from South Africa.

The chancellor intended to increase taxation sharply to pay for the Liberal government's groundbreaking social reform programme and meet its commitments on rapidly rising defence expenditure. In addition to the introduction of a new supertax for those with incomes in excess of £5,000 per annum, Lloyd George wanted to impose a new land tax and increase death duties. Long quickly emerged as one of the government's most vocal critics, claiming that the Liberals had adopted a socialist programme that would ultimately wipe out the landed class. A serious constitutional crisis followed when the House of Lords, breaking with parliamentary convention, voted against the budget on 30 November 1909. An election was inevitable, and it was widely anticipated that a wounded Liberal

Party would appeal to the electorate on the question of whether the wishes of the elected chamber should be blocked by an unelected group of hereditary peers. Certainly, the slogan "peers versus people" had a powerful impact, and Long was convinced that in such circumstances the Tory Party's best chance of success would be to focus on the Home Rule danger and its consequent threat to the Empire. Voting in the general election, which began on 15 January 1910, took place over a period of two weeks, with the final results tally available towards the end of the month. While the Conservatives recovered much of the ground lost in 1906, finishing just two seats behind the Liberals, it was clear that they would remain in opposition. There was a hung parliament but, assured of the IPP's support, the Liberals, who had won a total of 275 seats, continued in government. Moreover, with the IPP now holding the balance of power, it was widely expected that a move to introduce Home Rule would take place in the near future.

In the January 1910 general election, Long was returned as the MP for the Strand constituency in London. Earlier, he had informed both the constituency association in South Dublin County and his Unionist colleagues at Westminster that he would no longer be in a position to serve as Irish Unionist leader, but emphasised that his support for the Union would remain as steadfast as ever. Immediately after the election, Lonsdale, the MP for Mid-Armagh who acted as secretary to the Irish Unionist MPs, was directed to contact Sir Edward Carson, inviting him to become the chairman of the Irish Unionist Party. Carson, the MP for Trinity College, was an outstanding lawyer whose courtroom skills had given him celebrity status in Edwardian Britain. He took some time to consider Lonsdale's proposition. While the defence of the Union was the cause that initially drew Carson into politics, he must have been aware that by accepting the leadership of the Irish Unionist Party, he would be forsaking the possibility of future political or legal advancement. In spite of this, Carson conveyed

Sir Edward Carson (1854–1935), with his dog.

his willingness to lead the Irish Unionist Party, and this development was made public on 21 February 1910. The *Belfast News-Letter* reported that the choice would "give complete satisfaction", adding that Carson was "a brilliant debater, who can defend the Union against the attacks of its ablest opponents". Carson was a Southern Unionist who lived and worked in England. From the outset he recognised the importance of Ulster, where Unionist numbers, organisation and wealth would be crucial in any future struggle against Home Rule. Following the election, Carson led a group of 21 Irish Unionists in the House of Commons, though only three of these MPs represented Southern constituencies. Unionists were returned for both of the Trinity College seats, while Long's successor in South Dublin County, Captain Bryan Cooper, scraped home with a narrow majority. These Irish Unionists sat alongside their Conservative allies, though the relationship between Irish and British Unionists was never straightforward.

The January general election had been dominated by arguments over the budget and the future of the House of Lords. In Britain, Home Rule rarely featured as an issue during the campaign. Irish Unionists, by contrast, highlighted the dangers associated with Home Rule. An Ulster Hall rally in January heard that in the event of Home Rule becoming law a Nationalist-dominated parliament in Dublin would automatically look to Belfast, "the third great port in the UK", to raise the necessary finance to run the new system of government. Following the election, great concern was expressed about Redmond's role in the new parliament. The Irish leader was routinely accused of acting like a dictator, while Asquith was attacked for his weakness in fending off Redmond's demands. Of course, the constitutional crisis that had been triggered by the Lords' rejection of the budget and the outcome of the general election had presented the IPP with an opportunity which would be seized by Redmond. In a speech in Eastbourne on 21 April, Carson took aim at the Asquith, stating that he was "determined to drag the Crown in the mire" in an attempt to appease the Nationalists. He also suggested that his conduct marked "the blackest page in the history of our country". In fact, while Carson remained in high demand as a speaker at Conservative events across Britain, most of his energy during 1910 was devoted to his legal duties. The most high-profile case during this period was the Archer-Shee trial, which came to court in July 1910. Carson represented a young naval cadet, George Archer-Shee, who had been accused of stealing a postal order from another cadet before cashing it at the local post office. The case, which inspired Terence Rattigan's famous play, *The Winslow Boy,* captured the public's imagination, and it received widespread coverage in the national press. Carson's brilliant cross-examination of the postmistress proved decisive, as the court overturned a previous guilty verdict. The Archer-Shee trial clearly enhanced Carson's reputation, as he revelled in the role of fighting for the underdog against what appeared to be overwhelming odds.

Carson travelled to his favourite holiday destination, Homburg, a spa town in the Rhineland, to recuperate after the trial. His Irish Unionist colleagues were accustomed to such absences due to both perceived ill health and preoccupation with his legal work. Carson was in the High Court on 12 July 1910 at the start of the Archer-Shee trial and was, therefore, unable to attend the main "Twelfth" demonstration in Saintfield, County Down. In his letter of apology, which was read to the assembled Orangemen by the Belfast Grand Master, Col R. H. Wallace, Carson urged "all loyal men in Ireland [to] show their unaltered determination to resist any attempt to break up the Constitution of the UK". These words confirmed that Carson viewed the defence of the Union in an all-Ireland context. Indeed, this was reflected in one of the resolutions endorsed by the Belfast Orangemen on the day. It made reference to "the absolute unity of the Irish Unionist Party" and paid tribute to the party's MPs for "their defence of the interests of Irish Loyalists".

Although Carson was aware of the importance of Ulster to the Unionist cause, he did not make his first visit to the province as leader until the end of November 1910. In his address to a large body of supporters in the Ulster Hall, Carson relayed news of powerful support for the Unionist cause in England. Warning that the real danger with Home Rule was that it would inevitably lead to full independence, Carson went on to present a very detailed analysis of the financial prospects for Ireland under devolution, claiming that a Home Rule parliament would immediately face a shortfall of £2½ million. There had been recent speculation in the British press that opposition to Home Rule might be easing in Ulster, but Carson insisted, "I know my Ulster men." To the delight of his Belfast audience, the Unionist leader repeated Lord Randolph Churchill's famous words spoken at the same venue in 1886, "Ulster would fight and Ulster would be right." Still, Carson ended his speech with the call, "God save Ireland." During the course of his address, he had denounced the Liberal government, describing Asquith's Irish policy as a "nefarious conspiracy", a phrase he would use repeatedly in the 1910–14 period. Two days later, in a Derry speech, he would refer to the "nefarious treachery" of his opponents. On the following evening Carson was in more familiar territory when he spoke in Rathmines on behalf of Bryan Cooper, who was battling to retain the seat that he had won in January. In his address, Carson reassured his Dublin supporters that Unionists in Ulster "did not want and would not have separate treatment from the rest of Ireland", adding that "their cause was one with that of the south". At that moment the vast majority of Unionists in Ulster were fully supportive of this all-Ireland strategy.

In the December general election, Cooper was defeated in Dublin South County, and another Unionist candidate was unsuccessful in St Stephen's Green. In the recent past, Dublin Unionists had enjoyed a measure of success

Table 1: Selected January and December 1910 election results.

	Jan 1910		Dec 1910	
	Nationalist	Unionist	Nationalist	Unionist
Belfast West	4,631	4,139	4,543	4,080
Down South	3,815	3,180	3,668	3,040
Dublin South County *	5,006	5,072	5,223	5,090
Dublin St Stephen's Green	3,683	3,021	3,594	2,765
Londonderry City	2,378	2,435	2,310	2,415
Monaghan North	3,477	2,005	3,365	1,937
Tyrone Mid	3,314	2,475	3,102	2,379
Tyrone East	3,208	3,096	3,108	2,968
Totals	29,512	25,423	28,913	24,674
Total vote	54,935		53,587	
% of vote	53.7%	46.3%	54.0%	46.0%
Majority	7.4%		7.9%	
% change	-0.5%			

* Most marginal seat that changed hands

Table 2: Selected January and December 1910 election results.

	Jan 1910		Dec 1910	
	Unionist	Liberal	Unionist	Liberal
Antrim North	3,519	3,135	3,557	2,974
Down East	4,028	3,054	4,110	2,412
Fermanagh North	2,474	2,124	2,402	2,055
Londonderry South	3,985	3,678	3,845	3,513
Tyrone North *	3,136	3,238	3,038	3,170
Tyrone South	3,054	2,770	2,962	2,662
Totals	20,196	17,999	19,914	16,786
Total vote	38,195		36,700	
% of vote	52.9%	47.1%	54.3%	45.7%
Majority	5.8%		8.5%	
% change	-2.8%			

* Only seat won and held by Liberals

in each of these constituencies, but the December contest demonstrated that, outside Ulster, Unionists could only expect to win the Trinity College seats. Within Ulster, moreover, Nationalists were returned in all of the seats in Cavan, Monaghan and Donegal. A close inspection of the 1910 results demonstrates that in those constituencies where there was a straight fight between Unionism and Nationalism, Unionist candidates marginally increased their share of the vote from January to December on a slightly lower turnout. In another six Ulster constituencies, Unionist candidates were challenged by Liberals, with the latter victorious in North Tyrone. While the Liberal majority in this constituency increased very slightly in December, the overall pattern highlighted a modest increase in the Unionist share of the vote, suggesting that Ulster Unionists were able to take advantage of the increased risk of Home Rule that had become apparent during the course of 1910. There was, nevertheless, a stubborn rump of Liberal supporters in Ulster, with a strong Presbyterian influence, who defied the call for Unionist solidarity on the constitutional issue.

The Irish Question in British Politics

Following the Act of Union, the British government was required to assume greater responsibility for Irish affairs. At no point after 1800, however, did Ireland become fully integrated within the United Kingdom. Instead, a separate administration continued to operate in Dublin under the direction of a viceroy and chief secretary. For the most part, both main parties in Britain regarded Ireland as different to England, Scotland and Wales, with the result that specifically Irish solutions were attempted to deal with what the Westminster elite considered distinctively Irish problems. In the last fifteen years of the nineteenth century, the Liberals and Conservatives differed significantly in their approach to Ireland. With Gladstone in crusading mode, the Liberals favoured Irish Home Rule, a policy which acknowledged that Ireland should be viewed as a separate nation. In response, the Conservatives based their strategy on the practical, and very generous, policy of land purchase, assisting Ireland's tenant farmers to become owners of the land that they rented. Significantly, the Tories firmly rejected the Liberal argument that the Irish constituted a distinct nation. At the same time, both parties convinced themselves that their respective policies on Ireland would ultimately cement the Union. The Conservatives were confident that large-scale land purchase would create a new class of property owners in Ireland, who would be instinctively conservative and would, therefore, step back from the kind of agrarian agitation that had underpinned Irish Nationalism in the last quarter of the nineteenth century. Meanwhile, Liberals believed that the experience of devolution would encourage Irish voters to act with a greater sense of responsibility, which would curb any future demand for independence.

Gladstone's retirement in March 1894 following the emphatic rejection of the second Home Rule Bill by the House of Lords led to a reassessment of his party's Irish policy. The "Grand Old Man" had deployed moral and historical arguments in support of his Home Rule objective, though he also had an eye on the potential electoral support that the issue might generate in certain parts of the country. The reality, however, proved somewhat different. Irish Home Rule had not been a vote-winner in Britain. While there were other significant reasons, the Liberal Party was out of office for almost eighteen years in the two decades after the defeat of the first Home Rule Bill in 1886. This fact was not lost on Gladstone's colleagues. His immediate successor, Lord Rosebery, wanted to distance the party from the entire Home Rule project. However, a majority of senior Liberal figures favoured its retention with the proviso that it would no longer be at the heart of the party's programme. This was a recognition that the preoccupation with Home Rule under Gladstone had distracted the party from its focus on social reform, an outcome that clearly had negative electoral consequences. Overhanging such thinking was the obvious concern that Home Rule had split the Liberals, and might do so in the future, while, simultaneously, handing an advantage to their Conservative opponents. The result of the soul-searching was a decision to proceed slowly on the path to Home Rule. This was the strategy that was outlined by the new Liberal leader, Sir Henry Campbell-Bannerman, before the 1900 general election.

Clearly, there was little enthusiasm for Irish Home Rule among the party's leadership. Instead, there was an acknowledgement that devolution remained the ultimate answer to the Irish question and should, therefore, be the party's long-term goal. This implied that there was no need for the kind of sweeping measure that Gladstone had sought to carry in 1886 and 1893. Not only did this mean that Irish Home Rule was removed from the party's immediate agenda but it probably meant that the best way to achieve the party's ultimate goal would be by incremental steps. Such a cautious approach made it more difficult for the Tories to bang the pro-Union drum but also had the advantage of limiting the likelihood of a further split among Liberal MPs. Liberal leaders, moreover, were mindful that Irish support might be necessary to keep a Liberal government in office if an election produced a hung parliament. This had happened in the past, and the IPP's ability to take a bloc of 80-plus seats on a regular basis rendered such an outcome more likely. The final consideration for the Liberal front bench was the attitude of the House of Lords to any future Home Rule measure. While the Lords' veto remained in place, there was no possibility of an extensive Home Rule measure becoming law, even if the Liberal Party altered its position on the Irish question. Such circumstances ensured that the Liberals would adopt a pragmatic position on the Home Rule issue. It would be an aspiration but not one that needed to be vigorously pursued. This cautious approach was conveyed to the electorate in somewhat vague terms prior to the 1906 election.

What can be said with some certainty was that the Liberal landslide victory of 1906, ending a decade of Tory rule, could not be attributed in any way to the party's stance on the issue of Irish Home Rule. The party had campaigned on a social reform programme, and a talented cohort of younger ministers concentrated on the delivery of new welfare measures. Pressure to move forward on the Home Rule front was, of course, applied by the IPP, but the new Liberal administration, supported by a big majority in the House of Commons, respectfully declined to resurrect the Gladstonian formula on Ireland. In any case, the Lords' position on Home Rule had not altered, meaning that the ultimate success of any Home Rule measure would be dependent upon new restrictions imposed on the upper chamber. The time for such constitutional change was not yet at hand. Instead, the Liberal government sought to placate Irish Nationalism, and move a little closer to the final Home Rule objective, with the Irish Council Bill. Introduced in May 1907 by the chief secretary, Augustine Birrell, the bill proposed to give a largely elected Irish Council control over various aspects of the Irish administration. These included local government and education, but the powers to be transferred were strictly limited, and this led to their rejection by Nationalist leaders whose expectations continued to be shaped by Home Rule principles.

Nationalist disappointment with the Liberal government could not cloud the fact that future progress on the Home Rule objective was wholly dependent on Liberal support. This made the IPP's continued support for an alliance with the Liberals at Westminster essential, though it was difficult to defend such a stance in the wake of the collapse of an inadequate Irish Council Bill. While the Liberal government may have steered clear of a comprehensive measure of Irish Home Rule, it did, nevertheless, build on the reform programme that had been introduced by its Tory predecessors. The country's housing stock was significantly improved by new legislation passed in 1906 and 1909. A major grievance was redressed in 1908, when a national university was created by bringing together the colleges in Dublin, Galway and Cork. While this new institution was declared to be non-denominational, it was, in effect, the Catholic university for which the IPP had long campaigned. It was also backed by generous government funding. In the following year the Liberal government's Land Act, while seeking to impose tighter Treasury control, was an acknowledgement that the Conservative Party's policy of land purchase could not be jettisoned.

The 1903 Land Act had been the high point of the Tory administration's land purchase strategy. Overseen by the reforming chief secretary, George Wyndham, the 1903 Act had stemmed from an agreement between representatives of both landlords and tenants, and both sides had much to gain from the legislation. While the prime minister, Arthur Balfour, recognised that opponents of the Wyndham Act would present the legislation as an extravagant gift from the British taxpayer to Irish landlords and tenants, he viewed the measure as a major piece of social reform. Certainly, the land purchase policy represented a huge financial commitment from a Tory government at a point when it was looking to pay off debts incurred in the recent Boer War. The Treasury turned to the bond market to access the huge sums required to allow the transfer of land from landlords to tenants. The bonds allowed repayments to be staggered over a very long timescale in a way that was acceptable to early twentieth-century investors. The Tory leader continued to believe that social and economic grievances underpinned the demand for Home Rule and that if these could be redressed, then Irish Nationalists might become reconciled to the Union. He also estimated that there might be some electoral benefit for the Tory Party in Britain if it could demonstrate that it was striving to implement progressive polices in Ireland that would mean genuine progress for all its citizens. Growing support for the concept of conciliation among Irish landlords made it easier for Balfour's government to pursue such a course. At the same time, he never wavered from his belief that there was no such thing as Irish nationality. In Balfour's view, Ireland needed strong, but fair, government. Such a strategy might go some way towards placating Irish Nationalists while simultaneously reassuring Irish landlords. Interestingly, leading IPP figures such as John Dillon felt that the generous financial backing for constructive Unionism could easily dilute the demand for Home Rule and should be regarded as a threat to Nationalist goals.

Even the normally unflappable Balfour was caught off guard by the ferocious Unionist reaction to the publication of MacDonnell's devolution proposals in September 1904. While Wyndham moved quickly to distance himself from the growing storm around the devolution scheme, he faced a barrage of criticism from angry Ulster Unionists. This intensified when the chief secretary refused to dismiss MacDonnell. Unionist suspicions that the under secretary was attempting to undermine the Union by opening the door to eventual Home Rule could not be calmed, and there was a growing feeling among the Ulster hardliners that Wyndham could not be trusted on the constitutional question. Balfour responded by defending his chief secretary in the face of this Unionist onslaught. The prime minister had a high regard for Wyndham's ability, and he was one of his closest friends in cabinet. Balfour was also furious at the actions of the Ulster MPs, principally Moore and Lonsdale, who had orchestrated the campaign against the chief secretary in the House of Commons. By March 1905, however, with unease growing on the Tory backbenches, Balfour relented and accepted Wyndham's resignation. In spite of his outrage at the behaviour of Ulster

Unionists in hounding Wyndham from office, Balfour felt it prudent to assuage Unionist anger by appointing Walter Long as his replacement. Long would remain as chief secretary for Ireland for the final nine months that the Conservative government was in office. Clearly, the devolution crisis had placed a considerable strain on relations between the Tory leadership and Irish Unionists, particularly those in Ulster. Going forward, these Ulster Unionists sometimes displayed a lack of confidence in their Conservative allies' determination to maintain the Union at all costs. Significantly, the emergence of the Ulster Unionist Council, which had been a direct consequence of the devolution crisis, now provided Ulster with a more distinct voice within the broader movement of Irish Unionism.

Still, Ireland was far from Balfour's major concern during his premiership. He had a government, and a party, that was bitterly divided on the issue of tariff reform. One of his cabinet's most influential figures was Joseph Chamberlain, the ex-Liberal who had crossed the floor of the House of Commons in protest at Gladstone's adoption of Home Rule. A brilliant, but divisive, figure, Chamberlain had served as secretary of state for the colonies since 1895, a post that obviously encouraged him to develop his ideas on Britain's imperial future at a time of increasing challenge by the United States and Germany. In 1903 he went public with his tariff reform plan, essentially the creation of a protectionist British Empire trading bloc, which would mean tariffs on imported goods outside the Empire. In September 1903 he resigned from the cabinet to rally public support behind the tariff reform banner, but his initiative provoked an outcry from a large number of Tories who defended the principle of free trade. Chamberlain argued that his scheme of imperial preference would end unemployment in Britain, but his Conservative opponents, many of whom represented constituencies in industrial areas, warned that the working class would suffer from the higher food prices that would inevitably follow the imposition of tariffs. In October 1903 Balfour was forced into a cabinet reshuffle, as the most outspoken advocates on both sides of the argument were now outside government, but his failure to provide a clear course of action exacerbated the party's difficulties. The Tory premier spent the remainder of his time in office trying to hold these warring factions together. While he had retained a genuine interest in Irish affairs since his period as chief secretary in the 1880s, Balfour viewed the furore over the devolution crisis as an unwelcome distraction as he struggled to maintain some semblance of party unity. The Liberals would exploit this situation during the 1906 general election, as they stood on the free trade platform which highlighted the division among their Conservative opponents. It was also apparent that the Tory cry of "the threat to the Union", which was heard repeatedly during the campaign, made little impact on the final outcome.

The Liberal landslide victory in 1906 left the Conservative Party with much to ponder. Pessimists in the Tory ranks began to consider a future two-party Westminster system in which the Conservatives would find themselves relegated to the position of a minor party. With the party as bitterly divided as ever over the tariff reform issue, and Balfour clinging to the leadership, the road back to government seemed littered with obstacles. In such circumstances it was not surprising that Long, in his new role as Irish Unionist Party leader, struggled to promote genuine interest in the Irish question among Conservative supporters in Britain. To some observers, the introduction of the Liberal administration's Irish Council Bill that was largely, like the earlier Conservative devolution scheme, the work of Sir Antony MacDonnell, suggested that the two main parties at Westminster were pursuing parallel strategies in relation to Ireland. This accidental bipartisanship would not last. The collapse of the Irish Council Bill led the Liberal government to focus on less controversial issues. Asquith would subsequently highlight the university and land reforms as evidence of the Liberals' good intentions towards Ireland, and he repeatedly stressed that no part of the United Kingdom would benefit more from the recent introduction of the old age pension than Ireland.

It was, however, the rejection of the 1909 People's Budget by the House of Lords that relit the Home Rule flame. All the interested parties at Westminster knew that any move to curb the Lords' powers could facilitate the passage of a new Home Rule Bill. Moreover, Asquith, who succeeded Campbell-Bannerman in early April 1908, appeared to abandon his characteristic caution on the Home Rule question when he suggested that Ireland was "the one undeniable failure of British statesmanship" during a speech that he gave just one week before he assumed the premiership. Asquith returned to this theme during his famous Albert Hall speech on 10 December 1909. The prime minister used this pre-election rally, which drew an audience in excess of 10,000, to set out the Liberal programme for the new parliament. When he turned to Ireland, Asquith insisted that the only viable policy was the establishment of "a system of full self-government in regard to purely Irish affairs", though he emphasised that there could not be any question of Ireland separating from the United Kingdom. He then highlighted the importance of planned changes to the Lords by noting that while the present parliament had been "disabled" from making progress on the Irish question, the hands of the Liberal government would be "entirely free" in a new parliament. While the *Belfast News-Letter* took some comfort from the fact that the prime minister had stopped short of making a specific legislative commitment – he did not actually use the term "Home Rule" – Asquith had undoubtedly made Irish Home Rule an issue in the January 1910 general election. Certainly, it was the clearest expression of Liberal intent on Home Rule for many years. Not surprisingly, Redmond had demanded that the Liberal Party should make Home Rule an issue in the forthcoming election when he spoke to an audience of Nationalist supporters in Dublin three weeks before Asquith's Albert Hall performance. Behind Redmond's statement there was, of course, the threat that Irish voters in Britain could withhold their support from Liberal candidates, though such action would only have damaged the Nationalist cause. Significantly, Nationalist leaders were fully aware of the importance of the Irish working-class vote to the Liberal Party, confirmation of which was provided by outcome of the 1906 general election.

The results of the January general election put the Irish Nationalists in a much stronger position. Holding the balance of power, Redmond insisted that the government should press ahead with ending the Lords' veto, rather than making the budget its priority. The Liberal cabinet clearly disliked such dictation, but the alternative was resignation, and this was a step that Asquith was desperate to avoid. What followed was three months of cat-and-mouse activity between the IPP and the Liberals, as each side sought to exploit the other's weaknesses. Meanwhile, the Tory opposition expressed outrage at what it claimed was the corrupt bargain hatched by Asquith and Redmond, even though there had been no formal agreement between the two leaders. Instead, in spite of Redmond's close links to a number of cabinet members, suspicion and mistrust governed relations between the two parties, whose leaders never established the kind of personal rapport that might have worked to each party's benefit. Just before the election the *Pall Mall Gazette* predicted that Asquith's Home Rule commitment would be met by "uncompromising hostility" from his Conservative and Unionist opponents. This proved to be an understatement. The Westminster village knew that Asquith was, at best, lukewarm on Home Rule, and the sequence of events in the first half of 1910 appeared to confirm the charge that the prime minister was acting under Nationalist duress. Yet the reality was that Redmond's position was never quite as strong as it seemed. While the IPP leader understood his predicament, he chose not to share this with his followers. The most obvious problem that he faced was that while, like Parnell, he could make or break the Liberal government, removing it from office would mean a return for his Tory enemies. This would dash any early prospect of Home Rule.

Redmond's position was further exposed by the political reaction to King Edward VII's sudden death in May 1910. His successor, George V, who had little grounding in these delicate political matters, found himself thrust into the constitutional crisis with the future of the House of Lords in the balance. Anxious to prevent the monarchy being dragged into a major political debate, the new king pressed for a conference between the Liberals and Conservatives in the hope that a compromise could be found. In the circumstances, both parties could see advantages in such a move and readily acceded to the monarch's request. The conference held its first meeting in June. If the two parties could reach agreement on the Lords' issue, Redmond knew that the Liberals would escape from their dependence on the IPP. It was no secret that the Home Rule question was often at the centre of discussions as the Conservative delegates at the conference argued that major constitutional changes should be put to the people before becoming law. Although Redmond's leverage had been threatened by the prospect of the emergence of a bipartisan approach which would, of course, extend to the Irish question, the conference broke down without agreement in November. This paved the way for a fresh election in the following month. While Asquith attempted to bury the Home Rule issue during the campaign, his Conservative opponents took every opportunity to present the proposal as a threat to both the United Kingdom and the Empire. They also pointed to the "treachery", which was how they described the dealings between the prime minister and the IPP leader. The results put the two main parties level on 272 seats, leaving the IPP again holding the balance of power. Redmond and the Nationalists had survived the summer scare and now appeared poised to deliver Home Rule.

While the constitutional conference had posed a danger to the prospects for Home Rule, it also gave Carson and the Irish Unionists cause for concern. A consensus reached between the Liberals and the Conservatives on the future of the House of Lords might be extended to secure a meeting of minds on other controversial areas such as Ireland. The Conservatives could not lend their support to Home Rule, but they did give serious consideration to the concept of federal home rule, or "Home Rule All Round" as it came to be known. Such a scheme held attractions for both parties. Federal home rule meant separate parliaments for England, Scotland, Wales and Ireland, all of which would be subject to the imperial parliament at Westminster. Rumours that such a plan was being discussed were soon circulating. This alarmed the Irish Unionists who pressed Carson to use his influence with Balfour to ensure that the Conservative Party distanced itself from any federal project. Balfour, who had continued as Tory leader following the January general election, had been a resolute opponent of Home Rule since he entered parliament in 1874, but even he could see certain advantages in the federal scheme under discussion. While these may have been insufficient to convince the Tory leader that federalism offered a solution, younger members of his party were certainly supportive of the idea. Unlike Balfour, moreover, they did not feel constrained by previous commitments made to Irish Unionism.

Carson was also aware that delegates at the constitutional conference had considered the possible formation of a coalition government, and there was an understanding that a federal Home Rule scheme would form part of its programme. Even more worrying for Carson and the Unionists was the positive comment that the Home Rule All Round concept generated in the national press. The issue was only resolved in November when the conference failed to reach agreement on the action that should follow the Lords' rejection of a future Home Rule Bill. Balfour declared that he would consult senior figures in his party before any commitment would be given. Having met about twenty senior MPs, including Carson, it became clear that a majority of Conservatives wanted further safeguards on the Home Rule question. The result was the collapse of the constitutional conference, but Carson was determined to hammer home the message that Home Rule in any form posed a grave threat to the integrity of both the United Kingdom and the Empire. At the Conservative Party conference, held in Nottingham in the following week, the Irish Unionist leader moved a resolution. It called on all Unionists in the United Kingdom to maintain their "unalterable opposition" not just to Home Rule, but to any measure that might weaken the Union between Great Britain and Ireland. The resolution received overwhelming support, and Carson went on to condemn the recent speculation that had linked the Tory Party to the concept of federalism. Still, Carson's triumph was short-lived, as the

Ulster Unionist postcard attacking the Home Rule Bill.

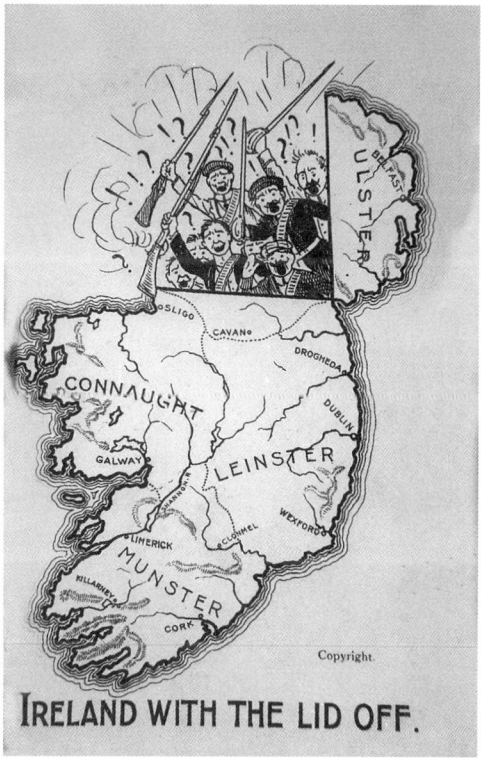

Ulster Unionist postcard Ireland with the lid off.

ensuing general election maintained the status quo at Westminster. A third Home Rule Bill now appeared to be inevitable.

Conclusion

At the close of 1910, the IPP appeared to occupy a powerful position. Redmond's leadership had struck the right balance between caution and firmness, while his personal rating in Ireland had never been higher. The 1910 elections had strengthened the Irish leader's hand at Westminster, leaving the IPP, with the embryonic Labour Party, holding the balance of power. Asquith and the Liberals clearly disliked having to follow a course laid out by Redmond, but there was no alternative if the Liberals wanted to remain in office. Therefore, an uneasy alliance emerged between the Liberals and Irish Nationalists, as Asquith's government reluctantly agreed to meet its Home Rule obligation. At the same time, of course, the likelihood of restrictions being imposed on the Lords' veto powers seemed to remove a major obstacle to Home Rule. With Nationalists' expectations raised, the Liberal cabinet's lack of genuine enthusiasm for Irish devolution did not always register with an Irish leader who stood ready to complete the work begun by Parnell. Respected rather than loved by his followers, this gifted orator had acquired a reputation for competence, while his aloofness helped him stand out from his fellow Nationalist MPs. Moreover, Redmond's authority in Ireland appeared to be absolutely secure. O'Brien's AFIL continued to be a source of irritation, but it had little appeal outside County Cork. Redmond was also alert to the potential threat posed by advanced Nationalists with their separatist programme, but the main radical Nationalist group, Sinn Féin, struggled to make any impression outside Dublin.

Like his Irish counterpart, Carson was somewhat detached from his parliamentary colleagues. Both men spent much of their time in London, where Carson's legal career presented a further distraction from his political responsibilities. Still, the Irish Unionist leader enjoyed a closer relationship with his Conservative allies than Redmond did with the Liberals. Carson was clearly an insider who was party to the thinking of leading Conservatives, and he was quick to act when he sensed that Conservative support for the Union might not be watertight. Both leaders sought to influence voters in Britain, though it was Carson who expended more energy in cultivating support for Unionism on the mainland. This had become even more necessary by 1910, as Unionists and Conservatives demanded that Home Rule must be put before the voters in some form before it could become law. While Carson had focused on galvanising opposition to Home Rule in Britain during the early months of his leadership, he quickly came to appreciate the importance of Ulster in the battle to maintain the Union. The events of 1904–5, when Ulster Unionists had reacted with fury to what were very mild devolution proposals, had provided an indication of the strength of feeling in the northern province on the Home Rule question. The devolution crisis also highlighted Ulster Unionist nervousness about the resolve of their Conservative friends when the question of the Union came under discussion. This would be a recurring feature over the next two decades and beyond. Still, the formation of the UUC, which had been a direct result of the crisis, would subsequently work in Carson's favour. Ulster Unionist leaders had broken with the past to create a modern, representative organisation that provided a direct link to their grass-roots followers. This enabled Ulster Unionists to mobilise support in a very effective manner in the struggle against a third Home Rule Bill.

Historiography

The pivotal role played by the United Irish League (UIL) in pressing for the reunion of the Irish Parliamentary Party (IPP) is analysed in Philip Bull's *Land, Politics and Nationalism: A Study of the Irish Land Question* (Dublin, 1996). Bull argues powerfully that the Land War ran from 1879 to 1903 and that the link between land and Nationalism provided the IPP with a social base – the tenant farming class. Fergus Campbell's *Land and Revolution: Nationalist Politics in the West of Ireland 1891–1921* (Oxford, 2005) highlights the relationship between the UIL and the Catholic Church. Initially, the bulk of the clergy distanced themselves from the movement. As the UIL became more established, however, these clerics recognised that only through participation could they hope to tone down the movement's more radical policies. Campbell claims that it was the UIL's effective intervention in the 1899 local government elections, when it successfully mobilised Nationalist support among new voters, that transformed it from "an isolated agrarian movement into a national political organisation". Thereafter, Campbell argues that the widespread UIL agitation of 1901–02 was the key factor in persuading the Conservative government at Westminster to reconsider its Irish policy. Tory ministers then reached the view that only legislation as far-reaching as the 1903 Wyndham Act could hope to quell this rural agitation. In its analysis of the Ranch War of 1906–10, Campbell's book suggests that it was essentially a conflict between landlord and tenant that had begun in 1879. This counters Paul Bew's *Conflict and Conciliation in Ireland 1890–1910 (Oxford, 1989)*, which sees the Ranch War as an example of class tension within Nationalism. For Bew, the clear target for Laurence Ginnell and those directing cattle-driving were the graziers, who were often prominent figures in local Nationalist politics. Looking more specifically at the British government's attitude to policing in Ireland before the Great War, Campbell's article, 'The social composition of the senior officers of the Royal Irish Constabulary, 1881–1911', *Irish Historical Studies,* Vol 36, No 144 (November 2009), makes the point that unlike police forces in the rest of the United Kingdom, RIC officers were not generally recruited from the ranks. This was, Campbell argues, because the RIC was "a semi-military force". It was also significant that after the Land War, few Catholics were appointed to senior positions in the RIC.

Senia Paseta's article, 'Nationalist responses to two royal visits to Ireland, 1900 and 1903', *Irish Historical Studies*, Vol 31, No 124 (November 1999) argues persuasively that while they did not create Sinn Féin, these royal visits "certainly contributed to its evolution". The visits also helped Arthur Griffith to fine-tune his propaganda skills and to establish himself as one of the IPP's main adversaries. Griffith's early political activism is analysed in Owen McGee's *Arthur Griffith*

(Dublin, 2015), which emphasises Griffith's determination "to act as a thorn in the Irish Party's side" following its reunion in 1900. To achieve this, Griffith was active in attempts to prevent the UIL establishing branches in Dublin. This led to his regular participation in street brawls (Griffith was a skilled boxer), and he was also at the forefront of a campaign to frustrate army recruitment during the Boer War. Maud Gonne was an enthusiastic political and financial supporter of Griffith's efforts. But it was his opposition to the IPP that defined his early career, as his writings expressed outrage at "the party's indifference to the urban working class". Soon after its formation, Sinn Féin boasted that it had the support of "one-fourth of the whole population, despite the opposition of the entire daily press". Griffith worked hard to give Sinn Féin a platform, but it faced other obstacles, as McGee points out, noting that C.J. Dolan's defeat in the 1908 North Leitrim by-election was a result of the movement's poor organisation and the opposition of the Catholic Church.

Frank Callanan's *T.M. Healy* (Cork, 1996) charts the bitterness that continued to plague constitutional Nationalism following the party's reunion in 1900. After the 1906 Liberal election landslide, Healy could boast that, unlike the IPP, he "was not beholden to the Liberals, or implicated in their secular, progressive programme". A rapprochement occurred when Healy and O'Brien re-entered the fold, but it was short-lived. Later, both men used the vehicle of the All-for-Ireland League, which was, as Callanan claims, "implacably opposed to the official Irish party and profoundly suspicious of the Liberals", but the IPP easily saw off such opposition. A. C. Hepburn's *Catholic Belfast and Nationalist Ireland in the Era of Joe Devlin, 1871–1934* (Oxford, 2008) emphasises the energy and political skills demonstrated by Joe Devlin in his analysis of the spectacular growth of the Ancient Order of Hibernians (AOH) in the first decade of the century. Devlin's leadership role in both the AOH and the UIL explains the harmony that existed between the two organisations. Hepburn also comments on the obvious sectarian character of the AOH and notes how this influenced perceptions of Irish Nationalism by Ulster Unionist leaders. Yet the AOH offered considerable social and economic benefits to Nationalists, while Hepburn states that a great strength of the organisation in Devlin's eyes was that it "offered the possibility of a lay-led and lay-controlled Catholic Nationalism". This allows the author to conclude that secular leadership rather than sectarianism was the defining characteristic of the AOH. Patrick Maume's *The Long Gestation: Irish Nationalist Life 1891–1918* (Dublin, 1999) views the IPP as a creature of the railways and the newspapers, noting that it interacted with a much more literate population. On Redmond, Maume highlights the tendency of historians to exaggerate the conservative influences on the party associated with its leader. Maume describes the reserved, respectful and mildly suspicious relationship between Redmond and Dillon. Moreover, he claims that Redmond was "vulnerable to charges of incompetence and double-dealing because he was a conciliator". He was also aloof and detached from his party colleagues and, as Maume stresses, a very private individual: "even his second wife's Protestantism escaped public mention in controversies on Catholic intolerance and mixed marriages."

Dermot Meleady's *John Redmond: The National Leader* (Dublin, 2014) offers an extensive and thoughtful overview of Redmond's career. Meleady notes that by 1908, when Redmond acquired his first motor car, criticism of his parliamentary strategy was developing following two years of Liberal rule "with little to show". With Campbell-Bannerman ill and Asquith poised to assume the premiership, Redmond attempted to establish a rapport with the future prime minister. However, as Meleady notes, he found Asquith "distinctly vague" on the Home Rule question. In examining the outcome of the January 1910 election, Meleady points out that the failure of the Liberals to secure a significant majority weakened the mandate for firm action in relation to the House of Lords. As Liberal ministers debated over whether the People's Budget or the Lords should take priority, Redmond feared that "momentum would be lost in the struggle against the Lords". What followed was "frantic activity" by Redmond to ensure that the Asquith government agreed to a sequence of moves that worked to the IPP's advantage. Paul Bew's *The Politics of Enmity 1789–2006* (Oxford, 2007) notes that the Liberal government's introduction of welfare reforms "evoked an enthusiastic Irish popular response which worried Nationalist purists". Indeed, the old age pension introduced in 1908 proved very popular in Ireland, and the numbers of claimants were much higher than anticipated. (This was because there was no requirement to register births in the mid-nineteenth century). Yet, as Bew notes, the IPP was "given a new boost" by the outcome of the January 1910 general election. Previously, Bew's *Conflict and Conciliation* suggested that Redmond had little sympathy for reformist Liberalism, believing that old age pensions were too "extravagant". However, Redmond enjoyed good fortune with the timing of the Lords' crisis that inevitably led to an election.

In his carefully researched *The Irish Parliamentary Party and the Third Home Rule Crisis* (Dublin, 2013), James McConnel claims that Irish Parliamentary Party MPs "developed a sophisticated constituency service role in the first decade of the twentieth century, which had a major influence on the shape of the political landscape in independent Ireland". This was partly due to the increasing number of local MPs elected after 1900 and, as McConnel points out, it was a development that was not particularly welcomed by Redmond, who associated "localism" in Irish politics with "fragmentation of the Nationalist cause". Ronan Fanning's *Fatal Path: British Government and Irish Revolution 1910–1922* (London, 2013) probes the difficult relationship between Asquith and Redmond. Fanning claims that Asquith was anti-Catholic, a trait that was revealed in his reaction to the Eucharistic Congress that took place in London in September 1908, only months after he became prime minister. Indeed, as Fanning stresses, anti-Catholicism was just as prevalent among Liberals as it was among Conservatives. He notes that Redmond borrowed from the Parnell playbook by threatening to call on Irish voters in Britain to vote against Liberal candidates in his attempt to force the Liberals to make an official declaration on Home Rule prior to the January 1910 election. Still, as Fanning records, the prime minister was slow to consider the Irish issue. He states, "Asquith's Liberal imperialism, his ties of friendship with Grey, Haldane and Crewe and his personal distaste for depending on the Irish all contributed to his reluctance to come to grips with Redmond after the first election of 1910." Indeed, Fanning sees the relationship between Asquith and Redmond as "one of mutual mistrust". In Fanning's opinion this had a profound influence on the Conservative Party. The Tories knew Asquith was unenthusiastic about Irish Home Rule, and they knew of his personal dislike for Redmond. This convinced them that there was "a corrupt bargain" between the Liberals and the IPP. In fact, Fanning describes how Redmond was excluded from the deliberations over the constitutional crisis in 1910, which threatened to restore the bipartisan approach on Ireland and, consequently, shatter the prospects for Home Rule. Ultimately, as Fanning emphasises, the "Big Beasts" in Asquith's cabinet had "none of Gladstone's messianic fervour for Irish Home Rule".

There are a number of general histories that shed light on the opening decade of the twentieth century. Among the best is Roy Foster's *Modern Ireland 1600–1972* (London, 1988). Foster concludes that the tension that developed between the forces of old Nationalism, as represented by the IPP, and the new Nationalism, as represented by organisations such as the Gaelic League, mirrored the generational conflict that was evident in contemporary Ireland. Foster is also adamant that movements such as the AOH and the UIL clearly exhibited political energy and, had they chosen, would have presented a much more potent challenge to the IPP than "the minority rhetoric of cultural revivalism and revolutionary separatism". Indeed, as Foster argues, "more often than not" the cultural Nationalists "supported ... the devolutionary strategies of the Irish Parliamentary Party". Yet he contends that by the time of the fiasco over the Irish Council Bill there was a growing sense that "the young were no longer subscribing" to the IPP. Previously, Leland Lyons's *Culture and Anarchy in Ireland 1890–1939* (Oxford, 1979) had developed the thesis that the manner of Parnell's fall in 1891 had left Irishmen bitter and disillusioned to the extent that they turned their backs on the grubby world of parliamentary politics, finding a new outlet for their energy and talent in the various cultural Nationalist movements. The argument was firmly rejected by Alvin Jackson's *Home Rule: An Irish History*

1800–2000 (London, 2003), which claims that there is no evidence to suggest that the growth was directly linked to the troubles encountered by the IPP. He argues, moreover, that until at least 1910 cultural Nationalism was merely the "wayward child" of Home Rule, not its destroyer. George Boyce's *Nineteenth-Century Ireland: The Search for Stability* (Dublin, 1990) stresses that, "in spite of all that had been attempted by British legislation, constructive Unionism, literary and Gaelic movements, Unionist mavericks, Russellites, trade Unionists and all the rest of them", the deep divisions between the people of Ireland "remained fundamentally unaltered".

Alvin Jackson's *Judging Redmond and Carson* (Dublin, 2018) endorses Fanning's view of Redmond, noting that he "enjoyed workmanlike, but not intimate or especially sympathetic, connections with British politicians". Jackson also points out that while Redmond was a regular Mass-goer, he, like Parnell, was opposed to the influence of the Catholic Church in Irish politics. Yet, as Jackson highlights, he remained silent on the McCann case (discussed in Chapter 2). Jackson notes that the bitter divisions in the IPP during the 1890s "left a permanent mark on Redmond's style of leadership", ensuring that the preservation of IPP unity was a constant source of anxiety. Indeed, as Jackson claims, many within the party viewed Redmond as a "compromise chairman" and they looked to Dillon "as the true power". In an interesting take, Jackson argues that in 1908–9 Redmond was as much led as leading, adding, "He was reactive and defensive, rather than commanding, calculating and defiant in the manner of Parnell." In spite of these weaknesses, Jackson concludes that the "relative success and length of his time as chairman did mean that after 1909–10 his position was considerably strengthened". One reason for this was the decisive action taken by the IPP leader in the wake of the January 1910 election. Evidence of this is revealed in Dermot Meleady's *John Redmond: Selected Letters and Memoranda, 1890–1918* (Dublin, 2018). Redmond informed the government on 10 February 1910 that it must deal with the Lords issue before re-introducing the Lloyd George budget. Meleady cites a further letter of 24 February to the Liberal chief whip, the Master of Elibank, warning that unless the IPP received assurances on this "we wd. feel bound to vote agst. Govt. and oppose them insistently in the H. of C.".

Jackson's *Ireland 1798–1998: Politics and War* (Oxford, 1999) highlights similarities between Asquith and Redmond, both lawyers who were unwilling to offer major concessions in case they might prove unnecessary. In Jackson's *Home Rule*, he argues that in the early years of the twentieth century the IPP, and particularly Dillon, recognised that the prospect of successful Tory policies to stabilise the country represented a major threat to Home Rule and to the party's survival. It was, therefore, necessary to maintain "a semi-permanent protest", in which Dillon wanted "conflict above victory". An outstanding addition to recent historiography is the *Atlas of the Irish Revolution,* edited by John Crowley, Donal Ó Drisceoil and Mike Murphy (Cork, 2017). In his essay, 'The Home Rule Crisis' in the *Atlas of the Irish Revolution*, Frank Callanan memorably describes the Liberal Party's connection with Home Rule as a "Gladstonian albatross", adding that Home Rule was "no ordinary issue that could be handled using Asquith's conventional methods". McConnel's *The Irish Parliamentary Party* also examines the Fenian influence within the IPP, noting that a number of Redmond's backbenchers were current or ex-Fenians. While these MPs, and others in the party, certainly viewed Home Rule as "a stepping stone to greater autonomy", McConnel confidently asserts that this was a minority among Irish Parliamentary Party MPs, who "seem to have regarded devolved self-government as preferable to separation".

Patrick Buckland's pioneering research on Unionism remains an excellent introduction to the regional varieties of the movement. In Buckland's *Irish Unionism 2: Ulster Unionism and the Origins of Northern Ireland 1885–1922* (Dublin 1972), the argument is advanced that it was the reluctance shown by Ulster Unionists to place too much trust on British goodwill that became one of the major differences between the two varieties of Unionism. The best analysis of the impact of the devolution crisis on Unionism remains Alvin Jackson's *The Ulster Party: Irish Unionists in the House of Commons 1884–1911* (Oxford,1989), which argues that Irish Unionism went through a process of "Ulsterisation" in the early 1900s. Jackson examines the role played by Moore, Lonsdale and the Craigs, the younger, more radical bourgeois activists who had become frustrated by Saunderson's ineffective leadership. This led to the formation of the UUC and, in turn, paved the way for the development of a more militant strain of Unionism centred in Ulster that was much more closely connected to its grass-roots base. In examining Saunderson's leadership, Jackson's *Colonel Edward Saunderson: Land and Loyalty in Victorian Ireland* (Oxford, 1995) argues that Saunderson was ideally suited to the "crusade politics" that had proved successful in 1893, but he subsequently faced a new set of challenges. By the turn of the century, therefore, Unionism "was finding it hard to channel popular opinion". Jackson contends that these younger, proactive Ulster Unionists were desperate for change, when "Wyndham saved them". In his conclusion, Jackson claims that Saunderson was an Irish – not an Ulster – Unionist.

Previously, as Jackson notes, the Ulster bourgeoisie had been happy to allow Irish landlordism to take the lead in the defence of the Union, but this changed abruptly in the early 1900s. By 1906, moreover, only 25 per cent of Unionist MPs were landlords, and there was a significant influx of lawyers to the party ranks during this period. The importance of Presbyterianism in this emerging Ulster Unionist movement is highlighted by Graham Walker's *A History of the Ulster*

Unionist Party: Protest, Pragmatism and Pessimism (Manchester, 2004). It gave the movement a distinctive social, economic and cultural outlook. Walker also suggests that in giving the Orange Order 25 per cent representation on the UUC, the Ulster Unionist leaders were "signalling their willingness formally to embrace religious sectarianism and the militant ethnic politics which accompanied it". Following Saunderson's death, John Kendle's *Walter Long, Ireland and the Union, 1905–1920* (Dublin, 1992) describes Long as "the natural and logical choice" as his replacement. Kendle also emphasises Long's objectives of promoting greater unity within Irish Unionism and improving relations between Irish Unionism and the Tory Party following the devolution fiasco in 1905. Kendle points to Long's focus throughout his leadership on the necessity of maintaining law and order in the Irish countryside. When the Ranch War erupted, Long became a consistent critic of the Liberal government's Irish administration for its failure to protect property. During the campaign for the January 1910 election, Kendle notes that, in the event of Home Rule, Long warned "neither the Ulster nor southern Unionists would acknowledge the authority of the Irish parliament; they would neither obey its laws nor pay its taxes".

H. Montgomery Hyde's *Carson* (London, 1953) emphasises the sacrifices made by Carson in accepting the Unionist leadership, noting that it would "inevitably cut him off from all promotion, whether political or legal, and it would also involve him in substantial sacrifices of income, leisure and probably health as well". In Hyde's account, Carson took the leadership because the Union was in danger, and he claims that Carson felt that southern Unionists would need "guidance" should a new Home Rule Bill reach the statute book. In highlighting Carson's non-sectarian attitude to Irish politics, Geoffrey Lewis's *Carson: The Man Who Divided Ireland* (London, 2005) notes that Carson was a firm supporter of a Catholic university, believing that as Ireland had a Catholic majority, the country should have a Catholic university. Moreover, as Lewis explains, Carson's southern Irish background ensured that he "felt an instinctive sympathy for his Catholic fellow-countrymen". Still, the complexity of Carson's character is revealed as Lewis analyses Carson's approach to the Tory government's strategy of constructive Unionism. Carson disliked the principle of land purchase, and he was a vocal critic of what he regarded as the government's soft approach towards law and order, preferring what Lewis describes as "the smack of firm government". By early 1905 Carson was "the fiercest critic" of Wyndham's devolution proposals, and, as Lewis stresses, though he was a member of the government, he sided with the Ulster Unionist MPs and informed the cabinet that creeping Home Rule would not be tolerated. While Carson was an Irish Unionist, Lewis notes that on being invited to assume the leadership following Long's defeat in South Dublin County, he was aware that "leadership of the Irish Unionist Party must mean, in effect, leadership of the Ulster Unionists, for it was in Ulster that the real opposition to Home Rule was concentrated". Of course, by the time Carson assumed the leadership in February 1910, Ulster Unionism had undergone a transformation since the beginning of the century.

Ronald McNeill's *Ulster's Stand for Union* (London, 1922) provides an invaluable eyewitness account of events from a Unionist perspective. In stressing that the British public were denied a chance to vote on Home Rule, McNeill refers to Asquith's "one-sentence reference" in his famous pre-election Albert Hall speech on 10 December 1909. Almost exactly one year later, on 6 December 1910, McNeill records Asquith's response to a heckler in East Fife, when he said he would introduce Home Rule, enabling Balfour to complain that 500 contests had been declared before there was any mention of Home Rule. Theo Hoppen's *Governing Hibernia: British Politicians and Ireland 1800–1921* (Oxford, 2019) analyses the impact of constructive Unionism around the turn of the century. He argues that the range of reforms and state investment had no parallels in the rest of the United Kingdom but emphasises that these Tory leaders consistently refused to acknowledge that Ireland was a nation.

Andrew Gailey's *Ireland and the Death of Kindness: The experience of constructive Unionism 1890–1905* (Cork, 1987) describes how Wyndham's chief secretaryship saw a shift to a more radical conservatism, adding that he was "extremely sympathetic" towards Irish Catholicism. Gailey claims that Wyndham was appalled by the bigotry of Ulster Protestants, and that he was intent on making the Union tolerable, thereby increasing Catholic loyalty. Gailey concludes his analysis of constructive Unionism by suggesting that it did weaken the IPP and compelled it "to adopt an extremely narrow, inflexible but consolidating policy of absolute concentration on Home Rule". In its comments on the reaction of Unionism and Nationalism to Wyndham's devolution proposals, Bew's *The Politics of Enmity* points out that while Unionists viewed them as a Trojan horse for Home Rule, Nationalists regarded them as inadequate. He concludes perceptively that a pattern was being established, as "relatively sophisticated attempts to establish a *via media* in Irish politics were rejected by both Nationalists and Unionists". Stephen Evans's article, 'The Conservatives and the redefinition of Unionism, 1912–21', *Twentieth Century History,* Vol 9, No 1, (1998) argues that opposition to Home Rule was the cornerstone of Tory policy before 1910. Evans quotes Balfour's famous speech at Haddington on the eve of the 1906 general election, when the prime minister described Irish Home Rule as "the greatest of all questions", adding that opposition to Home Rule was the reason the Tory Party had been "called into existence". David Dutton's *His Majesty's Loyal Opposition: The Unionist Party in Opposition 1905–15* (Liverpool, 1992) argues that the Tory Party under Balfour lacked the necessary "identity of purpose and sense of direction" to deal with the new political challenges that emerged in the Edwardian era. Only the defence of the Union, claims Dutton, provided a rallying point, and it was, therefore, entirely predictable that the Tories should cling to this following their humiliating electoral defeat in 1906. In a discussion of the complex relationship between Unionism and the Conservative Party, Jeremy Smith's *The Tories and Ireland 1910–1914: Conservative Party politics and the Home Rule Crisis* (Dublin, 2000) argues that over the course of 1910 there was a good deal of sympathy for the concept of Irish devolution among leading Conservatives, especially Austen Chamberlain. At this stage, as Smith demonstrates, Conservatives were seriously considering a wider devolution scheme for the United Kingdom that incensed Irish Unionists. By November 1910, however, a pro-Union group of leaders, including Lansdowne, had asserted its authority in the shadow cabinet. One of these leaders, Arthur Balfour, is examined thoroughly in Catherine Shannon's *Arthur J Balfour and Ireland 1874–1922* (Washington, 1988). Shannon illustrates Balfour's deep commitment to the Union but records his frequent frustration with what he saw as the excesses of extremist Unionists in Ulster. This partly accounts for the often-difficult relationship between British Conservatives and Ulster Unionists.

G. K. Peatling's *British Opinion and Irish Self-government, 1865–1925: From Unionism to Liberal Commonwealth* (Dublin, 2001) points out that, in the first decade of the twentieth century, progressive Liberals believed that Home Rule would promote real political debate in Ireland and break down the sectarian barriers. Peatling describes the success of the Liberal policy of conferring self-government on the conquered Boer provinces of South Africa and the party's belief that the South African precedent should provide a blueprint for Ireland. The difficulty of achieving political progress in Ireland for Westminster governments is discussed in Eugenio Biagini's *British Democracy and Irish Nationalism 1876–1906* (Cambridge, 2007), with the author stressing that, after 1906, "Liberal governments initiated ground-breaking social legislation and managed to overcome all sorts of constitutional changes, but were unable to solve the Irish Home Rule crisis". Still, on a broader level, Biagini highlights the significance of the Irish issue for British politics which, he states, came to be identified with democracy, constitutional freedoms and "the remaking of popular radicalism in both Britain and Ireland".

Chapter 2
The Ulster Crisis, 1911–14

The Ulster campaign of resistance against the third Home Rule Bill was entirely predictable, but the scale of the opposition took the Liberal government by surprise. For much of the crisis Asquith and most of his cabinet worked on the assumption that Unionists were bluffing. By the close of 1913, however, a decision to press ahead with an undiluted bill appeared to be too great a gamble for the government. Consequently, the Liberals succumbed to Unionist threats, and partition emerged as the only realistic compromise. The Ulster crisis had contributed to the bitterness that characterised Westminster politics in the period before World War I. The Conservatives, led by a determined Ulster Unionist sympathiser, offered enthusiastic support for Carson's menacing tactics, and relations between the two main parties quickly became toxic. Indeed, the personalities and leadership styles of the principal actors would help to shape events as they unfolded. The Ulster crisis became a defining issue in pre-war British politics, but relationships between the Liberals and Conservatives improved greatly once war intervened. One lesson drawn from the crisis by the political elite at Westminster was a determination to prevent the Ulster question becoming a central issue in the future. Of course, this would not apply in Ireland where partition would reinforce the differences between Unionism and Nationalism.

Motives and methods

Following the December 1910 general election, the Ulster Unionist Council (UUC) proposed the revival of the Unionist Clubs movement that had been active during the struggle against the second Home Rule Bill. These Unionist Clubs were re-established from January 1912 and played a leading role in the organisation of Unionist resistance in Ulster over the next three years. By February 1914 there were 371 Unionist Clubs, and, while membership often overlapped with the Orange Order, the clubs were a distinct entity that facilitated the mobilisation of

Unionism at grass-roots level. The Unionist Clubs were particularly prominent at the Craigavon demonstration, with 100 represented at the great rally held in the grounds of Sir James Craig's home on the edge of Belfast on 23 September 1911. By this point, Sir James had established himself as Carson's senior lieutenant in Ulster. This impressive anti-Home Rule meeting had been organised by Craig in response to a letter he had received from Carson at the end of July. The Unionist leader had asked if "the people over there really mean to resist", before adding, "I am not for a mere game, and unless men are prepared to make great sacrifices which they clearly understand, the talk of resistance is no use". Craig quickly decided that he needed to convey the depth of feeling among the Unionist rank and file in Ulster. The demonstration was meticulously planned, and 50,000 Unionist supporters marched from the centre of Belfast to Craig's home overlooking Belfast Lough. This was a significant occasion, as it was the first time that Carson addressed a large audience of his Ulster supporters directly. These face-to-face meetings would become regular features of the Unionist campaign, and they would have a profound effect on both the leader and his followers. When he spoke at Craigavon, Carson made two memorable statements. First, he described the actions of the Liberal government as "the most nefarious conspiracy that had ever been hatched against a free people". He went on to express his confidence that this conspiracy and deception of the electorate could be overcome. He then warned that should the government press ahead with its plans, "We must be prepared … the morning Home Rule passes, ourselves to become responsible for the government of the Protestant province of Ulster." Two days later, in consultation with Carson, a meeting of the UUC established a commission of five members to draft a constitution for such a provisional government. The Unionist leader's stage performance and his clear statement of intent had two important consequences. Carson's language captured the attention of the media in Britain where the Ulster crisis would

Sir James Craig (1871–1940), photographed around 1911.

dominate the headlines in the national press until the outbreak of World War I. Moreover, as Craig was hoping, Carson's obvious passion had greatly impressed those assembled at Craigavon, and a powerful bond was established between the Dublin lawyer and his new Ulster supporters.

It was the Liberal government's decision to tackle the issue of the House of Lords that had exacerbated the difficulties facing Carson and Craig. The Parliament Act received royal assent in August 1911. The Act made provision for the payment of MPs and reduced the length of parliaments from seven to five years. However, the clauses limiting the powers of the House of Lords proved most controversial, and these would have major consequences for Irish Home Rule. In addition to preventing the upper house from rejecting or amending a Money Bill, the Parliament Act ensured that any other bill rejected by the Lords would still become law providing not less than two years had elapsed between its introduction and third reading in the Commons. In piloting the bill through parliament, Asquith had displayed sound judgement and impeccable timing. A major hurdle, of course, had been to cajole the House of Lords into passing a bill that would seriously curtail its powers. The prime minister achieved this by persuading the king to help bring about a resolution of the constitutional crisis. When it became clear that George V was prepared to create the requisite number of Liberal peers to pass the measure in the Lords, enough existing Tory peers backed down and the Parliament Bill was passed in the upper chamber. This action had two important ramifications for British politics in the period up to the outbreak of war. Fierce arguments among the Tories at Westminster over strategy in the struggle over the House of Lords caused a split in a Conservative Party that had still to overcome the bitterness surrounding the tariff reform controversy earlier in the century. Moreover, the hostility between Liberals and Conservatives generated by the constitutional crisis poisoned relations at Westminster before the outbreak of war, making bipartisanship on any policy area impossible. This was the political context for the emergence of the Ulster crisis, and all the key players at Westminster fully understood the implications of the Parliament Act for Home Rule. Before August 1911, Unionists could relax, confident that the Conservative-dominated upper chamber would never concede any measure granting Home Rule to Ireland. The Parliament Act had removed this safety net and reminded Irish Unionists and their Conservative allies that Home Rule was now a much more realistic prospect. This was the background to the Craigavon demonstration.

Carson's speech at Craigavon, particularly his reference to a provisional government, caused a storm in Liberal circles. The home secretary, Winston Churchill, responded promptly, informing his Dundee constituents on 3 October that the government intended to introduce a Home Rule Bill in the next parliamentary session and would "press it forward with all their strength". For his part, Carson was aware that his focus on Ulster at the Craigavon rally could leave him open to the charge of ignoring his fellow Irish Unionists in the three southern provinces. The establishment of an Ulster provisional government, of course, meant some form of exclusion or partition, but Carson's advocacy of such a strategy was only tactical. In November 1911 he indicated in private correspondence that north-east Ulster was the key to the Union. He believed that if this part of Ireland could successfully resist Home Rule, then the Liberal government would not proceed, as Home Rule would have to be on an all-Ireland basis to meet the demands of Redmond and his Nationalist supporters. Carson was committed to the Union in its existing constitutional form, and he intended to use Ulster resistance to kill any new Home Rule Bill. Earlier, he had attempted to reassure southern Unionists, when he told a meeting in Dublin on 10 October 1911, "You need fear no action of Ulster which would be in the nature of desertion of the Southern Provinces … if Ulster succeeds, Home Rule is dead." Carson was fully aware of Unionism's electoral strength when he declared this strategy. Figures from the 1911 census showed that there were 250,000 Protestants living in the three southern provinces, comprising just under 10 per cent of the total population. In the nine counties of Ulster, meanwhile, Protestants outnumbered Catholics by 891,000 (56 per cent) to 691,000 (44 per cent), though they were unevenly distributed. These Ulster Protestants were really concentrated in the four "plantation" counties of Antrim, Down, Londonderry and Armagh, but there were clear Catholic majorities in the other five counties, overwhelmingly so in Cavan, Monaghan and Donegal.

The Unionist leadership received an unexpected boost when Andrew Bonar Law became leader of the Conservative Party. Criticism of Arthur Balfour had been mounting during the summer of 1911, and as momentum shifted decisively against the intellectually gifted, but increasingly ineffective, opposition leader, he resigned suddenly on 8 November. The two leading candidates for the top position in the Tory Party, Austen

Bonar Law (1858–1923).

Chamberlain and Walter Long, cancelled each other out in the sense that neither was acceptable to the other's supporters. This left the door ajar for a third candidate, and Bonar Law grasped the opportunity, brushing aside the disadvantage of having no cabinet experience. Before that summer, Bonar Law had made little reference to Ireland in any of his speeches, but this would change when the Parliament Bill was about to be passed. Bonar Law christened the measure the "Home Rule in Disguise Bill". He attacked the strangulation of the Lords' veto, because it opened the door to Home Rule. Demanding that the electorate must have a say on such a vital constitutional issue, Bonar Law warned that if Asquith pressed ahead with Irish devolution, he would be courting disaster. On 9 August 1911 he told the House of Commons, "I could never, if I were one of those Irish loyalists, consent to have a system forced upon me as part of a corrupt Parliamentary bargain." But it was Ulster that stirred Bonar Law's passion. His father, a Presbyterian minister, had served in a County Antrim church close to Portrush before moving to New Brunswick in Canada. There, Andrew was born in 1858. When he was twelve years old, he returned to Helensburgh on the Firth of Clyde, where he was looked after by his aunt, Jane Kidston. The Kidston family were prominent figures in Glasgow's business community, and Bonar Law left school at the age of sixteen to work in the family firm. Later, he was made a partner in a business that acted as agents in the well-known Glasgow "Iron Ring". His role as a metal trader in the famous Scottish iron and steel industry enabled Bonar Law to acquire considerable wealth. His father's failing health saw the old clergyman return to Ulster in 1877, and he would spend his remaining years in the province. This, together with the fact that his brother practised as a doctor in Coleraine, led Bonar Law to make frequent visits to the province to spend time with his family. Undoubtedly, Bonar Law acquired an instinctive understanding of the Ulster Unionist mentality, and this empathy would influence many of his political judgements as the crisis over the third Home Rule Bill unfolded.

Bonar Law became leader of the Conservative Party on 13 November 1911, having been proposed by Walter Long and seconded by Chamberlain. He offered a complete contrast to his predecessor in both personality and leadership style. Where the aristocratic Balfour exuded charm and easy confidence, Bonar Law made up for his lack of experience with great energy and real courage. While Balfour often appeared detached and aloof, Bonar Law was prepared to attack Asquith and the Liberals at every opportunity as he sought to reunite his party. The determination to put the Tories on the front foot in their battles with the government proved a welcome advantage for Irish Unionists. Soon after his appointment as leader, Bonar Law met Carson to exchange views. Lady Londonderry, the leading society hostess in the capital, encouraged such political meetings at her London home, and both men, particularly Carson, were regular visitors. The Unionist leader quickly recognised Bonar Law's devotion to the Ulster cause and his obvious empathy with Ulster Unionist thinking. He promised Carson that he would visit Ulster at the earliest opportunity. It was also evident that Bonar Law viewed Ulster and its resistance to Home Rule as the one issue that could unite his party after the bitter divisions caused by the tariff reform controversy and the more recent Lords' wrangling. Bonar Law himself had been a passionate supporter of tariff reform, but now recognised that the issue had to be shelved in the interests of party unity. From this time on, the Conservative Party would focus on opposing the government's policy on Ireland.

Bonar Law's forthright views on the Union were eagerly endorsed by the rest of the Conservative leadership. Of course, Long, a former Irish Unionist leader, was supportive, and Balfour, who retained considerable influence in the party following his resignation, renewed his commitment to the Union. The Conservative leader in the House of Lords, Lord Lansdowne, was another who was full of enthusiasm for the party's more direct approach to the Home Rule issue. Indeed, particularly in this early phase, Bonar Law almost saw Lansdowne as co-leader of the party. Lansdowne, who owned a huge estate in County Kerry in addition to his lands in England and Scotland, was happy to see the defence of the Union becoming the centrepiece of Conservative Party strategy. Still, there was a difference in emphasis between Lansdowne and Bonar Law, whose primary concern was Ulster. Lansdowne mainly represented the southern Unionists, a group whose influence he frequently exaggerated, and was anxious to save all of Ireland from Home Rule. The new leader's first major speech on the Home Rule issue was delivered on 26 January 1912. Bonar Law told supporters that the Liberals were guilty of deceiving the electorate and were now clearly under Redmond's thumb.

A core principle uniting all Irish Unionists and British Conservatives was the belief that Home Rule would never satisfy Irish Nationalists and that an unstoppable campaign for full independence would inevitably follow any concession of devolution. This was in spite of the fact that Home Rule was the limit of Redmond's aspirations and that the Irish leader's wish for Ireland to remain in the British Empire was genuine. However, many Nationalists repeatedly quoted Parnell's words, suggesting that Irishmen would not be satisfied until the last link binding Ireland to Britain had been destroyed. Irish Unionists also questioned the capabilities of potential Nationalist ministers in a future Home Rule executive. In particular, southern Unionists warned that social and economic chaos would follow the implementation of Home Rule. Such arguments were based on class thinking, as the landlord class in the south and west dreaded the formation of a Home Rule parliament that would be dominated by their former agrarian enemies. Indeed, southern Unionists had a long-standing concern about the threat that Home Rule would pose to their privileged position in Irish society. This expectation that Home Rule would inevitably produce inferior government by individuals who lacked the necessary educational background and social status was a regular theme for discussion in the Unionist big houses.

However, Unionists in the three southern provinces were also capable of taking a broader view of the Home Rule threat. Their anti-Home Rule propaganda frequently highlighted the long-term damage that Irish Home Rule could inflict on the Empire, arguing that granting devolution to Ireland was certain to spark demand for self-government in parts of the Empire such as India. Many southern Unionist families, of course, had developed close ties with the Empire, either from their military careers or from their experiences in the administrative and diplomatic services. Fear of the likely consequences of Home Rule for the Empire was a powerful factor behind the Conservative Party's opposition to Home Rule, and the close family links between the landed gentry in Ireland and Britain meant that southern Unionists and Conservatives on the mainland shared these concerns about the stability of the Empire. Ulster Unionists, too, identified strongly with the Empire. A number of their leaders, such as Craig and Fred Crawford, the chief strategist behind the Larne gun-running (discussed later in this chapter), had served in the army during the Boer War. Ulster emigrants had also made a major contribution to the Empire, and this was a great source of pride for Unionists in the north. The most prominent of these, William Massey, a native of Limavady, would serve as prime minister of New Zealand from 1912 to 1925. The image of Empire was frequently highlighted in speeches, and Unionist propaganda routinely described Ulster as "the imperial province".

Not surprisingly, the bourgeois leadership of Ulster Unionism was very anxious about the prospects for the north's economy should Home Rule be implemented. They argued that Ulster's economic prosperity was due, in large measure, to the Union. They were also convinced that Nationalists had little understanding or appreciation of business and that a Home Rule parliament would inevitably seek to impose higher taxation on successful Ulster enterprises. Belfast was, of course, home to renowned linen, shipbuilding and engineering industries. It also had a number of world leaders in the Belfast Ropeworks, Gallaher's Tobacco, the Sirocco Works, which made fans and ventilation systems, and Mackie's, which produced textile machinery. Many of the products manufactured by these companies were exported, and Unionist leaders warned that a Home Rule parliament would impose protective tariffs that would damage Belfast's export-oriented businesses. This argument struck a chord with Protestant skilled workers, who eagerly supported their Unionist employers, and there was a widespread fear that Ulster's wealth would be used to subsidise inefficient agriculture in the south and west. There was, moreover, a powerful feeling that north-east Ulster was fully integrated into the wider United Kingdom economy and was part of an industrial zone that extended to Lancashire and Lanarkshire. Home Rule threatened to disrupt the free flow of capital and goods in this economic triangle, and there was a real concern that business leaders in Belfast would find it more difficult to access the capital markets when seeking funds for major investment projects. Many of these businessmen could recall the financial impact of the 1886 and 1893 Home Rule Bills, which caused a fall in prices on the Belfast stock exchange. In truth, they had spent their business lives looking east rather than south to source raw materials and market their finished goods.

Despite the weight given to the economic case against Home Rule, it was the claim, "Home Rule means Rome Rule", that did most to mobilise rank-and-file Unionist supporters in Ulster. In setting out the religious objection to Home Rule, Unionist propaganda made frequent reference to the McCann case that had captured the public's attention. On 2 December 1910, the *Northern Whig* carried an extensive report under the headline, "Clerical kidnapping in Belfast". The story was directly linked to the 1908 Papal decree, *Ne Temere*, which stated that all children of mixed marriages must be raised as Catholics. In May 1908 Agnes Jane Barclay had married Alexander McCann, a Belfast Catholic, in Second Presbyterian Church, Antrim, and the couple had two children. The husband and wife each attended their respective churches, but the newspaper claimed that Alexander, encouraged by a local priest who did not recognise the Protestant wedding ceremony, left his wife and removed the two infants. They were never seen again by their mother. The case caused a political storm, as Irish Parliamentary Party (IPP) MPs chose to ignore the incident and refused to condemn the decree. The *Northern Whig* suggested that such a failure was because the Nationalist MPs were either in full agreement with the church's actions or were "so completely under her thumb" that they dare not express their own opinions. Unionist leaders were quick to link Agnes McCann's predicament to their campaign against Home Rule, claiming that the Catholic Church's influence over any future Dublin parliament would inevitably curtail the religious freedom currently enjoyed by Ulster's Protestant community. Significantly, the McCann case also engaged the public in England and Scotland, where Protestant clergymen frequently attacked the *Ne Temere* decree, arguing that it was incompatible with British law. Anti-*Ne Temere* meetings were held across Britain, and Rev William Corkey, the minister who had married the McCanns, was given special leave by his kirk session to address a series of these meetings in England. All of the main Protestant churches in Ulster were active in the campaign against Home Rule, and the fallout from the McCann case provided church leaders with a specific focus. Their broader objections were clearly articulated at the Presbyterian General Assembly in February and the General Synod of the Church of Ireland in April 1912. These were special gatherings held solely to discuss the Home Rule threat. At such events it became commonplace for participants to warn that Protestants would be subjected to discrimination under a Home Rule parliament and would, for example, be excluded from the government and the civil service.

The prominent role played by the Catholic clergy in Nationalist politics in Ulster exacerbated Unionist fears about the likely clerical influence on a Home Rule parliament. The term "priest-ridden" was routinely used in Unionist speeches and propaganda, though the irony that this criticism was often made by Protestant clergy, who were very active in Unionist politics, was somehow overlooked. One reason for the involvement of Catholic clergy, particularly at local level, was the absence of lay leadership due to the presence of a relatively small Catholic bourgeoisie in the north. In these circumstances local Catholic clergy often filled the void. Many northern Unionists, moreover, viewed Irish Nationalism through the prism of the Ancient Order of Hibernians (AOH) and ignored the more moderate and reasoned stance adopted by Redmond and other IPP MPs. The AOH was, in some senses, a mirror image of the contemporary Orange Order, and both movements grew rapidly in the decade after 1903. Like its Orange counterpart, the AOH was strongly associated with sectarianism and was regarded by Unionists as the militant wing of Irish Nationalism. Closely linked to the religious fears was the Ulster Unionist adherence to the "Two Nations" theory. Northern Unionists claimed that if the Irish were entitled to self-determination, then so too were the people of Ulster, who could claim to have a separate identity. This argument formed the basis for a series of articles which appeared in *The Times* between February and April 1912 and were published in an influential book, *The Two Irish Nations*. The journalist W. F. Moneypenny had been sent to Ulster and remained there while he produced the articles. His conclusion that Irish history was the story of "the clash of two rights" was based on his sincere belief that the arguments advanced by both Nationalism and Unionism had a good deal of merit.

The Third Home Rule Bill

The war of words between the government and leading Conservatives and Irish Unionists had raised tension to new levels by the beginning of 1912. Both Carson and Bonar Law had provoked angry responses from Liberal ministers. Churchill, in particular, was scathing in his description of the Unionist leader's attempts to rouse his followers, dismissing his dire predictions in Ulster as an empty threat. Never one to step back from confrontation, Churchill, who had moved from the Home Office to become First Lord of the Admiralty on 23 October 1911, accepted an invitation from the Ulster Liberal Association to join

Redmond and the leading Ulster Nationalist, Joe Devlin, at a Home Rule rally in Belfast. The invitation would allow Churchill to gauge opinion on the issue in Ulster for himself and demonstrate to his opponents that he was dismissive of Carson's extreme rhetoric. However, Churchill was totally misled about the strength of the Ulster Liberal Association, which mainly attracted support from Ulster Presbyterians who had remained loyal to the Liberal cause following Gladstone's conversion to Home Rule. Two of the association's most prominent members were Rev J. B. Armour, the Ballymoney Presbyterian minister, and Lord Pirrie, the engineering genius and Harland & Wolff director. While both men were very vocal in their support for Home Rule and were a constant source of embarrassment to the Unionist leadership, the reality was that the association's numbers had dwindled. Its officers caused a stir when it was announced that the Ulster Hall had been booked on 8 February 1912 for Churchill's visit. This angered Belfast Unionists, many of whom could recall Lord Randolph Churchill's famous speech at the same venue in February 1886, when he stated that Unionists should "fight" against Home Rule. The UUC reacted quickly, declaring that it would take action to prevent the Home Rule rally taking place. The plan was to hire the Ulster Hall for the previous evening and then occupy it for the following 24 hours, thus forcing the Home Rulers to find an alternative venue. The sit-in meant that Churchill addressed several thousand Home Rule supporters at Celtic Park football ground in the west of the city. Before he reached the ground, however, Churchill's motor vehicle was almost overturned by angry shipyard workers who had assembled outside his hotel. After the rally it was decided that, rather than return to his hotel, Churchill should be smuggled out of the city and taken to Larne, from where he could sail to the mainland. Carson, who had crossed to Belfast to direct the anti-Churchill operation, claimed a great victory for Unionism.

In the week after Churchill's Belfast foray, a new session of parliament opened, and the government confirmed its intention to introduce a new Home Rule Bill. To highlight their outright opposition, Unionists in Ulster planned a monster demonstration that would be held in Belfast during the Easter holidays. This allowed Bonar Law to make good his earlier promise to Carson, and he was one of several keynote speakers who addressed a crowd of 100,000 supporters in the Royal Agricultural Society's showgrounds at Balmoral on Easter Tuesday, 9 April 1912. Again, Craig's organisational ability was in evidence. Men marched into the grounds, dividing neatly into ranks of four as they passed the platform, close to which a giant Union Jack, measuring 48 feet by 25 feet, had been unfurled. In his address Bonar Law described Belfast as a "besieged city", but argued that by defeating Home Rule successfully, Ulster Unionists would "save the Empire". Significantly, a very large body of Tory MPs had accompanied Bonar Law to

Balmoral, where they joined their leader on the platform. After Carson had spoken, the two leaders grasped each other's hands in full view of the crowd, a dramatic gesture that symbolised the bond between British Conservatives and Ulster Unionists.

Two days later, on 11 April 1912, Asquith introduced the third Home Rule Bill in the House of Commons. It was, in essence, very similar to Gladstone's 1893 bill. Asquith confirmed that Ulster would not be granted special status, as four-fifths of the Irish MPs wanted Home Rule on an all-Ireland basis, while only an "irreconcilable minority" in Ulster, where Unionist representatives controlled 17 of the 33 seats, opposed this demand. Their wishes, he argued, could not be allowed to deny the majority in Ireland of their rights. Yet the prime minister's apparently firm rejection of special treatment for Ulster concealed certain misgivings that had been expressed in cabinet by a number of his senior colleagues. Still, Ulster had not featured significantly in the deliberations of the cabinet committee that had been formed in January 1911 to consider the Home Rule issue. There had been some interest expressed in the concept of "Home Rule All Round", a federal scheme that could have seen devolution extended to Scotland and Wales, but this was rejected by the cabinet. Thereafter, the committee concentrated on Irish Home Rule, focusing specifically on the future financial relationship between Westminster and Dublin. Thus, finance, not Ulster, was viewed as the main problem if the government were to proceed with its Home Rule plans. While Birrell, the Chief Secretary for Ireland, was broadly sympathetic to Nationalism, he worried that the talk of resistance to Home Rule in Ulster was not simple bluff. Accordingly, he considered the idea of some form of exclusion for at least part of Ulster, but he did not reveal these concerns to his fellow ministers.

In fact, the cabinet did not consider the Ulster situation until February 1912, when the general framework of the bill was already in place. Birrell remained anxious, but it was the views of two senior ministers, Lloyd George and Churchill, which shaped the cabinet discussion. On 6 February 1912, just two days before Churchill's Belfast visit, the two presented new proposals to the cabinet, arguing for Ulster's exclusion from the forthcoming bill. These memoranda provoked a lively debate among cabinet ministers, with Asquith apparently swaying both ways before deciding against exclusion. His letter to the king on the following day indicated the uncertainty at the heart of the government's Irish policy. While the cabinet had voted in favour of all-Ireland Home Rule, it would keep its options open to take account of potential developments. Indeed, Redmond was warned by Asquith that it might be necessary to alter the bill after its introduction if "fresh evidence of facts, or the pressure of British opinion" dictated. This might mean special treatment for the Ulster counties. Not surprisingly, the government did not publicise this strategy and Redmond chose not to share the information with his Irish MPs. The prime minister had explained that such special concessions on Ulster could be achieved either by amending the Home Rule Bill or by not pressing on with the legislation under the provisions of the Parliament Act. It was apparent, therefore, that the government did not rule out special treatment for Ulster as a matter of principle. Rather, Asquith preferred to sit back, waiting to see if such a compromise was necessary and then seeing if it would be sufficient. He also stated that the government had made its position clear, thereby putting the onus on the Conservatives to produce an amendment if they wanted to see changes to the bill.

It is easy to see how such a strategy appealed to Asquith. A premature concession on Ulster would have undermined Redmond and the Nationalists, but it also may have been unnecessary should Ulster Unionist threats of resistance have dissipated as the bill made its way through parliament. The major problem for the government in following this line was its lack of detailed knowledge about the real state of affairs in Ulster. Ministers were hearing from Redmond and his Belfast lieutenant, Devlin, that dire warnings of violent opposition were mere rhetoric. Yet the government, having initially failed to give serious consideration to the Ulster issue, now failed to gather accurate intelligence about the likelihood of trouble in Ulster if Home Rule was imposed. In this sense the government was badly served by Birrell who, though concerned by developments in the province, proved unable to draw firm conclusions about Unionist intentions. Consequently, matters were allowed to drift. Of course, ultimate responsibility lay with the prime minister, but his strategy was to play down the Ulster issue and hope that Carson's rhetoric would turn out to be an empty threat. This meant that Asquith handed the initiative to his Conservative and Unionist opponents, but such tactics fitted the premier's personality. Never one to seize the initiative, Asquith preferred to wait on the sidelines, allowing a situation to develop before he would make a timely intervention. This approach had served him well in previous crises. Such procrastination, however, was rooted not just in Asquith's lack of initiative or imagination; it also reflected his very laid-back style. His famous dictum, "we had better wait and see", neatly summed up Asquith's counter-attacking style, but it left the way open for Carson and Bonar Law to make the running as the Ulster crisis unfolded. On a number of occasions Asquith's procrastination clearly exasperated Lloyd George and Churchill, two ministerial colleagues who sought to dictate the course of events. While Lloyd George's attention was preoccupied with other problems for the remainder of 1912, Churchill continued to press the case for some form of Ulster exclusion in cabinet. He was not persuaded by Asquith's argument that if a compromise had to be made, it should be delayed for as long as possible.

Both sides were caught off guard by the intervention of a Liberal backbencher, Thomas Agar-Robartes, the MP for the St Austell constituency in Cornwall. During the debate on the bill's second reading in late May, when it received a majority in excess of 100, Agar-Robartes had called for the exclusion of northeast Ulster from Home Rule. Then, on 11 June 1912, during the committee stage, he moved an amendment proposing the exclusion of the four Ulster counties with Protestant majorities. The Agar-Robartes amendment caused some embarrassment to the government, but it also presented Asquith with the opportunity to wrong-foot his Conservative and Unionist opponents by seeking an early compromise based on exclusion. A number of historians have suggested that Asquith's rejection of this course of action was a missed opportunity, as it might have prevented the further escalation of the crisis. To have accepted the Agar-Robartes amendment while the bill was on its first parliamentary circuit would, of course, have been an admission that the Home Rule Bill had a major flaw. However, Asquith's principal reason for dismissing the amendment was that it would not halt Unionist opposition to the bill. Another obvious reason for the government's approach was that acceptance of the amendment would have unnecessarily, at this point anyway, left Redmond and the IPP disaffected. They had reacted with fury to the amendment, insisting that Ireland had to be treated as one distinct entity. Yet the initiative caused even more problems for the opposition parties. If the Ulster Unionists supported the amendment, they would have been accused of abandoning their fellow Unionists in the other 28 counties, when Carson had repeatedly claimed that they rejected Home Rule for any part of Ireland. There was, however, a possibility that the amendment, if passed, could destroy the entire Home Rule project. After some hesitation Carson persuaded his fellow Unionists to back the amendment, and they were joined in the division lobby by Conservative MPs who viewed the proposal as a "wrecking amendment" that might kill the bill. Leading Tories, such as Bonar Law and Balfour, were thus persuaded to support the amendment even though they did not like it. For others who had strong southern Unionist connections, such as Walter Long, this proved more difficult but, after much soul-searching, he too backed the amendment.

By the summer of 1912, therefore, the possibility of a solution to the Home Rule crisis based on some form of exclusion or partition had entered the political discourse. But it was also clear that neither side was keen on compromise. The Liberals, though they had privately agreed on a fallback position on Ulster if the need arose, were not prepared to disappoint the Irish Nationalists at this stage. Asquith was by now even more convinced that if a concession was deemed necessary, it should be delayed until the bill was on its final parliamentary circuit. The Conservatives, meanwhile, had bought into Carson's strategy of using Ulster to destroy the entire Home Rule scheme, and they were in no mood to compromise. Their key argument was that the 1912 Home Rule Bill had been the product of a "corrupt bargain" between Asquith and Redmond and that this unscrupulous deal had been deliberately hidden from the electorate during both elections in 1910. They demanded a fresh election to give the voters a say on the crucial question of Irish Home Rule. In his defence, of course, Asquith could point to the Liberal Party's long-standing association with Home Rule, while highlighting the fact that the Conservatives certainly had made Home Rule an issue in the 1910 contests. Beyond this, Bonar Law and Balfour had begun to consider other ways to thwart the bill. One line they pursued was the claim that with the Parliament Act now on the statute book, royal assent should no longer be viewed as a mere formality. Thus, the possibility of the king withholding royal assent or dismissing the Liberal government to allow a general election was mooted for the first time.

Evidence that Bonar Law was prepared to adopt an extreme position came on 27 July 1912, when the Conservative leader addressed a large anti-Home Rule demonstration at Blenheim Palace in Oxfordshire. Tensions had been raised by Asquith's historic visit to Dublin on the previous weekend, when he delighted his audience by pouring scorn on Unionist threats of civil war before adding, "Ireland is a nation, not two nations, but one nation." In his speech to 13,000 supporters at Blenheim, Bonar Law's anger at the prime minister's dismissive attitude was obvious. He warned the government that if it pressed ahead with Home Rule without putting the issue to the electorate, then Ulstermen "would be justified in resisting by all means in their power, including force". But what grabbed the headlines at Blenheim was the Tory leader's unequivocal stance on Ulster Unionist threats of violence. He informed his audience, "I can imagine no length of resistance to which Ulster will go, in which I shall not be ready to support them, and in which they will not be supported by the overwhelming majority of the British people." Another of the speakers at Blenheim, F. E. Smith, had reflected growing Tory confidence when he claimed that the present government lacked the necessary resolve to see off the Ulster challenge. Smith was a brilliant lawyer and Liverpool MP who was closely associated with the city's powerful Orange Order network. The Blenheim demonstration confirmed that opposition to Home Rule was clearly centred on Ulster, but Bonar Law had caused a storm with his apparent encouragement of violence. Asquith and the Liberal press were shocked by the bluntness of his language and by his obvious disregard for the constitutional process. Earlier, on 18 June, Bonar Law had informed the House of Commons that there were "things stronger than parliamentary majorities". Naturally such language caused alarm, but it reinforced the views held privately by Churchill and Lloyd George that special provision would ultimately be required for Ulster. There were a number of factors that explain Bonar Law's adoption of such a militant stance. As a new party leader, he was anxious to avoid the mistakes made by Balfour, whose lack of clarity had exacerbated divisions in the Tory ranks. Clearly, the defence of the Union was an issue on which the party could unite, and, by taking a tough line and ruling out compromise, it became easier to maintain this unity. It had also become evident that Ireland was an issue on which the party could press the government, with the ultimate objective being a return to office. There was, moreover, lingering bitterness from the passage of the Parliament Act, and many Conservatives were convinced, with little justification, that the Liberals, in tandem with their Irish allies, had been acting subversively since 1909. This kind of thinking made the prospect of agreement between the two parties very unlikely in 1912. On the positive side, most Conservatives viewed the defence of the Union as vital for the long-term stability of the British Empire, while, on a personal level, Bonar Law's attachment to Ulster led him to move his party to a more extreme position alongside the Unionists.

Ulster resistance

The introduction of the third Home Rule Bill had raised sectarian tension in Ulster. In early July, 2,000 Catholic workers were forced out of their jobs in the shipyards. This action had been sparked by an incident in Castledawson on 29 June. A party of children on a Sunday school excursion from their Presbyterian church in Belfast encountered a group of Hibernians who had returned from an AOH demonstration in nearby Maghera. A disturbance ensued and some of the terrified children fled into the unfamiliar countryside outside the village. Although none had been seriously injured, the rumour mill in Belfast painted a picture of innocent Protestant children being attacked by drunken Catholic men, with the consequences being wildly exaggerated. The result was the expulsion of the Catholic shipyard workers, with further violence following over the Twelfth holiday period. Sectarian trouble continued into September, when violent clashes broke out at a football match in the city. The scale of the unrest alarmed Carson who, from the outset, recognised the importance of maintaining discipline among his supporters in Ulster. Indiscriminate violence, such as occurred in Belfast during July 1912, only handed the advantage to the Liberal government and damaged public support for the Unionist cause in Britain.

It became essential to find a way to control and focus such intense popular feeling in Ulster, and it was Craig who devised a solution. From the spring of 1912, a number of leading Unionists had been considering the idea of an oath, which their supporters could take in order to demonstrate their determination to resist Home Rule. Craig worked closely with Thomas Sinclair, and they produced a document that was based on the Scottish National Covenant of 1638. Sinclair was a leading Belfast Presbyterian businessman who had played a prominent role in opposing the 1886 and 1893 Home Rule Bills. When Carson was presented with the wording of the document in late August, he declared, "I would not alter a word in the declaration, which I consider excellent." The Covenant allowed its signatories to profess loyalty to the king, but warned His Majesty's government that the men of Ulster, and the reference was to all nine Ulster counties, would use "all means which may be found necessary to defeat the present conspiracy to set up a Home Rule parliament in Ireland". Craig assumed responsibility for the organisation of what was designated "Ulster Day" on 28 September 1912. Carson and other leading figures were to sign the Covenant in the City Hall following another mass rally in Belfast, as nearly a fortnight of campaigning across the province reached its climax.

Carson opened the campaign on 18 September, addressing a crowd of 40,000 on Portora Hill in Enniskillen. This meeting set the tone for the entire Covenant campaign. It was the first of seven public meetings at which Carson spoke, and special trains were laid on to transport Unionists from Tyrone, Cavan, Monaghan, Donegal, Sligo and Leitrim. A huge platform was constructed to seat 1,000 special guests. Carson travelled by motor car from Crom Castle in the company of the Earl of Erne, Thomas Sinclair and Lord Hugh Cecil, a leading Tory. What transformed the event into a great spectacle was the large, mounted escort organised by William Copeland Trimble, a prominent Fermanagh Unionist and owner of the *Impartial Reporter,* which met Carson outside the town. In his speech, the Unionist leader acknowledged his followers' support, claiming that it led him to believe that "a mutual confidence" existed between him and them. This would allow him "to help the people of Ulster to defeat a most nefarious, a most unprovoked conspiracy against their civil and religious liberty". The purpose of these demonstrations, as Carson and others readily confirmed, was to convince the Liberal government that Ulster Unionists were serious when they warned of resistance to Home Rule. For his part, Cecil informed the crowd that "the cause of the Union" was winning increasing support in England and Scotland, a development that was confirmed by recent Tory successes in a number of by-elections. Cecil was joined in Ulster by other major right-wing Tory peers such as Lord Salisbury and Lord Willoughby de Broke. The other leading Conservative politician who generated great enthusiasm among Unionist supporters with his brilliant oratory was F. E. Smith, who spoke at five of these great public gatherings.

On Wednesday, 25 September, the organisers dispatched copies of the Covenant across the province where they were signed, often in local Orange halls, by Unionist supporters. On the Friday evening a great rally was held in the Ulster Hall, and Carson gave one of his finest performances on an Ulster

Signing the Ulster Covenant, Belfast City Hall, 28 September 1912.

platform, with each phrase carefully crafted and carrying great significance. Outside the venue, he dramatically unfolded before the expectant crowd a yellow silk banner, which was reputed to have been carried by Williamite troops at the Battle of the Boyne, while exclaiming, "May this flag ever float over a people that can boast of civil and religious liberty." The following day, a holiday in Belfast, a series of religious services was followed by the procession to the City Hall, where the leading Unionists signed the Covenant in another piece of carefully constructed theatre. Carson signed using a special silver pen which had been formally presented to him by Craig. In towns and villages across the province, local organising committees had arranged special church services, which were held before official signing ceremonies. In Belfast the Presbyterian Moderator, Rev Dr William McKean, preached at a morning service in the Ulster Hall and opened his remarks by stating, "We are plain, blunt men who love peace and industry." McKean's address illustrated the significance of religion in the Unionist rejection of Home Rule when he declared, "The Irish question is at bottom a war against Protestantism; it is an attempt to establish a Roman Catholic ascendancy in Ireland to begin the disintegration of the empire by securing a second parliament in Dublin." Similar sentiments were expressed throughout Ulster.

Ulster Day had been a propaganda triumph. The press was there in force to witness events first-hand, and senior reporters from all the leading English newspapers conveyed the image of an emotional, determined and defiant mass. There was also a distinct "God's chosen people" feel to the proceedings that was attributable to the deeply religious nature of the day's events. Here were God's people, as they presented themselves, just like the Old Testament Israelites, defying injustice and, as the Covenant stated, "humbly relying on their God". Clearly, this powerful religious undertone, together with the presence and participation of so many Protestant clerics, added to the emotional excitement of the day. More than 218,000 men signed the Covenant, and over 228,000 women signed a parallel Declaration. The grand total, when over 20,000 signatures from people of Ulster birth in Britain were added, reached 471,414. The campaign, which saw Carson criss-crossing the province, resulted in the Dublin-born Unionist leader being recast as an honorary Ulsterman. When he left the docks in Belfast on the evening of 28 September on board the overnight steamer to Liverpool, a crowd of 70,000 gave him a rousing send-off. The following morning, he was greeted by 150,000 supporters in Liverpool. This was the largest outdoor Unionist demonstration in the entire campaign, and it illustrated the level of support for the Unionist cause in Britain. The Covenant had achieved the goals set out by Carson and Craig. A highly disciplined mass movement had engaged in a carefully stage-managed act of defiance. In doing so, the Unionist rank and file in Ulster had demonstrated their resolve by taking their solemn pledge to resist Home Rule.

The events of the summer had raised Conservative and Unionist spirits, and this was evident when the Commons reassembled for the autumn session in October 1912. The committee stage of the Home Rule Bill's first circuit was the cue for a succession of stormy incidents in the chamber. Enraged by the use of the guillotine, a parliamentary process deployed by the government to limit the time allocated for debate and to speed the bill's progress, opposition MPs denounced the tactic as tyrannical, and Bonar Law renewed his demand for a general election. On 1 January 1913 Carson moved an amendment to have the entire Ulster province removed from the bill's operation. This adoption of exclusion appeared to be a logical step, building on sentiments expressed in the Covenant, but it was not without risk. Carson still clung to the hope that Ulster resistance could yet kill the whole bill, and his speech to the Commons made clear that even if the amendment was passed, opposition to the bill would be maintained. Naturally, any proposal for the exclusion of Ulster raised great concern among supporters of Unionism in the other three provinces, and they had to be persuaded that this was yet another tactical manoeuvre. Under no circumstances, they were assured, would they be abandoned. Still, Carson's amendment reflected the Ulster-based opposition to Home Rule that had become so predominant over the course of 1912. In private, many Unionists now conceded that they would be unable to block the entire measure. Accordingly, it made political sense to focus on saving Ulster from Home Rule. When the cabinet met to discuss the situation, Lloyd George and Churchill favoured using the Carson amendment as a route out of the Ulster impasse, but the majority remained committed to the "no compromise" policy. In the end, the amendment was rejected by 294 to 197 votes. On 16 January the bill was passed at third reading by a majority of 110. Almost immediately, as expected, it was thrown out by the Lords.

With events in parliament taking a predictable course, Unionists in Ulster felt it essential to demonstrate that they had both the desire and the means to resist the imposition of Home Rule. Already, Orangemen across the province had begun to drill, and groups of men marching in military style became a common sight on the country roads outside Orange halls. On 31 January 1913 the UUC announced that these men would come together in a new body, the Ulster Volunteer Force (UVF). Recruitment for the new force, which was to be capped at 100,000, was limited to men between the ages of 17 and 65 who had signed the Covenant. While recruitment was slow initially, the new force had grown to 90,000 members by the close of 1913. It also had a small full-time staff of ex-British Army officers who were based in the UVF's headquarters in Belfast's Old Town Hall. The force was organised on a county-by-county basis, with a varying number of regiments, battalions and sections, depending on the strength of recruitment in each of the nine counties. A key feature of the force was its cross-class membership. The great landowners, many of whom had military experience, often served as officers, and many allowed their estates to be used for weekend training camps. In Belfast, businessmen featured prominently, while support was particularly strong among shipyard workers. In the provincial towns, manual workers frequently served alongside their employers, while small farmers and labourers were heavily represented in rural areas. Dummy wooden rifles were regularly used for drill practice during this early phase. This caused great amusement for their opponents, but the UVF was eager to prove that it represented a viable military force. The measures taken to attract experienced soldiers to serve on its full-time staff indicated Unionist intent. Its leaders turned for advice to Lord Roberts of Kandahar, the most famous living British military leader, who responded with great enthusiasm. Through Roberts, the UVF obtained the services of Lieutenant-General Sir George Richardson, who had enjoyed a distinguished career with the army in India. Richardson assumed command of the UVF in July 1913, and his priority was the organisation of training for the 50,000 men who had already been recruited. A huge UVF parade was held on 28 September 1913, the anniversary of Ulster Day, when 12,000 men marched before 25,000 spectators at Balmoral. Soon, various support units, including a medical corps, a nursing corps and a motor car corps, were established, and these helped to develop the image of a well-organised military force. Of course, the force required a large cache of arms; early moves to acquire guns had been small-scale and only a handful of rifles were available. Still, the existence of the force gave some substance to Carson's increasingly militant rhetoric, which had developed over the course of 1913. At the same time, the emergence of the UVF imposed the kind of discipline among his followers that Carson had deemed to be essential.

The search for a solution

Campaigning against Home Rule in Britain also moved outside parliament. In March 1913 Lord Willoughby de Broke, who had been prominent in the preparations for the Covenant, wrote to a number of London newspapers announcing the formation of the "British League for the Support of Ulster and the Union". The letter bore the signatures of 100 peers and 120 MPs, and the movement soon attracted the support of a number of famous figures outside politics, such as Rudyard Kipling and Edward Elgar. This heightened awareness of the Ulster crisis in Britain. In parliament the reintroduced Home Rule Bill received its third reading in the Commons on 7 July 1913. Asquith was still adopting the "wait and see" approach and leaving it to the Conservatives to bring forward an amendment. Others, however, lacked the prime minister's coolness under pressure. In particular, the king was anxious that he might be drawn into the controversy if a compromise acceptable to all the parties could not be found. Bonar Law had stepped up the pressure, demanding a general election and suggesting that the king might exercise his constitutional power to dissolve parliament to force the issue. Towards the end of July, the king asked Tory leaders to clarify their views, prompting the dispatch of a lengthy memorandum by Bonar Law and Lansdowne. Their central argument was that the king should use the royal prerogative to dissolve parliament before Home Rule was enacted. The suggestion was that the king should withhold royal assent and then call for a new government that would put the issue to the voters. Significantly, A. V. Dicey, the brilliant Oxford academic and constitutional expert, had opined that His Majesty would be acting within his powers in taking such a course.

Still, other leading Conservatives were nervous about drawing the monarch into party politics, as it could establish a dangerous precedent that could ultimately undermine the king's role in the Constitution. Balfour was firm on this point, though he was adamant that the king could still send for new ministers. There could be a role, he proposed, for an elder statesman to steer a path through the crisis, and he made it known that he was available for such a task. With the king being placed under such pressure, Asquith's reaction was crucial. On 11 August, George V personally handed the prime minister a memorandum running to

400 words, which he had prepared after considering the Bonar Law–Lansdowne document. The king's memorandum highlighted the difficulties facing the monarchy, and he suggested an all-party conference to explore the possibility of a settlement. Asquith's response was unequivocal. He warned that the king must not depart from constitutional convention by intervening in the Home Rule crisis. The prime minister then presented an analysis of the situation in Ulster, suggesting "tumult and riot" as the likely outcome of Home Rule becoming law. Furthermore, he suggested that the doom-mongers who were predicting civil war were being alarmist. Moreover, any all-party conference could not succeed unless the opposition conceded the principle of Irish Home Rule, though the prime minister offered the possibility of a reasonable compromise being found on Ulster should this principle be acceptable. The king's concerns must have been an unwelcome distraction for Asquith, but, whatever his other mistakes in dealing with the Ulster crisis, the prime minister demonstrated a sure touch in handling the royal intervention. Recognising that senior Conservatives were placing the monarch under great pressure, Asquith was both tactful and decisive in steering the king away from controversy.

On the ground in Ulster, meanwhile, resistance to Home Rule was intensifying. The Twelfth celebrations in July 1913 drew large crowds, and Carson was present at the main demonstration which was held in the grounds of Craig's home. Both men were pleased that a repeat of the previous year's unrest had been avoided, and Carson attributed this to the discipline instilled by the UVF. Surprisingly, in spite of the time he devoted to the cause of Unionism, Carson continued with his high-profile legal career. In June he and F. E. Smith represented Lloyd George and Lord Murray of Elibank, the Liberal chief whip, in a famous libel case, which led to apologies being secured for the government ministers. In taking the brief at a time when relations between the two main parties at Westminster were so acrimonious, Carson stunned many of his closest colleagues, including Bonar Law. Returning to Ulster in September for a series of political engagements, Carson indulged in his most militant rhetoric to date. By this point Carson had sensed that the government's resolve was weakening, and he was eager to press home his advantage. On 23 September he attended a meeting of the UUC at which the 500 delegates formally approved plans for the immediate establishment of a provisional government if Home Rule was enacted. Even at this stage Carson retained the hope that Ulster resistance could derail the Home Rule project, as there was a chance that Redmond and the IPP would prefer a general election to some form of exclusion.

Certainly, the idea of partition was anathema to Redmond. He had emphasised this when he spoke against Carson's proposal for Ulster's exclusion from the bill. Although he described Carson's speech as "serious and solemn", the

Irish leader was quick to dismiss any prospect of armed insurrection in Ulster. From the Home Rule Bill's introduction in April 1912, Redmond insisted that Home Rule had to be on an all-Ireland basis. He was slow to come to terms with Ulster opposition to the bill, believing that there was no substance to Unionist arguments. The Irish leader also assumed that the dire threats issued by Carson were mere bluster and largely depended on the support Unionism received from a desperate and impatient Bonar Law. Moreover, the result of the Derry City by-election in January 1913 gave credence to one of Redmond's key arguments that Unionists did not speak for Ulster. The by-election provided a victory for a pro-Home Rule Liberal candidate, David Hogg, a Scottish-born shirt manufacturer in the city. The seat had been in Unionist hands since 1900, but Hogg stood on a clear Home Rule ticket and won by a majority of 57 votes. In his post-election address to the press, the triumphant candidate stated that he was "proud to have been the standard-bearer of self-government for Ireland in one of the most historic elections ever fought in Ireland". The by-election was significant not just because the Unionists surrendered the "maiden city" seat but because Hogg's victory gave Home Rulers the majority of Ulster's 33 seats, leaving the Unionists with 16. The Derry victory provided a boost for Nationalists in Ulster, but it probably contributed to Redmond's complacency on the Ulster issue, and he continued to dismiss Carson's rhetoric on armed resistance as fantasy.

While Redmond shouldered most of the burden during the Ulster crisis, he confided in three principal lieutenants who stood head and shoulders above the rest of the party. T. P. O'Connor acted as the key link between the IPP and the Liberal government, and he enjoyed a close relationship with Lloyd George. In spite of developments in Ulster during the first half of 1913, O'Connor remained confident that the Home Rule Bill would become law and that Unionist threats of armed resistance were bluff. Joe Devlin, the Belfast MP, had built on his reputation as a brilliant parliamentary performer during the Home Rule proceedings in the Commons. In addition, his influence with the AOH ensured that he remained a powerful figure among rank-and-file Nationalists. Like O'Connor, he downplayed warnings about civil war in Ulster, informing the Commons in June 1913 that such talk was "humbug, sham and hypocrisy". Privately, too, Devlin advised a number of his parliamentary colleagues that Unionists were not serious about using violence to block Home Rule. Devlin was close to John Dillon, Redmond's deputy and former rival. Dillon had an intimate understanding of grass-roots Irish politics and was a veteran of the agrarian struggle in the Parnell era. For much of 1913, when Redmond was often busy in London, Dillon toured Ireland, addressing Nationalist audiences and reassuring them that there was little likelihood of violent resistance to Home Rule in Ulster.

Therefore, when the Ulster crisis blew up in the autumn of 1913, the IPP was taken by surprise. It had no policy on Ulster beyond its insistence that Home Rule had to be on an all-Ireland basis, and Redmond left it to the government to defend the IPP's position. The obvious problem with this was that the Nationalists relied too much on the Liberals and had no contingency plan should the government retreat from the position outlined by Asquith on the introduction of the Home Rule Bill in April 1912. This was a critical error, as Redmond was privy to the decision at the crucial cabinet meeting on 6 February 1912 that the government retained the freedom to offer some form of protection to Ulster if the circumstances dictated. Throughout 1912–13, moreover, the IPP leadership had enough contact with ministers such as Lloyd George, Churchill and Birrell to detect that the government might give way on some form of exclusion. Still, Redmond clung to the belief that if the government stood firm, Ulster Unionist opposition would evaporate. The alternative would have been to take the initiative by offering Ulster some kind of safeguard, such as "Home Rule within Home Rule", or perhaps a Unionist veto in a new devolved parliament. While Carson would most probably have dismissed either of these proposals, such a gesture might have split the opposition forces and made a compromise settlement more achievable. Some of the blame for this can be laid with Asquith and his ministers who preferred to reassure Nationalists on their commitment to all-Ireland Home Rule rather than encourage some engagement with the Unionists.

Both Asquith and Redmond were caught off guard by the fallout from the Loreburn letter, which was published in *The Times* on 11 September 1913. Loreburn had served as lord chancellor in the Liberal government up to June 1912, and it was known that he was a firm supporter of Irish Home Rule. His letter urged the party leaders to go the extra mile in search of a settlement. Failure to do so, he warned, would lead to serious disturbances in Ulster. The Loreburn letter was a bombshell, because it was assumed, wrongly, by Conservative and Unionist leaders, that it had its origins in the Liberal cabinet. While the influential Loreburn was acting alone, his dramatic intervention altered the terms of the debate. Behind the scenes, meanwhile, Asquith met the king at Balmoral where he indicated to George V that he had not anticipated the scale of opposition to Home Rule that was now evident in Ulster. Yet he remained unwilling to make concessions in the face of Ulster threats. During September and early October 1913, the king welcomed political leaders from both parties to his Scottish castle. Bonar Law was one of the first to arrive, and he again pressed the king to use his powers and dissolve parliament. While the king baulked at taking such a drastic course of action, he was, nevertheless, prompted to send a further memorandum to the prime minister that raised several difficult questions. First, the king made it clear that there should, in his opinion, be a general election before Home Rule became law. Secondly, he asked Asquith about the possibility of the army being used to suppress potential disorder in Ulster given that a large number of senior officers were sympathetic to the Unionist cause. Although the prime minister responded by stating that the troops would follow orders, the king's enquiry had highlighted the growing disquiet generated by the Home Rule issue among high-ranking army officers.

Bonar Law's visit to Balmoral coincided with Churchill's attendance, and the two men took the opportunity to discuss the Ulster crisis. Churchill was encouraged by the moderate line taken by the Conservative leader, who expressed his concern about Carson's plan to establish a provisional government if Home Rule was enacted. Bonar Law stated his willingness to accept Home Rule if Ulster were excluded from its operation. His only reservation was that this would be viewed as a betrayal of Unionists in the three southern provinces. Partition now seemed a workable compromise, and Bonar Law wrote to Carson with news of his talks with Churchill. Carson's reply on 23 September fully endorsed the Bonar Law line and went on to focus on the actual area to be excluded from the bill: "My own view is that the whole of Ulster should be excluded but the minimum would be the six plantation counties, and for that a good case could be made." This exchange of letters confirmed that Bonar Law and Carson took a much more moderate stance in private than their public pronouncements suggested. Carson had closely identified with, even embodied, the spirit of defiance that had become such a feature of Ulster Unionist opposition. By the autumn of 1913, however, he was clearly worried about the consequences of such defiance should the government force through the Home Rule Bill. In Ulster, Craig and a number of his colleagues were adopting a more militant position and wanted to use the UVF to threaten the government. This had increased the pressure on Carson to reach a negotiated settlement.

Bonar Law, too, was keen on a more cautious approach. He faced internal party problems, many of which stemmed from his bellicose Blenheim speech. While many Tory backbenchers were delighted by their new leader's provocative posturing, a number of the party's senior figures expressed alarm, partly as he had not consulted his colleagues before addressing the Blenheim audience. While he was happy to cultivate this combative image, his primary concern had been to save Ulster, and the government learned, in the autumn of 1913, that he would accept a compromise based on partition. Bonar Law's problem was the phalanx of senior party figures, notably Lansdowne, Long, Curzon and the Cecils, who saw partition as the abandonment of southern Unionists. It was entirely possible that this group could scupper any attempt at a solution based on partition. With the southern Unionists emerging as a probable obstacle to a compromise, Carson chose to address the problem directly. He met a southern Unionist delegation at his London home and secured a commitment from them not to obstruct

Ulster's demand for exclusion from Home Rule. News of this exchange provided some reassurance for Bonar Law, though he remained concerned about southern Unionist reaction. For his part, Carson, while retaining an emotional attachment to Irish Unionism, had changed his strategy. In 1912 he was using Ulster to smash the entire Home Rule scheme, but, by the autumn of 1913, he was trying to save the greater part of Ulster from an unstoppable Home Rule Bill.

Both Carson and Bonar Law were encouraged by a Churchill speech in his Dundee constituency on 9 October. Churchill recognised this most recent development and stated that Ulster's "claim for special consideration" could not be ignored by the government if it was made with genuine sincerity. T.P. O'Connor was first among the Nationalist leadership to appreciate the dangers behind Churchill's stance, and he urged Redmond to reinforce the IPP's outright opposition to the exclusion of any part of Ireland from the Home Rule Bill. He did so in a memorable speech in Limerick on 12 October, when he warned the government against accepting a compromise based on partition, adding, "Irish Nationalists can never be assenting parties to the mutilation of the Irish nation, Ireland is a unit … The two-nation theory is to us an abomination and a blasphemy." Still, Redmond reaffirmed his conviction that all the rhetoric forecasting civil war in Ireland was a gigantic bluff. In a speech in Navan, one week later, he likened Ulster threats of resistance to the bravado of the drunken man desperately seeking restraint before he "attacks" his enemy. Two days after Redmond's Limerick speech, Churchill developed the theme he had articulated in Dundee, when he proposed in cabinet that there should be a five-year exclusion of the Protestant part of Ulster from the bill. However, Asquith was not tempted.

Still, the prime minister was keen to reach some kind of compromise. While he was not in favour of formal negotiations with the Conservatives, he wrote to Bonar Law suggesting confidential meetings between himself and the Tory leader. The offer was a reaction to pressure from the king and from Lloyd George and Churchill. The two leaders met on three occasions, 14 October, 6 November and 10 December, at Cherkley Court, the home of Bonar Law's close friend, Sir Max Aitken. Although nothing was agreed at the first of these secret meetings, the prime minister learned that Bonar Law's private stance was more moderate than his public statements indicated. He also discovered that Bonar Law would accept Home Rule if Ulster was excluded, but no attempt was made to define "Ulster". The prime minister was now aware of the difficulties confronting Bonar Law should he advocate a settlement based on exclusion. Lansdowne was cast as an uncompromising figure who had already informed Carson that he viewed this confidential dialogue between the two leaders with profound mistrust. Yet it was evident that despite the recent bitter acrimony between the Liberals and Conservatives, the two leaders were drawn towards a compromise based on the exclusion of Ulster. Obviously difficulties remained, not least securing agreement on the area of Ulster to be excluded, but this first meeting offered some hope of a solution. Significantly, as a number of leading Conservatives had feared, Asquith proved to be the more skilful negotiator, concealing his own problems while probing Bonar Law's readiness to consider possible concessions, which would, of course, require the endorsement of his Conservative colleagues.

At their second meeting on 6 November, Asquith pressed Bonar Law on the area to be excluded from the Home Rule Bill. When the Tory leader stated that Carson would accept nothing less than six counties, the prime minister reminded him that Tyrone and Fermanagh had narrow, but significant, Nationalist majorities. By this stage it was clear that the Nationalists would have to give ground if the government chose to pursue the exclusion idea. For some time the Conservatives had criticised the government's dependence on Redmond and the IPP, though it was slowly becoming apparent that a complacent Redmond was totally dependent on the Liberal government for the delivery of Home Rule. At the end of the second meeting, Asquith agreed to Bonar Law's request to put the question of Ulster exclusion before the cabinet, though the latter wrongly assumed that the prime minister would personally present the arguments in favour of such a course. When the cabinet did meet, it was Lloyd George who grasped the initiative by proposing an amendment, whereby those counties with Unionist majorities could opt out of Home Rule for a period of five years. Although Lloyd George presented the case for exclusion with his customary enthusiasm, not all of his colleagues were willing to make such a major concession, though it was now clear that the balance in cabinet had swung in favour of exclusion.

On 17 November 1913 Asquith belatedly met Redmond to discuss the unfolding situation. The Irish leader now learned of Lloyd George's plan to exclude part of Ulster for a fixed period, after which it would automatically come under a Dublin parliament. The prime minister also conveyed the impression that the proposal was really a delaying tactic to prevent the outbreak of serious violence in Ulster. Redmond was alarmed by the suggestion, though he indicated that he might consider it if it was put forward by Bonar Law. After the meeting he dispatched a memorandum to Asquith that forcefully argued against partition and stated that the immediate threat of violence in Ulster was being grossly exaggerated. The memorandum appeared to have the desired effect, as Redmond received an assurance on 26 November that the government would not introduce the Lloyd George plan. On the following day, moreover, Asquith rejected demands for a compromise on Ulster when he addressed a public meeting in Leeds: "We are not going to be frightened or deflected by menaces of civil war. We are not going to make any surrender of principle. We mean to see the thing through." Still, Lloyd George remained optimistic that the Nationalists could be pressed into accepting some form of exclusion. A meeting with Dillon on 17 November confirmed this, provided his scheme of temporary exclusion was delayed until the Home Rule Bill was on its final lap. Lloyd George then met Redmond on 25 November and urged him to accept his temporary exclusion plan. This left the Irish leader confused and angry. Over the course of a few days, he had received different interpretations of the government's thinking from Asquith, Birrell and Lloyd George, but it was clear that opinion in the cabinet was shifting in favour of exclusion. However, Bonar Law flatly rejected the scheme for temporary exclusion when it was presented by Asquith at their third and final meeting in December. Relations between the two leaders had been soured by Asquith's Leeds speech, and Bonar Law was becoming increasingly angry at the prime minister's procrastination, which he correctly assumed was a deliberate tactic. Bonar Law's expectation was that the government would offer Home Rule within Home Rule in the hope that the likely rejection of this proposal would turn public opinion in Britain against the Conservative Party. For his part, Asquith assumed that Redmond would accept Home Rule within Home Rule, as it maintained the integrity of a 32-county Ireland. Again, he was likely to delay any such offer, fearing that premature action would result in further demands from the opposition.

Asquith explored the Home Rule within Home Rule concept in two meetings with Carson on 16 December 1913 and 2 January 1914. While these meetings were more cordial than the Asquith–Bonar Law interviews, Carson firmly rejected the new proposal. Still, the prime minister remained upbeat, as he felt that his opponents had been backed into a corner, where they would now have to make their own detailed counter-offer, something that he had consistently sought to engineer. Yet Carson's response echoed Bonar Law's analysis. Both men argued that there was no point in working out specific proposals on the administration of any excluded area unless the government first accepted the principle of exclusion. Astonishingly, during all of these private discussions, the prime minister had left his cabinet colleagues in the dark, and he only reported the breakdown of his negotiations with Bonar Law and Carson on 22 January 1914. With little prospect of a negotiated settlement, the two opposition leaders revived their militant rhetoric. On 15 January Bonar Law informed a Cardiff audience that he had been in private discussion with the prime minister, but no progress had been made. He then fired off a letter to the king's private secretary, Lord Stamfordham, setting out his personal analysis of a deteriorating situation. In Bonar Law's opinion, the government had two options: "Either they must submit their Bill to the judgement of the people or prepare for the consequences of civil war." He ended with the bleak assessment that compromise had been tried, and it had failed. Still, a number of Bonar Law's Conservative colleagues remained optimistic, clinging to the hope that if the Liberals could be pressed into offering the exclusion of Ulster, it would be met by a Nationalist rejection which, in turn, would precipitate the collapse of the entire Home Rule scheme.

With the new parliamentary session due to open, Asquith and Redmond had a crucial meeting on 2 February 1914. This was their first contact since their meeting on 17 November. By this stage the prime minister was gauging how far he could push Redmond, and he highlighted the great difficulties facing his government. Asquith was clearly anxious to prevent violence erupting in Ulster, and extracting concessions from Nationalists provided a likely solution. Yet Asquith was less than truthful with Redmond, assuring him that his cabinet colleagues were all firmly opposed to the exclusion of Ulster, even on a temporary basis. He followed this worthless assurance, however, with a devastating blow, subsequently recording, "My visitor shivered visibly and was a good deal perturbed", when he delivered his assessment. The prime minister detailed the failure of his talks with Bonar Law and Carson before warning that the king was terrified of civil war in Ulster and that there could be serious problems with the army should violence erupt in Ulster. Consequently, Asquith explained, that he had no alternative but to offer some concession to Ulster, specifying Home Rule within Home Rule. While he suggested that the likely rejection of this compromise by Unionism would undermine the Ulster cause in Britain, the weakness of Redmond's position was now obvious. He had been joined in London by Devlin and Dillon, and together they penned a reply to the prime minister on 5 February. Again, they stressed that the threat of civil war in Ulster was wildly exaggerated and warned that an early announcement of any concessions would pose grave difficulties for the IPP, which would inevitably be accused of abandoning Nationalists living in Ulster. For three months Redmond had been sidelined by Asquith, and he was now being targeted by a government that regarded him as the weakest link in the Ulster crisis.

Asquith refrained from presenting a compromise formula when the Commons returned from its winter recess on 11 February. This gave Lloyd George the opportunity to break the stalemate. He believed any potential solution had to meet two criteria. First, any concession to Ulster should be an offer which, if rejected, would put the Unionists in the wrong as far as public opinion in Britain was concerned. Secondly, it should not result in any alteration of the general principles in the Home Rule Bill. By this point the Home Rule within Home Rule solution was much less appealing to Lloyd George than his original idea of the temporary exclusion of particular Ulster counties, the scheme that he had presented to Redmond and Dillon in the previous November. Progress depended on the Nationalists giving some ground, and Asquith, Lloyd George and Birrell met the "Big Four" – Redmond, Dillon, Devlin and O'Connor – on 2 March 1914 for a discussion of the Lloyd George initiative. Following the meeting

Redmond drew up a memorandum outlining the solution that his party had been urged to accept. Individual counties could, after a plebiscite, opt out of Home Rule for a period of three years, and Redmond reluctantly decided to accept the proposal as "the price of peace". The Irish leader insisted that this concession, which also gave Belfast and Derry the opportunity to vote against Home Rule, could only be made if it was fully accepted by Unionists, and added that it must be "the last word of the government". Yet within days Redmond conceded further ground by agreeing to an extension of the time delay from three to six years. This was an attempt by Asquith to secure Unionist acquiescence, as a general election was bound to take place in the interim following the changes made by the Parliament Act. This held out the prospect of certain counties avoiding Home Rule after the six-year time gap, if the Conservatives were returned to power.

This was a major concession by the IPP. Redmond had abandoned the "one Ireland" principle. There were several reasons behind his endorsement of the county option scheme. On the one hand, he had been influenced by a Carson speech in the House of Commons on 11 February 1914. Carson had adopted a statesmanlike tone and appealed to Redmond and his own "Nationalist fellow countrymen" to win over Ulster by persuasion rather than by force. The speech convinced Redmond that it was worth going the extra mile to find a solution. The Irish leader, moreover, wanted to believe that the likely exclusion of four Ulster counties would be a temporary state of affairs and that time would help to heal the bitterness which had intensified during the Ulster crisis. Redmond was also a parliamentarian who believed in compromise and constitutional action. He was never comfortable with the power of extra-parliamentary pressure that Carson used to such effect, and with Home Rule now within touching distance he was prepared to forego Irish unity in the short term. Devlin, from his Ulster base, had pressed Redmond not to shelve the one-Ireland principle, but even he was prepared to swallow temporary exclusion if the prize was Home Rule. Of course, it had been the campaign of resistance directed by Carson and Craig that had forced the government to seek a solution based on the exclusion of an area of Ulster. Redmond had succumbed to government pressure, but Carson refused to endorse the county option scheme. When Asquith announced the government's plan on 9 March, when moving the second reading of the bill that was now on its final parliamentary circuit, Carson contemptuously dismissed the offer. He warned the House that Unionists in Ulster would not accept a "sentence of death with a stay of execution for six years". One week later, in another piece of parliamentary theatre, Carson led his followers from the Commons and returned to Belfast, where it was assumed that he would establish an Ulster provisional government. This left the ball in the government's court. If Asquith was going to deliver the assurance given to Redmond that the county option scheme with the six-year time limit was the government's final offer, then Ulster would have to be coerced.

The crisis deepens

The formation of the Irish Volunteers in November 1913 was clearly inspired by the appearance of the UVF at the beginning of the year, but it was also an indication that a section of Nationalist opinion was dissatisfied by Redmond's handling of the Home Rule crisis. The key figure behind the Irish Volunteers was the Gaelic scholar, Eoin MacNeill, who, in tandem with Douglas Hyde, had founded the Gaelic League in 1893. The new movement was formally established at a public meeting in Dublin on 25 November 1913. MacNeill had recognised the success of Carson's extra parliamentary tactics and the

Poster advertising the launching of the Irish Volunteers, 25 November 1913.

central role played by the UVF. While the Irish Volunteers immediately caught the eye of the clandestine Irish Republican Brotherhood (IRB), many of whose senior figures joined the new movement, mainstream Nationalist supporters displayed little early enthusiasm. Certainly, Redmond was not comfortable with the new force. He did not want Nationalists to imitate a strategy that he had repeatedly condemned, and he genuinely distrusted any movement that was not entirely constitutional.

The appearance of a second citizen militia was an unwelcome development for the Liberal government, which issued two royal proclamations in December 1913 banning the importation of arms and ammunition to Ireland. The move angered the Irish Volunteers, as the UVF had been bringing in guns for much of 1913 without, it seemed, any interference by the authorities. The UUC had, in fact, established a secret committee as early as November 1910, which was tasked with overseeing all gun-running activity. This had been the brainchild of Fred Crawford, a militant Unionist from a business background, who had an impressive technical knowledge of guns and military experience gained in the

Boer War. By 1913 Crawford had been appointed as Director of Ordnance on the UVF Headquarters Staff, and he had formulated plans for a major gun-running enterprise. Such a venture would require considerable funding, but support from the Belfast business community, which was currently funding the UVF, was guaranteed. Money was also received from wealthy patrons in England. Interest in the Unionist cause was stimulated by the British League for the Support of Ulster and the Union, which had 10,000 members by the beginning of 1914. Its profile had been raised significantly by the efforts of Lord Milner and his able lieutenant, the Conservative MP for South Birmingham, Leo Amery. Under the umbrella of the British League and the Union Defence League, Milner and Amery organised a British Covenant that was signed by nearly 2 million supporters between March and July 1914. Both men also encouraged financial donations, which were used to purchase arms. The biggest sum was £30,000 from Rudyard Kipling, the great literary figure, who was an enthusiastic supporter of the Ulster Unionist cause.

Milner was also one of the establishment figures who had attempted to influence the thinking of British Army officers in relation to Ulster. While many of the officer class came from landed stock and were instinctively conservative, a good number were from Anglo-Irish families, and they were sympathetic to the Unionist cause. Army officers, of course, were expected to stay out of all political controversies, but many were active in the British League for the Support of Ulster and the Union. There was speculation that a number of these officers would resign their commissions if the army was issued with orders to move against the UVF. By early 1914 Bonar Law and Carson were considering the army's role in the crisis, and it was evident that a number of senior Conservatives were engaged in exploiting the sympathy for Ulster's position from many within the officer class. Naturally, any doubt about the army's readiness to play its part in imposing Home Rule on Ulster weakened the Liberal government's position. Yet this did not prove sufficient for Bonar Law. By early 1914 he had decided that the Tories should use their majority in the House of Lords to amend the Army (Annual) Bill to ensure that the army could not be used in Ulster until a general election had been held. The Army Act was an anachronism that had survived since 1689. Its purpose was to prevent the government from depriving any citizen of his rights, and its passage had always been a formality. Bonar Law's intention to amend the Army Bill before its deadline in April would have proved a grave risk for the Conservatives, and the shadow cabinet deferred a decision on the matter when it met on 4 February 1914. In the end such a decision was unnecessary due to a remarkable sequence of events.

Churchill had already raised the temperature when he spoke in Bradford on 14 March following Carson's rejection of the county option scheme. Describing the Ulster provisional government as a "self-elected body ... engaged in a treasonable conspiracy", Churchill intimated that the government would deploy the army in Ulster if Unionists continued to reject its final compromise offer. On the same day, Lieutenant-General Sir Arthur Paget, the commander-in-chief in Ireland, received instructions from the War Office to tighten security at a number of army barracks in Ulster, which might be potential targets for arms raids carried out by the UVF. Four barracks – Omagh, Enniskillen, Armagh and Carrickfergus – were viewed as high risk. Paget was summoned to London on 18 March to report on the precautions that had been put in place. In London, Paget met Churchill, who had planned to intimidate the UVF with a sudden show of military strength in carefully selected locations. Colonel J.E.B. Seely, the secretary of state for war, was enthusiastic, and Asquith reluctantly approved the plan. Churchill, who was by then First Lord of the Admiralty, had also arranged for several warships to sail from Lamlash in the Firth of Clyde to Belfast Lough to demonstrate the government's intent.

In his meeting at the War Office, Paget asked how he might deal with officers who refused orders to march on Ulster. Seely's reply laid the foundation for future confusion, as he stated that such officers would face instant dismissal, before adding that special consideration would be given to those officers whose homes were in Ulster. When he returned to his Curragh base on 20 March, this lack of clarity clearly clouded Paget's judgement. Meeting his seven senior officers, Paget, who had no written orders, speculated unnecessarily on the consequences of troop deployments which, he warned, would leave Ulster "ablaze". He also indicated that officers domiciled in Ulster would be exempt but that others refusing to march north would be dismissed. Paget's clumsy handling of this delicate situation provoked an immediate response from one of the senior officers, Brigadier-General Hubert Gough, the commander of the 3rd Cavalry Brigade. Following a meeting with his junior officers, Gough informed Paget that 58 officers would refuse to participate in an Ulster operation. When this explosive news reached the War Office, Gough and the other cavalry officers were summoned to London, where they were interviewed on 22 and 23 March. It quickly became clear that the situation was primarily due to Paget's incompetence, and Gough and his subordinates were requested to return to the Curragh and forget the entire incident. Gough, however, was not satisfied, and he demanded a written assurance that the army would not be used to coerce Ulster into acceptance of the Home Rule Bill. He had been urged to take this hardline approach by Major-General (later Field Marshal) Sir Henry Wilson, a native of County Longford and the Director of Military Operations at the War Office. Wilson was an ardent Unionist who had been intriguing with opposition leaders, including Bonar Law and Carson, for months, using his influence to raise doubts about the army's role in any possible coercion of Ulster. In response to Gough's request, the cabinet offered a written statement. However, Seely, acting on his own initiative, added two further brief paragraphs which he believed would be necessary to assuage Gough. His final paragraph stated that the government had no intention of using troops "to crush political opposition to the policy or principles of the Home Rule Bill", but Gough wanted even greater certainty. Using a sheet of official War Office paper, Gough wrote the following statement: "I understand the reading of the last paragraph to be that the troops under our command will not be called upon to enforce the present Home Rule Bill on Ulster, and that we can so assure our officers." He then showed the note to Field Marshal Sir John French, the Chief of the Imperial General Staff, another highly placed Unionist sympathiser, who endorsed Gough's interpretation and added his signature.

By the time Asquith realised what had transpired, the "Curragh incident", as it became known, had seriously damaged the government, greatly limiting its capacity to exert pressure on the Ulster Unionists. Still, in spite of Churchill's eagerness to stage a display of overwhelming military power, the cabinet had little appetite for coercing the Unionists. Certainly, Asquith was reluctant to use the army in Ulster. Yet his government had come close to sparking a full-scale mutiny, as Paget's blunder had been compounded by Seely. Not surprisingly, the Curragh incident led to the resignations of both Seely and French. In an attempt to restore calm, Asquith took over the War Office portfolio, but the opposition in parliament claimed that a conspiracy against Ulster had been the intention. The government was accused of hatching a "plot against Ulster", as the reason for the troop movements had been to provoke the UVF into taking rash action, thereby providing a pretext for the military to crush the movement. Such a scenario appears unlikely. Rather, Churchill's bravura and Seely's ineptitude, together with Paget's incompetence, are sufficient to explain the extraordinary events of March 1914.

Within a month attention had shifted from the Curragh crisis, as the UVF successfully landed a very large consignment of arms and ammunition, procured on the continent, on the night of 24–25 April. In January 1914, a full calendar year after the UVF's formation, the Unionist leadership had finally given the go-ahead to Crawford's audacious gun-running plan. Previously, these leaders had hoped that their militant rhetoric would cause the government to amend the Home Rule Bill, but they were forced to acknowledge the failure to extract major concessions from Asquith during the series of abortive meetings that the prime minister had conducted with Bonar Law and Carson. By January 1914 the Unionist leaders felt they had no alternative but to accede to the demands of the extremist faction within the UVF and sanction Crawford's scheme. The various county commanders were reporting poor morale among the rank and file, and this was another argument in favour of the gun-running. Still, Carson and many

Ulster gun-running. Discharging the Fanny. *The convoy of motor cars at Larne Harbour, 24/25 April 1914.*

of his colleagues recognised that this was a huge risk. The importation of weapons was, of course, illegal, and there was a fear that the escalation of their resistance campaign might turn public opinion in Britain against the Unionists. Crawford purchased the weapons in Hamburg, and they were transferred at sea to avoid detection in a difficult operation. The ship, a former coal vessel, had been bought specifically for the gun-running. Small quantities of arms and ammunition were landed in Bangor and Donaghadee, but the bulk of the cargo was unloaded at the port of Larne. The UVF had taken control of the town, and the weapons were transferred across Ulster by a fleet of cars and lorries. The gun-running had been a propaganda coup, and news that a total of 24,600 rifles and 3,000,000 rounds of ammunition had been imported received huge coverage in the British press. Both Bonar Law and Carson were quick to announce full responsibility for the operation. In reply, Asquith described the gun-running as "a grave and unprecedented outrage", and he threatened that the full force of the law would be used against those who had engaged in this illegal and, indeed, treasonable action. It was assumed that Carson and the other leaders would face criminal charges, but the intention to have leading Unionists prosecuted was quickly dropped.

These back-to-back "victories" at the Curragh and Larne appeared to hand Unionists a new lever in their quest to wring further concessions from the government. Nationalists, not surprisingly, were outraged by these events, which prompted a surge in recruitment for the Irish Volunteers. In March 1914 the Irish Volunteers numbered 7,000, but the figure increased dramatically during May with recruitment particularly strong in Ulster. Soon the movement had grown beyond 100,000 members, and this naturally made a civil war in the north more likely. This spectacular growth reflected rising anger at a Liberal administration that had refused to face down Unionist threats. Nationalist leaders were convinced that the authorities, particularly the police, had colluded with the UVF in the Larne operation, and the government's subsequent failure to prosecute the ringleaders appeared to confirm this suspicion. The swelling of Irish Volunteer ranks created problems for Redmond. He had never been comfortable with the presence of a Nationalist citizen militia, and he recognised that swift action was necessary to prevent the burgeoning movement becoming a rival to his own party. On 10 June he moved to take control of the Volunteers by demanding that the group's provisional committee be expanded to give the IPP a controlling interest. With reluctance, the Volunteer leaders gave way and Redmond's nominees took their places on the committee.

In spite of Redmond's coup, however, it soon became apparent that the original leaders of the Irish Volunteers were pursuing their own agenda. Here the initiative was taken by Sir Roger Casement, a former British consular official who had been born in County Antrim. Working closely with a number of wealthy advanced Nationalists, including Alice Stopford Green, Erskine Childers and Darrell Figgis, Casement organised a gun-running operation for the Irish Volunteers without informing Redmond. A total of 1,500 rifles and 45,000 rounds of ammunition had been procured in Hamburg and brought to Ireland on the *Asgard,* a yacht owned by Childers. The *Asgard* arrived at Howth, County Dublin on 26 July 1914, and the Irish Volunteers had

Erskine Childers (1870–1922), in November 1920.

The voyage of the Asgard, *July 1914. From left to right: Mrs Childers, Mary Spring-Rice, Captain Gordon Shephard, Pat McGinley.*

organised a fleet of taxis to transport the cargo the short distance to Dublin. This appeared to be a copy of Larne on a greatly reduced scale, but the parallels ended when the guns were landed. The Dublin Metropolitan Police (DMP) were made aware of the operation and intervened to seize the arms. Lacking sufficient numbers, the DMP had requested military reinforcements, and a small detachment of troops marched out to Howth. On their journey back to Dublin the troops were followed by an angry crowd and taunted for their failure to disarm the Volunteers. By the time they reached Bachelors Walk on the River Liffey, a rowdier element had joined the crowd and stones were thrown at the troops, who opened fire. Three civilians were killed and others were wounded. Nationalists were furious. The contrast with Larne was striking, and it was evident that the authorities were applying double standards.

It was obvious that the group behind the Howth gun-running had been influenced by events at Larne. These more advanced Nationalists were also convinced that the Unionist campaign of resistance orchestrated by Carson was proving more effective than the strictly constitutional approach directed by Redmond. However, the Unionists' extra-parliamentary strategy created its own problems. Larne had given the UVF a decisive military advantage over the Irish Volunteers, but more than half of its 100,000 members were still without weapons. After Larne, Carson was concerned about the increased potential for sectarian violence in the north. This was a development that Carson was desperate to avoid because of its likely impact on public opinion in Britain. Significantly, Carson adopted a more moderate tone in his public speeches after April 1914, expressing the hope that Home Rule would prove a success for the south and west of Ireland. Indeed, he went further, speculating that if the circumstances were right it might be in Ulster's interests "to come in under it and form one unit in relation to Ireland". If Carson was hinting at a settlement, Redmond did not respond. Larne, the Curragh incident and the rapid growth of the Irish Volunteers had limited his room for manoeuvre, as he assumed that any further concessions would intensify criticism of his leadership from advanced Nationalists.

On 5 May Asquith had a further secret meeting with Bonar Law and Carson. Although the exchanges confirmed that a settlement was still out of reach, the leaders did come to an understanding on procedure. It was agreed that any changes to the Home Rule Bill should not be made by amendment to the bill, but by a separate amending bill that would receive royal assent on the same day as the Home Rule Bill itself. There was, however, no agreement on the content of any amending bill. In fact, when the bill to amend the Home Rule Bill was introduced in the House of Lords on 23 June 1914, it was almost identical to the county option terms that Carson had rejected in March. The Conservative response highlighted the gap that still existed between the two main parties. On 8 July Lansdowne moved an amendment to the government's amending bill that permanently excluded all nine Ulster counties from Home Rule. This was passed by the House of Lords on 14 July and sent back to the Commons. With this certain to be thrown out by the lower house, the government had reached an impasse. Parliamentary time had almost run out, as the Home Rule Bill would soon be ready for royal assent under the terms of the Parliament Act. It was only at this point that Asquith finally agreed to the king's persistent requests for an all-party conference. The prime minister could have taken up the king's suggestion in the previous March when there was a deadlock on the county option scheme. Yet Asquith chose to delay until the last possible moment, believing that negotiations were more likely to succeed when the pressure for a settlement was at its most acute. Still, when Asquith eventually agreed to a conference, he did so with little hope of success. Indeed, the Buckingham Palace Conference, which ran from 21 to 24 July 1914, only highlighted the differences between the parties. Two representatives from each of the four parties attended the conference – Asquith and Lloyd George for the Liberals, Bonar Law and Lansdowne for the Conservatives, Redmond and Dillon for the IPP and Carson and Craig for the Unionists. Following a brief address from the king, in which he expressed his desire for a settlement, the conference proceeded under the chairmanship of James Lowther, the speaker of the House of Commons. The crucial topics for discussion were the area to be excluded from Home Rule and the duration of that exclusion. At the conference the area of exclusion was examined in great detail, but the time limit was never considered.

At the Buckingham Palace Conference, Carson and Redmond, recalling their days on the Leinster legal circuit, immediately established friendly relations. Each had genuine respect for the other, but they could not reach agreement on the future of Tyrone and Fermanagh. At the outset Carson demanded the exclusion of all nine Ulster counties, arguing that such a generous offer by the Nationalists would increase the likelihood of Ulster eventually accepting a United Ireland. Bonar Law subsequently claimed that Redmond and Dillon would have been agreeable if they had been free agents, but they knew that such a concession would have caused the evaporation of their support in Ireland. In fact, Redmond informed the conference that the exclusion of Ulster was "quite impossible", and Carson responded by demanding "a clean cut" to exclude permanently six counties from the operation of the Home Rule Act. This, he claimed, was his "irreducible minimum". Of course, both Tyrone and Fermanagh had narrow Nationalist majorities, but the Ulster Volunteers were particularly strong in these counties and Carson refused to budge on his demand. At this point, therefore, it was clear that power outweighed democratic niceties in the Unionist leader's thinking. Naturally, Redmond argued that only those areas with a Unionist majority could be excluded from Home Rule. To support his case, the IPP leader produced a series of maps, pinpointing the precise location of both communities in the two counties. These piebald maps illustrated the complex religious configuration and only highlighted the problems in drawing a border that was acceptable to both sides. Asquith sought to break the deadlock with a suggestion that south Tyrone and north Fermanagh could be added to the excluded area, but neither Redmond nor Carson was in agreement. His cabinet colleague, Lloyd George, favoured a decision based on the Poor Law Union districts, but this was dismissed as impracticable. Soon the conference, in Churchill's words, ground to a halt along "the muddy byways of Fermanagh and Tyrone". As the negotiations were breaking up, Redmond and Dillon agreed to give way on the time limit for exclusion, but they refused to surrender Tyrone and Fermanagh. Two days later, the IPP's room for manoeuvre was greatly curtailed by the Bachelors Walk killings.

Meanwhile, the amending bill, which was due in the House of Commons, was postponed until 28 July, but events were overtaken by the rapidly deteriorating situation in Europe. Asquith continued his hopeless search for a solution. He welcomed the offer of a further postponement from Bonar Law and Carson. With the country on the brink of war, the opposition leaders were anxious to create the impression of national unity. When the Home Rule Bill was finally passed on 18 September 1914, it was accompanied by a Suspensory Act that postponed the operation of the legislation. By the time war broke out, therefore, there had been no agreement on Ulster, though the IPP had made significant concessions on exclusion, and these would become a starting point for future negotiations. Asquith's delaying tactics had boosted Nationalist morale, but it was clear, even before 1914, that the Liberal government would be unable to deliver Home Rule on an all-Ireland basis. Yet Carson, too, had given ground. His original objective had been to use Ulster opposition to Home Rule to keep Ireland in the United Kingdom. When he realised that this was not feasible, he abandoned Unionists in the south and west and campaigned for the exclusion of Ulster. By the autumn of 1913, however, he privately acknowledged that saving six counties would be his maximum. This meant Carson turned his back on supporters in Cavan, Monaghan and Donegal who had signed the Covenant and enlisted in the UVF.

In early March 1914, Redmond had agreed to give up four counties, indicating that the gap between the Unionists and the IPP was bridgeable. A compromise might have been reached in 1912 had the government seized the initiative, but neither the Liberals nor the Nationalists appreciated the strength of feeling in Ulster; neither group saw any need for concessions at that stage. This, in turn, prompted Carson to raise the stakes during 1913 in an attempt to demonstrate to the government that his supporters would go to any length to resist Home Rule. In taking such an approach, Carson was greatly assisted by Bonar Law, whose endorsement of Carson's extra-parliamentary tactics gave wavering Unionists the confidence to contemplate violence, even if Carson only intended this to be a threat. For the Unionist leader, violence was clearly a last resort and only to be considered when every other option had been exhausted. There was, of course, the possibility that Carson might have been deposed as leader in favour of a more militant candidate if it became apparent that he was unwilling to risk violence in the event of the Liberal government forcing Ulster to accept Home Rule. Carson certainly appreciated this and was prepared to adopt a hardline approach in order to contain the Unionist extremists in Ulster. The Curragh incident, therefore, was of crucial significance for Carson's leadership. It eliminated the possibility of a clash between the army and the UVF, and it nudged the Liberal government further in the direction of a compromise on Ulster. While the cabinet remained divided on the Home Rule issue, key ministers, including Lloyd George, Churchill and Birrell, favoured some form of exclusion for Ulster. This would be the focus for all the key players at the Buckingham Palace Conference and beyond.

Conclusion

Throughout the Ulster crisis, Redmond, whose position was never as strong as it appeared, had placed his full trust in the Liberal administration to deliver Home Rule. In doing so he was badly served by O'Connor, the IPP's key insider at Westminster, who assured his leader of the Liberal government's determination to face down Conservative and Unionist opposition. The tragedy for Redmond was that when Asquith sought concessions in an attempt to ease the situation from 1913 onwards, he looked to Irish Nationalists for movement. Both the Liberal government and the IPP had underestimated the strength of Unionist resistance to the third Home Rule Bill. From his base in Belfast, Devlin was convinced that Unionist rhetoric was mere bluster, and he confidently shared this judgement with party colleagues and Liberal ministers. This contributed to Redmond's complacency during the critical period of the crisis and contrasted sharply with the urgency being consistently demonstrated by Carson, a development that was not lost on grass-roots Nationalist supporters in Ireland. Under severe pressure from his Liberal allies, Redmond was prepared to break the one-Ireland principle, and, though he insisted that any form of exclusion must be temporary, Carson was quick to seize the advantage. It was also apparent that the awkward relationship between Asquith and Redmond worked to the IPP's disadvantage, whereas Carson was secure in the knowledge that he could rely on Bonar Law's full support whatever the circumstances.

Although leading Tories had different priorities on Ireland, with some sharing Bonar Law's fixation with Ulster while others, such as Lansdowne, were more concerned about the fate of southern Unionists, the manner in which the Ulster crisis dominated British politics in the 1912–14 period clearly worked in their favour. By uniting in opposition to Home Rule, the party was able to set aside the deep divisions over both the tariff reform issue and the controversy over the House of Lords. Consequently, morale on the Conservative backbenches was restored. The Liberal Party, on the other hand, was damaged by the Home Rule crisis. Asquith's "wait and see" strategy had encouraged his opponents to abandon any caution they might have felt and to take an increasingly militant approach on the Home Rule question. This made any resolution of the crisis less likely.

Historiography

Redmond's discomfort with extra-parliamentary tactics is alluded to in the very first sentence of Denis Gwynn's huge biography, *The Life of John Redmond* (London, 1932). He states, "John Redmond's entire life was centred in the House of Commons", adding that he was following in the footsteps of his father who had been one of the founders of the Home Rule movement. Charles Townshend's *The Partition: Ireland Divided 1885–1925* (London, 2021) provides a perceptive analysis of the key issues relating to partition. Townshend notes that for Nationalists, "Ulster's move towards a separate path was, if not initiated by, certainly dependent on Britain." He also claims that the separation of Ulster and southern Unionists was well advanced by 1910. At times Conservatives in Britain were embarrassed by some Ulster Unionist excesses, and Townshend records A. V. Dicey's description of the action of Belfast Unionists in attempting to prevent Churchill's Ulster Hall speech in February 1912 as "deplorable stupidity". He then carefully analyses the Agar-Robartes move in 1912, pointing out that it was based on the clear assumption that there were two nations in Ireland and observing that it led to "a major adjustment of Unionist thinking". He concludes that the Agar-Robartes amendment "was a crucial moment in the crystallization of partition". The author is also critical of Birrell's actions as chief secretary, claiming that for months he oscillated between "smug dismissal" of Ulster resistance and alarm about the possibility of civil war. By March 1914, Townshend claims, Redmond found that northern Nationalists, and indeed the province's senior Catholic clergy, were not as hostile to temporary exclusion as he had feared. *The Partition* also supports the view that there was a high level of support for Ulster in Britain.

The influence that T.P. O'Connor exerted on his party leader is examined in Erica Doherty's essay, '"Ulster will not fight": T.P. O'Connor and the third Home Rule crisis, 1912–14' in Gabriel Doherty's (ed) *The Home Rule Crisis 1912–14* (Cork, 2014). It highlights O'Connor's repeated assurances to Redmond that the Liberal government would honour its commitment to all-Ireland Home Rule. In addition, O'Connor consistently brushed off Unionist threats as "bluff" and, along with Devlin, "publicly ridiculed" warnings of impending civil war. Yet Doherty shows that O'Connor, the IPP man in London, was routinely kept in the dark by Liberal ministers. In the same volume, Laurence Kirkpatrick's essay, 'Irish Presbyterians and the Ulster Covenant', points out that the Covenant set out the four grounds on which Ulster Unionists objected to Home Rule: economic, religious, civil liberty and imperial cohesion. Professor Kirkpatrick also emphasises the prominent role of Protestant church leaders in the organisation of the Covenant, noting that 63 per cent of Presbyterian clergy signed (345), 74 per cent of Church of Ireland clergy signed (392), while 42 per cent of Methodist ministers signed (61). On the Saturday, Ulster Day, eighty-six Presbyterian church halls and 97 Church of Ireland halls were centres for the signing process. In the volume's final essay, Martin Mansergh looks at the main figures, 'The role of the leaders: Asquith, Churchill, Balfour, Bonar Law, Carson and Redmond'. Mansergh claims that the Parliament Act was a major achievement for Asquith, and he sums up Churchill's complex relationship with Ulster by insisting that while he favoured partition, Churchill "was always instinctively pugnacious in dealing with challenges to authority".

Chris Dooley's *Redmond: A Life Undone* (Dublin, 2015) demonstrates that it was not just Ulster Unionists who could organise huge rallies. On 31 March 1912, over 100,000 attended a great Home Rule demonstration in Dublin, which was addressed by Redmond, Dillon and Devlin. Four months later Asquith was cheered by huge crowds when he visited Dublin. Dooley goes on to examine the Agar-Robartes amendment which, he states, was greeted with "silence" in the Commons. Birrell waited for a Unionist response before dismissing this "somewhat fantastic proposal". Yet, as Dooley states, Birrell had written to Churchill in August 1911, suggesting that each Ulster county should decide by referendum if its inhabitants wanted Home Rule. Indeed, the author argues that, as early as the summer of 1912, the Unionist argument was gaining ground with the government. A year later, in September 1913, Dooley declares that the Loreburn letter "dropped a hand grenade into the Home Rule controversy" and changed the terms of the debate. Dooley highlights the frustration felt by Redmond in November 1913 when, within two days, he heard very different accounts of the government's position, with Lloyd George demanding concessions from the IPP and Birrell offering reassurance. However, Redmond was an optimist and placed too much faith in the government. In his examination of the Buckingham Palace Conference, the author uses Redmond's verbal report to Stephen Gwynn, his friend and colleague, stressing that Carson quickly asserted his authority but caused surprise in respect of his lack of knowledge about Ulster.

The importance of Conservative support for Ulster Unionism is highlighted in Alan Parkinson's *Friends in High Places: Ulster's resistance to Irish Home Rule, 1912–14* (Belfast, 2012). Parkinson takes trouble to place Bonar Law's Blenheim speech in perspective by pointing out that the speech did not dominate press coverage in the days that followed. Rather, Tory by-election successes took the headlines in the British press. Looking at the development of Ulster Unionism, Parkinson asserts that, "Despite the initial emphasis on all-Ireland Unionism, the objections of Ulster Protestants to Home Rule were governed by their loyalty to their own community and regional unit, Ulster." In the province, he claims, the Unionist clubs, not the Orange Order, were "the face and voice of Unionism at local level". Ulster Unionism had undergone a transformation in the first decade of the twentieth century, leaving the anti-Home Rule movement on a sound footing. For Parkinson, the only missing ingredient was a charismatic leader, a void filled by Carson. Thereafter, he notes that Unionist propaganda was "slickly professional", adding that one strength of the Covenant was its "classless appeal". The Covenant also stirred interest in Britain, and Parkinson concludes that political isolationism in this period would have been "the death-knell for Ulster Unionists". Consequently, Unionist MPs drew large audiences as they toured England and Scotland, significantly larger, as Parkinson states, than trade union or suffragette gatherings. The author also draws attention to the importance of the support given to Carson by the editors and owners of the Tory press in Britain. When he claims that the Covenant gave Ulster Unionists a "moral righteousness", this was effectively relayed to British opinion, and sympathy was extended to this embattled minority.

Geoffrey Lewis's *Carson: The Man Who Divided Ireland* (London, 2005) stresses that his subject, unlike Bonar Law, had carefully refrained from giving a commitment that he would abide by the electorate's wishes in an election on the Home Rule issue. The author also makes the controversial claim that Carson had been considering special treatment for Ulster from at least November 1911. In his conclusion, Lewis is adamant that Carson did more than anyone else to create a divided Ireland, including Bonar Law and Craig, though he adds that partition was created by necessity. Timothy Bowman's *Carson's Army: The Ulster Volunteer Force, 1910–22* (Manchester, 2007) notes that Birrell was "blasé" on Ulster Unionist intentions, concerning himself with the prospect of riots and disregarding RIC reports of military preparations that he believed were "one-sided". Significantly, Bowman emphasises that there was no real rush to join the UVF. In fact, Carson did not review any UVF units until July 1913, and the UVF really had a "relaunch" in September 1913 when its headquarters staff was appointed. Yet, as Bowman explains, there was often a poor turnout at UVF events. On the other hand, the movement was particularly popular among Belfast's shipyard workers, and it allowed Carson to present Ulster Unionism as "a solid and united movement". Ronald McNeill's *Ulster's Stand for Union* (London, 1922) provides an invaluable analysis of contemporary Unionist thinking. He describes the Unionist defeat in Derry city in the January 1913 by-election, stating that it "wounded loyalist sentiment far more deeply than the loss of any other constituency". Later, in a by-election in the English constituency of Altrincham in May 1913, the Conservative candidate claimed that he had "won the contest entirely on the Ulster Question". McNeill also explains that when the county option was discussed in 1914, it was the time limit, not the area to be excluded, that was crucial. He states that Carson would have submitted the county option proposals to a convention in Belfast if the government had dropped the time limit. Andrew Scholes's *The Church of Ireland and the Third Home Rule Bill* (Dublin, 2009) provides an authoritative account of the church's role, particularly in relation to the growing divergence between southern and Ulster Unionism. During the 1910 elections, Church of Ireland clergy became more politically active, frequently chairing public meetings and taking positions in the revived Unionist clubs. On the Covenant, Scholes notes that the southern bishops privately opposed Ulster Day, while northern Church of Ireland clergy led many of the church services that took place on 28 September 1912. From that point there was a division between clergy who supported Ulster exclusion and those who feared partition. Scholes also argues that the UVF helped to bring the Protestant denominations closer together. Charles Frederick D'Arcy, Bishop of Down and Connor and Dromore, was a "very public supporter" of the UVF and welcomed its ability to discipline grass-roots Unionists. However, other Church of Ireland clergy were uncomfortable with the movement and, fearing violence, urged restraint. Scholes highlights the example of Kilrea's Rev A. E. Sixsmith as one of the most fervent clerical Unionist supporters. He had warned his local Unionist club that if they accepted Home Rule, they would become "slaves of masters who would trample on them".

Tom Bartlett's *Ireland: A History* (Cambridge, 2010) emphasises the pivotal role played by Belfast in the struggle against Irish Nationalism: "It was Belfast that was to be the core of resistance to Home Rule; it was Belfast that made determined opposition to Home Rule possible; and, ultimately, it was Belfast that made partition feasible." For Bartlett, this was a "central truth" – "it was Belfast's commercial wealth and Belfast's muscle that saw off the threat of the imposition of Home Rule for all Ireland". Tim Bowman's essay 'Ulster will fight' in the *Atlas of the Irish Revolution* (Cork, 2017) emphasises Carson's commitment to a "parliamentary strategy", stating that "at no point did Carson abandon his parliamentary strategy". He adds, it is "a measure of the genius of Carson's leadership ... that he managed a campaign which remained militant enough to maintain the unity of Ulster Unionism, without alienating wider British and Irish Unionism". Diarmaid Ferriter's *The Transformation of Ireland* (London, 2004) puts the focus on Carson's brilliance as an orator who knew how to exploit fully the "perceived honesty" of Ulster. Earlier, Alvin Jackson's *Sir Edward Carson* (Dublin, 1993) claims that his subject favoured the deployment of "moral strength" and viewed the use of violence in "icily realistic terms", believing that while such a course was honourable, it would also be "suicidal". In his previous work, Jackson also suggests that Ulster Unionism was ready to take the extra-parliamentary route before Carson's accession to the leadership.

Paul Bew's *Churchill and Ireland* (Oxford, 2016) notes that from the beginning of the Ulster crisis, "Churchill's position had been complex and, in a sense, conflicted." Within days Churchill shifted from arguing the case for special treatment for Ulster to a public defence of all-Ireland Home Rule, and then combined a call for special treatment in his Dundee speech with the threat of crushing the UVF until the Curragh officers intervened. In spite of this inconsistency, Bew argues that his subject came to the decision that Nationalists had to persuade Ulster to accept unity. Churchill's interest in Irish history ensured that he was better briefed than most of his colleagues but, as Bew demonstrates, he underestimated the religious zeal at the heart of Ulster Unionism. During the Home Rule crisis, Bew states, the Ulster Unionists "loathed" Churchill. George Dangerfield's *The Strange Death of Liberal England* (New York, 1935) remains an important study of the impact of the Ulster crisis on the fortunes of the Liberal Party. The author's key argument is that the Liberal Party was in serious decline by 1909, after which it had to confront the constitutional crisis, the suffragette campaign, a new wave of industrial strife and the Home Rule crisis. Together these destroyed the ailing party. Numerous historians have since taken issue with the Dangerfield thesis, but it remains a significant work.

The Liberal government's handling of Home Rule is expertly tackled by Patricia Jalland's *The Liberals and Ireland: The Ulster Question in British Politics to 1914* (Brighton, 1980). In the preparation of the Home Rule Bill in 1911, finance, rather than Ulster, was regarded as the principal difficulty, and Jalland highlights the government's complacency on Ulster opposition until it was forced to accept reality in the autumn of 1913. In particular, Asquith failed to recognise the potential gravity of the Ulster question and, as Jalland observes, he tended to prevaricate and be ambiguous in his statements on the issue. Therefore, Asquith's cabinet "failed totally to comprehend the extent of the Ulster problem", and the Liberal press tended to ignore Ulster. Consequently, as Jalland states, the government raised expectations about Home Rule that could not be fulfilled, partly because of its ignorance about "the real condition of Ulster" in 1911–12. Birrell was aware of developments and was the first to suggest, if very tentatively, that special treatment should be given to Ulster, but he failed to press his views in cabinet with sufficient vigour. The result, in Jalland's view, was that the government failed to grasp the opportunity presented by the Agar-Robartes amendment, which was "an honest, if politically misguided, attempt ... to persuade his party leaders to reconsider their Ulster policy". For Jalland, Asquith failed to deal with Ulster "on his own terms" during 1912. By the time the cabinet took Ulster resistance seriously in the autumn of 1913, Jalland claims, "it was far too late to avert the growing crisis". Had Asquith offered concessions to Ulster in 1912, such a settlement would at least have "provided a starting point and offered better prospects for the evolution of a more stable, non-violent relationship between the north and south of Ireland and Great Britain". Jalland speculates that this might have developed into dominion status for the south and perhaps, in time, have led to a united Ireland. Earlier, Roy Jenkins's *Asquith* (London, 1964) dismissed the argument that the Agar-Robartes amendment was a missed opportunity, stating that "no arrangement for exclusion, however extensive it had been, would in 1912 have destroyed the opposition to Home Rule". Jenkins claims half of the Tories were more interested in Dublin than in Belfast, while the other half, represented by Bonar Law, "although genuinely concerned with Ulster, were still more concerned with smashing the Liberal government". For Jenkins, opponents of Home Rule would have pocketed any concession in 1912 and then renewed their hostility to the bill. Jenkins's sympathetic view of Asquith's handling of the Ulster crisis is echoed in Alvin Jackson's *Home Rule: An Irish History 1800–2000* (London, 2003), which suggests that Asquith's leadership at the time had a much greater logic than has hitherto been assumed.

R.J.Q. Adams's *Bonar Law* (London, 1999) gives some indication of the growing animosity between the two main parties from the moment that Bonar Law became Tory leader. Adams states Bonar Law "both disliked and distrusted most of the leaders of the Government, and meant to test them with heavy blows". Much of Bonar Law's fury was directed at the government's refusal to allow the electorate to have a say in what he described as "the most controversial legislation of recent memory". He was quick to convey this feeling to the king. In fact, as Adams records, George V was "stunned" by Bonar Law's directness. Of course, the author confirms that his strategy throughout was "to use the Ulster crisis to force an election concentrated on Home Rule, which the voting trend of by-election victories convinced him the Unionist Party would win". Ultimately, Adams believes that Bonar Law was confident that the government would opt for an election "before they had embraced calamity". Bonar Law's leadership of the Conservative Party during the crisis over the third Home Rule Bill is carefully assessed in Robert Blake's *The Unknown Prime Minister: The Life and Times of Andrew Bonar Law, 1858–1923* (London, 1955). Blake stresses that Asquith's intellectual background saw him treat Bonar Law with "a touch of condescension", and this partly explains why he underestimated the Tory leader. The author looks closely at Bonar's Law's confrontational style, declaring that this intensified the growing bitterness between the two main Westminster parties. Despite the rhetoric, however, Blake argues that Bonar Law was frequently pessimistic, believing that civil war was very likely if the government pressed ahead with Home Rule on an all-Ireland basis. While he was certainly more moderate in private, Blake stresses that he "threw himself heart and soul into the support of the Ulster cause", and he demonstrated his commitment at Blenheim in 1912. However, Blake puts the Blenheim speech in context, arguing that his appeal to force was made on the assumption that the Liberals would impose Home

Rule without an election. The author concludes by highlighting the pressure that Bonar Law experienced from his own party when there was any discussion of a compromise. Blake puts Bonar Law's actions in context, but he is critical both of Bonar Law's interference with the army and of his attempt to involve the monarchy in the crisis.

A very different argument is presented in Jeremy Smith's *The Tories and Ireland 1910–1914* (Dublin, 2000), which claims that what Bonar Law was actually engaged in was "a pragmatic or theatrical extremism" with the objective of securing better terms from the Liberal government on the Ulster issue. For Smith, Bonar Law moved the party sharply to the right in response to growing disunity and increasing grass-roots disenchantment. This leads Smith to assert that the Ulster crisis was "constructed" and "invented" by Tory politicians who believed that opposition to Home Rule was the only way to reunite the party. The priority was to force an election, which they were confident they could win. Smith describes Bonar Law as a leader who lacked authority over his party. He was a Canadian by origin, spoke with a Scottish accent, was Presbyterian and had no land connections, all characteristics that rendered him unsuitable as a Tory leader. Yet, in the period immediately before the war, the Tories were deeply concerned about the survival of British society as they saw it, and this, for Smith, explains why they were prepared to follow Bonar Law on such a dangerous course. He credits Bonar Law with maintaining Tory unity in these years. However, his argument that Bonar Law took up the exclusion idea in 1913 because he assumed it had little chance of success ignores his empathy with Ulster Unionism. In his study of the Conservative Party, David Dutton's *His Majesty's Loyal Opposition* (Liverpool, 1992) offers an overview of the party's difficulties with the Lords issue. He argues that the division created by the constitutional crisis was even more serious than the bitter wrangling over tariff reform. This left opposition to Home Rule as the only avenue to restore party unity. Finally, Nicholas Mansergh's *The Unresolved Question: The Anglo-Irish Settlement and Its Undoing 1912–72* (London, 1991) places Bonar Law at the heart of the crisis. While he agrees with Blake's assessment that Bonar Law, albeit as a last resort, was ready to back an Ulster rebellion against Home Rule, Mansergh regards Bonar Law's accession to the leadership as crucial to the Unionist campaign of resistance. No other Tory leader, in Mansergh's opinion, would have given such a commitment to the Unionists. For Mansergh, therefore, Bonar Law was the key to the successful campaign for partition.

Alvin Jackson's *Judging Redmond and Carson* (Dublin, 2018) offers a brilliant analysis of the challenges facing both leaders as they negotiated the Ulster crisis. At the outset Jackson acknowledges that Carson was a "risk-taker" in a way that Redmond was not, adding that the Unionist leader was "spiritually and sentimentally distant from the cautious Redmond". The author also concurs with historians who have stressed that Carson was, first and foremost, a lawyer. In Jackson's opinion, "politics were an extension of his court-room performance". Moreover, as Jackson argues, Carson possessed "a killer instinct", a quality not shared by Redmond. One feature that distinguished Carson from the Unionist leadership group in Ulster was his lack of concern about Unionist unity. Craig and his northern allies had experienced electoral battles with Russellite candidates and, therefore, "retained an abiding preoccupation with the unity of Unionism". In assessing their contrasting styles, Jackson sees Redmond as a parliamentary "insider", whereas Carson was emphatically not. In reading Redmond's private correspondence, the author suggests that the IPP leader "sometimes allowed courtesy to disintegrate into the appearance of servility", adding later that he was guilty of "wheedling", as he pleaded for personal assistance. This was very different to Carson's relationship with the political elite at Westminster. Yet Redmond was, like Asquith, "honourable but reserved" although, in Jackson's view, lacking in initiative and daring. The author also points out that the prime minister "gave excessive weight to intellectual and professional attainment". Consequently, he was much more impressed by Carson. Jackson considers the autumn of 1913 as "the high water-mark of Redmond's success in terms of political engagement", but Carson's threat of violence at this point tipped the balance in the Unionists' favour. Redmond was adamant that such threats were a bluff, but Liberal ministers were not prepared to join Redmond in taking that risk. What clearly weakened his position was, Jackson states, Redmond's unwillingness "to disclose any contingency plan of his own, in the event of Unionist resistance worsening". The problem, of course, was that he did not have such a plan. In passing judgement on Liberal strategy, Jackson describes the county option as a "brilliant move". It overcame Nationalist demands as it was temporary, and there was no chance of violence if Home Rule was not due for another six years. Redmond loathed the idea of exclusion, believing that it could not seriously be advocated. Even in late 1913, he thought Carson was still trying to use Ulster to smash Home Rule. As Jackson states, "he did not grasp the significance of Carson's strategic evolution after the autumn of 1913, when the means became the end." Essentially, Redmond relied on the Liberal government to meet the Unionist challenge, which meant that leaders of Unionism and Nationalism could avoid negotiating with each other. Ultimately, as Jackson stresses, "Carson was much better integrated within the high politics of British Toryism than Redmond was within British Liberalism". Indeed, he claims that some Tory MPs treated Bonar Law as secondary to Carson.

Jackson also dwells on the increasingly strained relationship between Carson and the southern Unionists, a flavour of which was revealed in a despairing letter to Lansdowne in October 1913. Carson asked what southern Unionists expected from him when all they did was "talk in generalities". The Unionist leader aired his frustration when he stated that he did not think that they realised that he could not stop the Home Rule Bill. What he could do, of course, was save all or part of Ulster. The exclusionist case was strengthened by the Curragh and Larne, though Jackson notes that Carson's caution in regard to each of these events should be emphasised. Clearly, Larne strengthened Carson's negotiating hand over exclusion, but Jackson repeats his 1993 assessment that only one-third of the UVF had access to arms. In assessing the situation in the summer of 1914, Jackson comments on the deadlock, explaining, "Carson and the Unionists knew that Liberal ministers were probably unwilling or unable to move against them, and they believed too that Asquith was committed to delay. Asquith and Redmond suspected both that Carson needed a swift resolution, and that he was simultaneously unwilling to risk precipitate action." Overall, Jackson states that while the Tories had come to be politically dependent on Carson during the Home Rule crisis, Redmond grew ever more dependent upon the Liberal government. In his judgement of Carson, Jackson emphasises that he was a moderating influence, though he was capable of taking aggressive and impulsive stands. Jackson reveals that at a December 1912 secret meeting of senior Unionists in Belfast, Carson and Craig advocated an initiative for political compromise, but they were opposed by the majority present. Later, Carson did sanction the gun-running, but the author suggests that he expected the venture to fail. Finally, Jackson makes two interesting observations. First, George V enjoyed much friendlier relations with Redmond who, in the author's opinion, would have pursued reconciliation with the monarchy under Home Rule. Secondly, Redmond had developed much closer ties with the Empire than Carson, whose travels usually took him to German spa towns.

The high politics of the Home Rule crisis is expertly analysed in Ronan Fanning's *Fatal Path: British Government and Irish Revolution 1910–1922* (London, 2013). The author is particularly critical of the contribution made by Birrell, the chief secretary, who for the sake of political expediency concealed "his conviction that the exclusion of Ulster was essential", a decision that undermined the Liberal cabinet. Fanning contends that his failure to support Lloyd George and Churchill at the crucial cabinet discussion on 6 February 1912 had consequences that were "profound and enduring". The author also highlights the abstention by Lloyd George, Churchill and Grey in the vote on the Agar-Robartes amendment, which, he claims, cloaked the "partitionist reality". In assessing the strategy of the Liberal government, Fanning demonstrates how Asquith underestimated the depth of resistance in Ulster, admitting to the king that his government's Home Rule policy "was unEnglish and contrary to all Liberal and democratic principles". Yet he insisted that Carson's actions and rhetoric during 1913 made negotiations impossible. Fanning also claims that over the course of his secret meetings with Asquith, Bonar Law recognised that acceptance of exclusion might split his party. At that time, however, as Fanning emphasises, three successive Tory by-election successes in November 1913, with each registering a significant swing to the Conservatives, hardened Bonar Law's attitude. In the same month, Fanning reveals, Brig. Gen. J. E. Gough, a brother of the officer at the centre of the Curragh incident, visited Lord Stamfordham, the king's secretary, to inform him that unless there was a compromise on Home Rule, there would be major problems in the army. Less than a week later, Lloyd George had persuaded a number of senior ministers to back his county option scheme, and, Fanning contends, this "marked an irreversible step towards partition". Carson's bitter rejection of the scheme has "deafened historians" to the Unionist leader's welcome for "the irrevocable partitionist shift in Irish policy", though Fanning argues that his angry rejection in the Commons encouraged Churchill and Seely to behave more belligerently, leading to the Curragh crisis. Fanning's assessment of the Larne gun-running was that it made it impossible for the Unionist leaders to accept anything less than "the permanent exclusion of at least the six north-eastern counties of Ulster". By July 1914, when it was evident that Asquith was focused on the area to be excluded, Fanning points out that "the deluded Redmond" still felt the prime minister had an open mind on the crisis. In preparation for the Buckingham Palace Conference, which Fanning sees as "a landmark on the path to the partition of Ireland", the king had sought Balfour's attendance, but Asquith successfully objected, claiming that he was a "wrecker". Fanning notes that Lloyd George took the same course seven years later during the Treaty negotiations.

Among the interesting points made by the general histories in relation to the Ulster crisis, Diarmaid Ferriter's *The Transformation of Ireland* comments on the "remarkable" Unionist unity of the period considering the obvious class tensions. For Ferriter, Unionists had a clear understanding that what they had in common was far more important than their differences. In his review of the period, R.F. Foster's *Modern Ireland 1600–1972* (London, 1988) views Unionist opposition to Home Rule as ludicrously extreme, but explains that this was because both Unionists and Conservatives were convinced that the Liberal government was acting unconstitutionally. They also believed that the Liberals were not fully committed to Home Rule. Joe Lee's *Ireland 1912–1985: Politics and Society* (Cambridge, 1989) is more critical of Unionist actions. He claims that the Unionist case against Home Rule was built on a sense of racial superiority, and he draws parallels with white South Africans and their rationale for minority rule. Lee also casts doubt on the economic justification for the anti-

Home Rule case, suggesting that by contemporary standards in Europe, Ulster, or more particularly Belfast, was not the economic success story that was routinely highlighted in Unionist propaganda. Its staple industries of textiles, engineering and shipbuilding were each in decline. Richard English's *Irish Freedom: The History of Nationalism in Ireland* (London, 2006) emphasises the power of the religious motive, arguing that the IPP's identification with Catholicism, mainly through the AOH, was very significant. He suggests that Unionists saw Nationalism as "a clerically-led culture seeking its own ascendancy and likely to deploy power intolerantly". This issue is carefully examined in Paul Bew's *Ideology and the Irish Question: Ulster Unionism and Irish Nationalism 1912–16* (Oxford, 1994), which looks in detail at the reaction to *Ne Temere* and the McCann case in Ulster. Bew emphasises that the IPP "lapsed into silence" on this crucial issue. While the economic case against Home Rule was a significant consideration for the Ulster bourgeoisie, Bew argues forcefully that it was the religious motive that was most important. The author goes on to highlight the Unionist perception that they were misunderstood in Britain, and he pays particular attention to Carson's fear of the impact that sectarian violence would have on public opinion in Britain. Ultimately, he argues, it was Carson's desire to keep the lid on Unionist violence that saw him giving his backing to Crawford's gun-running scheme. Jackson's *Home Rule* adds weight to the argument that a concession of a four-county exclusion in April 1912 would probably have driven a wedge between the Ulster Unionists and British Conservatives. When Asquith rejected this, Jackson argues that the Liberal strategy would then be determined by the "ferocity of Ulster Unionist resistance".

There is some debate among historians on the strength of the IPP in the years before the Great War. Its decline was so sudden that many argue it was a hollow shell long before its final collapse. One of the best studies remains Michael Wheatley's *Nationalism and the Irish Party 1910–16* (Oxford, 2005), which examines five counties: Leitrim, Longford, Roscommon, Sligo and Westmeath. Wheatley confidently illustrates how the IPP still reflected broad Nationalist opinion before the war. Moreover, it retained a powerful organisational presence in these counties. Wheatley uses statistics on the United Irish League (UIL) collated from Royal Irish Constabulary (RIC) quarterly reports to show that the organisation remained, on paper at least, stable in the period from December 1909 to December 1913. That said, Wheatley notes the impact of the absence of significant land agitation on the UIL's part. Indeed, the author describes the years 1910–13 as a quiet period for Nationalist politics, adding that there was no real "grievance" to stimulate politics beyond the local area. While Redmond enjoyed the loyalty of grass-roots Home Rule supporters, only a minority sympathised instinctively with Redmond's cautious, moderate approach. Wheatley claims that reaction to the eruption of the Home Rule crisis in 1912 was confident (even "apathetic"), and this confidence was only shaken in the second half of 1913, when grass-roots Nationalists began to fear that Home Rule might not be passed. Significantly, the IPP could not provide an outlet for the "fierce Anglophobia", which had always existed but came to the fore towards the end of 1913 and found expression in the Irish Volunteers. At local level Redmond's moderation could create problems, but the AOH remained a powerful vehicle in the years preceding the war. However, as Wheatley points out, the formation of the Irish Volunteers "partly marginalized" Redmond's party. In examining Redmond's views about the likely outcome of Home Rule, Paul Bew's *John Redmond* (Dublin, 1996) argues that the Irish leader sought to allay Unionist fears by predicting that the IPP would wither away once Home Rule was implemented. In its place a new power elite would emerge, drawn from "the well-heeled upper classes", including, in all likelihood, significant numbers of ex-Unionists. Patrick Maume's *The Long Gestation: Irish Nationalist Life 1891–1918* (Dublin, 1999) argues that Healy, who had some contact with Unionist leaders, was the first senior Nationalist to recognise that the Liberal government's hesitancy in the autumn of 1913 made partition in some form inevitable. Maume is, therefore, critical of the IPP's failure to ensure that the excluded area would be under direct rule from Westminster, as this would have facilitated future reunification. In collaboration with Cornelius O'Leary, Maume's *Controversial Issues in Anglo-Irish Relations, 1910–1921* (Dublin, 2004) emphasises that at the close of 1912, Irish Nationalists assumed that Home Rule was a certainty and, consequently, ignored the potential for Ulster Unionist resistance.

Chapter 3
The Path to Separation, 1914–18

World War I was a catalyst for significant change in Irish politics. It exposed the frailties of constitutional Nationalism and encouraged a militant minority to stage a rebellion against British rule. Within a year of the outbreak, a coalition government was in place, which included some of the most strident opponents of Irish Home Rule. It had also become evident that the war would be protracted. The British reaction to the Easter Rising displayed little understanding of Irish political sensitivities. Within weeks the situation in Ireland was transformed, as a retrospective legitimacy was conferred on the leaders of the rebellion. The Irish Parliamentary Party (IPP) was one of the main casualties of the rising, and the door was opened for a more radical Nationalist movement that would reflect the views of the patriot dead. The authorities at Westminster were slow to recognise this sea change that was underway in Irish politics, and their attempts to reassert their authority only fuelled the demand for Irish freedom. The separatists were handed a further advantage when the Lloyd George government attempted to impose conscription in Ireland in the spring of 1918. This would guarantee Sinn Féin victory in the postwar general election. The results of the election confirmed that Ireland was well down the road to separation.

Ireland and World War I

On 3 August 1914 the foreign secretary, Sir Edward Grey, confirmed MPs' fears when he informed the House of Commons that Britain was preparing for war against Germany. Grey spoke for an hour, and his sombre mood only lifted when he considered the implications of the conflict for Ireland. His comment that "the one bright spot in this dreadful situation is Ireland" appeared to be a reaction to the news that the Irish political leaders had agreed to park their differences in light of the rapidly deteriorating international situation. Grey's speech struck a chord with John Redmond who was present in the chamber but had not intended to speak in the day's proceedings. On hearing the foreign secretary's speech, however, the IPP leader rose to his feet, informing the government that it could remove its troops from Ireland for the duration of the war. Their place would be filled by the Irish Volunteers in the south who would "join arms" with the Ulster Volunteers to defend the Irish coastline. In pledging Irish Nationalist support for Britain and the Empire Redmond looked to a brighter future, asking "Is it too much to hope that out of this situation there may spring a result which will be good not merely for the Empire, but good for the future welfare and integrity of the Irish nation?". Redmond had gambled in making this commitment, but he sensed an opportunity. Irish support for Britain in its hour of need would copperfasten Ireland's claim for Home Rule, and Redmond's intervention was enthusiastically endorsed the next day in the Nationalist press. This was by no means a foregone conclusion, as emotions in Dublin remained high following the Bachelors Walk killings in the previous week (see Chapter 2). He also won acclaim on all sides of the House for his courageous stand, as he looked to have stolen a march on his Unionist rival.

Redmond was, of course, fully aware that his action did not meet with the full approval of other senior figures in the party. Dillon or Devlin would have wanted to secure specific concessions from the Liberal government before offering Nationalist support in the coming war. Yet Redmond favoured a unilateral gesture. A major reason was the position of Belgium in the grave situation on the continent. Redmond saw a parallel with Ireland, another small Catholic country situated close to a powerful neighbour. The defence of Belgium against German aggression gave Ireland, and by extension Britain, the moral high ground in the forthcoming struggle. The fact that Britain was poised to deliver justice to Ireland was clearly another significant factor. Beyond this, Redmond believed that the European conflict would provide the context for the healing of the old animosities between Unionism and Nationalism, as both traditions could work together to ensure victory for Britain and the Empire in a just war.

Such thinking underpinned Redmond's approach when he addressed a Nationalist meeting in Maryborough (Portlaoise) on Sunday, 16 August. This was his first public speech since his dramatic intervention in the Commons on 3 August. He appealed to all Volunteers in Ireland to unite for the purpose of defending the country. While this sentiment appealed to his Nationalist supporters, Redmond knew that he had to secure Home Rule as soon as possible to retain this support. On 4 August he had written to Asquith, highlighting the great risk he had taken and warning the prime minister that should the enactment of Home Rule be further delayed, "I would be unable to hold the people." Not surprisingly, the prime minister was also feeling the pressure from Bonar Law and Carson who insisted that the status quo be maintained. They warned Asquith that any rash move on Home Rule would destroy the new spirit of cross-party cooperation that had been fostered by the European conflict.

At the start of the war Asquith handed over his responsibility as secretary of state for war, a post he had held since Seely's resignation, to Lord Kitchener. Soon, Kitchener was hosting a meeting with Carson and Craig at the War Office. The Unionist leaders offered to provide at least one division of trained Ulster Volunteers for Kitchener's army, though they demanded that the Ulster Volunteer Force (UVF) men should remain together as a fighting unit and have the prefix "Ulster" added to the division's official name. Initially, Kitchener was lukewarm but, by early September, he was ready to accept the Unionist offer. Carson then crossed to Belfast where he played a major role in the recruiting campaign that would lead to the formation of the 36th (Ulster) Division. Though it was based on the UVF, it was neither exclusively Protestant nor solely recruited in Ulster. Meanwhile, Redmond and Dillon had also been to the War Office. There they endured a difficult meeting with Kitchener who informed them that he intended to launch a general recruiting campaign in Ireland to secure new troops for the regular army. Later in August, General Sir Bryan Mahon, who had crossed to Ireland to assess recruiting potential across the country, sought Redmond's advice on the role of the Irish Volunteers. Redmond's response was unequivocal. If they were to be enlisted, they should only be deployed in Ireland for the purpose of home defence and they should not be required to take the oath of allegiance. Mahon's retort that Britain's, and indeed Ireland's, fate was presently being decided in Flanders failed to shift Redmond from his insistence that the Irish Volunteers must remain in Ireland. Within a month, however, he had changed his mind.

Redmond did not want to be outbid by Carson who was appealing for the Ulster Volunteers to enlist for service overseas. However, he was also keen to display his gratitude to the Liberal government, which had decided to put Home Rule on the statute book. Asquith took this decision in early September, though the evidence that this was a cautious, tentative step was clear from the fact that it would be accompanied by a Suspensory Act that would freeze its operation until the end of the war. Furthermore, the prime minister also gave an undertaking that Home Rule would not be implemented until the question of Ulster had been resolved by way of an amending bill. In spite of this assurance, Carson and Bonar Law reacted with fury on learning of the government's plan. Asquith then informed the House of Commons of his administration's intention on 15 September, prompting a bitter response from Bonar Law, who accused the government of betraying the Unionists at such a critical moment. On 18 September the Home Rule Bill was finally passed into law and given royal assent, though a Suspensory Act deferred its operation because of the war. Nationalist

MPs celebrated in the chamber, waving the old green flag with the golden harp and congratulating Redmond. Home Rule now appeared to be a formality, though there was a recognition, which had been evident from the Buckingham Palace Conference, that some form of exclusion would be required for Ulster.

Following the triumph of 18 September, Redmond made the slow journey back to his base in County Wicklow. His destination was the old shooting lodge at Aughavanagh, which he had purchased from the Parnell family. On Sunday, 20 September, Redmond had reached Woodenbridge where, by chance, the East Wicklow Volunteers were holding a review. It was here that the Irish leader delivered an impromptu speech in which he called on the Volunteers to serve "not only in Ireland itself, but wherever the firing line extends, in defence of right, of freedom and religion in this war". While Redmond retained the hope that cooperation in the war effort would promote reconciliation between Unionism and Nationalism, his endorsement of overseas service was based on cold political reasoning. Redmond had always maintained that once Ireland attained Home Rule, it would become one of the strongest links in the Empire. Consequently, English public opinion would expect Ireland to stand behind England in what, Redmond was convinced, was a just war. In thinking this way Redmond saw a clear parallel between Ireland and South Africa, an imperial power that had endured a recent history of conflict with Britain but was now fully committed to the war effort. Aside from the question of honour, however, the Irish leader convinced himself that a clear stand on the issue of overseas service was necessary in order to guarantee the completion of the Home Rule project.

Yet Redmond also anticipated that such a change of strategy would create difficulties with the leadership of the Irish Volunteers. In the immediate aftermath of the Woodenbridge speech, twenty members of the original 27-man committee that had controlled the movement prior to Redmond's intervention in June issued a press statement repudiating the new policy. They also expelled the 25 Redmondite nominees who had been added to the committee and accused Redmond of acting without the committee's approval in calling for Irish Volunteers to serve under a foreign government. Eoin MacNeill was to the forefront in arguing that the Volunteers should instead maintain a state of readiness to insist on the implementation of Home Rule at the end of the war. He was adamant that fighting for Britain would not advance the Nationalist cause, and he accused Redmond of treachery for his Woodenbridge stance. Among the Volunteers who opposed Redmond was a small group of Irish Republican Brotherhood (IRB) figures who had infiltrated the Volunteer movement and worked their way into positions of influence. These IRB militants followed the old Fenian philosophy, "England's difficulty is Ireland's opportunity", and they hoped the war might create the right circumstances for a rebellion against British rule. For this minority grouping Britain, not Germany, was the obvious enemy.

In the months following the Woodenbridge speech, Redmond's National Volunteers, as they became known, maintained a visible presence throughout the country. Numerous Sunday parades were well attended, and enthusiasm for the Volunteers among Redmond's supporters remained strong. A new governing committee was elected with Redmond as president and Colonel Maurice Moore as inspector-general, and a weekly newspaper, the *National Volunteer,* was launched. Redmond reiterated his support for overseas service, and he was informed that 16,500 National Volunteers had enlisted by 1 November 1914. However, many of these were drafted into English regiments, highlighting the fact that Ulster Unionists were given more favourable treatment by the War Office. Kitchener had reluctantly agreed to Carson's demand for a separate Ulster division, but Redmond's request for similar treatment met with a negative response. The Irish leader wanted his National Volunteers to be drafted into a new Irish Brigade, complete with their own officers and insignia. He subsequently appealed to the prime minister, who expressed his sympathy, but Kitchener remained obstructive. The War Office insisted on retaining the existing regular army structures, though these were later amended to encourage large numbers of Nationalists to enlist. In time, the 16th (Irish) Division, which was in addition to the regular 10th (Irish) Division stationed at the Curragh, was recruited following constant pressure from Redmond, and Nationalists immediately came to identify with this unit. Redmond and Devlin were prominent in raising the 16th Division, although, like the 36th Ulster Division, it included significant numbers of non-Irish recruits. Not surprisingly, it attracted many of the most enthusiastic National Volunteers, a development that contributed to the movement's decline.

It gradually became evident that Redmond's difficulties with the War Office undermined his position in Nationalist Ireland. The generosity of spirit that he had demonstrated both in the Commons and at Woodenbridge six weeks later was not reciprocated, as Redmond was frustrated on almost every issue in his dealings with Kitchener's officials. Still, Redmond appeared to be at the peak of his powers during this early phase of the war. The vast majority of the nearly 180,000 Volunteers supported Redmond following the Woodenbridge split. Consequently, the National Volunteers dwarfed MacNeill's apparently ineffective Irish Volunteers, which now numbered around seven per cent of the movement. However, this uneven split masked the potential significance of this minority group. While Redmond commanded overwhelming support in rural Ireland, the situation was different in Dublin. There, 2,000 of the city's 6,700 Volunteers defied Redmond and sided with MacNeill. It was from this group, of course, that the 1916 insurgents would be drawn. Significantly, this smaller group under MacNeill provided a much more manageable number for the conspiratorial IRB that sought to control the Irish Volunteers for its own purposes. Senior IRB figures now occupied key positions in the smaller movement, and they operated secretly, keeping the vast majority of the 12,000 Volunteers in the dark. A meeting of the IRB Supreme Council in August 1914 confirmed the group's intention. They agreed in principle to use the opportunity presented by Britain's distraction with the European conflict to stage a rebellion in Ireland. IRB men now dominated the General Council that controlled the Irish Volunteers, but MacNeill, the chief of staff, was not aware of this nor of the IRB's plans to launch a rising during the war. MacNeill, for his part, believed that the Irish Volunteers should maintain a state of readiness in order to insist on the implementation of Home Rule at the end of the war. This was a view that was shared by a majority of his followers. When the General Council discussed the possibility of rebellion, MacNeill was firmly opposed, arguing that military action without a reasonable prospect of success was out of the question. For the chief of staff, the only circumstance in which violence could be contemplated would be in retaliation against any attempt by the authorities to suppress the Irish Volunteers. Thus, both groups of Volunteers were committed to Home Rule, though MacNeill's followers probably viewed devolution as simply the first instalment en route to independence. This latter group comprised an IRB minority that was prepared to use physical force to achieve Irish freedom, and a much larger body of constitutional separatists who aspired to that same freedom but were against the use of violence. Up to the outbreak of war, these constitutional separatists were prepared to accept Home Rule as a step on the road to full independence. As the European conflict dragged on, however, these separatists were becoming increasingly reluctant to accept the very limited freedom conferred by Home Rule.

Thus, the Irish Volunteers emerged as one of a number of groups that became identified with opposition to the war. At the same time, the more advanced elements of the Nationalist press criticised what they regarded as Redmond's imperialism, causing the Dublin Castle administration to express its concern at the pro-German stance being adopted by some newspapers. As Sinn Féin was the best known of the more advanced Nationalist groups, the Castle routinely referred to such newspapers as the "Sinn Féin press". Soon the Irish Volunteers under MacNeill's command acquired the title Sinn Féin Volunteers. Initially, however, this group made little impact outside Dublin. Lacking clear political direction, the movement drifted under MacNeill's leadership and this allowed the IRB element to extend its influence. Yet, in spite of this early failure to capture the public's attention, John Dillon, Redmond's deputy and a shrewd observer of political trends in Nationalist Ireland, viewed the Sinn Féin Volunteers as a potential challenger to the IPP. This conclusion led Dillon to issue repeated warnings to the Castle authorities to ensure that no attempt would be made to suppress these advanced Nationalist groups or their newspapers. He was also convinced, as was Redmond, that the War Office was undermining support for constitutional Nationalism because of its attitude to Irish recruitment. Such action also raised the profile of the anti-war Sinn Féin Volunteers.

During the first six months of the war, over 50,000 Irishmen enlisted in the British Army. Although the pace of recruitment slackened considerably thereafter, approximately 200,000 would see service overseas over the course of the war. One third of the total number were regular soldiers or reservists, but the remainder were volunteers who were motivated by a variety of factors. For many of the urban poor, the prospect of being well fed, while their dependants were being looked after, proved to be attractive. Others were clearly motivated by a sense of duty or by the feeling that they were advancing a political cause, whether that was as a supporter or an opponent of Home Rule. Certainly, Redmond's recruitment campaign can be judged a success, particularly in the early part of 1915. By the end of that year, over 25,000 National Volunteers had enlisted, though a quarter of this number were reservists who had been called up in August 1914. Significantly, recruitment had slowed towards the close of 1915, when Nationalist perceptions of the war had altered. On paper the National Volunteers still numbered over 100,000, and the movement continued to organise Sunday parades and reviews, but enthusiasm was clearly in short supply by the end of 1915. Redmond's lack of interest in the Volunteers was one reason, but it was the increasing unpopularity of the war that proved to be the crucial factor in the movement's rapid decline. The war, of course, presented Redmond's opponents with the ideal campaign issue. Galvanised into action by their anti-recruitment stance, this myriad of advanced Nationalist groups was drawn closer together by their opposition to what they regarded as Britain's war. The IPP, by contrast, had been left in limbo by the government's decision to put Home Rule on the statute book. This had left the party without a programme of action apart from its support for an increasingly unpopular war. Crucially, many of the party's MPs were ageing figures who had risen to prominence in the earlier phase of the agrarian struggle. By this stage, these men were happy to sit back and oversee the running of their constituencies. It was also true that the resolution of the land problem, which had witnessed the transfer of land from the landlord class, had weakened the bond between the IPP and the tenant farmers who had constituted the party's powerful support base. While these new owner-occupiers continued to give their allegiance to the IPP, the removal of the land question had tempered the crusading zeal that had characterised Nationalist politics in many parts of rural Ireland. An important consequence of this development was the decline of the United Irish League (UIL), the IPP's principal organisational presence across Ireland. The war did not lead to the collapse of the party's political machine.

Instead, it provided the context against which the IPP's Home Rule success began to be viewed. Increasingly, it came to be regarded as a hollow victory.

In spite of these problems, however, the IPP retained its electoral supremacy. In the period between the outbreak of the war and the Easter Rising, there were eight by-elections in Nationalist-controlled seats in Ireland. Three of these, Wicklow West, Galway East and Derry City, saw the return of IPP candidates without a contest. Of the remaining five seats, three were in rural constituencies, King's County (Offaly) in December 1914, Tipperary North in June 1915 and Louth North in March 1916. Each was won by a loyal Redmondite. In Louth North the party's candidate faced a radical Nationalist, but P. J. Whitby had almost 500 votes to spare over Sinn Féin's Bernard Hamill. Although the party enjoyed facile victories, it was apparent that its organisation at constituency level was poor. Consequently, steps were taken to address the problem throughout the country. The IPP also fought two urban by-elections. In a very low turnout in Dublin's College Green division, the party's candidate, T. D. Nugent, defeated Labour's nominee by 2,445 to 1,816 votes in June 1915, a result that highlighted the party's difficulties in urban areas. The Labour candidate, Thomas Farren, who was backed by James Connolly, was a committed separatist, and he was unequivocal in his opposition to the war. In the other urban by-election in Dublin Harbour, the seat was easily retained by the party's official candidate who faced two other enthusiastic Redmond supporters. The separatists were unable to field a candidate. Taken together, these by-elections confirmed that Redmond and the IPP still enjoyed the support of a clear majority across Nationalist Ireland. While the party may have shed much of the dynamism associated with its past, it was also true that the more radical strains of Nationalism had failed markedly to challenge the IPP's electoral authority in the period before the Easter Rising.

However, growing disenchantment with the war had created difficulties for Redmond and his party. The drop in recruitment after the summer of 1915 also indicated that Sinn Féin's anti-war propaganda was having some influence. Enthusiasm for the war was strongest among the mostly Protestant, gentry families whose sons filled many of the officer ranks in the 10th and 16th Divisions. The death toll on the Western Front decimated these landed families, but their service alongside Nationalist recruits, together with Redmond's full commitment to the war, did go some way towards healing the old divisions between Nationalists and southern Unionists. The majority of recruits came from the urban working class, particularly Dublin, where pay and living conditions were well below standards in Britain. Moreover, Dublin's economic fortunes were hit hard by the war. Many of the distilleries were forced to close, and even Guinness, the one firm where good wages and job security were the norm, moved to half-time working. This deteriorating economic situation proved a key factor in persuading workers to

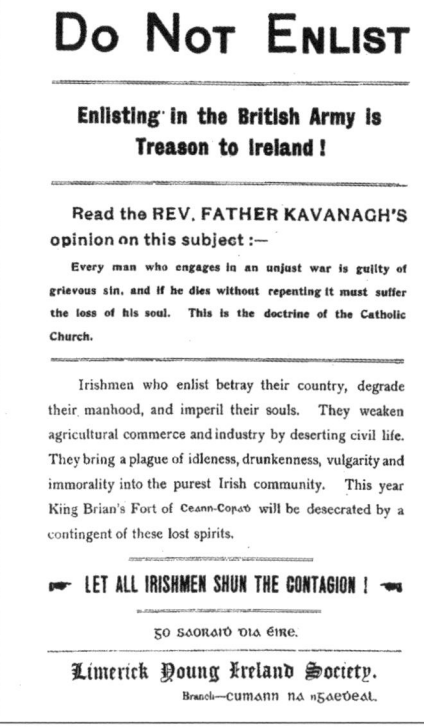

Cumann na nGaedheal anti-enlistment poster.

enlist in the army. Joining the army meant ignoring calls from James Connolly who appealed repeatedly in the pages of the *Workers' Republic* for workers to stand aside from this capitalist war. Connolly's frustration with the thousands of working-class Irishmen who joined the British Army proved to be a crucial factor in his support for a rebellion. In rural Ireland, by contrast, the war brought economic gains. Agricultural prices rose as demand for Irish produce soared, and this encouraged Irish farmers to adopt more intensive farming practices. The result was that many farmers' sons could now be gainfully employed at home. This was, of course, the cohort that the War Office considered ideal recruiting material, but these young men had little interest in enlisting for service overseas. This was particularly evident in the more prosperous rural areas, where farmers' sons were increasingly drawn to the various separatist groups that had been energised by their opposition to the war. Indeed, the authorities frequently highlighted the reluctance of the "middling classes", which included clerks and shop assistants from the market towns in addition to the farmers' sons, to come forward for recruitment. Sinn Féin, the most prominent of the anti-war separatist groups, naturally appealed to these younger elements.

The causes of the rising

World War I provided the necessary backdrop for the Easter Rising, as the IRB had been determined to stage a rebellion when Britain's full attention was fixed on the European conflict. In addition to providing the "opportunity", the war also deepened divisions within Nationalist ranks. Previously, Home Rule had operated as an umbrella ideology that could accommodate moderates who saw Home Rule as the limit of their aspirations and more advanced Nationalists who viewed Home Rule as the first step on the road to full independence. However, with Home Rule on the statute book but postponed, a growing number began to consider the act's limitations. MacNeill's quip that "Home Rule was a cheque continually post-dated" further emphasised constitutional Nationalism's wartime dilemma and caused many Nationalists to question the wisdom of Irish support for the war. The war had contributed to a political vacuum that worked to the advantage of the separatists and to the disadvantage of the Redmondites. While contemporary opinion had been overwhelmingly supportive of Redmond's Woodenbridge pronouncement, it soon came to be regarded as a misjudgement. The fact that the war was not over within a year, as was widely anticipated, further undermined Redmond's position. The Irish leader had been damaged by the War Office's dismissive attitude to Nationalist recruitment in the early part of the war, but an even greater blow was struck when a coalition government was formed in May 1915. A series of setbacks in the war had forced Asquith into accepting the need for a coalition. The prime minister ensured that Liberal ministers held the key cabinet posts, but the government at Westminster now included arch enemies of Irish Nationalism such as Bonar Law, Carson, Long, Chamberlain and Balfour. Asquith had offered Redmond a cabinet post, but this was declined on the principle that it would have compromised the IPP's tradition of independent parliamentary action. While his supporters endorsed Redmond's decision, D. P. Moran, one of his sternest critics, used *The Leader* to argue that by refusing a seat at the cabinet table, Redmond passed up the opportunity to influence the government. Of course, it was to be expected that any cabinet with Carson in its ranks would find a way to delay further the implementation of Home Rule. This assessment clearly weighed on the minds of more advanced Nationalists in Ireland, and these separatists were provided with a further boost when the coalition government introduced conscription in Britain in January 1916. The appalling loss of life on the Western Front, and the pressing need for manpower, had convinced the authorities at Westminster that compulsory military service was now essential. Naturally, the fear that this would soon be extended to Ireland was exploited by the separatists.

With conscription in Ireland appearing as a real threat, Redmond's Woodenbridge commitment came under renewed criticism. Furthermore, the war undermined constitutional Nationalism in other ways. It curtailed emigration, which had previously acted as a safety value by removing many of the most disaffected elements in Irish society. These men, many of whom were the younger sons of farming stock, had rejected recruitment, and their opposition to the war and fear of conscription pushed them into the arms of the more radical Nationalist groups. The war, meanwhile, had removed many of Redmond's staunchest supporters who had filled the ranks of the National Volunteers. From the spring of 1915 it was evident that the Redmondite movement was in decline.

That Easter, the review of National Volunteers saw 27,000 men on parade, but this was virtually the last occasion that the movement made a significant impression. While the war clearly contributed to the growing difficulties challenging Redmond and constitutional Nationalism, it did not by itself lead to a rebellion in 1916. Certainly, the war energised more militant Nationalism and intensified anti-British feeling, but only a small number of these extreme separatists were pro-German and were contemplating an insurrection. In analysing the causes of the rising, therefore, perhaps the most significant aspect of the war was that it provided the ideal opportunity for insurrection.

A second cause of the rising was the impact of Carsonism in the period immediately before the war. In leading Ulster resistance to the third Home Rule Bill, Carson had developed an extra-parliamentary strategy that pointed the way for militant Nationalism. Ulster Unionists had formed a huge private army and obtained 25,000 rifles from Germany. Their aim was to defy Asquith's Liberal administration. This action had inspired the formation of the Irish Volunteers, and the Ulstermen had demonstrated that only force, or the very real threat of force, proved effective in influencing government policy. For the men behind the formation of the Irish Volunteers, Carson's readiness to engage in violence contrasted sharply with Redmond's scrupulously constitutional tactics, and they were in no doubt about which example to follow. MacNeill had taken the initiative with his article, "The North Began", which can be read as a firm rejection of Redmond's constitutionalism. Of course, a small number of IRB militants were quick to take advantage of the subsequent formation of the Irish Volunteers, seeing the potential for revolutionary action in the new organisation. These militants also viewed MacNeill as an appropriate figurehead to lead a movement that they intended to nudge towards a rebellion. What Carsonism had done, therefore, was to convert a significant number of Home Rulers into radical Nationalists while, simultaneously, breathing life into a practically moribund IRB. Patrick Pearse, like many younger Nationalists, underwent this transformation. As late as 1912, Pearse was a committed Home Ruler, but the militarisation of Unionism altered his thinking. The concept of arms in the hands of Irishmen appealed to Pearse, who would write in November 1913, "I think the Orangeman with a rifle a much less ridiculous figure than the Nationalist without one." Clearly, Carsonism had a profound influence on the development of militant Nationalism in the period before the rising.

Years earlier, however, Pearse and his colleagues in the Gaelic League had been inspired by the prospect of a free and Gaelic Ireland. Thus, the new Nationalism that emerged around the turn of the century made a significant contribution to the rising. The Gaelic League, which was the pre-eminent organisation in the movement for cultural revival, brought a new generation of young men to Irish Nationalism.

In particular, the language movement attracted young men of talent and ambition who felt excluded by the older generation that dominated constitutional Nationalism. It was from this group that a new revolutionary elite would emerge. Their sense of nationality had been nurtured in the Gaelic League's language classes, where the romantic revolutionary spirit that was so apparent among the 1916 leaders was allowed to develop. Pearse articulated this shift in an essay entitled "The Coming Revolution", which appeared only days after MacNeill's article, "The North Began". He acknowledged the League's role in educating a new generation of Irish revolutionaries and claimed that these individuals had "an ulterior motive in joining the League", but Pearse insisted that the League's work was now over. A new generation, he argued, now had to assert Ireland's right to nationhood, a task that could only be accomplished through force. There was also the glorification of sacrifice in Pearse's writing: "We may make mistakes in the beginning and shoot the wrong people; but bloodshed is a cleansing and sanctifying thing, and the nation which regards it as the final horror has lost its manhood. There are many things more horrible than bloodshed; and slavery is one of them." The League's president and founding father, Douglas Hyde, wanted the movement to remain aloof from politics, but it became increasingly difficult to separate the desire for both cultural and political independence. Since the League's formation, moreover, a significant number of branches, particularly those in Munster, had been infiltrated by the IRB. In the summer of 1915 Hyde suddenly resigned the presidency, criticising the League's shift to a more overt political stance. For some time, Tom Clarke and Sean MacDermott, the two most important figures in the IRB, had been pressing the Gaelic League to identify with the aim of political freedom. They were successful, as the organisation's constitution was amended in July 1915 to state that the League should also "devote itself to realising the ideal of a free Gaelic-speaking Ireland". The new Nationalism, therefore, had strengthened the separatist movement and provided a leadership group that formulated both a rationale for rebellion and,

Patrick Pearse (1879-1916), by Sean O'Sullivan RHA.

significantly, a programme that was reflected in the content of the 1916 Proclamation. Even more crucially, perhaps, the new Nationalism helped to develop an atmosphere in which a rebellion might take place, though both Carsonism and the war were necessary to make the insurrection a reality.

While the new Nationalism, Carsonism and the war were important elements in bringing about a rising, a rebellion in 1916 was, by no means, inevitable. A crucial factor was the contribution of the IRB conspirators operating within the clandestine Fenian movement, particularly Clarke and MacDermott. Clarke, with his abiding hatred of Britain, best typified the indomitable Fenian spirit. His desire for an insurrection led him to support a group of young northern militants, principally Bulmer Hobson, Denis McCullough and Sean MacDermott, who were actively plotting to seize control of the IRB. Although they realised this objective by 1912, the IRB remained a largely ineffective and marginalised organisation. It gained a new sense of purpose, however, with the formation of the Irish Volunteers in November 1913. Senior IRB figures immediately joined the movement with the intention of manipulating the Volunteers for their own purposes. Of the 30 committee members chosen to oversee the Irish Volunteers, 12 were IRB men. Their influence was further increased when a number of others, including Patrick Pearse, Joseph Plunkett and Thomas MacDonagh, were sworn into the movement. Redmond's decisive action to bring the Volunteers under the IPP's control in June 1914 temporarily upset IRB planning and led to a spectacular falling-out between Tom Clarke and Bulmer Hobson. Both men sat on the ruling Supreme Council and Hobson was editor of the IRB's monthly newspaper, *Irish Freedom*. Hobson had been the prime mover in the IRB revival since 1910, but his acceptance of Redmond's takeover of the Volunteers ended his friendship with Clarke, who never spoke to him again. Subsequently, Hobson resigned from the Supreme Council and from the editorship of *Irish Freedom*, leaving the stage clear for the militants – Clarke, the Treasurer, and MacDermott, the Secretary – to direct IRB strategy. Together with the president, these three

Thomas Clarke (1857–1916).

formed the IRB Executive, which acted on the Supreme Council's behalf and effectively controlled the secret organisation.

The split in the Volunteers following the Woodenbridge speech left the IRB holding key positions in MacNeill's minority movement. Pearse was director of military organisation, MacDonagh was director of training and Plunkett was director of military operations. MacNeill remained chief of staff, and while he and his two closest colleagues on the headquarters team, Hobson, the quartermaster, and Michael Joseph Rahilly (The O'Rahilly), the director of arms, must have been suspicious of the IRB's intentions, they probably underestimated the IRB's ability to launch a rebellion. There was a widespread belief, even among leading IRB figures, that any rising must attract popular support, but the Executive was determined to stage an insurrection irrespective of public opinion. Indeed, James Deakin and Denis McCullough, the successive presidents from 1913 to 1916, discovered that they had little influence, as Clarke and MacDermott took all the crucial decisions. Even McCullough, who became president in late 1915 and was a close friend to both men, was kept in the dark about plans for a rising. In May 1915 the Executive had appointed a three-man military committee, comprising Pearse, Plunkett and Eamonn Ceannt, to draw up detailed preparations for a rebellion. Clarke and MacDermott had turned to this younger generation, each of whom was a recent recruit to the IRB, convinced that they were absolutely committed to staging an insurrection. Only Clarke and MacDermott were aware of this development, as their obsession with secrecy ensured that even the Supreme Council had no knowledge of their activities. In September 1915 these two formally joined the military committee, which was renamed the Military Council, and this was the body that made the rising a reality. Pearse was the figurehead put forward by Clarke. Although Pearse was unpopular with many IRB men who suspected him of political opportunism, Clarke was convinced that Pearse possessed the necessary leadership qualities. He was a gifted communicator with an air of nobility and revolutionary purity that appealed to Clarke. Plunkett was a fellow writer who acted as the Council's chief military strategist, while the less prominent Ceannt, an employee of Dublin Corporation, had become the Irish Volunteers' director of communications in August 1915. By late 1915, therefore, Clarke was content to take a back seat, confident that his life's ambition of instigating another Fenian rebellion would be realised by this youthful cohort. His confidant, MacDermott, assumed the role of key conspirator in planning the rising. He approved all the major decisions, ensured that total confidentiality was maintained and excelled at the cloak-and-dagger activity that underpinned the insurrection. The decision to choose Easter Sunday was probably taken by the Military Council later in 1915, and MacDermott ensured that the rising went ahead without reference to the Military Council.

While the Military Council, under direction from Clarke and MacDermott, was determined that the opportunity for a rising presented by the war should not be missed, the individual roles played by Pearse and James Connolly also proved significant. They were two of the four acclaimed writers who signed the Proclamation. Pearse, Plunkett and MacDonagh shared a common approach. They were romantic revolutionaries who had initially been inspired by the Gaelic League. Their observations of the war in Europe had further radicalised their sense of patriotism and developed the concept of a noble sacrifice for a holy cause. All three were intensely religious young men who were still in their thirties at the time of the Easter Rising. Pearse was born in 1879 into a conventional Dublin lower middle-class family. In September 1908 he opened St Enda's, a bilingual school that attracted pupils from many of the best-known families in Gaelic revival circles. The school specialised in the promotion of both the Irish language and Ireland's Gaelic past. All the boys learned of Cúchulainn, the mythical hero who was alleged to have said, "I care not though I were to live but one day and one night, if only my fame and my deeds live after me." This principle of sacrifice was part of the school's ethos, and Pearse also highlighted the historical importance of Wolfe Tone and Robert Emmet, two more recent heroes whose names were synonymous with martyrdom in the cause of Ireland. Once he had cast aside his Home Rule political philosophy in 1913, Pearse's writings displayed a powerful Messianic tone that was easily intertwined with the doctrine of blood sacrifice. Pearse saw Ireland's struggle for redemption in terms of Christ's sacrifice at Calvary. Plunkett and MacDonagh shared this belief in a parallel between Christ's death on the cross to save men's souls and the need for a similar sacrifice to save Ireland's soul and resurrect Irish nationality. This spiritual theme was at the heart of his graveside oration at the funeral of Jeremiah O'Donovan Rossa on 1 August 1915, when Pearse spoke on behalf of "the new generation that had been rebaptised in the Fenian faith". The veteran Fenian, who had died in the United States, was brought home to Dublin for burial, giving the IRB, and Pearse, the perfect propaganda stage. He ended his oration with a hint of a forthcoming rebellion:

> Life springs from death; and from the graves of patriot men and women spring living nations. The Defenders of this Realm … think they have pacified Ireland … but the fools, the fools, the fools! – they have left us our Fenian dead, and while Ireland holds these graves, Ireland unfree shall never be at peace.

Plunkett and MacDonagh also shared this revolutionary zeal and were equally willing to sacrifice themselves for Ireland's rebirth. Before the war they had collaborated on various theatre and literary projects, and both were drawn to the increasing militancy associated with the formation of the Volunteers. As with Pearse, the war had a profound effect on Plunkett and MacDonagh, propelling them towards a rebellion and self-sacrifice. Indeed, Plunkett, who was the chief military expert on the Military Council and who, incidentally, was dying from tuberculosis, visited Berlin in the spring of 1915 in an unsuccessful attempt to persuade the Germans to support an IRB rebellion with a powerful invasion force. Crucially, the overwhelming military odds stacked against the IRB conspirators did not cause them to reconsider their plans for an insurrection. Their belief in the blood sacrifice doctrine ensured their support for a rebellion whatever the likely outcome, and this proved vital for Clarke and MacDermott at the hub of the conspiracy. Eamonn Ceannt, another of the seven signatories of the Proclamation, was the least well known of the insurrectionist leaders. He had joined Sinn Féin in 1907 and was active in the Gaelic League, but he subsequently took issue with both movements, the former for its moderation and the latter for its reluctance to become involved in militant Nationalist politics. For Ceannt, the threat of violence deployed by the Ulster Unionists during the Home Rule crisis convinced him that it was "the duty of all men to be skilled in the use of arms". From that point Ceannt viewed armed conflict with the British as inevitable. With his colleagues on the Military Council, he was fully committed to a strategy of rebellion.

The final member of the Military Council was the socialist activist and writer, James Connolly. In his analysis of Irish history, Connolly's criticism of English landlords, and then English capitalists, had a discernible Nationalist undertone. Yet his objective of a socialist republic did not equate to the Gaelic republic sought by the other writer-revolutionaries. Likewise, his attitudes to the war were very different. In December 1915 Connolly angrily rejected Pearse's glorification of the European conflict. When Pearse argued, "The old heart of the earth needed to be warmed with the red wine of the battlefields," Connolly

James Connolly (1868–1916), at the age of 34, taken on his first visit to the United States.

Anti–British Imperialist cartoon of the early 1900s.

dismissed him as a "blithering idiot". Connolly was deeply disillusioned at the actions of the Dublin working class in responding to the government's recruitment campaign to fight for imperialist Britain in what he believed was a capitalist war. The large banner that was draped across the front of Liberty Hall, the headquarters of the Transport Union, proclaimed the labour movement's stance on the war: "We serve neither King nor Kaiser, but Ireland." Yet this expression of neutrality concealed Connolly's burning desire to strike a blow against Britain while the war was providing an all-consuming distraction. In early September 1914 he and the six other signatories of the Proclamation attended a meeting with senior IRB personnel at which the prospect of a rising was discussed. Connolly was enthusiastic, convincing himself that Nationalism and socialism complemented each other with a Nationalist revolution as a necessary precursor to a socialist takeover. In spite of their different perspectives on the carnage on the Western Front, Connolly found himself sharing Pearse's vision of an Irish blood sacrifice. Yet all through 1915 he remained outside the tight circle of IRB conspirators and was unaware of the Military Council's existence. The increasingly impatient Connolly assumed that the IRB's talk of a rising would not translate into action, and he began to make his own preparations for an insurrection. This would be spearheaded by the Irish Citizen Army (ICA), the 200-strong trade-union militia that had remained in existence following the Dublin Lockout. A rifle range had been installed in Liberty Hall and training was intensified under the ICA Chief of Staff, Michael Mallin. By the close of 1915 Connolly was publicly advocating revolutionary action, claiming that if the IRB took cold feet, the ICA "would advance by itself if needs be".

Connolly's determination to stage a rebellion alarmed the Military Council, whose members feared that precipitate action by the ICA would not only ruin their own plans but also result in the suppression of the Volunteers. Consequently,

Connolly met secretly with the Military Council over a four-day period from 19 to 22 January 1916. Apparently, it took some time for Connolly to be convinced that plans for a rising were well advanced, with a date set for Easter Sunday, some three months away. The clandestine gathering ended with Connolly being brought on board the Military Council, as he agreed to shelve his plans for an ICA-led rebellion. Connolly had to concede that the rising would not be undertaken in the name of socialism, but the additional numbers under IRB control obviously increased the prospect of success. It was also apparent that Connolly was coming under Pearse's influence. He had been impressed by Pearse's oration at the O'Donavan Rossa funeral. In a *Workers' Republic* article, published in February 1916, Connolly called on his generation to make "the supreme act of self-sacrifice to die if need be that our race might live in freedom". This confirmed Connolly's endorsement of the blood sacrifice concept advocated by Pearse and his fellow writer-revolutionaries. In one of his final articles, Connolly sought to justify his decision to join forces with bourgeois Nationalism: "The cause of labour is the cause of Ireland, the cause of Ireland is the cause of labour. They cannot be dissevered." Connolly wanted action, and he was convinced that the present opportunity must not be wasted. Of course, the content of the Proclamation, which was mostly Pearse's work, illustrates Connolly's influence. The document guaranteed "equal rights and equal opportunities to all its citizens", while declaring "the right of the people of Ireland to the ownership of Ireland". These lofty ideals were not delivered, but the eagerness of Connolly and Pearse to stage an insurrection and sacrifice themselves in the process helped to deliver a rebellion. Clarke and MacDermott were the key drivers, but the blood sacrifice ideology, along with Carsonism, the new Nationalism and World War I, combined to produce the Easter Rising.

Insurrection

While regular speculation about sedition could be heard from a number of quarters, MacDermott's obsession with secrecy ensured that only a small circle was aware of the precise plans for the rebellion. Still, the authorities at Dublin Castle chose to ignore the rumours of a possible insurrection. Birrell still held the post of chief secretary, but he left much of the day-to-day running of affairs to his under secretary, Sir Matthew Nathan, who had occupied the role since October 1914. On his appointment Nathan banned a number of militant Nationalist newspapers, including *Irish Freedom,* though they quickly reappeared under new titles. He also studied the monthly Royal Irish Constabulary (RIC) reports, enabling him to compile a long list of militant Nationalists who were suspected of engaging in subversive activity. Nathan was, however, willing to listen to the advice of Redmond and Dillon who were adamant that the best course of action was to ignore the activity of the militants. This meant ignoring Unionist demands for a crackdown against anti-British agitators. Indeed, Birrell and Nathan continued to reject a policy of coercion even when it became clear that support for the more extreme Nationalist groups was on the increase. Outside Dublin there were sporadic incidents in a number of areas in which the Volunteers fired on the RIC, while in the capital in October 1915, the ICA staged a series of mock attacks on Dublin Castle, and these continued at regular intervals until March 1916. Still, the authorities continued to ignore such regular provocation even as rumours of an impending rising circulated in the city

Although the Castle administration continued to reject Unionist demands for the disarming of the Volunteers and an end to parading, the army in Ireland was becoming increasingly nervous. Officers had been alarmed by the increased Volunteer and ICA activity in March 1916 and, more specifically, by a warning from the director of military intelligence in Britain that information, most probably from intercepted German code messages, indicated that a rising with German assistance was being planned for Easter Saturday, 22 April. This led to the arrest of Ernest Blythe and Liam Mellows, two prominent IRB figures who were deported to England. By this stage senior military personnel in Ireland were pressing Nathan for his assessment of the situation. On 10 April 1916 he wrote to the adjutant general, acknowledging the increased level of Volunteer activity but concluding, "I do not believe that its leaders mean insurrection or that the Volunteers have sufficient arms if the leaders do mean it." While the military authorities remained nervous, Nathan's assessment was accepted. He believed that the deportations had eased the situation and he was mindful of Dillon's advice that tough action by the government would only increase tension across the country. It was also true that while rumours of rebellion were growing almost daily, the government had no specific information from its agents within the Volunteer movement. Clearly, the Military Council's determination to maintain secrecy was contributing to the authorities' complacency. Even on 17 April, when information was passed to Nathan from the officer in command of defences at Queenstown Harbour in County Cork, indicating that a shipment of arms was to be landed somewhere on the south-west coast in preparation for a rising, scepticism prevailed. The RIC in the neighbouring counties were put on alert, but Nathan was convinced that there would be no insurrection. The under secretary was stunned by events leading up to the rising, although they unfolded in a way that persuaded the authorities that the danger of a rising had passed.

A combination of good fortune for the authorities and incompetence on the part of the Volunteers appeared to crush any possibility of an Irish rebellion. On Thursday, 19 April 1916, the *Aud*, a German ship disguised as a Norwegian trawler, arrived in Tralee Bay. However, it was unable to make contact with Volunteers waiting on the shore. The skipper waited for 24 hours before moving off, but his vessel was intercepted by the Royal Navy and escorted into Queenstown. On approach to the harbour, the ship was scuttled and with it sank the cargo of 20,000 rifles and any chance of a successful rising. On that same Good Friday, Sir Roger Casement was put ashore in County Kerry by a German submarine. Casement had been the IRB's man in Germany, but he was quickly apprehended by two alert RIC officers and taken to Tralee jail. He had originally travelled to Germany in October 1914 with the intention of forming an Irish Brigade drawn from Irish prisoners of war in Germany, but this proved to be a hopeless task. His other objective was to enlist German support for the IRB. However, Casement had quickly become disillusioned by German indifference, and he informed Plunkett in 1915 that any rising without German assistance would be futile. In truth, the Germans were not impressed by Casement, whose reputation was undermined by the presence of his servant, Alder Christensen, an unscrupulous Norwegian seaman who travelled in his company. Casement's German mission was not productive, and this exasperated John Devoy, the principal IRB conspirator in the United States, who had played a role in the decision to dispatch Casement to Germany. When Devoy was informed of the Military Council's plan for an Easter rebellion in 1916, he contacted the German embassy in Washington, bypassing Casement and requesting a shipment of arms to be sent to the south-west coast of Ireland at some point between Good Friday and Easter Sunday.

The intervention of this third party complicated the planning and contributed to the *Aud*'s capture and Casement's arrest. It was with some difficulty that Casement persuaded his German hosts to deliver him to Kerry. His intention was to meet the IRB leaders in Dublin and dissuade them from launching the rebellion. Casement's capture, of course, ensured that the Military Council, which was committed to an insurrection with or without German aid, never had the opportunity to hear his argument. However, when news of Casement's detention reached the authorities in Dublin, they assumed that the plot to launch a rebellion had been foiled. Casement was assumed to be the leader of the insurrectionists, and his arrest and rapid transportation to England convinced the authorities that a rising had been averted. Nathan was aware that the Volunteers were to be mobilised on Easter Sunday, but a notice in the leading Sunday newspaper cancelling the manoeuvres planned for that afternoon, together with the knowledge that Casement was in custody, reassured the authorities that the danger of a rising had passed.

Still, these late setbacks did not deter the Military Council. Its seven members hoped for German rifles to give the rebellion a real chance of success, but the capture of the *Aud*, if anything, only strengthened their resolve to proceed with a blood sacrifice. Their dilemma now was to mobilise sufficient insurrectionists to ensure that any rising was feasible. They were also aware of the fierce opposition to a doomed rebellion by MacNeill, Hobson and The O'Rahilly, three key figures in the Volunteer leadership. Indeed, by early April, such was MacNeill's fear that the IRB was about to stage a rising that he persuaded the Volunteer leadership to support his demand that only instructions that had been countersigned by him could be issued to the Volunteers. This appeared as a major obstacle to the IRB leaders who knew that MacNeill and his colleagues would oppose any rising unless the government attempted either to suppress the movement or to impose conscription on Ireland. In such circumstances the Military Council decided to deceive the Volunteer leadership by using the "Castle Document", which appeared on 19 April. It was almost certainly a forgery organised by MacDermott, Plunkett and MacDonagh, and it contained details of a government plan to suppress the Volunteers. MacNeill was persuaded of the document's authenticity, and he issued orders to prepare for resistance. On the following day, however, Hobson learned that the IRB had also issued instructions to prepare for a rising on Easter Sunday. This prompted Hobson and MacNeill to drive to St Enda's, where they confronted Pearse and heard for the first time of the Military Council's plans for Easter Sunday. An angry MacNeill wanted to halt the mobilisation of Volunteers planned for Easter Sunday, but Pearse, MacDonagh and MacDermott talked him out of it, arguing that German arms were about to be landed in Kerry. None of those present had any knowledge of the *Aud*'s sinking earlier that Good Friday. Over the course of the following day, however, MacNeill became more aware of the scale of deception undertaken by the IRB conspirators, and he issued orders late on Easter Saturday evening with the aim of stopping the rising. To ensure that his message was received, MacNeill also published his countermanding orders in the *Sunday Independent,* suspending all Volunteer activity scheduled for that day. As chief of staff, MacNeill naturally assumed that his action had prevented a rising but, unknown to him, the Military Council met at Liberty Hall on Easter Sunday morning and agreed to launch the rebellion on the following day.

On Easter Monday, just under 1,600 insurgents assembled to stage a rising that the Military Council recognised was certain to fail militarily. The confusion caused by the orders and countermanding orders, together with the secrecy guarded by MacDermott, greatly reduced the number of participants. Even McCullough, the IRB president, had been deliberately kept in the dark. The sight of Volunteers marching through the city centre caused little excitement among the city's population that had become accustomed to the frequent parades and manoeuvres conducted by both the Volunteers and the ICA. The centre of the city was quiet, with many attending the traditional holiday race meeting at Fairyhouse, an event that also attracted a significant number of army officers. With the authorities confident that a rebellion plot had been uncovered, the insurgents met minimum resistance. Led by Pearse, the president of the provisional government and the commandant-general of the Dublin Division, the insurgents occupied the city's key buildings. The General Post Office (GPO) in O'Connell Street, then known as Sackville Street, became the headquarters. Although Pearse, Clarke, MacDermott and Plunkett, the Military Council's chief strategist, were in the building, it was James Connolly who effectively assumed command. The insurgents quickly raised two flags over the GPO. One was the old green flag with the gold harp, while the other was a tricolour of orange, white and green, a more obscure emblem but one that provided a link to an earlier insurrection. After the occupation of the GPO, Pearse marched outside to read the Proclamation from the provisional government to a small crowd of bemused onlookers. All seven members of the Military Council had signed the Proclamation, which emphasised Ireland's right to establish her freedom through force of arms. It also sought to connect the 1916 insurrection to the tradition of past rebellions against British rule. Significantly, the Proclamation's final sentence made it clear that the 1916 leaders were ready "to sacrifice themselves for the common good". More controversially, there was a reference to their "gallant allies in Europe", a term that ensured that the rising would be viewed by the British as an act of treason.

Easter Rising: British armoured car (heavily improvised) in Dublin.

In the opening phase of the insurrection, an ICA unit approached the gate at Dublin Castle, shooting dead a policeman, Constable James O'Brien, and capturing a group of soldiers. However, they failed to press home their advantage against the largely undefended seat of British rule in Ireland. Instead, the insurgents concentrated on other key targets. Edward Daly was in charge at the Four Courts, while another group led by MacDonagh occupied Jacob's biscuit factory. Michael Mallin commanded the ICA unit at St Stephen's Green, while a young mathematics teacher, Éamon de Valera, was in command at Boland's Mill. The tactics employed by the insurgents involved holding the positions and waiting for government forces to dislodge them. During the first few days of the rebellion the poorest elements in the city took advantage of the Dublin Metropolitan Police's withdrawal to remove the contents of many city-centre shops. As the fighting intensified towards the end of the week, many parts of O'Connell Street were ablaze. The army used artillery to attack the insurgents' positions, forcing the occupants to withdraw but causing major structural damage to many of the city's buildings. By Thursday evening the GPO was in flames. The insurgents abandoned the building and Connolly, who had been seriously wounded, had to be stretchered to a house in nearby Moore Street. On Friday the British tightened the cordon around the insurgents. To prevent further loss of life, Pearse and Connolly decided to surrender, and instructions to this effect were relayed to other Volunteer positions. By Sunday, 1 May, the rising was effectively over.

Over 200 civilians and more than 100 British troops were killed in the fighting. The insurgents, whose losses stood at 64, were immediately arrested following their surrender. Among the prisoners were a number of women. About 90 women had participated in the rising, 60 of whom were members of Cumann na mBan, the women's equivalent of the Irish Volunteers, which had been formed in April 1914. While many of the Volunteer leaders did not want women involved in the fighting, Cumann na mBan personnel provided a support network for the insurgents. One very dangerous role that they performed was acting as couriers, transferring messages and supplies, often under heavy fire, to the various Volunteer positions. Sometimes food had to be commandeered as van drivers were forced to hand over supplies to armed Cumann na mBan activists. The remaining 30 female participants were members of the ICA, and they played a more prominent role in the fighting. One of their number, Countess Constance Markievicz, acted as Michael Mallin's second-in-command at St Stephen's Green. The sight of the 48-year-old countess, armed with a revolver that she did not hesitate to fire, remains one of the most powerful images of the fighting in Dublin. Outside the capital there were isolated engagements and a few minor successes, but the obvious absence of coherent planning limited the impact made by the insurgents. The failure to secure the shipment of rifles and the false start caused by MacNeill's countermanding orders presented insurmountable obstacles. In the west 1,500 Volunteers under the leadership of Liam Mellows held the town of Athenry for a brief period, while the Wexford Volunteers controlled Enniscorthy for three days. Mellows proved to be an enterprising officer who, using a clever disguise, had returned from his deportation to England to play his part in the rebellion. The most notable success outside Dublin was at Ashbourne in County Meath, where Volunteers commanded by Thomas Ashe engaged in a five-hour gun battle with the RIC. Eight policemen were killed and a further 16 were wounded, as Ashe's men seized control of four police barracks containing large quantities of arms and ammunition. They were still in control of part of the county when Pearse issued his order to surrender. In spite of these minor successes, however, the Easter Rising had been a military disaster, and the failure of the insurgents to win the support of the wider population, particularly in Dublin, was clear to both sides in the fighting. Yet the insurgents had displayed great courage in the face of overwhelming military odds, and their claim to have stood up in the cause of Irish freedom could not be denied. The main question now was: how would the British authorities respond to the rebellion?

Countess Constance Markievicz (1868–1927).

Executions and martial law

Dublin citizens demonstrated genuine hostility towards the captured insurgents as they were taken into detention. The prisoners were jeered and abused by large groups of civilians. Many were furious at the loss of civilian life, the terrible destruction of property and the serious disruption to their lives that had continued for six consecutive days. It was also evident that many of the women who vented their anger were the wives of men serving with the British Army on the Western Front. Yet this early rage was short-lived, and attitudes to those engaged in the rising underwent a dramatic transformation. The primary reason for this radical shift of opinion was the misguided and badly judged British response to both the insurgents and the wider Irish population. Both Birrell and Nathan resigned their positions as chief secretary and under secretary, taking responsibility for the failure to foresee, and prevent, the rebellion. The chief decision-maker was now Major-General Sir John Maxwell, who had arrived in Dublin just in time to oversee the concluding stages of the fighting. The powers of the civil authority were suspended indefinitely, and Maxwell acted as a military governor when martial law was imposed over the whole country. This was an overreaction, as the Easter Rising had essentially been a Dublin affair but the implementation of martial law throughout the country imposed unnecessary restrictions and caused great resentment among the people. However, the British took a narrow view of recent events. Their focus was on the dire international crisis, and their priority in Ireland was to make an example of the 1916 leaders in an attempt to prevent any repetition of the rebellion. Maxwell oversaw the British response to the rising, but he was a second-rate soldier who lacked the political nous to carry out what was a very delicate task. The military governor and his subordinates, moreover, had little understanding of Irish affairs and demonstrated little concern for the potential consequences of their actions. Ireland's history of suffering at English hands, together with the general feeling of sympathy for the large body of insurgents who had been coaxed into a rebellion by hopelessly misguided, yet patriotic, leaders, made Maxwell's task extremely sensitive. His subsequent actions displayed no understanding of these circumstances.

From the outset the British were convinced that the rising was a "Sinn Féin rebellion". They were clearly unaware of the leading role played by the IRB, and, as Sinn Féin was the most prominent militant Nationalist group, they attributed the rising to Arthur Griffith's movement. This misjudgement meant that when Maxwell ordered large-scale arrests across the country, many of those detained were Sinn Féin members who had no part in the rebellion. While some 1,500 of these were quickly released, nearly 2,000 were shipped to Britain where they were detained either in English jails or in a special internment camp at Frongoch in north Wales. This would prove counter-productive, as these detention centres became training establishments for radical Nationalism. While the internment of Irish prisoners created sympathy for the various militant Nationalist groups, most attention was concentrated on the work of the courts-martial that Maxwell had ordered at the conclusion of the rising. Trials were held in secret and executions followed, and this transformed the political atmosphere in Ireland. On 3 May the authorities issued a brief statement, confirming that Pearse, Clarke and MacDonagh had been shot by firing squad that morning. More such announcements were made over the next nine days. Plunkett, Edward Daly,

Willie Pearse and Michael O'Hanrahan were executed on 4 May, and Major John MacBride suffered the same fate on the following day. On 8 May it was the turn of Ceannt, Mallin, Con Colbert and Sean Heuston, while Thomas Kent was executed in Cork. Finally, on 12 May, Connolly and MacDermott faced the firing squad at Kilmainham Jail.

In total, fifteen executions were carried out. These included, as anticipated, all seven who had signed the Proclamation, but a number of minor figures, most notably Willie Pearse, Patrick's devoted younger brother, were also shot. Yet it was the protracted nature of the executions, the cruel secrecy and the uncertainty surrounding both the identity and numbers of those who might be added to the list that shook Nationalist Ireland. In fact, 90 prisoners had been sentenced to death, but 75 had their sentences commuted to penal servitude. Among those to escape the firing squad were de Valera and Countess Markievicz. Naturally, there was an outpouring of sympathy for the condemned men, and the publicity surrounding each individual increased this powerful emotion. The terminally ill Plunkett was married to Grace Gifford on the eve of his execution, while the gravely wounded Connolly had to be strapped to a chair so that he could face his executioners. The military authorities were also unnecessarily prickly in their relations with the Catholic clergy who administered Holy Communion to the condemned men. The publicity surrounding these events increased public fascination with the stoicism of those who had nobly faced the firing squad. Almost immediately a cult of the dead leaders developed. Requiem masses drew large congregations, and these were usually followed by sombre processions through the Dublin streets. The executed men had become martyrs who took their place in the Tone–Emmet tradition.

These developments created new difficulties for the IPP. The first to appreciate the seriousness of the situation was John Dillon, the party's deputy leader, who had been present in Dublin during the period of the rising. As his biographer states, Dillon had identified the real threat of "how to prevent the reaction in favour of the revolutionaries from becoming a reaction against the parliamentarians". Redmond, who had been in London, pleaded that the authorities should show restraint in the aftermath of the rebellion, though he was outraged by the actions of the insurgents. Dillon, by contrast, directed his full fury at the government in a famous speech that he delivered in the House of Commons on 11 May 1916, denouncing the secret trials and demanding a halt to the executions. He closed his emotional address by providing a moral endorsement for the insurgents who had "fought a clean fight, a brave fight, however misguided, and it would have been a damned good thing for you if your soldiers were able to put up as good a fight as did these men in Dublin". Dillon was desperately seeking to shore up support for the IPP but, in spite of his appeal, the final two executions went ahead

Hanna Sheehy–Skeffington, widow of Francis Sheehy–Skeffington (1878–1916).

as scheduled on the following day. On the night of 11 May, Asquith crossed to Dublin and spent a week in the country trying to gauge opinion. It was only at this point that his government urged caution on the military authorities. Maxwell, who had been given discretion in individual cases, took a narrow view of the rising, seeing it as a German-inspired plot that was designed to deflect British attention at a critical moment in the war. The authorities were still in the dark about the IRB conspiracy at the centre of the Easter Rising.

Dillon had also used his Commons speech to expose an atrocity that had occurred in Portobello Barracks, where three detainees were summarily shot on the orders of Captain J. C. Bowen-Colthurst. Thomas Dickson and Patrick MacIntyre, both journalists, and Francis Sheehy-Skeffington, the leading pacifist, had been arrested previously and were shot by firing squad without any kind of trial. Bowen-Colthurst was subsequently deemed to be insane, but Dillon shocked the House with his exposé of the murders, and the case was covered extensively in the English press. Maxwell's decisions were being increasingly called into question, and the spirits of the separatists were raised in Ireland when the Bishop of Limerick, Dr Edward O'Dwyer, attacked Maxwell's reaction to the rising, describing it as one of "the blackest chapters in the history of the misgovernment of this country". Writing to Maxwell, O'Dwyer, who regarded the insurrectionists as "poor young fellows", informed the general that his action had "outraged the conscience of the country". O'Dwyer had been a consistent critic of Redmond's wartime support for Britain, but his willingness to condone the rising further distanced the cleric from other members of the hierarchy. Attention now shifted to London where Casement was tried for high treason at the end of June. One of the most prominent political figures involved in the prewar resistance to Home Rule, F. E. Smith, was now attorney general, and he led the prosecution, an irony that was not lost on Irish Nationalist observers.

It was no surprise when Casement was found guilty, and he was hanged in Pentonville Jail on 3 August. A campaign to earn a reprieve was unsuccessful, even though Casement had come to Ireland in an effort to prevent a rising. His execution, however, proved to be a significant blunder. It further inflamed opinion in Ireland and had a negative effect in the United States at a moment when the British government was desperate to persuade the Americans to enter the war.

In Dublin, meanwhile, Asquith was keen to smooth the return to civil government. A new chief secretary, H. E. Duke, was appointed on 31 July, but Maxwell continued to dominate the administration. The government hoped to restore calm across the country to allow it to focus on the war, but Maxwell's presence ensured that anti-British feeling remained high. Moreover, the continued detention of prisoners in jails and internment camps and the retention of martial law with its consequent arrests, house-searches and curfews needlessly infuriated Irish opinion. While the authorities at Westminster measured their response to the rising in the context of a war in which they had executed 350 of their own troops on the Western Front for alleged cowardice, this was never considered in Nationalist Ireland. The British may have viewed the 16 executions of key figures in a German-backed rising as entirely justified, but their action was seen by Nationalists throughout the country as vengeful and vindictive. Indeed, bitterness engendered by the executions, the mass arrests and the imposition of martial law suggests that a powerful, if latent, feeling of antipathy towards the British government was already present in Ireland. This changing mood in the wake of the Easter Rising provided a timely boost for the separatists and a huge challenge for Redmond and the representatives of constitutional Nationalism.

The 1916 Lloyd George negotiations

Asquith returned from his fact-finding visit on 18 May and resolved that his government should make a fresh attempt to reach a political settlement in Ireland. He turned to Lloyd George to conduct the negotiations, even suggesting that he should take the post of chief secretary, as the Welshman had an intricate understanding of Home Rule politics. After some hesitation, Lloyd George accepted the challenge, though not the chief secretaryship, and opened the talks process on 23 May. The government recognised that an agreement would not only bolster constitutional Nationalism, which was coming under increasing pressure from the separatists, but also placate American opinion. The British ambassador in Washington, Sir Cecil Spring-Rice, was warning London that the executions had shaken the American public and, with a presidential election due later that year, his fear was that Irish-American voters might force a new administration to take a more pro-German stance. In opening the discussions Lloyd George, mindful of the failure of the Buckingham Palace Conference, negotiated separately with the leaders of Unionism and Nationalism. He began by warning Carson, who had resigned from the coalition government in the previous October, that the twenty-six counties would be granted immediate Home Rule but that the remaining six would be excluded. On 29 May, in a letter to the Unionist leader, he confirmed that the exclusion of Antrim, Down, Londonderry, Armagh, Tyrone and Fermanagh would be permanent.

In dealing with Redmond, Lloyd George highlighted the attraction of immediate Home Rule for the twenty-six counties, adding that the exclusion of the remaining six would be temporary. The negotiations exposed old tensions within the IPP. Redmond and Dillon had differed in their response to the rising, and the deputy leader wanted his party to step back from such risky negotiations and resume open and active opposition at Westminster. Yet he was persuaded to shelve his doubts, as Redmond staked his political future on a successful outcome to the Lloyd George negotiations. Lloyd George had secured agreement on the area of Ulster to be excluded from Home Rule, but the uncertainty over the time limit continued to create problems. He did manage, for a brief period, to persuade both groups that their objectives could be realised. When he produced his draft proposals, they were ambiguous on the question of a time limit, as Lloyd George hoped to leave a final decision on temporary or permanent partition to a postwar imperial conference. It was against this backdrop that Carson and Redmond sought to sell the peace initiative to their respective supporters. First up was Carson, who addressed a private gathering of the Ulster Unionist Council (UUC) on 6 June. The Unionist leader, who was fully aware of the American angle, gave his backing to the proposals, arguing that the rejection of the six-county partition would result in serious damage to the Unionist cause in Britain. He was savagely attacked by Unionist delegates from Cavan, Monaghan and Donegal, who reminded the meeting that they had signed the Covenant and were now being sacrificed by the leadership. These "border" Unionists only relented following a private meeting with Carson. When the UUC reconvened on 12 June, Carson received the unanimous, albeit reluctant from certain quarters, backing to continue the negotiations based on the exclusion of the six counties.

Redmond faced a more difficult task in delivering Nationalist support for the Lloyd George deal. His main problem was in securing northern Nationalist support for the six-county partition proposal. A number of Ulster bishops had already voiced their opposition to any form of partition and Nationalists in Tyrone and Fermanagh had reacted with predictable fury to news of the Lloyd

George proposals. Redmond had to lean on Joe Devlin and another northern Nationalist, Jeremiah MacVeagh, the MP for South Down, when the issue was settled at a special conference that met in St Mary's Hall in Belfast on 23 June. Redmond struggled to control the rival factions during a bitter five-hour debate in which Dillon was almost shouted down. In his address, the IPP leader warned that rejection of the Lloyd George scheme would ultimately destroy the party. It took an impassioned appeal by Devlin to carry the conference, which voted by 475 to 265 in favour of the exclusion proposals. The Belfast Nationalist insisted that exclusion would be temporary and, while the twenty-six-county area would have its own parliament, the excluded area would continue under the control of the Westminster parliament. Devlin's intervention had secured a majority of Nationalist delegates, but it was evident that the partition scheme caused deep resentment. Ulster Nationalism was divided, as representatives from Tyrone, Fermanagh and Derry city were overwhelmingly opposed to the Lloyd George initiative. The split resulted in the formation of the Irish Nation League following a meeting of anti-Redmondites in Omagh on 5 August 1916. The new movement was unequivocal in its rejection of partition, and it immediately attracted support from the Catholic clergy in west Ulster. Although the Irish Nation League could not establish itself as a genuine rival to the IPP and was subsequently swallowed up by Sinn Féin, it did provide a focus for opposition to Redmondism at a critical juncture and certainly helped to undermine the IPP in Ulster.

Redmond had staked his political future on the successful implementation of the Lloyd George plan, but his gamble failed following fierce opposition from an unexpected quarter. Lloyd George's handling of the negotiations had raised concerns among a number of the Conservative members in Asquith's coalition government. In particular, Walter Long and Lord Lansdowne, two cabinet ministers with very strong southern Unionist connections, were angry that Lloyd George had exceeded his brief by offering Redmond immediate Home Rule for the twenty-six-county area. Disagreement on the peace plan first surfaced at a cabinet committee meeting on 1 June, which was attended by Asquith, Lloyd George and Lord Crewe, who joined Long and Lansdowne. Long maintained that the full cabinet had never endorsed any proposal that would confer immediate Home Rule on the south and west, while Lloyd George countered by claiming that political progress in Ireland was essential to retain current American support for the war effort. As the minister of munitions, Lloyd George fully appreciated the importance of wartime supplies shipped across the Atlantic, but the argument failed to impress the cabinet's two guardians of southern Unionism. In fact, southern Unionists had been alarmed by the government's commitment to a fresh political settlement, viewing it as a reward for the Easter insurgents. Their chief spokesman, Lord Midleton, had raised their concerns in a meeting with

Lloyd George on 29 May. At the meeting Lloyd George hoped to appeal to the patriotism of the southern Unionists and to assuage their fears by emphasising that a new Home Rule government for the twenty-six counties would be of a "purely provisional character". Moreover, it would be reviewed at the end of the war. He also sought to soften the blow by promising the southern Unionists additional representation and influence in a new Home Rule parliament. Midleton, however, remained cautious, correctly assuming that Lloyd George had gone further in his negotiations with both Redmond and Carson. The southern Unionist leader was also perturbed by the sudden rise of more militant Nationalism in the wake of the rising, but his greatest fear was the implementation of a partitionist settlement. By 1916 southern Unionists viewed partition as a much greater concern than Home Rule. Partition would leave them as a tiny minority in a potentially hostile state, and the southern Unionists were intent on deploying their considerable influence at Westminster to obstruct any immediate Home Rule settlement based on partition.

In spite of Midleton's prompting, Long and Lansdowne were slow to appreciate the impending threat to southern Unionists. This was, in part, due to Lloyd George's strategy for circumventing potential opposition in cabinet. His objective was to keep the cabinet in the dark through the early stages of the negotiations and then force through acceptance of immediate Home Rule once he had reached agreement with the two Irish parties. While he expected opposition from Long and Lansdowne, it was not until his plan was made public on 10 June that the two launched a sustained attack on the proposals. Long had already been stung by criticism from some of his old Irish colleagues, and he was attacked in the press by the right-wing *Morning Post* for betraying the trust of the southern Unionists in accepting the Lloyd George plan. In a letter to Lloyd George on 11 June, Long admitted that he had been slow to spot the dangers inherent in the proposals and warned that he would not support any agreement based on the adoption of Home Rule. Subsequent correspondence with Lloyd George and other members of the cabinet reiterated his contention that Lloyd George had not been authorised to offer immediate Home Rule. Long's position was made more difficult by the discovery that the Conservatives in the government were divided on the Lloyd George scheme. Long and Lansdowne were the principal opponents of the initiative, and they were supported by Lord Selborne and Lord Robert Cecil, but Bonar Law, Balfour and F. E. Smith each supported the plan. Austen Chamberlain, meanwhile, sat on the fence, though he was critical of Lloyd George's rather cavalier approach when the issue was discussed in cabinet on 21 June. What had become clear to the prime minister was that the Lloyd George scheme might lead to the resignation of a number of Conservative ministers, a development that would have had grave consequences for his coalition government.

In preparation for the next cabinet meeting on 27 June, Long and Lansdowne prepared memoranda that forcefully laid out their objections. The most serious of these was the allegation that the proposals were a breach of the party truce that had been in place since the outbreak of war. They also claimed that responsibility for the general state of affairs in Ireland, and the rising in particular, rested with the hopelessly compliant Birrell-led Castle administration. Both Long and Lansdowne seriously contemplated resignation, a course taken by Selborne, their principal supporter in the cabinet, on the day prior to the crucial meeting. When the cabinet convened on 27 June, Long and Lansdowne maintained their outright opposition to the Lloyd George scheme. Their concerns, however, were dismissed by Balfour who urged his colleagues to seize a "unique opportunity" to resolve "peaceably and permanently the problem of Ulster". Balfour's analysis was endorsed by Bonar Law, as the pair warned that the rejection of immediate Home Rule would boost radical Nationalism at the expense of the IPP. Bonar Law also reminded his colleagues that the permanent exclusion of a six-county "Ulster" had been the extent of Carson's demand at the Buckingham Palace Conference. At this point Asquith, urged on by Lloyd George, decided to forge ahead with the partition scheme. He was confident that Conservative fears could be allayed through the establishment of a new cabinet committee that would ensure the maintenance of law and order in southern Ireland for the duration of the war and impose additional safeguards to the Home Rule settlement. Lansdowne backed the committee idea, and it appeared that Long, the main obstacle to a settlement, could now be isolated. On 5 July Asquith informed the cabinet that Redmond had agreed to the new condition. In the discussion that ensued, Long and Lansdowne articulated their reservations, but each indicated that they would not resign and risk collapsing the government. The southern Unionists, meanwhile, were determined to block the proposals, and they sought to persuade Tory parliamentarians, especially in the House of Lords, to oppose the initiative. Although Bonar Law had indicated his support, a meeting at the Carlton Club on 7 July highlighted the party's fears about the immediate implementation of Home Rule. The situation became more strained when Asquith informed the House of Commons of the recent developments on the Irish question. In his speech the prime minister appeared to suggest that the partition arrangement would be temporary. On the following day Lansdowne was eager to clarify the situation in a speech to the House of Lords. He stated unequivocally that the new arrangement would be permanent and caused a sensation by suggesting that the government would consider extending the emergency powers granted to General Maxwell to maintain the rule of law in the twenty-six-county area.

A furious Redmond viewed Lansdowne's speech as "a gross insult to Ireland", adding that Nationalists would never consider partition unless they had a cast-iron guarantee that it would be temporary. The change in tone about Lloyd George's handling of the negotiations now convinced Long, Lansdowne and Midleton that the government would be taking a major gamble if it persevered with such a controversial measure. When the cabinet next discussed the issue on 19 July, Long and Lansdowne were unwilling to compromise, as they intended to thwart the scheme. Each reflected southern Unionist fears, but they were confident that if they could persuade their colleagues to make permanent the exclusion of the six northern counties, then Redmond was certain to walk away from the negotiations. This is what transpired. Redmond angrily rejected the notion of permanent partition, and the negotiations collapsed amid bitter recriminations. The decisive factor had been the role played by Long and Lansdowne who, encouraged by their southern Unionist friends, had successfully exploited the fears of a Conservative party that was uneasy about the prospect of Home Rule so soon after the Easter Rising. For his part, Asquith recognised that Tory support was essential for the success of any new political settlement in Ireland. To have forced the issue risked the fall of the wartime coalition government.

In Ireland the collapse of the 1916 negotiations proved to be a disastrous blow for the IPP. In his desperation to deliver Home Rule and shore up support for constitutional Nationalism, Redmond had gambled by agreeing to new demands on the partition issue. The failure of the negotiations and, more particularly, the manner in which they had collapsed, appeared to confirm that Redmond had been outmanoeuvred by Carson and betrayed, once again, by the British government. Clearly, the IPP leader did not command the same influence as he had in 1914. Moreover, the failure of the Lloyd George plan prompted Nationalists to re-evaluate the wisdom of Redmond's enthusiastic support for the war. The Woodenbridge commitment, so popular at the time, was now viewed as a serious misjudgement, and there was a growing fear among Nationalists that the Westminster government could extend conscription to Ireland, as it tried to balance the appalling losses on the Western Front. This was the case after the disastrous opening day of the Battle of the Somme on 1 July 1916, when the British Army suffered a total of 60,000 casualties, 21,000 of whom died. Significantly, the 36th (Ulster) Division had been involved in some of the heaviest fighting that day, leaving 2,000 of its men dead and a further 3,000 wounded. Unionist propaganda was quick to contrast their blood sacrifice in the service of the king and the Empire with the treachery of the German-backed Easter rebels. One consequence of this publicity drive was a hardening of opinion in Britain in response to Irish Nationalist demands.

Sinn Féin gains momentum

The impact of both the rising and the collapse of the Lloyd George negotiations had placed the IPP in a perilous position. However, it was not yet clear how the radical opponents of constitutional Nationalism would take advantage of their good fortune. These various groupings clearly lacked cohesion, but, ironically, it was the government's incorrect labelling of the rising as a "Sinn Féin rebellion" that helped to pull the disparate factions together under the Sinn Féin banner. Still, this was not a straightforward, nor indeed a rapid, process. This was illustrated by the outcome of the West Cork by-election in November 1916. The seat had been won previously by Lawrence Gilhooly, a follower of William O'Brien's All-for-Ireland League. Significantly, Sinn Féin was unable to field a candidate, and the contest saw a three-cornered fight between D. L. O'Leary, the IPP candidate, Frank Healy, the O'Brienite, and an independent Nationalist, Dr Shipsey, who put his name forward in protest at Healy's nomination, which had not been the result of the normal selection procedure. In the campaign, the IPP was fiercely criticised for its concessions during the Lloyd George negotiations, while Healy described Redmond's parliamentary followers as "traitors". When the votes were counted, O'Leary emerged triumphant with a majority of 116 over Healy. A bitter O'Brien complained that the intervention of the independent candidate, who polled 370 votes, had cost the All-for-Ireland League the seat. While there was clear justification for this claim, O'Leary's vote proved that the IPP was not finished. Although Sinn Féin did not enter the contest, newspaper reports were adamant that O'Brien had specifically selected Healy to attract the separatist vote in West Cork. Indeed, O'Brien had earlier dismissed the IPP as a political force, suggesting that the Irish people would have to turn to Sinn Féin for leadership. Yet the 1,866 votes garnered by O'Leary demonstrated the strong party loyalty that might sustain the IPP in spite of all its difficulties. There was an interesting footnote to the West Cork by-election. On the eve of the poll Tomás MacCurtain, the commandant of the Cork Volunteers, who was interned in Reading Jail, informed the president of the "Sinn Féiners" in Cork that Healy did not represent their views. The Cork prisoners reinforced this contention by taking out an advertisement in a local newspaper, claiming "neither Mr Healy nor any of the other candidates for Parliament in West Cork represent the views of either the interned prisoners or Sinn Féin". Though the turnout was over 70 per cent, it was possible that Healy's narrow defeat was due to Sinn Féin abstentions. It was also instructive to note that the interned prisoners claimed to speak for Sinn Féin.

While the public mood had been transformed in 1916, radical Nationalists were slow to see the opportunity and organise a separatist political movement using the Sinn Féin label. This would change following the release of a large number of internees from Frongoch and Reading in December 1916. Lloyd George had just replaced Asquith as prime minister and, still with an eye on American opinion, one of his first acts was to sanction the prisoner releases in time for Christmas. Previously, most of the Sinn Féin activists had been low-ranking Volunteers, but the December releases provided the movement with new leadership material. An early opportunity to test Sinn Féin's potential occurred when the North Roscommon seat fell vacant early in 1917. The vacancy was created by the death of the veteran Parnellite, J. J. O'Kelly. Separatist feeling ran high in the constituency, and local Sinn Féiners, under the direction of the radical priest, Father Michael O'Flanagan, were determined to challenge the IPP. Having been turned down by Michael Davitt Junior, they turned to Count George Noble Plunkett, the father of the executed 1916 leader. Although Plunkett stood as an independent, voters in North Roscommon were left in no doubt that he represented Sinn Féin. Undoubtedly, his connection with the rising was an electoral asset, though he did not arrive in the constituency until two days before the poll. While the campaign conducted on his behalf may have been amateurish, it was noteworthy for the enthusiasm generated by youthful Volunteer activists. The election took place on 3 February 1917, and Plunkett secured 3,077 votes to the IPP candidate's 1,708 votes. Plunkett attracted votes from a collection of groups, including the old Sinn Féin movement, the Irish Nation League and the Volunteers. Indeed, the Volunteers had made a significant contribution to Sinn Féin's success. Some of the men released before Christmas had journeyed to the constituency and they brought energy and dynamism to the campaign. This number included Michael Collins. The contest was marked by the image of elderly voters being carried to polling booths through deep snow on the shoulders of young Volunteers. Another notable feature was the involvement of the younger clergy who had been mobilised by O'Flanagan to gather support for Plunkett. O'Flanagan ran a largely negative campaign that targeted the IPP, though he stressed that Plunkett would seek Irish freedom at a postwar peace conference, when Ireland would join smaller countries such as Serbia, Czechoslovakia and Romania in pressing the case for independence.

Sinn Féin's triumph in North Roscommon set the movement on its way to a landslide victory in the postwar election. Before the by-election the different separatist elements such as the old Sinn Féin, the Gaelic League, the Volunteers, Cumann na mBan and the IRB were without a clear strategy. Soon after the by-election victory, however, leading figures in the separatist movement, including some of the recently released prisoners, came together in an attempt to secure greater cooperation. These included Volunteers, many of whom were suspicious of politicians but recognised that politics represented the best way forward in 1917. They had also gained valuable experience in the art of electioneering.

The result was the emergence of a new movement that used the existing Sinn Féin organisation. It grew rapidly but was hampered by divisions between its two leading personalities, Count Plunkett and Arthur Griffith. Plunkett was not content to play the figurehead role envisaged by Griffith and sought to dominate the emerging movement. He was dogmatic and soon quarrelled unnecessarily with the Irish Nation League, one of the groups that had contributed to his by-election success.

When Plunkett called a convention in April 1917, he chose not to invite the Irish Nation League, dismissing the group as being too moderate. He also wanted to sideline the old Sinn Féin movement, and this drew him into conflict with the formidable Griffith. At the April convention in Dublin's Mansion House, the cantankerous Plunkett announced the formation of the Liberty League, an entirely new organisation committed to full independence. However, Griffith refused the Liberty League's demand to take over the existing Sinn Féin clubs. For a brief period in the early summer of 1917, Liberty clubs and Sinn Féin clubs fought for supremacy at parish level, but this was an unequal struggle from which Sinn Féin soon emerged as the clear winner. The Liberty clubs were swallowed up by the Sinn Féin movement, a fate that would also befall the Irish Nation League. Plunkett continued as a Sinn Féin representative, but he was no longer in the movement's front rank. Sinn Féin had, of course, the advantage of an existing organisational network, an efficient central office and two influential newspapers. It also possessed the magic of the Sinn Féin name towards which separatists naturally gravitated. The movement now grew rapidly at local level. In July it registered 11,000 members, a figure that would double within a month. By October 1917 Sinn Féin could claim to have over 200,000 members spread across its 1,200 clubs. This represented a club in nearly every parish in Ireland, the result of spontaneous local initiative as Irish separatism became the new political doctrine.

The ambition to achieve electoral success was a key factor in drawing the disparate separatist elements closer together. A second opportunity to demonstrate its ascendancy over the IPP was presented in May 1917, when a by-election took place in South Longford. For this contest Sinn Féin nominated a prisoner, Joe McGuinness, who was being held in Lewes Jail in the south of England. While this illustrated the importance of the Volunteers in the separatist movement, it prompted a reaction from the prisoners in Lewes who were among the most senior figures in the Volunteers. They frequently viewed parliamentary politics with contempt but, in spite of their objection, local Sinn Féin organisers began to canvas for McGuinness. Again, Collins was active in a campaign that used a poster carrying the slogan, "Put him in to get him out", combining the election campaign with the demand for the release of the remaining prisoners. Although

McGuinness was a local man, the contest on 9 May 1917 was very close, with Sinn Féin winning by 37 votes following a recount. Dillon had taken personal charge of the IPP campaign, and he ensured that every effort was made to retain the seat. His campaign was undermined by the actions of the Westminster government, which had ordered the arrest of prominent Sinn Féin leaders following the North Roscommon contest. In a memorable Commons' speech on 26 February, Dillon attacked Lloyd George, accusing him of "manufacturing Sinn Féiners by tens of thousands" and, in the process, destroying constitutional Nationalism. Dillon shared none of Redmond's complacency, as he recognised that the South Longford contest was pivotal to the party's future. From the constituency he wrote to Redmond with a warning about the party's predicament, "We have the Bishop, the great majority of the priests, and the mob and four-fifths of the traders of Longford. And if in the face of that we are beaten, I do not see how you can hope to hold the party in existence." Unfortunately for Dillon, his efforts were scuppered by a late intervention by Dr William Walsh, the Archbishop of Dublin. On the day before polling, he issued a statement in the *Irish Independent* which, though it did not specifically endorse McGuinness's candidature, bitterly attacked the IPP for its concessions on Ulster. It was abundantly clear where the cleric's sympathies lay, and this must have influenced a significant number of voters.

Sinn Féin were fortunate to take the South Longford seat. The IPP candidate had been declared the winner after the first count, but a bundle of uncounted votes was subsequently discovered, giving McGuinness his narrow victory. There were also allegations of vote rigging that may well have affected the outcome. Of course, South Longford was crucial, as it maintained momentum for the rapidly expanding Sinn Féin movement. As with the previous victory, the Volunteers had played a key role, highlighting the generational gap that had recently developed in Irish politics. In South Longford it was evident that the majority of the younger clergy supported Sinn Féin, and this reflected a more general trend in which younger voters were attracted by the energy and dynamism of the party's electoral machine. After the South Longford victory, Sinn Féin received a further boost with the release of the Lewes prisoners. They were greeted by an ecstatic Dublin crowd on their return on 18 June 1917. These were the senior surviving figures who had fought in the Easter Rising, and their number included Thomas Ashe and Éamon de Valera. Both must have been surprised at the contrast with the reception to which they had been subjected only a year earlier. While a number of the prisoners remained sceptical about political involvement, it was clear that Sinn Féin's growing stature offered an alternative to exclusively physical force in the struggle for Irish freedom. Another chance to test this strategy appeared soon after the prisoners' release. Willie Redmond's death on the Western Front at the Battle of Messines on 7 June had created a vacancy in East Clare. De Valera was selected as the Sinn Féin candidate, and he emphasised his leading role in the Easter Rising during the campaign, canvassing in his Volunteer uniform. His opponent, Patrick Lynch, was a well-known figure in the constituency, but de Valera won the seat by 5,010 votes to 2,035. The scale of his victory shocked his own election team. The portrayal of de Valera as one of the Easter heroes, who would refuse to take his Westminster seat if elected, was popular with the voters. As before, the Sinn Féin campaign focused on the IPP's shortcomings, though it did sound a positive note in its demand for Irish representation at the postwar peace conference.

A new slogan, "self-determination" was widely used, and it featured prominently in another by-election when W. T. Cosgrave romped home in a straight fight with the IPP to take the Kilkenny seat in August. That same month the British authorities drove another nail in the IPP's coffin when they introduced a new wave of oppression. Among those detained for making seditious speeches was Thomas Ashe, the Volunteer leader of the successful attacks in County Meath during the rising. In prison Ashe demanded to be categorised as a "political prisoner" and, when this was refused, he began a hunger strike, using the tactic that had been deployed by the suffragettes. In order to keep such prisoners alive, the authorities in Mountjoy Prison authorised forcible feeding, a painful process during which liquid food was pumped into a prisoner's stomach though a long rubber tube that was inserted through either the mouth or the nostrils. After one of these experiences Ashe was taken ill, and he died on 25 September 1917. The Sinn Féin movement now had another martyr, and Ashe's funeral in Dublin was attended by an estimated 40,000 mourners. Michael Collins had made the necessary arrangements and gave the graveside oration, after which Volunteers fired a volley of shots over the coffin in Glasnevin cemetery. Ashe's funeral released a new outburst of popular feeling that threatened to overwhelm the IPP. Sinn Féin had successfully exploited the IPP's catalogue of failures since the outbreak of war. Yet this had taken time, and the new political landscape only began to take shape following the release of the middle-ranking prisoners being held in Frongoch and Reading. Internal disagreement and Plunkett's attempt to create a new separatist organisation delayed this political transformation, but Griffith's temporary stewardship and the spectacular growth of Sinn Féin at grass-roots level produced a dynamic national movement that can be described as a broadly-based popular front. It was at this point that de Valera emerged as leader of this impressive umbrella movement. Tension, however, remained between the various coalition groups that constituted Sinn Féin, and some of these factions, such as the Volunteers and the IRB, succeeded in retaining their separate identities. Still, the four successive by-election victories and Sinn Féin's spontaneous expansion at parish level masked many of the problems facing the new party. However, the Volunteers were determined to assert their authority at a planned Volunteer

The funeral of hunger-striker Thomas Ashe (1885–1917), at Glasnevin. The hatless figure in uniform (above the Celtic cross) is Michael Collins. The four hatless men to the right of the earth mound are Ashe's brothers.

convention. The principal Volunteer leaders were de Valera, Ashe, Collins, Cathal Brugha, Diarmuid O'Hegarty and Diarmuid Lynch, and they decided to hold the convention at the same time as the Sinn Féin convention in October. Before this took place, a number of Volunteer commanders defied the authorities by organising drilling and political meetings, and it was one of these events that led to Ashe's arrest.

Ashe's death galvanised the Volunteer companies and increased the desire of their leaders to extend their influence within the Sinn Féin movement. This threatened the party's unity. There was also a feeling within the broader Sinn Féin movement that the party's aims should be more clearly defined. This appeared to signal a struggle between the political and military wings of the separatist movement, but it was essentially a clash between the republicans and the non-republicans that threatened to split Sinn Féin. Among the republican faction were de Valera, Collins, Brugha and Rory O'Connor, and they argued that Sinn Féin stood for the republic that had been proclaimed by the 1916 leaders. The key voice on the non-republican wing belonged to Arthur Griffith who continued to highlight the merits of the old Sinn Féin constitution, which was monarchist. Griffith and his supporters sought a powerful independent Irish parliament. They viewed a republic as unobtainable, warning that committing Sinn Féin to the goal of a republic was unnecessary and unrealistic. These differences threatened to spill over at the forthcoming convention, or Árd-Fheis, which convened in Dublin on 25 and 26 October. A few days before the meeting, however, the Sinn Féin Executive met to resolve some of the problems. One issue was settled when Griffith readily agreed to stand aside as Sinn Féin president, enabling de Valera to fill the position. This was reaffirmed at the Árd-Fheis, and Griffith became vice-president. Perhaps more significantly, a new Sinn Féin constitution was agreed following a number of executive meetings in the week before the Árd-Fheis. When a split on the wording appeared likely, de Valera produced a compromise formula that both moderates and extremists found acceptable. The crucial clauses stated, "Sinn Féin aims at securing the international recognition of Ireland as an independent Irish Republic. Having achieved that status, the Irish people may by referendum freely choose their own form of Government." Clearly, the new constitution leaned towards the republicans, but it left sufficient room to maintain unity among the respective elements of the separatist movement. De Valera hinted at this ambiguity in the course of his long address to Árd-Fheis delegates, when he claimed, "We are not doctrinaire Republicans", a phrase that his opponents would subsequently seize upon. Over 1,000 delegates had gathered for the convention, and the new president appreciated the importance of presenting a united front to the electorate.

The focus on unity continued on the day after the Árd-Fheis closed, when the Volunteer convention met secretly in Dublin. There was, of course, considerable overlap in membership, and the Volunteer delegates elected de Valera as president of the Volunteers. As president of both Sinn Féin and the Irish Volunteers, de Valera symbolised the unity of the reconstructed, broadly based separatist movement. More particularly, his dual role fused together the political and physical force elements, and this became a powerful feature of the struggle for independence. This tie-up drew attention to the movement's ambivalent attitude to the use of force. While the Volunteers clearly did not rule out the use of violence, others in the separatist movement favoured a return to the tactic of militant constitutionalism that had proved so effective in the Parnell era. De Valera was non-committal in discussing potential violence, but he made frequent reference to the use of "moral force" in his speeches. This carefully crafted ambivalence was politically astute for a party that was seeking the support of voters, many of whom had been steadfast supporters of Redmond's constitutional and parliamentary strategy. While a majority now rejected the IPP's attempts at compromise with both the Ulster Unionists and the Westminster authorities, few were prepared to support anything resembling a rerun of the 1916 rising. The spectacular rise of Sinn Féin over the course of 1917 suggested that the Irish people wanted freedom, though its precise constitutional form generated little interest. By the end of the year, moreover, Sinn Féin had a popular charismatic leader in de Valera. This gifted mathematician and former teacher and the senior surviving figure from the rising was viewed as the personification of the entire separatist movement.

The Irish Convention

A notable feature of de Valera's victorious campaign in East Clare in July 1917 had been Redmond's lack of engagement. While the loss of his brother was a factor, Redmond had, by this stage, turned his attention to the prospects for the Irish Convention, which was due to meet at the end of the month. While Lloyd George had given his full attention to the war effort since becoming prime minister in December 1916, the cabinet was ready to consider the formulation of a new Irish policy by the spring of the following year. In May 1917 the government offered a choice to the respective leaders of Unionism and Nationalism. They could have immediate Home Rule with the exclusion of six counties, or they could meet in a convention to produce an internal settlement, and the prime minister promised to give legislative effect to their recommendations, provided "substantial agreement" was achieved. Lloyd George was enthusiastic about the Irish Convention, as the principle behind it appealed to Irish-Americans, and the United States had entered the war on the Allied side in April 1917. The government knew that Redmond would be willing to participate in the Convention, but the attitude of the Ulster Unionists was less predictable. Following some hesitation, they too agreed to participate, but only after they had received an assurance that no party would be bound by the Convention's decisions.

When the UUC discussed the issue on 8 June, Carson's attitude was crucial. He argued in favour of participation in order to secure Ulster's position and to fight for safeguards to protect their southern Unionist brethren. The southern Unionists had already agreed to take part provided they received adequate representation. Midleton had convinced his colleagues on the Irish Unionist Alliance (IUA), when they met on 1 June, that they had more to gain than lose by participating in the Convention. Indeed, Midleton and his closest associates believed that a radical shift in their approach was essential, and they had been moving in a new direction since the outbreak of the war. The "Midletonites" had reconciled themselves to the fact that some form of Irish self-government was inevitable. Consequently, they needed to secure the best outcome for southern Unionists. The way to achieve this was to establish common ground with Redmond and constitutional Nationalism. Such a course of action might produce a workable settlement that appealed to southern Unionism while, simultaneously, undermining Sinn Féin and the brand of militant Nationalism that southern

Unionists viewed as a serious threat. However, not all southern Unionists were prepared to back such a new departure, and there remained a significant group that was opposed to any tampering with the Union.

The 95 members of the Irish Convention held their first meeting at Trinity College, Dublin on 25 July 1917. In addition to the 52 Nationalists, there were 26 Ulster Unionists, 9 southern Unionists, 6 Labour representatives and 2 others. Horace Plunkett, the ex-Unionist MP who had more recently drifted into the ranks of constitutional Nationalism, was elected as chairman. Nationalists dominated proceedings, and in Redmond and Devlin they had two impressive leaders. Midleton was the chief spokesman for the southern Unionist group, while the prominent businessmen, Hugh Barrie and George Clark, led the Ulster representatives. A major drawback was the non-attendance of Sinn Féin. The party had dismissed the Convention as irrelevant. From the outset the absence of Sinn Féin and the reluctance of the Ulster Unionists to play a full and constructive part in the proceedings proved to be major obstacles for the Convention. It was also clear that there was a lack of trust between both groups of Unionists. This had been apparent since 1913, when the Ulster Unionists had acted in their own interests during the Home Rule struggle. By 1917 they were firmly partitionist, and this created tension with the Midletonite representatives who, by this stage, feared partition much more than Home Rule. During the Convention's early proceedings, it was evident that the southern Unionists and IPP representatives were more natural allies. Redmond's obvious loyalty to the Empire and commitment to the war had impressed these southern Unionists, but they were also motivated by the fear that any southern parliament would be dominated by Sinn Féin.

Prior to the Convention, Midleton intended to play the role of a mediator, bringing together the Nationalists and Ulster Unionists, but this never materialised. Instead, Ulster Unionists were furious at the level of cooperation between Nationalists and southern Unionists whose constructive approach generated considerable goodwill. An indication of this was given in November, when there was a serious difference of opinion on the contentious issue of fiscal control. Nationalists insisted that fiscal control had to be transferred to a new Dublin parliament, while the Ulster Unionists were adamant that Westminster should retain control over fiscal matters. With an impasse developing, Midleton produced a compromise, proposing that Dublin should be given control of internal taxation while Westminster retained its powers over customs duties. This had been a key sticking point, but Redmond and the more moderate Nationalists appeared willing to accept the Midleton formula. Thus, by December, there were good grounds for believing that a settlement was within reach.

From the beginning of 1918, however, the Irish Convention faced growing headwinds. The split between the two Unionist groups became more pronounced, and divisions emerged among the constitutional Nationalists. Many of the IPP representatives were uncomfortable with Midleton's fiscal compromise and did not want to surrender control of customs duties to the imperial parliament. Still, Midleton sensed that there was an opportunity for a settlement. In early January he travelled to London to meet the prime minister. Lloyd George assured him that if the fiscal compromise scheme attracted widespread support in the Convention, with only the Ulster Unionists dissenting, then the government would give it legislative effect. The ball was now in Redmond's court. His choice was either to hold out for fiscal autonomy or to side with the southern Unionists and abandon an Irish parliament's right to levy its own customs duties. Having gone this far down the conciliation road, Redmond favoured making one final concession in an attempt to reach a settlement, even though he surely harboured doubts about Lloyd George's guarantee to give such an agreement government support.

On 4 January Redmond indicated his willingness to take this final risk when he addressed the Convention. He highlighted the sacrifices Nationalists were willing to make and contrasted this with the negative approach taken by the Ulster Unionists. Unfortunately, Redmond took ill and withdrew to County Wicklow for ten days. During this time he had no contact with party colleagues. When he returned to Dublin for the crucial Convention debate on 15 January, Redmond learned that two of his most trusted colleagues, Devlin and Bishop O'Donnell, had decided to oppose the Midleton compromise. Both had been in consultation with Dillon, who regarded the surrender of fiscal autonomy as one concession too far. All three, moreover, felt that such a move would leave the IPP at the mercy of a ruthless Sinn Féin movement keen to exploit further concessions by the constitutionalists. When Redmond discovered that Devlin, O'Donnell and the other bishop representatives had swung against him, he withdrew his support for the compromise. Redmond was humiliated, and he quickly informed the Convention that he felt he could no longer be of service. The failure to support the Midleton initiative ensured the Convention's failure.

Thereafter, the debates became more heated and the parties more intransigent. Lloyd George tried a number of manoeuvres to break the deadlock, but there was no resolution of the key problems – Ulster and fiscal control. With no agreement, three conflicting reports were eventually submitted in April 1918. The majority report, endorsed by 44 to 29 votes, was backed by the southern Unionists and more moderate Nationalists. Of the 29 delegates who opposed the compromise, 18 were Ulster Unionists and 11 were Nationalists. Each of these groups submitted their own minority reports. The more advanced Nationalists recommended fiscal autonomy for Ireland, while the Ulster Unionists restated their demand for exclusion.

Whereas the Ulster Unionists refused to consider change, Midleton's progressive approach put a strain on southern Unionist unity. Outside the Convention, opposition to Midleton was beginning to organise. On 20 February a group of irreconcilable southern Unionists met in Dublin's Shelbourne Hotel, where they concluded that Midleton's acceptance of self-government was a grave error. Together they formed the southern Unionist Committee, and they issued a celebrated "Call" in the press on 4 March, calling on all Unionists to confirm their conviction that Ireland's only hope rested in the maintenance of the Union. The "Callers" sought to persuade the Irish Unionist Alliance's executive committee to block Midleton's Convention policy. They failed in their attempt but subsequently took control of the IUA, leading to a split with the Midletonites. During the Convention, southern Unionists, principally Midleton and Dr John Henry Bernard, the Church of Ireland Archbishop of Dublin, often influenced proceedings with their pragmatic and liberal approach. Redmond's war record had diluted their concerns about Irish Nationalism and, while the Easter Rising had temporarily shaken southern Unionists, the rise of Sinn Féin convinced many that some form of self-government was inevitable.

In these circumstances Midleton sought cooperation with moderate Nationalism, and the Irish Convention provided the stage to test this new strategy. As the 1916 Lloyd George negotiations had confirmed, southern Unionists feared partition more than Home Rule. The desire to reach accommodation with the IPP on the political framework for a new Ireland opened up divisions in southern Unionist ranks that accelerated their decline. Their predicament was not helped by Ulster Unionist interference, as the northerners urged them to stand firm on the defence of the Union before abandoning them to their fate in a Sinn Féin-dominated Irish Free State. Significantly, many of Midleton's supporters had considerable British interests, usually in land or business, and they were willing to work with Home Rule and seek to safeguard their influence in the new Ireland. If this did not work to their advantage, they could, of course, withdraw to the mainland. Their opponents, by contrast, were mostly Irish-based land and business owners who genuinely feared Home Rule and viewed the Union, and British security, as their only safeguard. Therefore, while the Convention appeared to highlight the continued influence of southern Unionism, it also marked a significant point in the movement's decline. Indeed, many southern Unionists viewed the Irish Convention as their last opportunity to shape a new political settlement.

Having personally experienced failures to negotiate an Irish settlement in 1914 and 1916, Lloyd George had backed the idea of a conference of Irishmen to agree on a new political framework. In truth, the Irish Convention stood little chance of success. The Ulster Unionists would not countenance any form of

Home Rule and they refused to play a fully constructive role in the discussions. In his desperate efforts to secure an agreement, Redmond was prepared to concede fiscal autonomy, but this put him at loggerheads with his closest colleagues in the constitutional Nationalist movement. Redmond had battled illness during the Convention's proceedings, and he died on 6 March 1918. Not only had he, once again, failed to deliver Home Rule, but the IPP had suffered further damage from its participation in the Convention. Sinn Féin denounced the Convention as a futile exercise and claimed that it was an arrangement made by Lloyd George and Redmond to mislead the Irish people. It was certain to benefit from the failure of the parties to produce workable proposals.

Sinn Féin triumphant

By dismissing Redmond's concession on fiscal autonomy, Dillon and Devlin sought to preserve the IPP for a final showdown with Sinn Féin. The IPP faced a powerful national movement with an extensive grass-roots presence and a coherent, if not very specific, political strategy. Yet this did not ensure an overwhelming victory for Sinn Féin in any postwar election. The IPP did not roll over, and it demonstrated signs of life with three successive by-election victories in the early part of 1918. The IPP enjoyed specific advantages in each of the contests, but the three defeats had a sobering effect on de Valera and temporarily halted the Sinn Féin bandwagon. Two of these by-elections took place in Ulster, where the IPP was still a force and could count on the electoral muscle of the Ancient Order of Hibernians (AOH). Both of the seats, South Armagh and East Tyrone, also lay within the archdiocese of Cardinal Michael Logue, the County Donegal-born cleric who was an outspoken critic of Sinn Féin. In the South Armagh by-election, the IPP's Patrick Donnelly defeated Dr Patrick McCartan by over 1,000 votes. The contest, with polling taking place on 1 February, was fiercely contested, and there were violent clashes between the Hibernians and Volunteers. A similar pattern played out in the East Tyrone seat, for which polling had taken place on 4 April. Seán Milroy, an old associate of Griffith's, won 1,222 votes, but the seat was taken by the IPP's T. J. S. Harbison, who won 1,802 votes. Both of these by-elections demonstrated that the IPP remained powerful in Ulster, where strong organisation at grass-roots level had always been essential to resist aggressive electoral challenges mounted by Unionists. Even though the younger clergy in both divisions sided with Sinn Féin, this appears to have been more than offset by Logue's support for the IPP. Moreover, the selection of Harbison as the candidate for East Tyrone was a shrewd move, as the Cookstown solicitor had voted against the Lloyd George partition proposals in June 1916. Indeed, for Catholic voters in Ulster whose main priority was partition, Sinn

Féin did not offer anything in advance of the IPP. If anything, the IPP's pledge to continue the fight against partition at Westminster proved more attractive than Sinn Féin's policy of abstention, which risked the partition argument being settled by default.

At this point de Valera's approach to Ulster was devoid of any subtlety. Campaigning in the South Armagh by-election, he had portrayed Ulster Unionists as "a rock in the road" that might have to be blasted out of Sinn Féin's path. Such physical force rhetoric failed to sway northern voters in sufficient numbers. The other by-election took place in Waterford on 22 March in the seat left vacant by Redmond's passing. His son, Captain William Redmond, took the seat by 1,264 to 764 votes in a straight fight with the Sinn Féiner. The family remained popular in a constituency that John Redmond had represented since 1891. In each of these three contests, particular circumstances worked to the IPP's advantage, but the victories offered the party some encouragement and, in the short term at least, shook the Sinn Féin movement. Any possibility of further progress, however, was shattered by the conscription crisis in April 1918. In response to the German offensive of March 1918, which had left the British Army short of manpower, the Lloyd George government looked to Ireland to produce the 150,000 troops that were urgently required. The Conservative and Unionist members of the cabinet demanded the immediate extension of conscription to Ireland in order to provide these desperately needed reinforcements. Lloyd George, with one eye on American opinion, hesitated momentarily. The authorities in Dublin had warned that huge numbers of troops would have to be sent to Ireland to enforce conscription, but Sir Henry Wilson, the army's chief of imperial general staff and a long-standing opponent of Irish Nationalism, insisted that the prime minister must take the initiative. Accordingly, he introduced the Military Service Bill on 10 April by Order in Council, a parliamentary procedure that curtailed debate. In an attempt to sweeten the pill, Lloyd George gave an undertaking that a Home Rule measure would precede any enrolment of Irish conscripts. The crisis that followed highlighted the Westminster government's extraordinary naivety and its catastrophic failure to empathise with Irish Nationalism.

By 16 April the bill had completed its parliamentary journey through the Commons. During the debate Dillon, who had replaced Redmond as IPP leader, warned the government that "All Ireland will rise against you" before leading his party from the House. Returning to Ireland, the IPP joined with Sinn Féin in launching an anti-conscription campaign. On 18 April a conference took place in the Mansion House at which all shades of Nationalist opinion were represented. The Mansion House Conference attracted Sinn Féin and IPP leaders. Labour representatives and William O'Brien, the leader of the All-for-Ireland League, were also present. All delegates supported an anti-conscription pledge that had been drafted by de Valera, promising "to resist conscription by the most effective means at our disposal". On the following Sunday the pledge was signed by huge numbers of Nationalists outside church doors in scenes reminiscent of Ulster on Covenant Day in 1912. Then, on 23 April, a one-day general strike was held that paralysed economic life everywhere in the country outside Belfast. Nationalist Ireland came together in opposition to conscription, but Sinn Féin drew most of the credit. Leading Sinn Féiners and Irish Parliamentary Party MPs shared platforms to denounce the government's action. While Dillon was just as vehemently opposed to conscription as de Valera, the people weighed the IPP's earlier commitments against Sinn Féin's consistent denunciation of Irish support for the war.

Anti-conscription poster, 1918.

Crucially, the Catholic Church was in the vanguard of the anti-conscription campaign. The bishops, meeting at Maynooth, declared that the Irish people had the right to resist conscription "by all means that are consonant with the law of God". The Catholic hierarchy's association with Sinn Féin during the conscription crisis conferred a new respectability on a movement that was seen by some as a dangerous revolutionary grouping that reflected many of the excesses of the Bolshevik party in contemporary Russia. Indeed, de Valera was more than comfortable in his relationship with the Catholic hierarchy, and this helped to project him as the dominant figure in the anti-conscription campaign. Evidence of Sinn Féin's pre-eminent role in the campaign was confirmed when the King's County (now Offaly) seat became vacant on the death of the sitting MP in April. The IPP withdrew its candidate, allowing McCartan an opposed run. The anger released by the extension of conscription shocked the government to such an extent that it shelved plans for its introduction. Sinn Féin had dominated the campaign against conscription, and its partnership with the Catholic Church removed any possible doubt about the party's moral qualifications to lead the Irish people. The chastened British government never implemented compulsory military service in Ireland, but the legalisation remained in place, allowing Sinn Féin to exploit the threat for most of 1918. For Sinn Féin the conscription crisis struck at the ideal moment, following three by-election defeats. Its direction of the anti-conscription campaign virtually guaranteed Sinn Féin victory over the IPP at the postwar election.

In the following month the authorities compounded their error by arresting leading Sinn Féiners. On the night of 17 May, the entire Sinn Féin leadership, with the exception of Michael Collins and Cathal Brugha, was arrested. Collins had received intelligence concerning the swoop. He was aware of the propaganda value of having Irish political leaders unfairly incarcerated in British jails, and he ensured that the targets would be present at the expected locations. The following day, the new viceroy, Lord French, declared that a "German plot" had been uncovered, in which the Sinn Féin leadership was conspiring with the Germans. While no hard evidence was produced to substantiate the claim that treasonable communication had taken place between Ireland and Germany, 73 Sinn Féin leaders were arrested and deported to England. Those arrested included de Valera, Griffith, Cosgrave, Plunkett and Countess Markievicz, but the public was convinced that the "plot" was a fabrication. Sympathy for Sinn Féin rose, and this was turned into an electoral advantage. The East Cavan seat had become vacant, and Sinn Féin, ignoring Dillon's wish to avoid a contest, was determined to run a candidate. Sinn Féin nominated Griffith, who was languishing in Gloucester Jail, and the Volunteers mobilised to spearhead the campaign, using the trusted slogan, "Put him in to get him out". Griffith took the seat by over 1,200 votes, confirming that government coercion played into their hands.

Further crackdowns followed, as French issued a proclamation on 3 July banning Sinn Féin, the Volunteers, Cumann na mBan and the Gaelic League. Even hurling matches were outlawed, but Sinn Féin responded to this repression with a campaign of passive resistance to British rule. Hundreds of public meetings were organised in the summer of 1918, and 1,500 hurling matches were played on one particular August Sunday as Sinn Féin and the GAA defied the government ban. RIC officers frequently attended such gatherings, where they attempted to record the names of the main participants, and they invariably received a hostile reception. It was during these months that Michael Collins established himself as a key figure in both the political and military movements. Although he was on the run from the authorities, Collins was active in helping to reorganise the Volunteers and in directing political opposition to Britain, while most of the Sinn Féin leaders were stuck in English jails.

In the early months of 1918, the Volunteers became involved in a fresh wave of land agitation. There had been food shortages during the winter of 1917–18, and rumours began to circulate that the country might even be close to experiencing a famine if food continued to be exported to England. Sinn Féin now added its weight to the Department of Agriculture's instruction that farmers should put at least ten per cent of their land under the plough. Local Sinn Féin clubs took the initiative by dividing up grazing land into small units ready for tillage, a practice that was most commonplace in the west where land hunger remained a dominant issue for rural dwellers. Volunteers were active in this "land-grabbing" and cattle-driving, and they frequently led large processions of enthusiastic local citizens out to the grazing ranches, which were to be ploughed up in the name of the "Irish Republic". Land-grabbing won new recruits for Sinn Féin among the rural proletariat, particularly in Mayo, Sligo and Clare. The activity, despite its popularity, incurred the wrath of Volunteer Headquarters, which viewed land-grabbing as socially divisive. The separatist movement wanted to represent all classes of Nationalist opinion and put a stop to Volunteers acting as social revolutionaries. Indeed, both the Sinn Féin Executive and the Volunteer leadership publicly stated their opposition to land-grabbing. On 2, March Volunteer headquarters issued an order to halt their members participating in cattle drives, "as these operations are neither of a national nor military character".

While the separatist movement distanced itself from social radicalism, Sinn Féin had to contend with a Labour Party that represented an electoral threat in urban areas. Labour had given some indication of its influence through the successful one-day strike that had been organised as a protest against conscription, though the all-party anti-conscription campaign had drawn the party closer to Sinn Féin. In the spring of 1918, Labour's most able leader, Thomas Johnson, announced the party's intention to field candidates in the postwar election. This drew it into conflict with Sinn Féin, which had made occasional noises in support of improved wages and conditions for workers but clearly lacked working-class appeal. There were suggestions of an electoral pact, but Sinn Féin exerted increasing pressure on individual Labour personnel to withdraw from the contest. At a special Labour conference on 1 November, the party's executive voted to stand down from the forthcoming election. This surprised many of its members and caused long-term difficulties for the party. Labour's withdrawal infuriated the IPP and delighted Sinn Féin, which was now able to focus exclusively on the national question.

The boost from the conscription crisis enabled Sinn Féin to extend its presence in all parts of the country. By the close of 1918 it had 1,354 clubs, and this gave the movement a significant organisational advantage over the IPP. Yet it was in rural areas that Sinn Féin was stronger, and this gave added significance to Labour's withdrawal from the election. The IPP was poorly equipped to fight the election, as the old UIL organisation had disintegrated in many constituencies.

In such circumstances Dillon had to rely on the press to appeal to voters, as he reminded the electorate of the IPP's achievements, while attacking the policy of abstention. However, even here the IPP was plagued by ill fortune. A paper shortage restricted production of the *Freeman's Journal,* the party's main organ, to between 20,000 and 25,000 daily copies, when its normal circulation would have been more than double this figure. The party was also sluggish in the selection of candidates, a reflection of the apathy and defeatist attitude adopted by many of its MPs. This contrasted sharply with the detailed preparations made by Sinn Féin. The war ended on 11 November, and the general election was arranged for 14 December. Sinn Féin issued a punchy, four-point manifesto. It would abstain from Westminster, establish its own constituent assembly, take Ireland's case for independence to the Peace Conference in Paris, and, more vaguely, use "any and every means available to render impotent the power of England to hold Ireland in subjection". Sinn Féin had not deviated from these objectives during the period of its rapid growth in 1917–18, and the programme clearly resonated with voters at the postwar general election.

When the results were announced on 28 December, Sinn Féin had won 73 seats, and the Unionists had triumphed in 26 seats, leaving the IPP holding only six seats. The party would almost have been obliterated but for an electoral pact in Ulster brokered by Cardinal Logue to prevent eight marginal seats falling into Unionist hands. This enabled the IPP to win North East Tyrone, South Armagh, South Down and East Donegal. The party's other two victories were in Waterford, where Captain Redmond held the seat with a majority of 474, and in the Falls constituency, where Devlin trounced de Valera by 8,843 votes to 4,451. Significantly, Sinn Féin won 25 seats, many of which were in Munster, without a contest. This highlighted the IPP's low morale and collapse in confidence, as it could not even field candidates to fight seats that it currently held.

A further factor that was crucial to the outcome of the 1918 election was the extension of the franchise. For the first time, all men over 21 and all women over 30 were eligible to vote. This trebled the Irish electorate to almost 2,000,000, and it seems likely that many of these first-time voters found the youthful and dynamic Sinn Féin to be an attractive proposition. Yet the party's landslide victory was not as complete as the seat returns indicated. In the twenty-six counties Sinn Féin won 65 per cent of the total votes cast, though this figure would have been higher had there been more electoral contests. Of course, many of those elected were in prison where they had been since the German plot arrests in May. Those arrested played no role in the election campaign, which was confirmation of the party's organisational effectiveness at local level. One notable victory came in Dublin's St Patrick's division where Countess Markievicz made history by becoming the first woman to win a Westminster seat. Elsewhere, Sinn Féin's successful candidates tended to be young men, most of whom had been born in the 1880s and 1890s, from middle-class Catholic families. It was this cadre of Sinn Féin leaders who, together with the Volunteers, would continue the struggle for independence.

Conclusion

When the war began in August 1914, the implementation of Home Rule would have satisfied the vast majority of Nationalists. By the end of the conflict, however, Nationalist Ireland had moved well beyond the concept of such a limited form of self-government and was now demanding full independence from Britain. Both external and internal factors combined to transform Nationalism during the period of the war. Prior to this, indeed, the eruption of the Ulster crisis had dealt a blow to Redmond and his moderate brand of constitutional Nationalism. In Carson he faced an astute and ruthless opponent who consistently appeared to be one step ahead of his Nationalist counterpart. Moreover, in his attempts to reach an accommodation on the Home Rule question, Redmond had bowed to government pressure to depart, however temporarily, from the one-Ireland principle, and this had raised new concerns among his followers. In truth, Redmond was more moderate than his rank-and-file supporters, and his public displays of loyalty to the Empire in the early weeks of the war tended to accentuate this gap. He had taken a major gamble at Woodenbridge, but it was a gamble that failed. The balance of the Volunteer split suggested that Redmond had called the situation correctly, but the much smaller group of Irish Volunteers formed a more determined and single-minded group that was, in turn, more amenable to IRB infiltration. This development would prove crucial to the IRB Military Council as it forged ahead with plans for a rebellion. Yet even before the rising the war had become unpopular. Again, the recruitment figures indicate a higher level of support for the war than was actually the case. The Dublin working class enlisted in very substantial numbers, but financial pressure, rather than a desire to serve king and country, was their obvious motivation. The workers' action encouraged a dismayed James Connolly to join forces with the bourgeois revolutionaries who had identified Easter 1916 as the perfect stage for a rebellion. Although the seven signatories saw Britain's distraction with the war as the ideal opportunity for an insurrection, it was their willingness to sacrifice their own lives in an attempt to resurrect the spirit of Irish nationality that was their defining characteristic.

While the British authorities had probably been numbed by the colossal numbers of young men who had been sacrificed during the first two years of the war, Irish Nationalists viewed the deaths of the 1916 leaders in a very different light. The sacrifice of the 1916 leaders was not a distant or remote occurrence. The people felt close to the men who were executed. Indeed, Irish citizens felt that they knew each of the sixteen as individuals. The executions, in addition to the blunders associated with the mass arrests and imposition of martial law, forced a reappraisal of Nationalist attitudes towards British rule. If the Easter Rising posed a huge challenge to the IPP, then the collapse of the 1916 Lloyd George negotiations proved to be a hammer blow. Southern Unionists had used their influence at the heart of government to block a scheme that would have delivered immediate Home Rule for the twenty-six counties. Redmond had once again resorted to reason, but found Long and Lansdowne to be completely unreasonable. The constitutionalists were abandoned and, in the changed mood across most of Ireland, became easy targets for an emerging Sinn Féin movement that had successfully signed up the various separatist organisations.

The British government was painfully slow to see this development, and Long, the cabinet's Irish "expert", was blind to the threat posed by Sinn Féin. Instead, the authorities were content to let the Irish Convention run its course, adhering to the logic that Westminster should not seek to impose a settlement but leave it to the Irish parties themselves to agree a solution. However, the combination of Sinn Féin's abstention and the Ulster Unionists' absolute refusal to look beyond their six-county stronghold rendered the Convention a failure. This left the British government's reckless decision to extend conscription to Ireland as the final guarantor of the separatist movement's overwhelming triumph at the 1918 general election. The contrast at the polls was striking. The IPP, in spite of Dillon's efforts, went through the motions with little expectation of victory. Its sitting MPs, some of whom struggled to conceal their sense of entitlement, were cast as yesterday's men, and they faced a phalanx of confident, youthful and energetic Sinn Féin candidates at the beginning of their political careers.

Historiography

One of the most perceptive books on the period is Fearghal McGarry's *The Rising Ireland: Easter 1916* (Oxford, 2000). The author stresses that Ireland's separatist minority was unable to counter the wave of enthusiasm for the war. While McGarry judges Redmond's Woodenbridge speech to have been a miscalculation, it was "consistent" with his personal and political principles. The Irish leader had always argued that a Home Rule Ireland would prove "one of the strongest bulwarks of the Empire", and he personally identified with the war, viewing it as a just struggle for the rights of small nations. McGarry also highlights Redmond's belief that cooperation against a common enemy would promote reconciliation between Unionism and Nationalism. In examining the Volunteer split, McGarry points to the weakness of the Irish Volunteers, concluding that, in early 1915, "it would have been difficult to see how England's difficulty was Ireland's opportunity". This leads McGarry to argue that had the war ended quickly, Redmond's strategy would have been vindicated. Charles Townshend's *Ireland: The 20th Century* (London, 1998) emphasises that, initially, there was support for the war in Ireland, "not patriotic but sympathetic". However, the author is convinced that the process of radicalisation that Irish Nationalism underwent predated the Easter rebellion. Townshend quotes Birrell's observation of a "change in atmosphere" in late 1915, when the chief secretary described the Irish situation as "one of actual menace".

Later, Townshend's *Easter 1916: The Irish Rebellion* (London, 2005) develops this thesis, arguing that from the early part of the war there was a kind of "mental neutrality" in Ireland and that the "fierce spasm of patriotism" that existed in England was not replicated across the Irish Sea. Townshend insists that the war undermined the IPP, as prices rose but wages were pegged and Ireland suffered from unemployment and low pay. He states that Redmond's image as a "recruiting sergeant" steadily corroded his public prestige. By the spring of 1915, Townshend notes, there was a marked drop in enthusiasm for recruitment, as the people realised that the conflict would be protracted and were angered by the lack of recognition from England for Ireland's contribution. He argues that Sinn Féin was a "minor force" in 1915, but the growing fear of conscription, which emerged in late 1915, altered this.

Michael Foy and Brian Barton suggest, in *The Easter Rising* (Stroud, 2011), that "the war quickly crystallised differences" between moderate and more militant Irish Nationalists, adding that the militants were very quick to see the opportunity presented by the war. In examining recruitment, the authors contend that sympathy for Belgium and the expectation that it would be a short conflict were the key factors influencing early recruitment. Alvin Jackson's

Judging Redmond and Carson (London, 2003) highlights Redmond's relationship with the army, noting that he had a grandfather and an uncle who were both British Army generals, and later a brother and a son who were decorated army officers. Carson lacked such connections. On the other hand, Redmond had been close to a number of militant Nationalists earlier in his career and had regularly pressed the authorities for the release of high-profile Fenian prisoners, including Tom Clarke. But, as Jackson declares, "Redmond and his colleagues drifted away from these active connections", which partly explains why the party was so out of touch with the Irish Volunteers. Indeed, both Redmond and Dillon saw the Volunteers as a challenge rather than an asset.

Paul Bew's *The Politics of Enmity* (Oxford, 2007) describes Redmond's keenness to support the war effort, as he wanted to demonstrate that Ireland could be loyal to Britain in an international crisis. Yet, as Bew notes, it seemed that "Ireland was being asked to make a huge blood sacrifice for a British war effort without sufficient return". In his analysis of wartime by-elections in Ireland before the rising, the author notes that in spite of the IPP's successive victories, "there is clear evidence of the weakness of the IPP's structures". Significantly, Ulster Unionists were grudging in their praise for Redmond's stance at the outbreak of war. Ronald McNeill's *Ulster's Stand for Union* (London, 1922) records how Ulstermen were "lukewarm" in praise of the Irish leader's House of Commons speech on 3 August 1914, noting that the Irish Volunteers offered by Redmond would be limited to service at home.

The more favourable treatment given to the Ulster Volunteers is highlighted in Timothy Bowman's *Carson's Army: The Ulster Volunteer Force, 1910–22* (Manchester, 2007). He notes that when they were offered the opportunity to form the basis for a new division, they also made demands for their own badge, own title (Ulster), local battalion titles and officers with Unionist sympathies, "most of which were conceded". For a time, Bowman states, optimistic Unionist leaders were considering the formation of two divisions from the UVF, but the members "were not that inclined to enlist", with rural recruitment in Ulster not that much ahead of recruitment in rural Ireland. Fergal McCluskey's *The Irish Revolution, 1912–23: Tyrone* (Dublin, 2014) claims that Ulster Volunteers joined up in "respectable numbers" across the county, but this was not sustained. Over the course of 1915, nearly 1,000 enlisted in Tyrone (340 National Volunteers, 523 Ulster Volunteers and 175 non-aligned). Gerry White's essay "'They have rights who dare maintain them': the Irish Volunteers, 1913–15 in the *Atlas of the Irish Revolution* (Cork, 2017) examines the decline of Redmond's National Volunteers. He states that the fact that over 23,900 members enlisted in the British Army clearly had "a negative impact" on the movement.

In assessing Redmond's speech in the Commons on the outbreak of the war,

Denis Gwynn's *The Life of John Redmond* (London, 1932) argues that no other Irish leader would have dared to make such a commitment only a week after the Bachelors Walk killings. Two days before his Woodenbridge speech, Redmond had stressed the unity of the Empire in its hour of need when he welcomed the Home Rule Act. Meanwhile, Patrick Maume's *The Long Gestation: Irish Nationalist Life 1891–1918* (Dublin, 1999) states that Redmond supported the war, believing that Ireland owed a "moral debt" to Britain in respect of Home Rule. Nicholas Mansergh's *The Unresolved Question: The Anglo-Irish Settlement and Its Undoing 1912–72* (London, 1991) is highly critical of Redmond's actions at the beginning of the war, claiming that he failed to get his hands on the levers of power. In Mansergh's view, Redmond should have established a "mirror image" Ulster provisional government in the south. A counter-argument is presented in Bew's *Ideology and the Irish Question* (Oxford, 1994), which firmly rejects the thesis that Redmond missed a real opportunity to advance the Nationalist cause in August and September 1914, when he could have exploited Britain's difficulties for political gain. Adopting such an opportunist strategy, Bew contends, would have implied a willingness on Redmond's part to "allow the triumph of German arms in France". R.F. Foster's *Modern Ireland* (London, 1988) views Woodenbridge as a disastrous miscalculation, arguing that Redmond's "misjudgement" can be regarded as a turning point in Irish history. Lee's *Ireland 1912–1985* (Cambridge, 1989) takes a different view, suggesting that Redmond had no choice but to act as he did, if he hoped to have any influence on a postwar Irish settlement.

More recently, Wheatley's *Nationalism and the Irish Party* (Oxford, 2005) states that in the five counties he has researched many IPP supporters expressed sympathy for the Allies and declared their support for Redmond. However, he claims that after a few months of hostilities most people were "anything but enthusiastic" in their support for the war. Still, only two weeks into the war, Wheatley illustrates the level of popular support for Britain, adding that Redmond's offer of the Volunteers for home defence was perfectly in tune with the popular mood. However, the Irish leader's position quickly deteriorated. Wheatley's central argument is that the IPP was destroyed by the Home Rule crisis and "mass militarism" in late 1913 and by its wartime support for recruitment. For Wheatley, the IPP had already run into serious difficulties in these five rural counties by Christmas 1914.

Jackson's *Home Rule* (London, 2003) emphasises the negative impact for Redmond of the War Office's discrimination in its treatment of Ulster and Irish recruits. The author declares that Redmond wanted a "blood sacrifice" by Irishmen in the war to demonstrate that the British could trust Ireland with Home Rule. By this stage, Jackson notes, the Irish leader had staked everything on the Liberal alliance, but the war created a new consensus between the Liberals and Conservatives, which clearly undermined the IPP. Maume's *The Long Gestation* addresses the question of support for the war effort among Nationalist MPs. Only seven MPs enlisted during the war, a low figure notwithstanding the party's age profile. Significantly, Maume points out that none of Dillon's sons joined the army. In his assessment of the reaction to the heavy losses sustained by Irish troops in 1915, Maume notes that difficult questions were asked about the delayed deployment of the Ulster Division. It had the reputation of a highly trained, formidable force, but Kitchener was rumoured to be holding them in reserve in Ireland in case of a rebellion by Irish Volunteers.

In analysing the causes of the Easter Rising, Laffan's *The Partition of Ireland* (Dundalk, 1983) stresses that Carson "rekindled the Fenian flame", as the UVF turned into an impressive example for the Irish physical force tradition. Tom Garvin's *The Evolution of Irish Nationalist Politics* (New York, 1981) highlights the importance of the new Nationalism, arguing that the Gaelic League had a "profoundly political purpose and was crucial to the development of an Irish revolutionary elite". This elite is put under the spotlight in Foy and Barton's *The Easter Rising*, which argues that Tom Clarke was an "autocrat", hence the need for tight control. He was also the "living link" between the old Fenian movement and the 1916 generation. The authors also contend that the Military Council sought a "posthumous victory" in 1916, predicting that executions would follow what they hoped would be a "creditable" military performance. In a further work, Michael Foy's *Tom Clarke: The True Leader of the Easter Rising* (Dublin, 2014) declares that Clarke and MacDermott complemented each other perfectly. When Clarke joined the Supreme Council, Foy argues, it was "his charisma, dynamism and commitment to transforming the IRB that explain his ascendency". He adds that Clarke was "thrilled" by the actions of the UVF, and he subsequently used his influence to promote Pearse and Plunkett to positions of influence. Foy describes Clarke's alliance with Connolly as a master stroke, "an inspired and audacious gamble that ended the danger that Connolly's inflammatory rhetoric posed to the IRB". Then to handle MacNeill, whom Clarke had hoped would resign and disappear, MacDonagh, a colleague of MacNeill's at UCD, was added to the Military Council in April 1916. Foy concludes by claiming that unlike Pearse, "Clarke and MacDermott's desire for a supreme sacrifice – a blood sacrifice – came not from any messianic desire to die but a coldly rational calculation that only through their executions could they snatch victory from military defeat."

Townshend's *Easter 1916* seeks to explain Connolly's involvement by suggesting that with the outbreak of war "national liberation" became the only path to socialism. In addition, Pearse's "inclination towards a cautious socialism" offered Connolly some hope that the rising might be a precursor to a social revolution. McGarry's *The Rising* argues that a rebellion was "a moral and historical imperative" if Fenianism was to have any future. He also claims that the leaders' awareness "that most Irish people disagreed with them made it more rather than less important to fight". Gerard MacAtasney's *Tom Clarke: Life, Liberty, Revolution* (Dublin, 2013) notes that Clarke was haunted by the IRB's failure to exploit the opportunity presented by the Boer War. For Clarke, argues MacAtasney, the outcome of the rising was irrelevant, as it was "necessary for its own sake". In his study of Tyrone, McCluskey's *The Irish Revolution* claims that republican support was growing in the county prior to the rising. Finally, Lewis's, *Carson: The Man Who Divided Ireland* (London, 2005) remarks that the Unionist leader's first thought on learning of the Easter Rising was that it had put paid to Home Rule.

The conventional view that the initial response to the rising was hostile, as Dublin residents poured scorn on the captured insurgents, is challenged in Lee's *Ireland 1912-1985*, which suggests that there was considerable sympathy for the participants. There was, in Lee's opinion, no sudden U-turn in public opinion. Rather, opinion "was not so much reversed as simply crystallised by a combination of the executions and better information". More particularly, Foster's *Modern Ireland* highlights the significance of the Sheehy-Skeffington murder, noting that it had an "enormous effect" on public opinion. McGarry's *The Rising* looks at the impact of the mass arrests in the wake of the rebellion, stressing that many of those arrested "in a frenzy of raids" had not been involved in the rising or even in separatist politics. While the rebellion had been largely confined to Dublin, the entire country was placed under martial law for the next six months. Although many of the "innocent" were quickly released, McGarry asserts that "the indiscriminate punishment of such a large number of people generated outrage, sympathy and protests ... and has probably been underrated as a factor in the alienation of public opinion from the British government and the growth of support for the republican movement". In his *Rebels: Voices from the Easter Rising* (Dublin, 2001), McGarry claims that the rebels were shocked by the "ferocity" of opposition to the rising, with women from the slums being most vocal. Of course, many of this group had husbands or sons serving in the British Army, but McGarry argues that "their anger also reflected the danger to which their families, homes and livelihoods had been exposed".

Townshend's *Easter 1916* confirms that Maxwell was highly regarded by Kitchener, but when it came to his response to the insurrection, Maxwell was only concerned with the guilt or innocence of the Volunteers, "not with the possible political effect of punishing them". Even when Maxwell recognised the seriousness of the problem in mid-June 1916, he remained convinced that the initial impact of the executions had been positive. As McGarry illustrates, Maxwell assumed that revulsion caused by his actions "had set in because his policies had been misrepresented by politicians, the priests and the press". Fanning's *Fatal Path: British Government and Irish Revolution 1910–1922* (London, 2013) claims that the Easter rebellion was swiftly suppressed and appeared to have been repudiated by Irish public opinion, but this was transformed by the executions, as the government "abdicated responsibility", leaving Maxwell in control.

Leland Lyons's *John Dillon* (London, 1968) contrasts the reactions of Dillon and Redmond to the rising. Redmond was horrified, but Lyons states that Dillon's neo-Parnellite Fenian sympathies ensured that he stopped short of condemning the rebels in his famous speech in the House of Commons on 11 May 1916. Thereafter, Dillon was opposed to entering fresh negotiations with the Asquith government, preferring a policy of "open and active opposition" at Westminster. Jackson's *Judging Redmond and Carson* claims that Redmond was "shocked" by the rising, as he was out of touch with popular opinion, unlike Dillon, who was present in Dublin during the insurrection. By contrast, "Redmond was in London, remote physically and emotionally from the action in Dublin, and could not generate the required passion."

McGarry's *The Rising* concludes by declaring that "British coercion created insurmountable challenges for the Irish Party." The author claims that rumours of Irish MPs cheering news of the executions in the Commons were widely circulated in Ireland, and the IPP was "inevitably, if harshly, seen as complicit in the executions". The truth, however, was that Redmond could exert little influence on the British authorities, though he did accept the necessity for some executions. Maume's *The Long Gestation* stresses that in the 1916 Lloyd George talks, Redmond accepted partition without banking the Home Rule prize. He states that by subsequently accusing the government of treachery, the IPP "convicted itself of folly" and was humiliated. However, Maume declares that by that stage there still was no rational alternative to the IPP. Jackson's *Judging Redmond and Carson* claims that the collapse of the Lloyd George peace plan "effectively destroyed Redmond's chances of a political recovery", a view that was confirmed by Stephen Gwynn, one of the Irish leader's closest colleagues.

Fanning's *Fatal Path* closely examines the thinking of Lloyd George in preparing for the negotiations. Initially, he knew that he must not offend the "Unionist powerbrokers" in the cabinet, Bonar Law and Carson in particular, "who would shortly determine the identity of Asquith's successor". Fanning argues that the Lloyd George negotiations were "the first illustration of the stranglehold Unionist ministers exerted on the Irish policy of the coalition governments of 1915–22, a stranglehold tantamount to a power of veto". In an interesting addendum, Fanning points out that Lloyd George's preference for dealing separately with Redmond and Carson was a guide to the coalition's preference for treating Ireland and Ulster as separate problems needing separate treatment. Chris Dooley's *Redmond: A Life Undone* (Dublin, 2015) describes how after the negotiations Redmond shut himself away at Aughavanagh where he read little of the criticism in the newspapers. Indeed, he did not make his first public speech until 6 October 1916, when he addressed an audience in Waterford.

The most detailed analysis of Ulster Nationalist reaction to the 1916 Lloyd George scheme remains Eamon Phoenix's *Northern Nationalism: Partition and the Catholic Minority in Northern Ireland, 1890–1940* (Belfast, 1994), which contrasts the more pragmatic strategies pursued by Nationalists in the east of the province and those in the west where the Catholic clergy were particularly active in leading opposition to partition. Phoenix also places the formation of the Irish Nation League in context, highlighting its failure to spread throughout Ulster and beyond. He concludes that the league offered "a slightly more aggressive form of constitutionalism", a factor that explains its inability to establish itself as a rival to the IPP. Devlin's role in the 1916 negotiations receives careful judgement in A.C. Hepburn's *Catholic Belfast and Nationalist Ireland in the Era of Joe Devlin, 1871–1934* (Oxford, 2008). In the week before the crucial Belfast convention, the five northern bishops informed Devlin that the plan would be defeated by "an overwhelming majority", a prediction that strengthened Devlin's resolve to carry the conference. Following the convention, Hepburn describes how a jubilant Devlin informed Lloyd George of the outcome by telegram immediately after the vote. When the scheme collapsed, however, the Belfast MP turned his fire on the government, furiously denouncing the administration for its mishandling of the whole affair.

Carson's anger at the collapse of the negotiations is expertly highlighted in Jackson's *Judging Redmond and Carson*. The author stresses that Carson had viewed Lansdowne with a degree of contempt since 1903, while Long had always been scheming and jealous of Carson, and this influenced both men in their opposition to the Lloyd George plan. Lewis's *Carson* describes Carson's two-hour speech to the UUC on 6 June 1916 as "one of the most uncomfortable episodes in Carson's life". He was furiously attacked by Cavan, Monaghan and Donegal Unionists, led by Major Saunderson, Colonel Saunderson's son. Carson, as Lewis notes, was also heavily criticised by Long. Furthermore, Lewis points out that relations between Carson and Lloyd George were positive during 1916, and both he and Bonar Law worked to ensure that the "Welsh wizard" replaced Asquith as prime minister in December 1916.

In his assessment of the 1916 negotiations, Michael Laffan's *The Resurrection of Ireland: The Sinn Féin Party 1916–1923* (Cambridge, 1999) emphasises that Lloyd George sought to exploit the IPP's weakness during the negotiations. The author also provides the best analysis of the emergence of a united Sinn Féin movement in 1917. Before 1917, Laffan argues, many people hated the government and rejected the IPP, "but they had as yet no alternative". For Laffan, the turning point came with the North Roscommon by-election and the sudden appearance of an electoral machine, which delivered Plunkett to victory. Yet the real achievement was "the emergence of a sense of cohesion and common purpose among a disparate group of people who, until then, had often suspected or disapproved of each other". Such a development, Laffan proclaims, largely explains why divisions within the movement subsequently appeared. He also stresses the importance for the emerging movement of the timing of the release of the senior prisoners, including de Valera and Ashe, in June 1917, because they found "a united, efficient and energetic party awaiting them". Laffan claims that the "more guarded" language used during the North Roscommon and South Longford contests was replaced by de Valera's strident rhetoric from the summer of 1917. Dooley's *Redmond: A Life Undone* declares that the formation of a new coalition under Lloyd George in December 1916 further undermined Redmond's influence. Carson, Bonar Law and Balfour were notable figures in the new government.

David Fitzpatrick's *Politics and Irish Life 1913–1921: Provincial Experience of War and Revolution* (Dublin, 1977) has set the standard for a number of local studies, which together indicate that there was no real national pattern through 1917–18. In accounting for the rise of the separatist movement in County Clare, Fitzpatrick highlights the central role played by the lower clergy who were brought on board by local activists in order to give Sinn Féin respectability in rural areas. In his comments on the East Clare by-election, the author highlights de Valera's eagerness to gather votes from all quarters, irrespective of views on constitutionalism. He clearly demonstrated much greater political acumen than Plunkett, concentrating on the twin policies of abstention and an appeal to the postwar peace conference. Fitzpatrick also stresses the negative approach of the emerging movement, suggesting that Sinn Féin was "more a mood than an organisation" and "a repudiation of the old political Nationalism more than a promise to replace it". Marie Coleman's *County Longford and the Irish Revolution 1910–1923* (Dublin, 2003) also dwells on the role played by the younger clergy in the rise of Sinn Féin during 1917–18. The author analyses the South Longford by-election, emphasising the impact made by 200 election workers who had arrived from Dublin. Redmond, as in North Roscommon, played no part in the by-election, but Dillon and Devlin directed the IPP campaign in South Longford. Interestingly, Coleman makes the point that the conscription crisis did not swell Sinn Féin ranks in Longford, as numbers had increased significantly during the by-election. However, she states that the Volunteers were certainly boosted in the county by the conscription crisis. David Fitzpatrick's *Harry Boland's Irish Revolution* (Cork, 2003) points out that Joe McGuinness did not belong to the

IRB and was sentenced to only three years for his "modest role" in the rising. The final word on the 1917 by-elections belongs to Jackson's *Judging Redmond and Carson*, which argues that the contests in North Roscommon, South Longford, East Clare and Kilkenny exposed Redmond's "apathy". Jackson also makes the contrast with Parnell's defiant by-election performances in 1890–91.

Phoenix's *Northern Nationalism* carefully explains that the IPP's two by-election successes in South Armagh and East Tyrone in the early part of 1918 should not be viewed "as evidence of a major upswing in the fortunes of the Home Rulers", though they did illustrate the importance of the partition issue for Ulster Catholics. Later, in the general election, Phoenix demonstrates that, Devlin apart, the IPP had little prospect of success in Ulster without an electoral pact. Devlin's overwhelming victory over de Valera in the Falls constituency is assessed in Hepburn's *Catholic Belfast and Nationalist Ireland*, which argues that the negative reaction to the collapse of the 1916 negotiations was much more keenly felt in the south, where concern for Catholic Ulster was "no more than skin deep". Sinn Féin's Ulster policy is superbly analysed in John Bowman's *De Valera and the Ulster Question 1917–1973* (Oxford, 1982). Bowman demonstrates that both communities in the north were "difficult missionary territory" for de Valera. Initially, the Sinn Féin leader had "a simplistic perspective on Ulster, which was based on his belief that Unionist opposition to any all-Ireland arrangement was primarily due to British influence and intrigue". This ignored the consistent approach of Fr O'Flanagan who, as Bew's *The Politics of Enmity* highlights, argued in this period that there were two nations in Ireland, each with a right to self-determination. Maryann Valiulis's *Portrait of a Revolutionary: General Richard Mulcahy and the Founding of the Irish Free State* (Dublin, 1992) argues that Sinn Féin and the Volunteers blended or "synthesised" the constitutional and physical force elements in Irish Nationalism. However, she contends that the importance of the 1916 executions in explaining the radicalisation of Irish Nationalism has been exaggerated. Rather, it was the actions of the insurgents, not the British reaction, that inspired young revolutionaries such as Mulcahy to take up arms against the British.

Laffan's *The Resurrection of Ireland* highlights the differences between the worn-out, apathetic IPP and the youthful, dynamic and energetic Sinn Féin movement. Noting that most of the delegates at the 1917 Árd-Fheis were under 40, Laffan stresses the significance of the part played by first-time voters in the 1918 general election. Laffan claims that the IPP retained much of its former vote but failed to attract new support. The author dwells on Dillon's own experience in East Mayo where he lost his seat to de Valera, recalling Dillon's assessment that the IPP's "lack of organisation and helplessness" faced "the most perfect organisation and infinite audacity". Laffan also makes the point that Sinn Féin's demand for a republic seemed "less absurd" in the context of collapsing monarchies in contemporary Europe.

Charles Townshend's *The Republic: The Fight for Irish Independence* (London, 2013) emphasises the role played by the conscription crisis in the rise of Sinn Féin. Using RIC reports, the author argues that this had been the crucial factor in attracting clerical support for Sinn Féin. He concludes that the "fusion of clerical and political leadership over the conscription crisis in April 1918 transformed Irish politics". A recent essay by Pauric Travers, 'The Conscription Crisis and the general election of 1918' in the *Atlas of the Irish Revolution* draws attention to the isolation and ineffectiveness of the IPP in the House of Commons during the war, declaring that this "was graphically illustrated during the parliamentary debate on conscription between 9 and 18 April 1918". He also reveals that de Valera's uncompromising attitude on the issue "convinced the hierarchy to take a strong stand". Travers argues that the conscription crisis was "an unmitigated disaster for the constitutional Nationalists" and demonstrated their "powerlessness". In the general election that followed, "the Irish Party was an ageing middle-class party faced with a younger, more populist rival".

The most comprehensive treatment of the Irish Convention remains R.B. McDowell's *The Irish Convention 1917–18* (London, 1970), which argues that its failure was due to Ulster Unionist intransigence and a Sinn Féin boycott. Jackson's *Home Rule* offers a very different interpretation, claiming that it had a genuine chance of success. For Jackson, Plunkett's appalling chairmanship was the primary reason for its failure. When the opportunity for a settlement appeared in January 1918, Plunkett, possibly intentionally, opted to delay proceedings. Jackson stresses that H.T. Barrie, the leader of the Ulster Unionist delegation, was a moderate with a real interest in reaching consensus. Indeed, Lewis's *Carson* claims that Carson had altered his thinking in the run-up to the Convention. He was now considering a long-term scheme to bring the north and south together, under which Ulster could be excluded from Home Rule but would participate in an all-Ireland council. Lloyd George was made aware of this development. Jackson's *Judging Redmond and Carson* declares that at the Convention Redmond "was extremely eloquent and judicious, consensual and magnanimous", but he did not have a coherent programme of his own. Dooley's *Redmond: A Life Undone* recalls Redmond's welcome for the announcement of the Convention, claiming it was "the first time in its history that Ireland has been asked to settle its own problems". The author also emphasises that Redmond really impressed the southern Unionists at the Convention, but the Ulster Unionist delegates could not reach a deal without reference to their political leaders.

Finally, Fanning's *Fatal Path* emphasises the importance of World War I for Irish politics: "It was the war that put Home Rule on ice; it was the war that restored the Unionists to office; it was the war that demanded the executions after the Easter rebellion and that then, and again in 1918, dictated internment without trial, thus empowering Sinn Féin and the Irish Volunteers while destroying the IPP; it was the war that conceived, brought forth and nourished the 'terrible beauty' of Yeats's 'Easter 1916'." In its assessment of Sinn Féin, Townshend's *The Republic* highlights Sinn Féin's flexibility, which allowed it to draw support from many strands of Nationalism: "It could be vague about its ends, but it had a coherent and persuasive conception of its means."

Chapter 4
The Emergence of the Irish Free State, 1919–25

Britain's reputation would be severely damaged by its disastrous actions in Ireland during the War of Independence. The postwar coalition government failed to develop a coherent political or military strategy that might have reduced public support for the republican movement and limited its military potential. Part of the reason for this was that Lloyd George, the prime minister who had led his country to victory in World War I, presided over a coalition whose members viewed Ireland from very different perspectives. Wholly reliant on the Tories for a majority, Lloyd George knew that any new initiative in Ireland would have to be approved by Conservative cabinet ministers such as Bonar Law, Birkenhead and Chamberlain. The principal reason for the government's muddled approach, however, was that Ireland was not viewed as a pressing concern during 1919. In addition to a host of domestic problems, the government's agenda was dominated by the Paris Peace Conference. It also faced serious disturbances in different parts of the Empire such as India, Egypt and Mesopotamia. Consequently, Ireland was overlooked, and Irish policy, such as it was, lacked direction. This can partly be explained by the nature of the conflict in 1919.

Rejection of British rule led a handful of young Volunteers, acting without authorisation, to seize the initiative and target the Royal Irish Constabulary (RIC). However, the violence was sporadic in the early stages and was confined to very specific geographical areas. Significantly, it lacked the necessary intensity to grasp the government's attention. This would change during 1920, but the government's insistence that it was facing a criminal conspiracy in Ireland contributed to the decision to reinforce the police with ex-servicemen who were tossed into the conflict with totally inadequate training and preparation. Their ill-discipline and use of reprisals increased public support for the IRA and damaged British authority irreparably. During 1920, both the Irish and British press began to refer to the Irish Volunteers as the Irish Republican Army (IRA). Towards the end of the conflict, the British threw men and resources at the problem, but the

IRA was able to sustain the struggle long enough for public opinion in Britain to turn against government policy in Ireland. When a truce was finally agreed in July 1921, it was a relief for both sides, particularly the British.

The War of Independence

The first military engagement of the War of Independence took place on 21 January 1919 at Soloheadbeg in County Tipperary. By coincidence, this was the same day as the Dáil's inaugural meeting at the Mansion House in Dublin. A party of Volunteers, including Séamus Robinson, Dan Breen and Seán Treacy, surprised two RIC constables who were escorting a load of gelignite to a local quarry. The plan was to seize the explosives and the policemen's weapons, but both constables were shot dead when they resisted. Robinson, Breen and Treacy had acted on their own initiative without sanction from either Volunteer General Headquarters (GHQ) or the Dáil. This had followed a pattern in which local bands of Volunteers in particular areas had engaged in activity, commonly raids for arms, which had not been authorised by GHQ. Such local initiatives would become a recurring theme for the duration of the conflict. Indeed, the reluctance of both GHQ and the Dáil to endorse the attack at Soloheadbeg undermined the authority of both groups in the eyes of the most active Volunteers. The lack

The members of the First Dáil outside the Mansion House, 10 April 1919. The front row consists of L Ginnell, M Collins, C Brugha, A Griffith, E de Valera, Count Plunkett, E MacNeill, W Cosgrave and E Blythe. The priest is Rev Father O'Flanagan and Terence MacSwiney is second left, second row.

of enthusiasm for such violence stemmed, in part, from the assumption that attacks on RIC officers, most of whom were Catholics who had settled in the local community, would prove counter-productive. Local press reports recorded that the two victims of the Soloheadbeg ambush, James O'Connell and Patrick MacDonnell, were popular figures in the local community, and the news that Constable MacDonnell was the father of five children clearly added to the sense of outrage. At Mass in Tipperary the following Sunday, Monsignor Arthur Ryan described the killings as "cold-blooded murders" and condemned the crime as "an offence against the laws of God". Such unequivocal clerical condemnation was widely shared, and the Volunteers found themselves shunned by the local community in South Tipperary in the immediate aftermath of the Soloheadbeg attack.

While Sinn Féin propaganda had increasingly targeted the RIC, many within the broader separatist movement were uncomfortable with the prospect of a fresh campaign of violence directed against the police. Indeed, as Diarmaid Ferriter has pointed out, many RIC officers subsequently stressed that relations between the local population and the police were "relatively good" before the War of Independence. It was also significant that the Tipperary Volunteers who carried out the Soloheadbeg attack were censured by Volunteer GHQ. There was a genuine fear among the leadership that any repetition of the Soloheadbeg violence by militant Volunteers would turn the public against the republican movement. What was required was an urgent clarification of the republican movement's policy on clashes between the Volunteers and the RIC. This appeared in an issue of the Volunteer journal, *An t-Óglach,* on 31 January 1919, and it signalled a new, more ruthless approach by the Volunteers. *An t-Óglach* claimed that the Volunteers constituted the legitimate army of the republic before declaring that "a state of war" now existed between Ireland and England. The article declared that in this conflict, "Every Volunteer is entitled, morally and legally … to use all legitimate methods of warfare against the soldiers and policemen of the English usurper, and to slay them if necessary."

In seizing the initiative at Soloheadbeg, the local Volunteers, who hoped that their operation would be a catalyst for similar Volunteer activity elsewhere, had forced the republican movement to adopt a clear position in its attitude to attacks on the Crown Forces. This meant disregarding condemnation of Volunteer actions from significant voices among the local population, though these soon dissipated as the authorities' reaction to the outrage quickly shifted public opinion. In designating South Tipperary as a special military area, the Irish administration imposed restrictions on the entire civilian population of the area in a manner that quickly stoked public resentment.

Evidence of this change in the public's attitude was soon apparent. When a party of Volunteers mounted an operation to rescue Seán Hogan, one of the Soloheadbeg attackers, from police custody at Knocklong, County Limerick on 13 May 1919, two more RIC men were killed. These killings elicited a more muted response from the local population. This trend was confirmed in late June when District Inspector Michael Hunt was shot dead on a busy Thurles street. Although there were many witnesses, the attacker was not identified. Other incidents which claimed the lives of RIC personnel took place in Westport and Limerick city. When two more constables were gunned down in August in County Clare, the government immediately placed the whole county under military rule. This had been the Irish administration's response to each of the earlier incidents, and there was little appreciation by the authorities of the impact of such repression on the wider population. From the security perspective, moreover, putting large areas in the south and west of the country under military rule did little to hamper the activities of the small number of militant Volunteers who were active during this initial phase. Public anger at the restrictions imposed by the authorities ensured that the revulsion expressed following the early killings quickly evaporated. It was also significant that the £1,000 reward for information leading to the arrest of Breen and his comrades was never claimed. In Clare, for example, some 7,000 troops were scattered across the county by the end of August 1919. Fairs and markets were cancelled, houses searched and curfews imposed, all of which increased the public's sense of oppression but failed to disrupt Volunteer activity.

While the attacks on the RIC in this early phase had been sporadic and uncoordinated, pressure on the force had clearly intensified. In April 1919 the Dáil revived the old Land League tactic by ordering a boycott of the RIC. A campaign of social ostracism was developed, supported by Volunteer intimidation where necessary, which aimed to both discourage recruitment to the force and exert pressure on serving members to consider resignation. The boycott allowed the wider public, many of whom continued to feel uneasy about armed action taken against individual RIC members, to play some role in the independence struggle. Although there was a large force of regular troops in Ireland, the police shouldered the heaviest burden during the conflict. While Dublin had its own force, the Dublin Metropolitan Police (DMP), the rest of the country was under the RIC's authority. Its officers were stationed in approximately 1,400 barracks that were scattered across Ireland. Most of these barracks served small rural communities, and a typical station housed a sergeant and four to six constables. As a force, the RIC was poorly prepared for the War of Independence. In spite of the prewar Volunteer activity and the Easter Rising, Ireland had enjoyed a long period of peace, and the officers who found themselves on the front line were, on average, significantly older than the Volunteers. As the violence gradually intensified, a growing number of officers resigned from the force. A small number, however, reacted violently to the challenge being thrown down by the Volunteers. In January 1920 a group of RIC men responded to an attack on one of their colleagues in Thurles by damaging the homes of local republicans and attacking the offices of the *Tipperary Star*.

A similar occurrence had taken place some months previously in County Cork. On 7 September 1919, a party of Volunteers led by Liam Lynch intercepted a group of soldiers from the King's Own Shropshire Light Infantry as they paraded to a local church in Fermoy for the weekly Sunday Service. The plan was to seize the soldiers' rifles, but as these were being loaded into waiting vehicles a melee ensued during which one of the soldiers was shot dead. This was the British Army's second fatality in the conflict following the killing of a soldier from the Nottinghamshire and Derby Regiment in Cobh, County Cork. At the subsequent inquest the jury, while expressing sympathy with the family of the deceased, refused to bring a verdict of murder, claiming that the raid had been staged to capture the rifles and the killing had not been part of the plan. That night, angry comrades of the dead soldier attacked properties in Fermoy, particularly those belonging to members of the jury. The controversy surrounding such acts of indiscipline worked to the advantage of the Volunteers. The Crown Forces were cast as the public's enemy, rather than its protector, and the republican claim to be acting as the people's defenders was given greater credence.

At the same time, the publicity generated by what were often characterised as daring operations raised the standing of the Volunteers in the eyes of the general public. In this way a relatively small number of native Volunteers was able to increase its control over the population. One such example took place at Ashtown, County Dublin, on 19 December 1919, when a party of Volunteers staged an ambush of a two-car convoy in broad daylight. Their target was the Viceroy, Lord French, who was fortunate to escape injury. Subsequently, an angry French ordered the arrest of all known Volunteer leaders and the deportation of those who could not legally be convicted. However, the Viceroy's appetite for such firm action was not matched by his officials in Dublin Castle. They insisted that the authorities must adhere to strict legal procedure with the result that deportations were delayed while other suspects, much to the military's annoyance, were released from custody.

Indeed, it was evident by the close of 1919 that cooperation between the police and the army in Ireland was problematic. Furthermore, French's reaction to the Ashtown attack had highlighted the weakness of the RIC's intelligence system. The information at the police's disposal was hopelessly out of date, and it was apparent that the public's willingness to assist the authorities by providing accurate intelligence was in short supply. An increasing number of the population supported the republican struggle, while many of those who did not approve of the violence viewed the Volunteers as patriotic, if misguided, in their efforts to advance the cause of Irish freedom. Moreover, intimidation could be forcefully deployed to dissuade the type of collaboration with the authorities that could undermine the guerrilla campaign against the British. There was also, of course, a tradition of non-cooperation with the authorities in many parts of rural Ireland that worked to the Volunteers' advantage. Clearly, the Volunteers derived huge benefit from the Crown Forces' lack of accurate intelligence, and Michael Collins was determined to press home this advantage. Collins had grasped the importance of supremacy in the intelligence battle if the Volunteers were to have any chance in a conflict against a much larger, more powerful military force. The key was to infiltrate the Castle system at every level, and four of his agents in the "G" (detective) branch of the DMP played a crucial role in this information war. These four men, Éamonn Broy, James Kavanagh, Patrick MacNamara and David Neligan, had access to the most sensitive security information. In addition, Lily Mernin, who worked as a secretary for military intelligence in Dublin's Ship Street Barracks, passed on relevant documents directly to Collins. This enabled him to identify those detectives who posed the greatest threat to Volunteer operations, and Collins dealt ruthlessly with these men. He formed an elite group of assassins, the "Squad", whose IRB connections ensured that they remained fiercely loyal to Collins. Their first victim was Detective Sergeant Harry Smith, who was gunned down near his home on 30 July 1919. A number of other assassinations were carried out before the end of the year. Although the Catholic Church in Dublin loudly condemned such attacks, they achieved Collins's aim of totally disrupting the police intelligence system in the capital.

The second half of 1919 had seen the Volunteers intensify their campaign against the police. Many local units engaged in activity such as road-trenching and the cutting of telephone and telegraph wires, and the RIC chose to abandon many outlying barracks during the winter of 1919–20. While this had occurred during earlier periods of tension, for example during the 1918 election, the RIC returned to the vacated barracks once the prospect of serious trouble had receded. From the beginning of 1920, however, the Volunteers systematically destroyed these unoccupied stations to ensure that the police could not return. During the first six months of 1920, over 400 such barracks were burned down. This increased the sense of demoralisation fell by many policemen, and the fact that the force was under-strength added to this problem. Although improved pay and conditions had helped to attract new recruits in the second half of 1919, this could not offset the flood of resignations being submitted during this period. Significantly, it was older officers close to retirement who were less likely to resign, as they wanted to enjoy a full pension at the end of their careers. For many others the dangerous nature of the job was becoming increasingly apparent, and Sinn Féin's campaign of social ostracism clearly made life difficult for serving policemen. At the beginning of 1920, RIC numbers totalled 9,500. While the lower ranks were mostly filled by Catholics who came from a farming background, the senior posts were disproportionately occupied by Protestants. Many of these joined as officer cadets rather than progressing through the ranks. Such a state of affairs, allied to the growing public antipathy towards the RIC, unsurprisingly made recruitment for the force increasingly difficult. The answer for an Irish administration that only belatedly recognised this problem was to seek recruits in Britain where there was a large pool of unemployed ex-servicemen.

Undoubtedly, the low level of violence in the early phase of the War of Independence partly explains the lethargic approach by the Westminster government to developments in Ireland. Over the course of 1919 fewer than twenty policemen had lost their lives. These attacks were frequently the result of local initiative, and only the Squad's targeting of DMP detectives appeared to be a result of coordinated planning. Indeed, the sporadic nature of the violence before 1920 makes it difficult to describe the conflict as a war. Significantly, however, the campaign mounted by the Volunteers was garnering public support, as it consistently provoked a disproportionate response by the authorities who were quick to place large swathes of the country under military rule. Such a strategy proved self-defeating, as it failed to take account of existing political and security realities. In general, each Volunteer operation prompted a show of strength by the police and military, action that only increased the popular perception of British oppression. The entire population, therefore, was being subjected to a mild form of coercion that failed to pinpoint the relatively small number of active Volunteers engaged in the violence. Thus the authorities failed to capitalise on the sense of public outrage that followed the early killings of RIC men, who were, for the most part, Irish Catholics, and isolate the militants. Rather naively, the government viewed the attacks as the work of criminal gangs that had exploited the general disorder in many parts of the country. A more imaginative and thoughtful political approach, in conjunction with a more surgical security policy, might have pushed the great majority of the separatists down a constitutional path and isolated the modest number of Volunteer activists. Instead, the British drifted into a security-focused policy that had neither clear political nor military objectives.

There were two principal reasons for this. While Lloyd George had returned as prime minister following the 1918 general election, he now led a coalition government that was dominated by the Conservative Party. The Conservatives had won 330 seats, almost double the number won by Lloyd George's coalition Liberals. Although the new chief secretary, Ian Macpherson, was a Liberal, the cabinet was dominated by Conservatives, including Bonar Law and Long, who favoured a tough security approach to the Irish disturbances. Differences in cabinet between the Liberals and Conservatives contributed to the drift in Irish policy during 1919. Some Liberal ministers urged the government to press ahead with Home Rule. However, by the time Lloyd George and Bonar Law reached agreement on the implementation of a new devolution scheme in October 1919, neither believed that it would be sufficient to satisfy the Irish. Significantly, it had taken until October for the coalition partners to agree on the formation of a cabinet committee that would consider the Irish question and outline a way forward.

A second reason for the government's failure to produce a coherent Irish policy following the outbreak of violence was its preoccupation with other affairs. Both Lloyd George and Bonar Law spent much of the first half of 1919 in Paris attending the Peace Conference. When they returned to London, moreover, they were confronted by the issues of postwar reconstruction and the growing tension in industrial relations that led to a series of strikes across Britain. Beyond these domestic problems, Lloyd George and his government had to deal with trouble in other parts of the Empire, notably in India and Egypt. Consequently, Ireland was pushed farther down the coalition's agenda and was not considered a priority in the immediate postwar period. This meant the Irish administration failed to adopt a clearly defined strategy, instead relying on mild repression punctuated with half-hearted attempts at conciliation. Such a development helped to maintain unity between the political and military wings of the separatist movement. It also enabled a relatively small number of militants to dominate Irish republicanism for the duration of the conflict. Still, there was tension both between the Volunteers and the broader Sinn Féin movement and within the Volunteers.

Dáil Éireann sought to control the Volunteers, but it met infrequently during the War of Independence. Only 28 teachtaí dála (TDs) were present at the inaugural meeting, as approximately half of the Dáil's members, including Éamon de Valera and Arthur Griffith, were in prison. Others chose not to attend, fearing arrest. Those present adopted a brief provisional constitution and listened to a reading of the Declaration of Independence. This linked the Irish Republic endorsed by the people at the recent general election to the one proclaimed by the signatories of the 1916 Proclamation. The TDs also approved the Democratic Programme, a left-leaning document that mirrored other idealistic statements of intent that had been drafted in a number of European capitals soon after the war. To many contemporary observers, the Democratic Programme was a demonstration of gratitude to the Labour Party that had stood aside in the 1918 election, thereby ensuring a landslide victory for Sinn Féin. It had been penned by the Labour leader, Thomas Johnson, but had been revised prior to the Dáil meeting by Seán T. O'Kelly, who diluted much of its socialist rhetoric. While the document contained the key principle that "all rights to private property must be subordinated to the public right", it would not be a catalyst for social revolution in Ireland. Indeed, the Sinn Féin leaders reflected a socially conservative mindset. They moved swiftly to prevent the emergence of class tension, especially in rural Ireland, and to focus on the struggle for national independence.

The other piece of business conducted at the Dáil's opening session was the appointment of three delegates to the postwar peace conference. De Valera, Griffith and Count Plunkett were selected to present the case for Irish independence in Paris, but the first two were in prison and O'Kelly, the Dáil's ceann comhairle (speaker), stepped in to act as the Irish envoy in Paris. O'Kelly arrived in Paris on 10 February with credentials describing him as the representative of the "Provisional government of the Irish Republic". However, Irish hopes of progress dissipated when President Woodrow Wilson made it clear that he considered the future of Ireland to be a question for the British government alone. Although O'Kelly persisted in Paris, it was clear that Ireland's claim for self-determination would not be heard. The appeal to the postwar peace conference had been the clearest element of Sinn Féin policy in the 1918 election campaign, and the manner in which this had been dismissed in Paris marked a significant political setback for the party. This encouraged the Sinn Féin leadership to adopt a more militant stance, a development that further strengthened the influence of the Volunteers.

De Valera's absence during this formative period was an obvious blow to Sinn Féin. He had been in Lincoln Jail following his arrest in May 1918, but he was sensationally sprung from prison on 3 February 1919 following an operation masterminded by Collins and his close IRB associate, Harry Boland. The dramatic escape had given the republican movement a propaganda boost, and de Valera returned to Dublin later that month to plan Sinn Féin's next move. The initial rejection of Irish independence claims at the peace conference encouraged the Sinn Féin president to consider a tour of the United States, where he intended to harness Irish-American support. Accordingly, de Valera travelled to the United States in June 1919 and did not return to Ireland until December 1920. For eighteen months, therefore, Sinn Féin was without its most astute political mind during the struggle for independence. This was another factor that contributed to the dominance of the Volunteers within the broader separatist movement. De Valera was, of course, present for the second session of Dáil Éireann from 1–4 April, when his first task was to appoint a new cabinet. De Valera selected Collins (finance), Cathal Brugha (defence), Griffith (home affairs), Plunkett (foreign affairs), William T. Cosgrave (local government), Constance Markievicz (labour) and Eoin MacNeill (industries). The release of all Sinn Féin prisoners in English jails in the previous month and the escape of a number of others from Mountjoy meant that 52 TDs were able to attend the second session where they heard de

Valera make two important pronouncements. Firstly, he poured cold water on the Democratic Programme, insisting that the priority had to be the overthrow of British rule in Ireland. Secondly, he addressed the growing state of unrest in the country and called for the RIC to be "ostracised socially by the people".

It was also clear that the Dáil cabinet was determined to act as an underground government by establishing an effective counter-state. The public vote in the 1918 election was highlighted both to support Sinn Féin's claim to be the legitimate government of Ireland and to endorse the Volunteers' military campaign against the Crown Forces. During the third session of Dáil Éireann, which took place on 10–12 April, the leadership laid out plans to undermine British attempts to govern the country. While these included the usual demands for international recognition of Irish independence, Sinn Féin leaders had previously indicated that they intended to raise funds in order to support the work of the Dáil government. Sinn Féin sought a total of £250,000 in the Dáil Loan, and the expectation was that a similar sum could be collected in the United States. In addition to the practical financial contribution to Dáil funds, Collins, the minister for finance, attached a political significance to the Dáil Loan. He anticipated widespread public participation with many citizens contributing small amounts. This would allow individuals to feel that they were actively contributing to the cause of Irish freedom. By the summer of 1920 the target had been surpassed. The Loan was collected on a constituency basis and it attracted more than 140,000 subscribers in Ireland. The constituency average was just over £4,000, and Munster was responsible for almost half of the total of £370,000 that was collected. The Dáil Loan proved a triumph both for Sinn Féin's organisational capacity at grass-roots level and for the personal leadership of Collins, who assumed full responsibility for the entire venture. The minister for finance understood the importance of marketing, and he appeared in a short promotional film produced by the Irish Film Company and shown in cinemas all over the country.

Yet in spite of the success of the Dáil Loan, Sinn Féin had encountered serious problems in establishing an alternative government. In September 1919 the Dáil was suppressed by the authorities and declared a "dangerous association". This followed the banning of Sinn Féin, the Volunteers and the Gaelic League, which was implemented on 3 July. This effectively weakened the political arm of the separatist movement. Such action raised doubts about Sinn Féin's ability to exert meaningful influence over the Volunteers. In theory, the Volunteers were under the control of the minister for defence, Cathal Brugha, but the reality was that many commanders exercised considerable local autonomy and were often resentful of political interference. Brugha was anxious to remedy this situation in an attempt to establish political control over the Volunteers. In August 1919 he insisted that each Volunteer had to swear an oath of allegiance to the Dáil. However, there was opposition to the oath in some quarters, particularly among IRB members, and substantial delay before it could be administered in certain areas, ensuring that Brugha's objective of forcing the Volunteers to accept the authority of the Dáil was never achieved. In fact, Brugha did not play an active role in the conflict during 1919. Instead, Collins emerged as the dominant personality in the revolutionary struggle. His dual role as a member of Volunteer GHQ and the Dáil cabinet helped to ease some of the tension that emerged between the political and military factions. Still, Brugha did not welcome Collins's growing power, and his move to force the Volunteers to accept the Dáil's authority was, in part, a move to check Collins's influence. He was also furious at Collins's use of the IRB to consolidate his power and sought to undermine the Brotherhood's role within the Volunteers. Brugha had enlisted de Valera's support in trying to end the IRB's influence, but he was frustrated by his own assistant, Richard Mulcahy.

The minister for defence had delegated much of the responsibility for overseeing the activities of the Volunteers to Mulcahy, but he worked closely with Collins. The two were IRB members, and both men believed that as the IRB shared the "aims and methods" of the Volunteers, its actions could only advance the cause of Irish independence. As chief of staff, Mulcahy was pragmatic enough to recognise that Volunteer GHQ exercised little direct control over the Volunteer brigades, and he was prepared to leave the development of military strategy to those local commanders who were actually engaged in the conflict. Volunteer operations were still sporadic and uncoordinated by the end of 1919, but a district pattern of guerrilla warfare, developed at local level, had become evident in certain areas of the country.

1920 – year of terror

During 1920 the Volunteers were frequently referred to as the Irish Republican Army (IRA). They conducted an increasing number of operations and the RIC remained their primary target. Barracks were routinely attacked and more ambushes of police patrols were mounted. These often led to gun battles that could last for several hours. The assassination of lone policemen had become a key tactic for the IRA, and this could lead to retaliatory attacks when police discipline began to slip. The first such retaliation had taken place in Thurles in January 1920, and it had the effect of terrorising the local population. One consequence of this development was that local Catholic clergy condemned both the IRA outrages and the police reprisals that followed. However, the nature of these reprisals handed the propaganda initiative to the IRA and helped to consolidate support for the Volunteers among the wider public. The clearest example of this in the first half of 1920 occurred in Cork city on 20 March, when Tomás MacCurtain, the commander of the Cork No 1 Brigade of the IRA, was assassinated in his own home. The MacCurtain attack followed the killings of a number of RIC personnel in the city, and it was widely believed that rogue elements of the RIC had carried out the shooting. MacCurtain was a very prominent local figure, having just been elected as Cork's lord mayor on 30 January, and his funeral, which drew a very large crowd, proved to be a highly successfully propaganda coup for the republican movement.

By stepping up their campaign, the IRA exerted further pressure on the RIC, and this led to a growing number of resignations from the force. The year had opened with an attack on Carrigtwohill barracks in County Cork. By the end of April 1920, three hundred RIC barracks had been destroyed in arson attacks. Individual members of the RIC were being shunned and boycotted in their local communities, and this, together with the increased danger associated with the job, had caused many to consider their future in the force. The authorities had already turned to England in order to recruit replacements for those leaving the RIC, as they confirmed their determination to overcome the challenge presented by the republican movement. In January 1920 Macpherson explained to an audience in Inverness that he regarded Ireland as "an outpost of the Empire" where they would maintain law and order "until they were asked by the people of this country to surrender it to the Irish Republic". While such sentiments were welcomed by Unionists who claimed that "drastic government" was now a necessity, the Nationalist press in Ireland was adamant that the growing unrest across the country was due to the British security presence. Recruitment in Britain for additional police personnel attracted an average of 100 men each month from January to June 1920. The first of these new recruits arrived in Ireland on 25 March, but a shortage of uniforms ensured that they stood out from their RIC comrades. They wore a mixture of police and military clothing and were described as the "Black and Tans", a name that was taken from a pack of foxhounds in County Tipperary.

The Black and Tans, 90 per cent of whom were ex-soldiers who had served on the Western Front, quickly acquired a reputation for brutality. They were given inadequate training for police work, and their lack of discipline served to heighten tension in many parts of the country where they faced a hostile civilian population. In spite of the attractive wage on offer (£3/10/0 per week with allowances, when the pay for the average constable serving in Britain was £2/15/0), recruitment for the new force was slow to take off in these early weeks. Indeed, it only accelerated following the sharp downturn in the British economy that occurred in the summer of 1920. In October more than 1,100 men signed up, and over 8,000 Black and Tans would see service in Ireland. Many were sent to trouble spots in Munster where they were frequently billeted in police barracks.

Black and Tans on guard duty in Dublin, 1920.

Relations between these new recruits and serving RIC men were often strained, as experienced policeman regarded the Tans' actions as adding fuel to the fire and aggravating the security situation in the south and west of the country.

Naturally, the Tans became targets for the IRA who could choose both the time and the most favourable location to conduct ambushes before disappearing into the nearby countryside. When they sustained casualties, the Tans retaliated by targeting the lives and property of civilians living in the locality. Several such incidents in late September 1920 confirmed that a new pattern of violence had come to define the conflict. In Trim, County Meath, a large force of Tans entered the town following an attack on the local police barracks on 26 September which resulted in the shooting of a head constable. A number of business premises owned by alleged Sinn Féin sympathisers were set on fire and the local population was terrorised. One of the firms, the local mineral water factory which was owned by the chairman of Trim Urban District Council, sustained damage estimated at £20,000. In the previous month the Tans had caused significant disruption and economic damage to the rural population around Knocklong, County Limerick, when they burned down one of the largest creameries in Ireland. This form of economic warfare was intensified as other creameries were targeted. Bacon factories and mills were also subjected to arson attacks conducted by the Crown Forces.

A few days before the incidents in Trim, an IRA shooting in Balbriggan had prompted a force of over 100 Black and Tans to descend on the County Dublin town, where they attacked local residents and set fire to a number of properties. Two civilians, including a local barber, were killed, and a large number of properties, including four pubs, were destroyed. The "Sack of Balbriggan" immediately became the focus of international attention. Its proximity to Dublin enabled dramatic photographs capturing the devastation to be widely circulated, and this ensured that the government's Irish policy was fiercely criticised. In Britain the *Scotsman,* while highlighting the cowardly nature of the attacks mounted by the IRA, denounced the Tans' response at Balbriggan as "wicked and deplorable". Even *The Times,* which had been broadly sympathetic to the coalition government at Westminster, had demanded an immediate halt to all reprisals by the end of September. These were described as a "national disgrace" in an editorial. While the authorities may not have explicitly authorised such practices, *The Times* accused the government of conniving at this unlawful deployment of force, adding that such a development had made the prospect of an Irish settlement even more unlikely. By this stage it was evident that interested observers of the conflict in Ireland regarded the reprisals strategy as counter-productive. It had eroded Westminster's moral authority and invigorated the republican movement.

The death of Terence MacSwiney on 25 October following a hunger strike that lasted 74 days provided a further boost for the republican cause. MacSwiney had succeeded his close friend, Tomás MacCurtain, both as lord mayor of Cork and commandant of the Cork Brigade of the IRA, following the latter's assassination in March 1920. In August MacSwiney was arrested at Cork's city hall and charged with possession of a number of documents including material that belonged to the RIC. Even before he had been sentenced by a military tribunal to two years penal servitude without hard labour, MacSwiney had begun to refuse prison food. The hunger strike would become a key weapon for republican prisoners who challenged the authority of the British legal system. Responding to the announcement of his sentence, MacSwiney had informed the military tribunal, "I have decided the term of my imprisonment. Whatever your government may do, I shall be free, alive or dead, within a month."

The statement of measured, but fatal, defiance produced a media storm, as the international and British press absorbed the story of this high-profile Irish political prisoner. His subsequent transfer to Brixton Prison in London added to the drama that surrounded the affair. MacSwiney's steady decline became front-page news around the world, drawing international sympathy and support for the republican cause and unnerving a Westminster government that would give serious consideration to ordering the prisoner's release. Two fellow prisoners,

Women protesting against the treatment of IRA hunger strikers, outside Mountjoy Jail, Dublin, 1920.

Michael Fitzgerald and Joseph Murphy, who had begun the fast with MacSwiney, remained in Cork and they too died in jail, but it was the demise of the lord mayor of Cork that seized the public's attention. His requiem mass in London became a major public event, and his funeral in Cork on 31 October was observed as a day of public mourning throughout Ireland. Cork now had a martyr figure on a par with Patrick Pearse, and the republican movement used MacSwiney's noble act of self-sacrifice both to provide an inspiration to the Irish people and to channel international pressure on Britain to withdraw from Ireland. On 1 November Kevin Barry, an 18-year-old medical student was hanged in Mountjoy Prison for his role in an IRA ambush in which three British soldiers were killed in Dublin. Barry had been captured during the engagement and was subsequently found guilty by a court-martial, even though there was no evidence that he had been personally responsible for any of the deaths. Barry's youth ensured that his execution had a profound effect on opinion both in Ireland and Britain. The Labour Party had championed Barry's cause in the House of Commons, and his execution led to a more sustained criticism of the government's record in Ireland by certain sections of the British press.

Dramatic though these events were, they were soon overshadowed by a surge in violence towards the end of November 1920. In Dublin the IRA had been engaged in an intelligence battle with the authorities, relying on Collins's network of informers to keep them one step ahead of their pursuers. When Collins received information that British agents operating in the capital were closing in around senior republican figures, the director of intelligence planned a decisive strike on his opponents. Such was the scale of this operation that Collins had to deploy specially elected men from the four Dublin battalions of the IRA in addition to members of the Squad who had experience in targeting and assassinating suspected British agents and informers. At 9 am on Sunday, 21 November 1920, groups of men arrived at designated addresses in the city, and a total of fourteen men were killed. While two civilians died as a result of mistaken identity, the majority of those killed were British agents who were taken by surprise in their lodgings and hotel rooms. The fourteen included two auxiliary Division of the RIC who had been passing one of the properties and had attempted to intervene. The Auxiliaries were viewed as an elite force recruited from ex-officers in the British Army. Easily recognisable with their distinctive tam-o'-shanter caps, the Auxiliaries were much more feared than the Black and Tans. News of this coordinated and bloody operation quickly spread across the city and a number of anxious officials and their wives sought refuge in Dublin Castle, fearing for their safety. It was inevitable, as Collins undoubtedly anticipated, that these audacious attacks would provoke a violent response from the Crown Forces based in the capital.

That afternoon Croke Park was the venue for a challenge football match between Dublin and Tipperary. The Tipperary team was viewed as the enemy by the Crown Forces, and it was assumed that the match would be attended by a number of IRA personnel who had participated in the morning's attacks. The military authorities hastily put together a plan in which troops would form a cordon around the ground to oversee the dispersal of the crowd. Before this, a group of RIC and Auxiliaries were to search all spectators after an officer had halted the match ten minutes before the final whistle. Not surprisingly, placing an angry force of RIC and Auxiliaries in direct contact with such a large hostile crowd ensured chaos. The Crown Forces opened fire, killing fourteen people and wounding a further sixty. Among the dead were three young boys and one of the Tipperary players, Michael Hogan. A subsequent military inquiry claimed that the Crown Forces had reacted to shots fired from the crowd, but, while some of the spectators undoubtedly had handguns in their possession, there was no evidence to support this contention. This was not the end of the killing. Before Bloody Sunday – as the day would become known – was over, three prisoners, Dick McKee, Peadar Clancy and Conor Clune, were killed while in police custody in Dublin Castle. While the authorities immediately released a statement insisting that all three had been shot during an escape attempt, Dubliners were in no doubt that the killings had taken place following the men's refusal to provide the names of those involved in the earlier shooting of British agents. The three had been arrested on the eve of Bloody Sunday and, though McKee and Clancy were senior IRA figures who had worked closely with Collins in planning the operation, Clune was a Gaelic Leaguer with no IRA connections.

The level of violence on Bloody Sunday shocked the public in both Ireland and Britain, and it undoubtedly stiffened republican determination to prolong the conflict. Before the end of November, another notorious incident, the Kilmichael ambush, gave the IRA a stunning success and, in the process, confirmed that the Volunteers had developed into a capable fighting force. On 28 November 1920, an IRA flying column of 36 men under the command of Tom Barry ambushed a motorised Auxiliary patrol at Kilmichael, near Macroom, in County Cork. Following a fierce engagement, three Volunteers and seventeen Auxiliaries lay dead or dying. The ambush has subsequently become a subject of great controversy, as differing accounts of the action have been recorded. In his recollection of the event, Tom Barry stressed that the Auxiliaries had used the "false surrender" tactic, whereby the Auxiliaries feigned surrender but then suddenly opened fire on their attackers. The first British officer on the scene noted that a number of bodies had been mutilated by bayonets, a finding endorsed by the doctor at the inquest. Barry's reputation as a resourceful and ruthless IRA commander was clearly enhanced by the Kilmichael incident. The son of an RIC constable, Barry had served as a gunner with the Royal Field Artillery during World War I. On his return to Ireland following his wartime service, Barry tried and failed to obtain employment in the British civil service. By the summer of 1920 his anger at the behaviour of the Crown Forces in his native Cork led him to join the IRA. His military experience and obvious ability as a guerrilla commander ensured that he quickly assumed a leadership role in the Volunteers.

This upsurge of violence towards the end of November marked the beginning of the final phase of the conflict, as each side responded to the other's actions with even greater brutality. A fortnight after the Kilmichael ambush, the IRA attacked an Auxiliary patrol as it made its way down the Old Youghal Road in Cork. Twelve Auxiliaries were injured, and one subsequently died from his wounds. That night, 11 December 1920, another party of Auxiliaries gathered in Patrick Street where they smashed shop windows and set fire to buildings. When they intervened to prevent members of the Cork Fire Brigade from tackling the fires, the result was the destruction of more than five acres of property. The buildings were valued at more than £20 million, and 1,000 workers lost their jobs as a result of the blazes. The burning of Cork sparked international condemnation, but the government's initial response saw Hamar Greenwood, who had succeeded Macpherson as chief secretary in April 1920, deny that the police had any involvement, instead claiming that the citizens of Cork were responsible for the wave of arson attacks. The absurdity of Greenwood's statement to the House of Commons was greeted by incredulity in large sections of the British press. Following a military inquiry, the Auxiliary company responsible for what was the most spectacular reprisal of the War of Independence was expelled from the city of Cork. Within days, however, the same unit was involved in further controversy, when they shot dead a youth and a 70-year-old priest outside Dunmanway. The fatal shots had been fired by an Auxiliary cadet named Harte and, though he was subsequently found to be insane, the murders deepened the feeling of revulsion felt in the county. Such actions were frowned upon by military commanders such as General Edward Strickland, who had insisted on the removal of the Auxiliaries from Cork city.

The burning of Cork and the Harte murders brought tension between the police and the military to breaking point. General Neville Macready, the general officer commanding (GOC) in Ireland, refused to assume responsibility for the RIC, the Black and Tans and the Auxiliaries and openly condemned their regular acts of indiscipline. This friction between the military and the police was a major factor in Britain's failure to implement an effective security policy during 1920. Lloyd George maintained that the trouble in Ireland was a "policeman's job", insisting that IRA attacks were mounted by criminal elements that he described as "murder gangs". This murder gang mentality, together with the cabinet's refusal to acknowledge that the situation in Ireland had developed into a small war, contributed to the decision to reinforce the police rather than make full use of the army. Over the course of 1920, however, the police became increasingly independent and proved difficult to control. The introduction of the Black and Tans and the Auxiliaries clearly exacerbated this problem.

When Macready issued orders to troops forbidding any form of retaliation, Major-General Hugh Tudor, the chief of police, refused to issue parallel instructions, claiming that such a course would impact negatively on police morale. Tudor had been appointed in May 1920, and Macready hoped that, with his military background, he would impose strict discipline on his rapidly expanding force. Instead, with the tacit approval of Lloyd George and Churchill, he allowed the policy of "unauthorised" reprisals to develop during the summer of 1920. Clearly, Tudor subscribed to the "murder gang" theory and, unlike Macready, he lacked political nous, a serious flaw that contributed significantly to the failure of Britain's Irish policy in 1920. Tudor's instinct was to overlook or excuse serious acts of indiscipline, believing that any other approach would only increase the level of despair within the force. He was convinced that the reprisals tactic would bring an end to the trouble in Ireland and was encouraged by the level of political support for this strategy in London. Speaking at the lord mayor's banquet on 9 November 1920, Lloyd George enthusiastically suggested that his government was turning the tide in Ireland by his claim that "we have murder by the throat". Such optimism, of course, was quickly shattered by the events of Bloody Sunday and Kilmichael.

The policy of reprisals associated with Tudor was a response to the development of the IRA's guerrilla war strategy in the summer of 1920. By this point special IRA units known as flying columns had been established. Each flying column averaged between 20 and 30 full-time fighting men, though, on occasion, they could be much larger. Flying columns began operating in Cork, Tipperary, Clare and Limerick, where they moved around familiar territory, billeting on local farms and staging ambushes on police and military patrols. To some extent the formation of these groups had been forced on the IRA, as the authorities intensified their efforts to arrest known Volunteers. This led targeted IRA men to "go on the run" and group together in these flying columns in order to sustain their campaign against the Crown Forces. Still, only a minority of Volunteers were attached to these columns. The majority in rural Ireland continued to be part-timers who worked on their farms and were occasionally mobilised by their local commander to complete a range of tasks. The main tactic of the flying column was the ambush, and it was in response to such attacks that the police carried out reprisals in which local communities suffered. In theory, the flying columns should have presented the police and the military with an obvious target, but the IRA's knowledge of the local terrain enabled the Volunteers to disappear into the surrounding countryside following an operation. The failure of the Crown Forces to combat this type of guerrilla warfare saw them rely increasingly on reprisals. While the cabinet was averse to the burning of property, as happened in Trim and Balbriggan, certain ministers were in favour of shooting "suspects". Naturally, this resort to police counter-terror increased the public's outrage and quickly turned opinion in Britain against the government's security policy.

Politically, the Lloyd George government was faring no better. While the 1920 Government of Ireland Act conferred Home Rule on Ireland, though it was delivered with partition, it was clearly too little, too late. The legislation had emerged from the deliberations of a cabinet committee which had been established in October 1919. Prior to this the cabinet admitted privately that it did not have an Irish policy, and the 1920 act illustrated just how far out of touch the government was with opinion in Ireland. By 1920 Home Rule belonged to the previous generation as far as the leadership of Sinn Féin was concerned. Moreover, the choice of Walter Long, the former Irish Unionist leader and the cabinet's recognised "Irish expert", to head the committee ruled out any new, imaginative approach to the Irish problem. In addition, Sinn Féin's policy of abstention ensured that, from an Irish perspective, the debate on the Government of Ireland Bill was dominated by Ulster Unionists. Yet the government assumed that constitutional nationalism retained significant support in Ireland, and the offer of Home Rule, with the prospect of an early end to partition, might appeal to Irish citizens. Such a belief hinged on the notion that most Irish people were firmly opposed to the IRA's military campaign. Policy, therefore, should have attempted to marginalise the perceived small number of extremists and then deal decisively with this group. This was the view endorsed by Greenwood, but he allowed his optimism to obscure his view of reality in Ireland. In July 1920, *The Times* warned that republicans would seize on the Government of Ireland Act to strengthen their claim to be the legitimate government of Ireland, as Sinn Féin was "all powerful, and … virtually synonymous with the Irish people". Greenwood rejected this analysis as too pessimistic, stubbornly retaining the view that "respectable Irishmen" were opposed to the IRA and welcomed the presence of the British Army.

Greenwood soon became associated with the policy of reprisals, and he was quick to voice his support for Tudor and the police. While he briefly considered easing coercion following his appointment, Greenwood's attitude had hardened by the summer of 1920, as he witnessed the repeated failure of the courts to bring guilty verdicts against captured IRA men. The government responded by introducing tough new legislation in August. The Restoration of Order in Ireland Act (ROIA) gave the authorities the power to try suspects through courts-martial. This circumvented the problem of finding juries willing to convict fellow Irishmen, an irony that was not lost on Sinn Féin. On the one hand, the government insisted that IRA attacks were the work of criminal murder gangs, but it now resorted to trying these "civilians" in military courts rather than through the normal criminal justice system. Moreover, only in cases where the death penalty was a likely outcome was there to be a bona fide legal officer in attendance. Naturally, this increased the likelihood of wrongful convictions and provided further ammunition for Sinn Féin's effective propaganda machine. Yet while the ROIA conferred wide-ranging powers on Macready, the military chief in Ireland, the cabinet stopped short of placing the whole country under martial law. In effect, the legislation gave the authorities the power to arrest and detain anyone associated with the republican movement, meaning that the bulk of the population became suspects. The deployment of the Black and Tans and the Auxiliaries to seek out and arrest suspects ensured that public anger at the government intensified.

Still, Greenwood persisted in the belief that Irish opinion could be won over by the authorities. This ignored the results of the local government elections held in 1920. Elections for urban and municipal councils were held in January, and these were followed by the county council elections in June. The government had delayed these local government elections and introduced the proportional representation (PR) system in an attempt to limit Sinn Féin's advantage. The Sinn Féin election campaign in January was also disrupted by the authorities. However, the party still polled strongly, winning 87,311 first preference votes to 85,932 for the Unionists, 57,626 for Labour, and 47,102 for the Home Rulers. More impressive was the overall result which left Sinn Féin in control of nine of the 11 corporations and 62 of the 99 urban councils. Of course, Sinn Féin's appeal was even stronger in rural Ireland, and the party won control of 29 of the 33 county councils (Tipperary was divided into two ridings) in the June contests. These results strengthened Sinn Féin's electoral mandate and its claim to be the legitimate government in Ireland. They also further undermined the British administration in Ireland. Cosgrave, the Dáil's minister for local government, sought to hammer home Sinn Féin's advantage by instructing the councils to impede the Castle administration and to take their direction from Dáil Éireann.

Aided by his deputy, Kevin O'Higgins, Cosgrave worked tirelessly to establish an alternative system of local government in the face of determined British opposition. Following the local government elections, Greenwood announced in July 1920 that he was withdrawing the annual grants paid to local authorities if the councils refused to recognise the authority of the British government. This action put the entire bill for the damage done by both sides during the War of Independence onto local ratepayers. Consequently, property owners faced sharp rises in their rates bills, a development that led to a rise in support for the republican movement among these wealthier, propertied families. Still, this created a huge problem for Cosgrave and O'Higgins as they sought to supplement local government finances. To increase revenue, they tried to levy their own rates. Although this was particularly successful in the more prosperous eastern half of the country, it met strong resistance in the west where opposition to any form of taxation was ingrained. Faced with this shortfall, the local government department implemented a number of economy measures, all of which made good sense in rural areas where the population was in decline. Workhouses were phased out and local cottage hospitals, most of which were underused and overstaffed, were closed and patients were transferred to county hospitals. Under Cosgrave's direction, therefore, local government became more efficient and cost effective.

Sinn Féin also sought to build a counter-state, supplanting British rule in Ireland by creating an alternative court system. Although the initial attempt to establish "national Arbitration Courts" following a Dáil decree in August 1919 proved ineffective, republican courts, which were largely the result of local initiative, began to spring up in many parts of the country from March 1920. These bodies immediately secured the public's confidence. Indeed, many of these courts went beyond straightforward arbitration, which was the extent of their powers sanctioned by the Dáil, as they assumed authority for civil and criminal cases. In this instance the Dáil struggled to catch up with such spontaneous developments and, on 29 June 1920, it permitted the new courts to try civil cases. In addition, the Dáil's minister for home affairs, Austin Stack, was given the powers to establish courts with a criminal jurisdiction. Yet, in spite of the Dáil's eagerness to bring these revolutionary courts under its direction, Stack proved to be a poor administrator and a largely ineffective minister. Consequently, many of these republican courts continued to operate independently with little reference to Dáil Éireann. This was particularly true in the west, where agrarian disputes dominated the legal proceedings, and the courts simply built on the tradition of the Land League tribunals. These courts dealt with cattle-driving, the division of grazing ranches among landless men and quarrels between neighbouring farmers. Their decisions were enforced by local IRA units. By coincidence, some of these disputes in the west indirectly involved the RIC, as one of the force's many duties was to keep an eye on cattle owned by graziers who had become the target of a cattle drive. Significantly, these Dáil courts gained a wide degree of acceptance, as they discharged their functions in an impartial manner, a fact emphasised by the willingness of Unionist landlords to have cases brought before the republican courts. Judges for these cases were often drawn from local solicitors or the Catholic clergy, but they ensured, for the most part, that justice was dispensed in an even-handed fashion.

Of course, the local IRA had a major role to play in the new justice system. The campaign against the RIC had forced the police to withdraw from many areas, leaving a void that the IRA had to fill. In those towns and villages where a police presence was maintained, fuel and provisions had to be commandeered for local barracks, and this frequently increased tension between the police and the local population. Those working as cooks or having any kind of association with the RIC were often subjected to intimidation. Women who fraternised with local policemen were particular targets, and they could expect their hair to be shaved by the Volunteers. With the police under increasing pressure, the crime rate increased in many areas, and local inhabitants often looked to the IRA to apprehend wrongdoers and deter others from engaging in crime. In June 1920 Mulcahy instructed the IRA to form a police force, and it won public approval. In addition to the detection of crime, the republican police took responsibility for the regulation of hours kept by public houses and clamped down on illicit whiskey distilling, a practice that had increased significantly with the absence of any police presence in many rural areas. Republican police also provided stewarding at public events such as race meetings and football and hurling matches.

Therefore, the Dáil had some success in building an effective counter-state, an achievement made all the more remarkable by the fact that it was conducted against a background of constant harrying by the police and military. Sinn Féin and the IRA had, in the process, demonstrated that they could be efficient administrators, not just revolutionaries. This was a significant factor in the republican movement's ongoing struggle to maintain a psychological hold over the people. While the actions of the Black and Tans and Auxiliaries had clearly been counter-productive, the IRA could not simply rely on the population's unconditional support. The desires for peace and a return to normality were powerful instincts, and the republican movement worked hard to ensure that it maintained its propaganda advantage over the British. To this end the Dáil had established the *Irish Bulletin,* which first appeared on 11 November 1919. It was issued several times each week and, in spite of numerous obstacles, it was widely circulated. Initially, under Frank Gallagher's editorship, the *Bulletin* concentrated on documenting British acts of aggression, and it had no shortage of reports with the wave of reprisals carried out in the second half of 1920. Significantly, the *Bulletin* exerted considerable influence in Britain, where excerpts from the news-sheets were occasionally carried by a number of newspapers, including *The Times.* In November 1920 copies of the *Bulletin* turned up on the benches in the House of Commons, and the publicity generated helped to turn public opinion in Britain against the coalition government's Irish policy. By February 1921 Erskine Childers had assumed overall control of Sinn Féin publicity, and the *Irish Bulletin* put much greater emphasis on challenging government claims that the IRA was simply a "murder gang". Thereafter, articles painted the IRA as the legitimate army of the Irish Republic engaged in a war against foreign oppressors.

Towards the truce

The final phase of the War of Independence witnessed an escalation of the violence with both the Crown Forces and the IRA sustaining heavy losses. Civilian casualties also rose significantly. Up to the end of November 1920, 177 policemen and 54 soldiers had been killed. Another 42 civilians, including IRA Volunteers, had also lost their lives. In the period from 1 January 1921 until the truce in July, a further 228 policemen and 96 soldiers died in the conflict. During the same months, 154 civilians were killed. This last figure includes both Volunteers and civilians shot either intentionally or accidentally by Crown Forces, and those deemed to have been "spies" who were killed by the IRA. These higher figures can be attributed to a greater number of ambushes mounted by IRA flying columns operating with an increased number of Volunteers. It was also the case that those attacks were now being conducted over a wider geographical area, as the IRA extended its operations beyond those areas in Munster that had hitherto experienced the heaviest fighting. The British responded to this escalation by deploying significant numbers of regular soldiers in those rural areas where flying columns were active. This greater use of troops gave the authorities some success. Carefully planned searches uncovered caches of weapons and ammunition, and the flying columns were put under more intense pressure, forcing them in many instances to withdraw to very remote areas. Naturally, this closer contact with the enemy resulted in a further upsurge in violence.

February 1921 saw two significant reverses for the IRA in County Cork where the Crown Forces stepped up efforts to contain Barry's flying column. On 15 February an attack was mounted on a passenger train at Upton Station, as it travelled from Cork to Bandon. Intelligence suggested that about 20 men from the Essex Regiment had boarded the train at Cork, but the attackers were oblivious to the fact that another 50 troops had joined the train at Kinsale Junction. They also wrongly assumed that the troops would be concentrated in the train's middle carriage. Consequently, when the Volunteers opened fire, they were surprised by the large body of troops that alighted from the train and returned fire. The leader of the ambush party, Charlie Hurley, was wounded and three of his men were killed in the gun battle. Unfortunately, a further eight civilians died, including three railway workers and a female cook, and the ambush sparked widespread condemnation, even from some quarters normally supportive of IRA actions. Five days later, at Clonmult, near Midleton, the Cork IRA lost twelve men, while four were wounded and a further four captured when a joint army/police force surrounded a farmhouse in which a group of Volunteers were hiding.

In the following month the IRA enjoyed mixed success in County Leitrim. On 4 March a British officer was killed in an ambush at Sheemore Hill close to Carrick-on-Shannon, and a local creamery was destroyed in a reprisal. A week later at Selton Hill, near Mohill, soldiers from the Bedfordshire Regiment, acting on a tip-off, used two Lewis machine-guns to attack a house in which eleven Volunteers were staying. Six of the IRA party, including their commander, the very capable guerrilla leader Sean Connolly, died in the attack. Before the end of the month, William Latimer, a local Protestant farmer and Orangeman suspected of providing the RIC with information on the whereabouts of Connolly's unit, was shot dead. Connolly's funeral in his native County Longford

Memorial at Selton Hill, County Leitrim.

drew a huge crowd, confirming the public's identification with the republican struggle. However, the officiating cleric, Patrick Finegan, the Bishop of Kilmore, had announced that he would only conduct the "funeral mass" as Connolly had been "shot escaping, not ambushing". In his Lenten pastoral only days earlier, Finegan had declared his opposition to violence "from whatever side or source it comes", warning his co-religionists that engaging in violence ran counter to "the teachings of our Catholic faith". Significantly, the lower clergy in many parts of rural Ireland were much less reticent in supporting the IRA.

While these incidents illustrate the wider geographical footprint of the conflict, traditional heartlands such as West Cork remained active. By March 1921 Tom Barry's flying column numbered more than 100, and it had become the primary target for General Sir Peter Strickland, the army's commander in Munster. On 19 March a large force of British troops attempted to encircle Barry's men at Crossbarry, near Cork city. Though hopelessly outnumbered, Barry's men managed to evade capture by marching for over 12 miles while using accurate covering fire to check their pursuers' progress. About ten soldiers were killed at Crossbarry. Such a close shave did not stifle Barry's determination to engage the enemy. On 30 March his men attacked Rosscarbery RIC barracks in Barry's home town, displaying ruthless efficiency as they destroyed a building that was considered impregnable. The attack began when a 400-pound bomb was detonated at the front door of the barracks, forcing the RIC men inside to move upstairs. When Barry's men burned the stairs, the policemen were forced to surrender. The attack had resulted in the deaths of two officers, while a further nine were injured. The dead and wounded had to be lowered from the ruined building via an upstairs window. The Rosscarbery attack reflected the growing terror in 1921, as both sides adopted more ruthless tactics.

Dublin city, meanwhile, also witnessed rising violence in 1921. During the first six months of the year, attacks on the police and military averaged one per day, and these were widely reported in both the Irish and British press. In some of these incidents, civilians, including children, were caught in the crossfire as gun battles developed. Outside the capital, indeed, civilians were deliberately targeted by both sides. Reprisal shootings by Auxiliaries and Black and Tans became a routine occurrence and an increasing number of civilians were shot by the IRA. As the Crown Forces enjoyed some degree of success in the early part of 1921, the IRA reacted with a new level of ruthlessness. Anyone suspected of colluding with the police or military became a target. Some businessmen who traded with the Crown Forces were killed, but, more often, "spies" were shot if they were suspected of passing information about the IRA to the authorities. In each case a message was pinned to the body to serve as a warning to others. In fact, many of those executed had not relayed information to the Crown Forces but were condemned either by local gossip or by their refusal to cooperate with the IRA. In parts of Munster, moreover, some of those identified as "spies" appear to have been killed because they were considered to be sympathetic towards Unionism. One of the most notorious killings occurred following an abortive IRA ambush at Dripsey, County Cork, on 28 January 1921, in which two Volunteers were killed and a further five captured. Acting on information relayed by Mrs Lindsay, who in the course of a journey from her home at Leemount House to the nearby town of Coachford had learned of the planned ambush, about 70 troops were dispatched to Dripsey to engage the IRA column. Once it became known that Mrs Lindsay had informed the RIC, both she and her driver, James Clarke, were kidnapped by the IRA and held hostage in an attempt to pressurise the authorities into releasing the five IRA captives. The British refused to meet the kidnappers' demand and the five Volunteers were hanged on 28 February. The hangings led to the execution of both Mrs Lindsay and her driver on 9 March 1921.

While the IRA intensified its operations against the Crown Forces, it continued to use the guerrilla warfare tactics that had been perfected during 1920. In Dublin, however, plans were hatched to stage much more ambitious attacks involving large numbers of Volunteers. Although some of these had to be abandoned due to unforeseen circumstances, such as the plan in February 1921 to lure government forces into an ambush at the city's Amiens Street railway station where over 160 Volunteers were waiting, one spectacular attack was staged. The strongest advocate for these major strikes was de Valera. On his return from the United States in December 1920, de Valera urged the IRA to organise a large-scale attack in the city which, he argued, would provide the republican movement with a propaganda coup. He had favoured an assault on Beggars Bush military barracks, but this was considered to be unrealistic. On 25 May, however, his wish was granted when a large force of over 100 Volunteers entered the Custom House, the headquarters of local government administration in Ireland, forcing staff to vacate the building. The Custom House was then set ablaze, while other IRA units delayed the attendance of the Dublin Fire Brigade. The eighteenth-century building was destroyed, but the Volunteers were quickly surrounded by Auxiliaries and regular troops. In the ensuing gun battle, six Volunteers were killed, 12 were wounded and about 70 were forced to surrender. As de Valera had predicted, the Custom House attack attracted huge publicity, but the losses incurred dealt a savage blow to IRA morale in the capital. Collins was furious that de Valera had used his influence to persuade officers in the Dublin Brigade to mount this high-profile attack which ended in military disaster. The fact that many of the Volunteers participating in the action did so with only a few rounds of ammunition increased Collins's fury. In the wake of the Custom House attack, neither Collins nor Mulcahy could hide their contempt for de Valera's failure to grasp the harsh realities of guerrilla warfare.

From early 1920, much of the south and west of Ireland was under martial law. While this increased the pressure on the IRA, it clearly exacerbated the sense of oppression felt by the population. Proclamations issued in General Macready's name warned that anyone found with arms or explosives would face a court-martial and a likely death penalty. In some areas local civilians were strapped to the front of police vehicles to deter attacks. With the application of martial law, official reprisals were sanctioned. This frequently involved the burning of properties belonging to those who were suspected of complicity in the planning of ambushes. During the first five months of 1921 these official reprisals were carried out at the rate of one per day. In response, the IRA engaged in counter-reprisals, warning that two Unionist houses would be destroyed in retaliation for each house burned by the Crown Forces. Not surprisingly, this led to a further escalation of the conflict, but the army was achieving some success in the martial law area. A new system of military intelligence had been established, and the increased use of foot patrols was proving more effective in negating the IRA flying columns. While Macready was encouraged by these developments, he was becoming increasingly frustrated by police indiscipline, which presented a propaganda advantage to the IRA. In December 1920, for example, shortly after Kilmichael, Auxiliaries stationed at Macroom had issued a "new Police Order", which warned all male inhabitants or those passing through Macroom that they must not "appear in public with their hands in their pockets". A further warning stated, "any male infringing this order is liable to be shot on sight". Naturally, such a proclamation caused outrage among the local population. Yet, in the early part of 1921, the authorities were relying on increasing numbers of Auxiliaries and Black and Tans, whose behaviour was clearly counter-productive.

Serious disagreements among police commanders, moreover, were adding to the problems facing the authorities. In February 1921 a party of Auxiliaries stole £325 worth of food and alcohol during the search of a grocery store in Trim, County Meath. When Crozier, the Auxiliary division commander investigated the incident, he immediately dismissed twenty-one Auxiliary cadets in the local company and placed a further five under arrest pending a court-martial. Astonishingly, Tudor, who as police chief had overall control, reinstated the men and ordered an inquiry. A furious Crozier then resigned, claiming that the Auxiliaries had only been reinstated when they threatened to make public information on a catalogue of atrocities carried out by the police. The furore caused by Crozier's resignation put the spotlight on the government's policy of repression in Ireland, and many sections of the British press demanded Greenwood's removal from his role of chief secretary.

While Greenwood retained his optimism that a military solution was still achievable, others in the cabinet began to consider the alternative. Certainly, Bonar Law's resignation on 17 March due to ill health allowed Lloyd George more room to manoeuvre. Still, he was committed to the Government of Ireland Act and the hope that elections for the southern parliament in late May might go ahead as planned. Though he had initiated peace feelers some months earlier, Lloyd George was not yet ready to place himself firmly among those in the cabinet who favoured a truce with the IRA. Therefore, while a number of ministers expressed grave reservations at the level of violence in the spring of 1921, a majority in the cabinet saw no alternative to coercion. Indeed, on 24 May, the government took the decision to extend martial law across all twenty-six counties in the south. This new security policy was planned to take effect from 14 July, and arrangements were put in place to dispatch additional troops to Ireland. Macready had informed the cabinet that if the martial law approach was to stand any chance of success, it would have to be applied ruthlessly. Yet the commander-in-chief was not confident about the outcome. He had previously informed a number of ministers and officials that coercion alone was unlikely to bring about a solution. In his memorandum, moreover, he was adamant that the troops under his command could not be expected to endure another winter in Ireland. He concluded that October 1921 should be the deadline for the achievement of a military victory. Thus, while the cabinet supported the imposition of full martial law in the twenty-six-county area, it did so with little enthusiasm or conviction. Both Lloyd George and Churchill were particularly concerned about the new direction of security policy, repeating their earlier pronouncements that the Irish problem was essentially "a policeman's job".

Such differences in emphasis over the government's security strategy failed to take account of the growing public anger at the direction of the cabinet's Irish policy. The reliance on reprisals was increasingly condemned, and this highlighted the overall failure of Lloyd George's approach in Ireland. In particular, press criticism of the government was mounting. Only the right-wing *Morning Post* stood firm, as it demanded an all-out assault on the IRA, but this brought little comfort to a beleaguered coalition government. *The Times* reflected public unease and had been critical of the government since the Balbriggan reprisal in September 1920. By the early summer of 1921 Lloyd George was being routinely accused of having no Irish policy. In the House of Commons Asquith seized every opportunity to highlight government own goals in Ireland, while the Labour Party established its own commission to investigate the situation. Its report, published on 29 December 1920, was scathing in its criticism of the government, and the party campaigned on the Irish debacle from January 1921. At the same time, a cross-party pressure group, the Peace with Ireland Council, which had been established in November 1920, and the Trades Union Congress loudly demanded reconciliation with Ireland, while exposing the moral vacuum at the heart of the government's Irish policy. Another significant source of criticism was the Anglican church. Church of England bishops repeatedly condemned excesses by the Crown Forces in the House of Lords. On 6 April a letter from the bishops appeared in *The Times* under the heading, "Force breeds Force", which deplored the use of indiscriminate reprisals. The correspondence also urged the government to conclude hostilities and reach a negotiated settlement with Sinn Féin. Speculation about the nature of any such settlement had centred on the possibility of granting Ireland the same status as the dominions. Indeed, both Asquith and the former foreign secretary, Viscount Grey, argued consistently that Irishmen should enjoy the same freedom as the inhabitants of the dominions, whose leaders also pressed the government to call a truce.

By mid-June the cabinet was clearly anxious about both the public and parliamentary reaction to the plans for the extension of martial law. Although the Conservative ministers in the coalition government were generally opposed to negotiations and in favour of continuing with coercion, Lloyd George was uncertain. However, he sensed an opportunity created by the intervention of the South African prime minister, Jan Smuts, who was in London to attend the Imperial Conference. Smuts, who was highly regarded, viewed the deteriorating situation in Ireland as a threat to the British Empire. He urged the government to abandon the use of force and reach a political settlement with the twenty-six counties. Arguing that the establishment of the Northern Ireland parliament presented the government with the pretext for a change of direction in Ireland, Smuts made the suggestion that the king should use the occasion of his speech at the opening of the Belfast parliament on 22 June to issue a plea for peace. Lloyd George had publicly stated on a number of occasions that he was unwilling to negotiate with Sinn Féin, but the unpalatable alternative now was the extension of martial law with no guarantee of victory. Clearly, the political will to carry on with and, indeed, intensify the use of coercion was diminishing rapidly. In these circumstances the prime minister judged that the time was right for negotiations. Moreover, the very positive reaction in Britain to the king's Belfast speech was significant. It allowed Lloyd George to respond to the king's call for peace and obscured the fact that this was a personal climbdown for the prime minister.

While the king's gesture had pulled the coalition government towards negotiations, Sinn Féin's position had still to be clarified. The republican movement had been wary about responding to several peace moves that had Westminster's sanction, in spite of the government's public position. Through the back channels, the republican movement had indicated that it would not consider either the surrender of arms or any dilution of its demand for a republic. Still, de Valera's return from the United States had offered some encouragement to those officials in Dublin Castle who favoured a political settlement. The president had played no part in the development of the IRA campaign, and he was viewed as a political rather than a military leader. For his part, de Valera was struggling to impose the Sinn Féin counter-state's authority, as it was facing growing difficulties by the end of 1920. The Dáil courts were in decline, while the department of local government was under significant financial pressure that seriously impeded its work. Although de Valera worked hard to halt this trend and give the underground movement a new focus, the Dáil government clearly suffered from the growing British security presence. This was apparent from the very low numbers who were able to attend the sittings of the Dáil. Although the Dáil met only infrequently, attendance sometimes dropped as low as 20, with the majority of Sinn Féin deputies either in jail or on the run.

The security squeeze was also disrupting the IRA's campaign, and the number of interned suspects rose from about 1,500 in January 1921 to almost 4,500 before the end of the conflict. This, in turn, had led the IRA to adopt more ruthless tactics, a development that led to some republicans questioning the IRA's military strategy. One of the critics, Roger Sweetman, the Sinn Féin deputy for North Wexford who had previously painted a negative picture of the actions of Collins's Squad on Bloody Sunday, was openly condemning the IRA's methods of warfare at the beginning of 1921. Yet Sweetman attracted little public support for his views, and he was bitterly attacked when he advocated a peace conference with the British. He would resign his Dáil seat before the end of January. Criticism of the IRA from other quarters was also becoming louder. While many of the bishops had denounced British repression, a number, such as Bishop Finegan who had officiated at Sean Connolly's funeral in County Longford, were equally unhappy with the level of IRA violence. Cardinal Logue, Dr Gilmartin, Archbishop of Tuam, and Dr Cohalan, Bishop of Cork, each criticised the campaign of terror. Cohalan also attracted public attention when he excommunicated all those Catholics in his diocese who had been engaged in acts of murder. In spite of the church's influence, however, the hierarchy did not reflect the wider public's perception of the conflict.

Yet, while the republican movement could disregard the views of the bishops, it had to take account of the growing war weariness that was becoming more discernible during the first half of 1921. The IRA's commandeering of food and other supplies became bitterly resented by many of those whose lives had been disrupted by the conflict. Moreover, tactics developed to obstruct the Crown Forces, such as the destruction of roads, bridges, railways and other communications, added to the problems facing many rural dwellers in their day-to-day lives. This disruption increased frustration in many of the most active areas and led to growing calls for peace. The commanders of the flying columns were well aware of the importance of retaining support among the local population, but they were reporting increasing public hostility to the IRA in a number of areas during the early part of 1921. Not surprisingly, this raised questions about how long the IRA could sustain its military campaign, particularly when the tightening of the security net was having an adverse effect on Volunteer morale. Naturally, these developments caused some leading figures in the republican movement to consider the advantages that might be gained at a peace conference.

On the British side, a number of prominent figures were also attempting to lay the foundations for future negotiations. In April 1921 the senior Conservative Lord Derby arrived in Dublin, suitably disguised, as an emissary of the British government. He met both Cardinal Logue and de Valera but made little headway. Much more significant than the Derby initiative were the actions of a peace faction based at Dublin Castle. These high-ranking officials, principally Mark Sturgis, Sir John Anderson and Alfred "Andy" Cope, had reached the conclusion that there was no prospect of a military solution in Ireland as repression had proved counter-productive. The most prominent of the three, Andy Cope, had already established lines of communication with the Sinn Féin leadership, and he worked tirelessly to promote negotiations. By the beginning of June 1921 Lloyd George was still hesitant, reluctant to offer the concessions that would be required for a truce. The prime minister was influenced by reports from senior military commanders that the IRA was being "hit hard", but he was also acutely aware of the pitfalls associated with the planned extension of martial law. The gloomy assessment offered by Macready and the growing anger over the use of coercion in Ireland was changing Lloyd George's mind, and he finally indicated that his government would consider negotiations if Sinn Féin would drop its insistence on a republic.

It was also apparent that the positive British reaction to the king's Belfast speech on 22 June demonstrated popular support for the idea of a negotiated settlement with Ireland. Sinn Féin had recognised this development and was aware, as far as its own supporters were concerned, that any rejection of a reasonable truce offer from Lloyd George would create its own problems. Indeed, the republican movement had its reasons for leaning towards a truce, as its military prospects were becoming bleak. By the summer of 1921 the IRA had an estimated 3,000 Volunteers on active service, but they were now facing a combined police and military force in excess of 40,000. The establishment of a more effective intelligence system and the greater flexibility shown by the army, which included the use of aircraft to track and attack flying columns, made life even more difficult for the IRA. Collins was certainly anxious about the deteriorating situation, and the prospect of the twenty-six counties being flooded with additional troops under the martial law plan caused him even more concern. After the truce came into force, Collins was to suggest that the IRA could only have survived for a further three weeks. At the other extreme, Tom Barry estimated that his flying column could continue its operations for another five years. Both men were exaggerating. Yet the assessment of the IRA's short- and medium-term prospects shared by Collins and other members of GHQ staff must have influenced de Valera as he groped his way towards a truce. The president knew that he had to bring the gunmen with him in order to avoid a split in the republican movement when he sat down to negotiate with the British. In such a scenario Collins's support would be essential.

While de Valera was not averse to the idea of peace talks, he insisted that the British had to make the first move. This came in a letter from Lloyd George on 24 June, inviting de Valera to a conference in London in order to explore the possibility of a settlement. Only two days earlier, on the same day as the king's address at the opening of the Northern Ireland parliament, de Valera had been arrested after troops had swooped on his rented Blackrock home. However, Cope intervened to secure his release. When the correspondence offering peace talks arrived the next day, a clearly stunned de Valera took several days before issuing a response. On 4 July he met Midleton and other representatives of southern Unionism and on the following day he entertained Smuts. All of these visitors urged de Valera to accept Lloyd George's invitation. Midleton then travelled to London to secure Lloyd George's consent to a truce, which de Valera had demanded as a prerequisite for any conference. Finally, on 8 July, the prime minister received de Valera's response agreeing to come to London to enter negotiations. The truce, which came into operation at noon on Monday 11 July, was signed by Macready in the Mansion House. The violence continued right down to the deadline. In the final week of the conflict, the IRA killed three civilians and three soldiers, while the Black and Tans shot a prominent local figure in Cork. On the morning of 11 July, two long-serving RIC men were killed in separate incidents. This brought the total killed during the War of Independence to over 1,400. British security policy in Ireland had been a failure, as the Lloyd George government had allowed the situation to drift out of control. The militarisation of the police in 1920 only served to escalate the situation and deliver overwhelming popular sympathy to the IRA. Yet this support was also running out of steam by the summer of 1921. Accordingly, both sides were grateful for a truce in July.

The Anglo-Irish Treaty

Following the truce, de Valera crossed to London on 14 July 1921, where he met Lloyd George. The British prime minister sought to use the occasion to impress upon the Sinn Féin leader the importance of the Empire. A large coloured map of the world hung on the wall, and de Valera took his place at the cabinet table, around which the dominion leaders had sat in conference only a few days earlier. In a theatrical performance, Lloyd George then invited Ireland, through de Valera, to take her place in this Commonwealth of "free nations". The purpose of the visit was to establish the basis upon which negotiations between Irish and British representatives might take place. The two leaders met on four occasions between 14 and 21 July. For the visit de Valera was accompanied by senior Sinn Féin members including Griffith, Stack and Childers. During these discussions Lloyd George, as de Valera had planned, did most of the talking, but he was crystal clear on the fact that, whatever constitutional settlement was reached, Ireland must remain part of the Empire. However, de Valera would not be drawn on the issue, knowing that any early concession by Ireland on this vital point could cause a split in the Sinn Féin movement. Instead, he was keen to concentrate on the partition issue. De Valera quickly sensed that Lloyd George was less comfortable in dealing with the Ulster question, and he accused the British government of following an indefensible and immoral course in establishing a statelet in the six-county area. This verbal sparring with the prime minister marked the beginning of the Sinn Féin tactic of using Ulster as a bargaining chip, as it sought to squeeze concessions from the British on the vital question of Irish independence. Lloyd George's position was made more difficult by the obstructive approach taken by Sir James Craig. While the discussions in London were ongoing, Craig arrived in the capital, declaring that de Valera's claim to speak for the whole of Ireland was an outrageous impertinence. Undoubtedly, Craig's presence in London was a distraction for the Lloyd George government, especially after he turned down an invitation from the prime minister to participate in the discussions. Craig's priority was straightforward: his only interest was to defend Northern Ireland's newly acquired constitutional position.

De Valera was not encouraged by these initial exchanges with the British, and he wrote to Collins warning him to prepare for a possible resumption of hostilities. The London discussions left de Valera in no doubt that there would have to be a compromise on Ireland's republican status. However, he was not yet ready to dilute the demand for independence, knowing that such a move would jeopardise Sinn Féin unity. Lloyd George recognised that the Irish leader was operating under this constraint, but he also sensed that de Valera was anxious for negotiations to proceed. On 20 July the prime minister briefed his cabinet on the talks and laid out his objectives. Lloyd George was clear that Ireland's demand for republican status would not be on the table. Instead, Sinn Féin would be offered dominion status, subject to its acceptance of specific undertakings on defence, finance and trade. Moreover, there would be no coercion of Ulster to end partition. The prime minister believed that this was a generous offer, but de Valera dismissed the proposals when they were put to him on the following day, adding that no other dominion would be asked to make such sacrifices. De Valera left this final meeting stating that he could not recommend anything in the British offer to the Dáil or to the Irish people. Lloyd George responded by warning that outright rejection would bring the truce to an end. In this game of brinkmanship Lloyd George's threat did not come as a shock, but it left the Sinn Féin leader in a difficult position.

De Valera returned to Dublin where a cabinet meeting to consider the British document was planned for Sunday, 25 July. Before he left, Smuts called to offer his advice. The South African prime minister urged de Valera to accept the offer of dominion status. Smuts was highly regarded by de Valera, and the two men exchanged correspondence over the following fortnight before the South African's departure from London. Of course, de Valera knew that Smuts had Lloyd George's ear, and he conveyed the message that progress could not be made unless the partition question was resolved. This prompted a reply from Smuts on 4 August in which he advised de Valera not to focus on the Ulster question, arguing that it would resolve itself when Unionists came to appreciate the advantages of being in a united Ireland. He also impressed upon de Valera that while a republic was the clearest characteristic of national self-determination, "it was not the only expression."

The debate within the Dáil cabinet on the British proposals laid bare the wide range of opinion on national status among the Sinn Féin leadership. At one end of the spectrum Griffith welcomed the British offer, while an angry Brugha reminded his colleagues that they were part of a government that had declared Ireland to be a "republic". In his reply to Lloyd George on 10 August, de Valera attempted to square the circle by promoting the concept of "external association", though he was vague about its precise meaning. "External association" was the ingenious suggestion that de Valera had been contemplating for some time. The crux of the idea was that Ireland would enjoy the freedom of an independent state but, simultaneously, be externally associated with the British Commonwealth. Its primary purpose was to keep militants such as Brugha and Stack on board. However, it was unacceptable to the British, who were not yet ready to consider the idea of a republic attached to the Empire. Over the next few weeks letters and telegrams were exchanged between London and Dublin, but it was evident that no progress had been made in bridging the gap between the two sides. While it suited de Valera to delay proceedings, Lloyd George was determined to bring matters to a head. Accordingly, he called his ministers to a cabinet meeting in Inverness Town Hall on 7 September. The prime minister was a regular visitor to the Scottish Highlands, but his cabinet colleagues must have been furious when they learned that they had to undertake such a long train journey to accommodate the prime minister's holiday arrangements.

In discussing the prospects for negotiations with Sinn Féin, the cabinet was unanimous in its insistence that the Irish had to accept undertakings on the Crown and Empire as preconditions for a conference. This was conveyed to the Irish, but it was not accompanied by an ultimatum, an indication that a majority in the cabinet remained committed to negotiations. The Irish reply, which was hand-delivered to the Highlands by Harry Boland and Joseph McGrath, stipulated Ireland's right to be reorganised as an independent state: "Our nation has formally declared its independence, and recognises itself as a sovereign State." Lloyd George's response reflected his frustration, as he warned, "The reiteration of your claim to negotiate with His Majesty's government as the representatives of an independent and sovereign State would make conference between us impossible." The deadlock continued until 29 September, when Lloyd George issued a fresh invitation to talks. His letter restated the government's firm position on the Empire but, strikingly, it made no reference to any previous correspondence.

The Dáil cabinet welcomed the development. De Valera sought to put a favourable interpretation on the prime minister's offer, emphasising that Sinn Féin had won a conference without preconditions. However, several of his ministers recognised that in agreeing to negotiations Sinn Féin had just made a crucial compromise. A republic would not be on the table, and it was on this basis that substantive negotiations would begin. Still, the Lloyd George invitation appeared to offer significant room for manoeuvre, as it stated that the conference would consider how Ireland's future relationship with the Empire might be reconciled with "Irish national aspirations". Significantly, the Irish negotiating team had already been selected, and de Valera's absence must have come as a shock to Sinn Féin supporters in the country. The cabinet had been split on his participation, but de Valera used his casting vote to ensure his omission. De Valera's action greatly angered Collins who viewed his unwillingness to serve on the Sinn Féin delegation as an abdication of his responsibilities. The cabinet returned to the issue on 14 September. Again, the decision to keep de Valera at home was reaffirmed, causing Cosgrave to comment memorably that they were sending a team but "leaving their ablest player in reserve". The reasons for him to attend were obvious. He was leader of Sinn Féin and should, therefore, act as a counter-weight to Lloyd George on the British team. Furthermore, as Cosgrave pointed out, he had more experience in conducting negotiations and, having met Lloyd George in July, was fully aware of the key issues.

However, de Valera had his reasons for remaining in Dublin. He argued that as "president of the Republic", a position that had only existed since 26 August, he was "the symbol of the Republic", and the office should not be compromised by "any arrangements" that the Irish delegation might have to agree in Dublin.

By staying at home, moreover, it meant that the delegates in London could delay British insistence to come to an agreement, as they had to refer back to their president. De Valera intended to be in constant dialogue with the Sinn Féin delegates, and there was an assumption that if negotiations broke down, he could intervene at the last moment to seek a resolution. The other key reason for de Valera's non-attendance was his determination to maintain Sinn Féin unity. In his cabinet, Brugha and Stack had to be kept in check, a task that could more easily be accomplished by his presence in Dublin. He was also keen to reduce the obvious tension that existed between Brugha, the minister of defence, and Mulcahy, the IRA chief of staff, a situation that had posed a major problem since the truce.

On balance, historians have been critical of de Valera's determination to absent himself from the negotiations. The fact that he was fully aware that a compromise on Ireland's status was inevitable and did not want to be the individual responsible for that compromise has sustained much of the criticism. There has also been some speculation that de Valera, acting with Machiavellian intent, had secured an advantage in a potential leadership struggle with Collins. The latter was on the Irish delegation and would therefore be associated with any compromise on the issue of the republic. On the other hand, it was common knowledge that Collins's acceptance of any compromise would be a crucial factor in determining the IRA's response, and de Valera recognised that any settlement endorsed by Collins had a better chance of being acceptable to Sinn Féin's support base in Ireland.

In de Valera's absence, Griffith led the Irish delegation, and he was joined by Michael Collins, whose influence would prove crucial. Collins was unhappy with his appointment to the Irish delegation, arguing that he was a soldier. De Valera had left him behind when he went to London in July, but he was confident that Collins would, out of a sense of duty, play his part, though Collins, too, knew that a compromise on Ireland's republican status

Michael Collins (1890–1922), in military uniform.

was inevitable. The Sinn Féin president anticipated that Griffith and Collins would work closely together, and he wanted to send a balanced delegation that reflected the divergence of views within the leadership group. To achieve this, Robert Barton, the Dáil's minister for economic affairs, was added to the team. An unlikely revolutionary from a wealthy Protestant family, Barton would collaborate with his cousin, Erskine Childers, who acted as secretary to the Irish delegation. Two other Dáil deputies, George Gavan Duffy and Éamonn Duggan, both of whom were lawyers, made up the five-man delegation, though Childers would play a more prominent role than the two legal experts. He was the most hardline republican among the Irish representatives and, as de Valera expected, would urge the Irish delegation to reject dominion status. Though the delegation reflected the differing views within Sinn Féin, this obvious division proved to be a significant weakness when negotiations commenced.

Personal bitterness among the delegates added to this problem. Griffith and Childers did not conceal their hostility to each other, and Collins distrusted Childers, whom he suspected of maintaining a secret channel of communication with de Valera. The other great disadvantage facing the Irish delegates was their lack of preparation. The limits of any concession they might accept were not clarified, and Griffith and Childers were clearly far apart on the crucial issue of national status. Of course, de Valera knew this and allowed matters to proceed. The Sinn Féin delegation would press for external association, a concept that none of the team really understood. Should the conference break down, the Irish strategy would be to try and ensure that the break would be due to an impasse on the partition question. A break on Ulster would be favourable to the Irish and cause major problems for the British.

Although he would not be in London, de Valera hoped to exert some authority over the Irish delegates, but this merely added to the confusion. The instructions issued to the delegation illustrated de Valera's attempt to direct events from Dublin. The Irish delegates were to be "plenipotentiaries" (envoys with full powers), but these powers were to be curtailed:

(1) The plenipotentiaries have full powers as defined in their credentials.
(2) It is understood before decisions are finally reached on a main question, that a dispatch notifying the intention to make these decisions will be sent to members of the Cabinet in Dublin, and that a reply will be awaited by the plenipotentiaries before the final decision is made.
(3) It is also understood that the complete text of the draft treaty about to be signed will be similarly submitted to Dublin and a reply awaited.

(4) It is understood that the Cabinet in Dublin will be kept regularly informed of the progress of the negotiations.

Having arranged to counter Griffith and Collins by balancing the Irish delegation with more uncompromising republicans, de Valera sought to use these instructions, particularly clauses (2) and (3), to allow him to veto any draft document that did not meet with his approval. Not surprisingly, Griffith and Collins disapproved of the instructions, which left them in an ambiguous position. When the crunch came, they chose to ignore them.

In spite of all these disadvantages, the Irish delegation was a formidable team. Griffith was able, experienced and determined, and he had played a key role in the evolution of the Sinn Féin movement. In Collins, he had a colleague of undoubted ability who could easily hold his own in the negotiations. While he may have regarded himself primarily as a soldier, Collins quickly gained the respect of his British counterparts. He proved to be open-minded and pragmatic, and he had the vision to take a long-term view. While the republic was a "sacred cow" for the Sinn Féin militants, Collins was more interested in securing practical changes that would confer considerable freedom on Ireland and enable her to extend that freedom. Crucially, he was opposed to a renewal of hostilities with the British because he was certain that it would result in a defeat for the IRA. This put him at odds with Brugha, who had accepted de Valera's idea of external association as a final compromise and favoured an end to the truce if the Irish negotiators failed to secure republican status. Collins believed that such a course was suicidal. During the negotiations hostility between the two intensified, and Collins assumed that Brugha was seeking to undermine the efforts of the Irish delegation. Certainly, Brugha pressed de Valera to curb Collins's power, and he remained furious about the influence of the Collins-directed IRB within the army. This was, indeed, an additional factor for Collins to consider, and he held regular meetings with the IRB leadership before and during the talks in London in order to keep the movement informed about the progress of the negotiations and to gauge reaction to particular developments. Collins made no secret of the IRB's role. While the rest of the Irish delegation lodged at Hans Place in London, Collins stayed at Cadogan Gardens in the company of his own IRB staff.

The Irish delegates, then, were able but divided. The British delegation, by contrast, was united in its objectives and superbly led by Lloyd George. The "Welsh wizard", as he was dubbed, was a gifted political leader with a quick, agile mind and a wealth of negotiating experience. He also possessed a compelling personality and had the confidence of a highly regarded, successful wartime leader. The prime minister was joined by the senior Conservative figures of Austen Chamberlain and Lord Birkenhead, both with formidable reputations.

David Lloyd George (1863–1945), pictured at Cannes, January 1922.   *Sir Austen Chamberlain (1863–1937), at Hendon RAF display, June 1925.*

Chamberlain had become party leader in March 1921, while the charismatic Birkenhead was one of the country's leading constitutional experts. Winston Churchill was the fourth member of the British delegation. He had long experience in Anglo-Irish relations and was considered to be the British team's defence expert. These four were joined by Laming Worthington-Evans, the secretary of state for war and a close confidant of the prime minister, Hamar Greenwood, the chief secretary for Ireland and former Home Ruler, and Gordon Hewart, the attorney general who was in attendance when his legal opinion was required. Tom Jones, Lloyd George's fellow Welshman and chief lieutenant, acted as secretary to the British delegation. The serving assistant secretary to the cabinet, Jones acted as a sounding-board for many of the prime minister's ideas, and he was to play a central role in the negotiations.

Notwithstanding the array of political nous on the British side, it was Lloyd George who dominated the proceedings. Ever alert to changes in the public mood, the prime minister had regained popular support for his Irish policy in the countdown to the negotiations. His offer of a conference seemed fair and

Winston Leonard Churchill (1874–1965), arriving at Downing Street for the Treaty negotiations, 11 October 1921.

Frederick Edwin Smith, 1st Earl of Birkenhead (1872–1930), in Judge's robes, April 1920.

generous, and it was welcomed by the same press that had been fiercely critical of the government's coercion policy in Ireland earlier in the year. Significantly, the public expected Ireland to remain in the Empire and agree to Britain's defence requirements. Thus, opinion was firmly behind Lloyd George as he pressed the Irish delegation to accept dominion status. The prime minister was also confident that he would have public support for the reopening of hostilities if the negotiations broke down on Sinn Féin's refusal to come into the Empire. This gave the British team a decisive advantage, and Lloyd George kept the real possibility of a resumption of the war on the table throughout the discussions. Yet it was equally apparent that such advantages might be more than outweighed by the partition issue, and the British delegation fully expected the Irish to exploit the Ulster question. Lloyd George and his colleagues knew that a breakdown of the conference on the refusal of the British to end partition would leave them in a very weak position. The expected Unionist inflexibility was another problem for the prime minister. As his coalition government was dependent on Conservative support for its survival, and with Bonar Law watching closely from the sidelines, the possible coercion of Ulster could not be contemplated, leaving Lloyd George with little room to manoeuvre on the partition issue. Ultimately, of course, the focus for the Conservatives was the need to secure Irish acceptance of the Crown and Empire. If his government was to survive, therefore, the prime minister had to ensure that Chamberlain and Birkenhead were satisfied with the direction of the conference.

The negotiations

The negotiations began on 11 October and a treaty was signed in the early hours of 6 December 1921. At the opening session, the Irish were presented with the British proposals, which were almost identical to those rejected by de Valera on 20 July. The British document made clear that Ireland would be offered dominion status but, as *The Times* stated on 11 October, "the Empire, in the old sense of the word, had passed, and a new relationship had succeeded it". The hope was that Ireland would accept this partnership, though the paper stressed that "the situation in Ulster remains an obstacle in the path of peace". From the outset, the Irish delegation was at a disadvantage. It was unable to table its counter-proposals, which included the external association concept, until 24 October. Consequently, the early discussions centred on the British document, and Lloyd George ensured that it set the parameters for the negotiations. When the Irish did present their document, the prime minister insisted that their proposals were outside the scope of the present discussions. The delay had allowed Lloyd George to seize the initiative.

In the early plenary sessions, the British were willing to be generous on the issues of trade and finance, but their insistence on the retention of specific defence facilities worried the Irish delegation. Childers stated that Ireland must have the right to remain neutral in any future conflict involving Britain. Still, it appeared that the problems relating to defence could be resolved along with the trade and finance issues, leaving only the questions of Ulster and Ireland's constitutional status outstanding. Childers repeatedly argued that Ireland must have the right to proclaim her separate nationality, while the British pressed hard for dominion status linked to allegiance to the Crown. Meanwhile, Griffith, who was the least hostile to the idea of dominion status, took every opportunity to move the negotiations onto the question of Ulster. The fourth plenary session was dominated by the Ulster issue, and the Irish delegates must have been encouraged by the negative attitude to partition demonstrated by their British counterparts. Griffith and Collins highlighted the suffering of the minority in the north, stressing that Nationalists in Tyrone and Fermanagh were being denied their democratic rights. While the prime minister suggested that Northern Ireland could be persuaded to join with the rest of Ireland of her own accord, Griffith demanded that the British should pressurise the Unionists to accept a reunified Ireland. Again, the Irish were encouraged by Lloyd George's willingness to apply such pressure. The Sinn Féin delegation finally presented its proposals, "Draft Treaty A", at the seventh plenary session on 24 October. Griffith pointed out that they had dropped the "republic" title but wanted "association with" rather than "membership of" the British Empire. When Lloyd George emphasised the genuine degree of freedom enjoyed by dominions such as Canada and New Zealand, the Irish delegates showed little interest, with Childers commenting that Ireland could not be in the same position as Canada.

By this stage the British had identified Childers as an obstacle to progress, and the principals on both sides agreed after this seventh round that more headway might be made if the plenary sessions were replaced by sub-conferences. This suited the British as it sidelined the prickly Childers, but it was also welcomed by Griffith and Collins, who had made the original proposal to continue discussions by sub-conference. After a fortnight the leading protagonists on both sides recognised that the dogmatic and inflexible Childers would have to be outflanked for a substantial agreement to be reached. Childers, together with Barton, his cousin, and Gavan Duffy, had formed a tight-knit group, but the switch to the sub-conference method of negotiation excluded all three from the important discussions. By this stage Griffith and Collins were also becoming increasingly frustrated by de Valera's actions. The president had intervened following an exchange of telegrams between King George V and Pope Benedict XV, in which the king had responded to the pope's good wishes for success in the negotiations by stating that he too hoped that the conference would "initiate a new era of peace and happiness for my people". This prompted de Valera to dispatch his own telegram to the pope, a copy of which he issued to the press on 21 October, warning His Holiness not to view the Irish people as the king's subjects. This snub for the pope angered Lloyd George, who felt that de Valera was attempting to undermine the negotiations.

Worse was to follow. After the seventh plenary session, Griffith reported to de Valera the content of a conversation that had taken place between himself and Lloyd George and Chamberlain. The senior British delegates had pressed him to recommend acceptance of the Crown, but Griffith had argued that this would be conditional on the British guaranteeing the "essential unity" of Ireland. This infuriated de Valera, who warned that the prospect of the Irish people becoming British subjects was out of the question. He concluded his message with the chilling statement, "If war is the alternative, we can only face it, and I think the sooner the other side is made to realise it the better." De Valera's letter provoked outrage from Griffith and Collins who viewed it as an attempt to curb their powers as plenipotentiaries. Both men threatened to abandon the negotiations, and calm was only restored when all the Irish delegates signed a reply repudiating de Valera's attempts to impose new restrictions on the plenipotentiaries. A chastened de Valera sought to ease the tension by issuing a fresh letter in which he claimed that there was no question of seeking to interfere with the powers of the Irish delegates, adding that his purpose had been to keep them informed on the views of the Dáil cabinet. Of course, the Irish delegation was fully aware of the cabinet's views, and Collins informed his colleagues that Brugha and Stack, with assistance from the president, were deliberately laying a trap for him.

By the time negotiations shifted to the sub-conference method, a clear pattern had been established. It was apparent that agreement could be reached quickly on the trade, finance and defence questions. This would leave the outstanding issues of Ulster and the Crown, and these had become intertwined. Under pressure, the Irish indicated that they were prepared to concede ground on Ireland's status, provided that the British could guarantee the essential unity of Ireland. At first, this appeared to be a clever strategy. If the conference broke down, it should have been possible for the Irish delegation to ensure that the break would centre on Ulster. Yet linking Ulster and national status muddied the waters, and Lloyd George added to the confusion by drawing the Irish into his own territory by persuading them to take an interest in the survival of the government. On 31 October the prime minister faced a vote of confidence in his government in the House of Commons. This had been tabled by the "Diehards", a group of right-wing Tories who opposed the coalition. The prime minister met Griffith on the eve of the censure motion, seeking personal assurances on Ireland's acceptance of the Crown and free partnership with the Empire. If Griffith agreed, Lloyd George would give him an undertaking that he would crush the Diehards and press Craig and the Unionists to accept essential unity. It was not difficult for the prime minister to gain Griffith's attention, as the no-confidence vote censured the government "for going into conference with the Sinn Féin delegates". In the end Griffith acceded to Lloyd George's wishes, and the prime minister led the government to victory on the vote of confidence.

On 1 November, however, Griffith made a further concession when asked for some form of documentary evidence confirming Ireland's willingness to come into the Empire that could be used to defend the government at the Conservative Party conference scheduled for Liverpool in mid-November. The Tory members of the government anticipated criticism for their participation in the negotiations, and Griffith signed a letter to Lloyd George stating that he would "recommend free partnership with the British Commonwealth", if he could be satisfied on Irish unity. Before it was dispatched, however, the letter was amended on the insistence of Childers, Barton and Duffy to "recommend free partnership of

Ireland with the other States associated within the British Commonwealth". This form of words left ample room for future discussion.

Previously, Childers had informed de Valera of his opposition to the sub-conference style of negotiation, but he failed to persuade the president to demand a return to the plenary sessions. At these sub-conferences, Griffith and Collins frequently faced Lloyd George and Chamberlain, though the latter was sometimes replaced by Birkenhead or Churchill. These discussions proved to be more open engagements, with each side prepared to outline its particular difficulties. The sub-conferences also provided the ground for the development of a powerful personal rapport between Collins and Birkenhead. These two charismatic and pragmatic figures quickly won each other's confidence, with Birkenhead demonstrating a real empathy for Irish decision-makers. He also convinced Collins that he really wanted the talks to succeed and did not want a return to war in Ireland.

By early November, therefore, the British were confident that the Irish would accept allegiance to the Crown if they received satisfactory concessions on unity. It was now time for Lloyd George to put pressure on the Unionists in Belfast. He had informed a delighted Griffith that if Ulster proved unreasonable, he would resign. The prime minister employed a combination of persuasion and threat in an attempt to move Craig, but he was rebuffed. This news was conveyed by Jones when he met Griffith and Collins informally at the Grosvenor Hotel on 8 November. The Unionist leader had been in constant communication with senior Conservatives outside the government, including Bonar Law, and he stuck to the position that the government could reach any arrangement with Sinn Féin that it desired, but he would not become involved and would hold on to his six counties. Jones then told the Irish duo that Lloyd George would make one final effort to persuade the Ulster Unionists to accept an all-Ireland parliament and, if they refused, he would resign. The cabinet secretary speculated that this would probably result in the establishment of a Conservative administration, led by Bonar Law, that would inevitably be hostile to Sinn Féin. Jones was anxious to demonstrate that the prime minister's demise would have serious implications for the Irish. It was at this point that he floated the idea of a Boundary Commission, which would redraw the existing border if Craig refused to accept an all-Ireland parliament. Griffith understood this to mean that Northern Ireland would lose a large chunk of its territory, with the rump eventually succumbing to Dublin rule.

The Boundary Commission proposal was relayed to de Valera who congratulated Griffith on the Ulster negotiations but cautioned him to hold his ground on the Crown and Empire. On the British side Jones and Lloyd George were now confident that the prime minister could escape from his resignation pledge should he fail to secure an all-Ireland parliament. Clearly, Griffith was anxious for Lloyd George to remain as prime minister and, at a further meeting on 9 November, indicated that Craig's refusal to accept an all-Ireland parliament was no longer crucial, as the Boundary Commission could resolve the Ulster problem. This was a major error. Ulster had been a headache for the prime minister, as it threatened to derail the negotiations, but Lloyd George turned this to his advantage by using the prospect of unity to keep Sinn Féin moving towards the British position on Crown and Empire.

As promised, Lloyd George renewed his attempts to cajole the Unionists. On 10 November he wrote to Craig urging the Unionists to accept an all-Ireland parliament. This would, he argued, enable his government to secure agreement with Sinn Féin on allegiance to the Crown and inclusion in the Empire. In the correspondence the prime minister also introduced an economic threat, warning the Unionists that taxation under the United Kingdom parliament would be considerably higher than anticipated taxation rates under an all-Ireland parliament. This was significant, and a private meeting with Craig in London raised Lloyd George's hopes that the Unionists were ready to consider some kind of all-Ireland relationship. However, while Craig may have been willing to provide some assistance for the government in its negotiations with Sinn Féin, his cabinet colleagues displayed no interest in taking a broader view of Anglo-Irish relations and the implications for the Empire. Safe in the knowledge that he could count on the support of Bonar Law, Craig resisted government pressure to move towards an all-Ireland parliament. He was also determined not to become embroiled in the negotiations. In these circumstances Lloyd George pushed ahead with his Boundary Commission idea, securing Griffith's commitment to the principle at a private meeting on 12 November. The prime minister then instructed Tom Jones to draw up a memorandum encompassing the Boundary Commission idea, and it was shown to Griffith the next day. The leader of the Irish delegation quickly agreed to the form of words in the memorandum, though there is no evidence that Griffith signed any document. This event raised two issues not grasped by Griffith at the time. First, the British had not defined on paper precisely how a Boundary Commission might work. Secondly, acceptance of such a concept weakened Sinn Féin's fallback position of engineering a break on Ulster should the negotiations collapse.

On 16 November the Irish delegation received a draft Treaty that included the Boundary Commission proposal. It would be established if Ulster refused to accept an all-Ireland parliament. Receipt of the document prompted a row among the Irish delegates. Duffy rushed back to Dublin to meet the cabinet and complain about the way that Griffith and Collins were conducting the negotiations. However, de Valera refused to call a halt to the use of sub-conferences, arguing that the Treaty could not be signed until it had been submitted to the cabinet for approval. In London, meanwhile, Childers and Barton presented a fresh document to the British. This asserted that legislative and executive authority in Ireland must have an exclusively Irish derivation, adding that Ireland would be associated with the Commonwealth and would recognise the Crown as "symbol and accepted head of the association". This was, in essence, external association, but a further sub-conference on 24 November made clear to Griffith and Collins that the British totally rejected the concept. What followed was a discussion on symbolism, which was clearly important to both sides, and agreement on the use of the title Irish Free State, a more literal translation of Saorstát Éireann, was reached.

Birkenhead requested that the Irish be accompanied to the next meeting by a constitutional lawyer for a discussion on the role of the Crown. Accordingly, John Chartres, the second secretary to the Irish delegation, attended, leaving Childers on the outside. Birkenhead sought to reassure the Irish that the Crown, as in Canada, would be a symbol only, and no future British government would attempt to influence Ireland against her will. That was crucial for the British, as Birkenhead explained, because it bound together all members of the Commonwealth in voluntary union. Chartres countered that, unlike Canada, Ireland's proximity to and history of conflict with Britain meant that interference by a future Westminster government, using those same constitutional powers that Birkenhead claimed were merely symbolic, was likely.

The issue of the Crown was discussed at a Dáil cabinet meeting on 25 November, when it was confirmed that the Crown could be recognised for the purposes of association, as symbol and accepted head of the combination of associated states. Significantly, both Brugha and Stack supported this new position on the Crown, though they remained firm on the principle of external association. This, of course, did not mean allegiance to the Crown, because in Ireland's case, for the historical and geographical reasons set out by Chartres, she could not enjoy the freedom which the dominions undoubtedly possessed. Yet the Irish experienced difficulties responding to the British offer to word any phrase which would ensure that the position of the Crown in Ireland would be no more "in practice" than it was in any other dominion.

On 1 December the British presented their final proposals, which showed only minor modifications to the original dominion status offer made by Lloyd George to de Valera on 20 July. The Irish delegation returned to Dublin to attend a crucial cabinet meeting that had been scheduled for Saturday, 3 December. On the sea journey from Holyhead, the vessel was in collision with a fishing smack, delaying its return to Dun Laoghaire until 10.15 am on the Saturday morning. With the cabinet due to meet at 11 am, Collins had to skip a meeting of the IRB Supreme Council. A copy of the Treaty proposals was passed to his IRB colleagues together with a request that the council should have a response ready by lunchtime. Collins actually met a representative from the Supreme Council during a cabinet adjournment. He learned of the IRB's objections to the oath, but provided Collins with an alternative form of words which they had agreed.

Back in the Mansion House, where the cabinet was meeting, individual ministers offered their opinion on the British proposals. Griffith, supported by Duggan, was adamant that this was Britain's final offer, but Barton and Duffy argued that further concessions could be squeezed from the British. The cabinet debated the issues for seven hours during which bitter personal exchanges regularly featured. In perhaps the worst of these, Brugha targeted Griffith and Collins, when he claimed that the British had "selected their men" for the sub-conference sessions. Both men reacted furiously, with Collins stating that Brugha himself should go to London to conduct the negotiations. During the meeting Collins made little contribution. Although he was clearly unhappy with the wording of the oath, he was in broad agreement with Griffith.

De Valera attempted to find a new form of wording for the oath of allegiance that could be endorsed by both wings of the cabinet, though there is no agreement on the precise wording that he suggested. The official record states:

> I ... do solemnly swear true faith and allegiance to the Constitution of the Irish Free State, to the Treaty of Association and to recognise the King of Great Britain as Head of the Associated States.

De Valera subsequently offered two versions of what he had said, but Childers was convinced that he had used the term "King of the Associated States". Certainly, Collins assumed that de Valera would accept a slightly modified oath, but it was clear that a good deal of confusion remained over who said what. Significantly, the president did not ensure clarity on this crucial issue, instead returning to the idea of external association which he wanted the Irish delegation to put forward again. Barton urged the president to join them in London for the climax of the negotiations. In the end, however, Griffith stated that he would not sign the Treaty, but would bring it back to Dublin and submit it to the Dáil. Such an undertaking, of course, would be dependent on the British granting additional time. Therefore, a tired Irish delegation returned to London without a clear plan.

There, Childers, Barton and Duffy hastily pulled together another draft based on the external association principle, but Collins absented himself from the Downing Street meeting, considering it a waste of time. Griffith led the team for the conference on 4 December, setting out the case for external association with considerable skill. In the back of his mind was the one clear instruction given to the plenipotentiaries. He would reject the oath as it stood and, if the conference was headed for a breakdown, seek to ensure that the break came on Ulster. However, Griffith's position was undermined by Duffy. During an exchange in which he stated that Ireland wanted to be closely associated with the dominions, particularly on the issue of defence, he added "our difficulty is coming into the Empire". This provoked a reaction from the British that may have been rehearsed. Led by Chamberlain, the British team walked out. They would send their final proposals on the following day and Craig was to be informed that the conference had failed.

In an attempt to revive the negotiations, Jones visited Hans Place that night, hearing from Griffith that the Irish needed some concession on the Ulster issue to help them push the Treaty through the Dáil. Griffith also suggested that the prime minister should meet Collins the next morning. Collins arrived at Downing Street on the morning of 5 December, and a discussion followed on both the Boundary Commission and the national status clauses. There was sufficient movement to restart the conference, and Griffith, Collins and Barton returned to Downing Street that afternoon. Birkenhead and Collins had already considered a revision of the oath wording that was closer to the IRB's recommendation, and the conference focused on the issue of national status.

At this final conference Griffith stuck to the argument that the provisional concessions on status agreed by the Irish delegations had been contingent on the satisfactory conclusion of the Ulster issue. Thus, they would not sign any Treaty until Craig had clarified his position. This stance infuriated Lloyd George who warned that it would be a serious breach of faith if Griffith tried to break on Ulster. While Griffith indicated his willingness to sign the Treaty, he insisted that Collins and Barton had not been privy to the document that had been drawn up by Tom Jones and were, therefore, under no similar obligation. Griffith was also adamant that a response on unity was required from Craig, but the prime minister simply ignored this demand. It was at this point that Lloyd George, in a piece of high drama, produced two letters from his pocket, claiming that he had promised to inform Craig of the negotiations' outcome. One stated that a Treaty had been signed and peace restored, while the other proclaimed that the conference had ended and war would be resumed. Brandishing both letters, the prime minister warned that those who declined the peace route must take "full responsibility for the war that would immediately follow refusal by any delegate to sign".

Griffith had already conveyed his willingness to accept the Treaty, and Barton was shocked when Collins revealed his intention to sign on the car journey back to Hans Place. Duggan, who had always been in the Griffith–Collins camp, was ready to sign, but Barton and Duffy resisted for an agonising few hours. Duffy finally relented following an emotional plea by Duggan who vividly recalled the sight of young Volunteers being hanged in Mountjoy Prison. Childers tried desperately to persuade Barton to hold out, but he too succumbed to the pressure and the Anglo-Irish Treaty was formally signed in the early hours of 6 December 1921. In the final exchanges, Lloyd George had dropped the British demand for free trade and conceded fiscal autonomy to the Irish Free State, but it was his threat of immediate war that had proved decisive. This was a considerable gamble on the prime minister's part because, despite Chamberlain's earlier musing, it was unlikely that public opinion in Britain would have accepted the reopening of hostilities in such circumstances.

By this stage, however, it was evident that the Irish delegation, whose members must have been under strain from the repeated rail and sea journeys between London and Dublin, were anxious for an end to the conference following eight weeks of intensive talks. The fact that it was a home fixture for the British gave them an important advantage, and they were able to dictate the direction of the negotiations from the opening of the talks. The Irish failure to table an alternative set of proposals on 11 October was crucial. Lloyd George and his team were clearly more united than their Irish counterparts and, though they believed they were making significant concessions, the British never lost sight of their objectives on the fundamental issues of Crown and Empire. Griffith, who had led the Irish delegation with considerable vigour and skill, was never as committed to the symbolism of a republic as some of his colleagues. Moreover, Collins did not want a return to a war that he was convinced would end quickly in defeat. Acting

Signatures on the Anglo-Irish Treaty.

under these constraints, neither leader was prepared to call Lloyd George's bluff on the reopening of hostilities in Ireland.

Reaction to the Treaty in Britain and Ireland

Throughout the negotiations, the prime minister had been careful to retain the backing of the Conservative Party on which his coalition government depended. By 1921 his government was increasingly unpopular, and unease was growing on the Tory backbenches. There was a genuine fear that Lloyd George might break the traditional party system and, in the process, destroy the Conservative Party's identity. At the same time, the Tories had moved on from their prewar obsession with the Ulster question, and this clearly worked to Lloyd George's advantage in his dealings with Sinn Féin. Previously, the Conservative Party viewed its support for the Ulster Unionists as a central plank in its defence of the Empire, but relationships had altered significantly in less than a decade. Indeed, many Conservatives had come to view Unionist inflexibility during the negotiations as a threat to the Empire. This was apparent in November 1921, when the Belfast administration resisted attempts to pressurise it into amending its constitutional position. Anger at this intransigence was reflected in most sections of the British press, which attacked the Unionist government for adopting such a narrow, self-interested stance. In the *Observer*, J. L. Garvin wrote that the "attitude of Ulster … has been a very deep disappointment to her friends". Significantly, Lloyd George's demand that the Ulster Unionists should accept legislative subordination to a new all-Ireland parliament, while retaining their devolved powers, seemed to be a reasonable request in the eyes of British public opinion.

Yet when the prime minister tried to exert pressure on the Unionists at a critical point in the negotiations, Bonar Law rushed to their defence. He had returned to frontline politics following his departure in March 1921 and immediately pledged his support for the Unionist position. Consequently, Lloyd George had to limit the pressure he could bring to bear on Belfast, and he turned his attention towards squeezing movement from Sinn Féin following the Ulster Unionist rebuff in November. Still, the commitment in the Treaty to establish a Boundary Commission outraged Unionist opinion and threatened, once more, to test Craig's resolve. Indeed, Unionists were subsequently shocked by Bonar Law's support for the Treaty, which he made clear when the parliamentary debate in both Houses opened on 14 December. In his speech, the former Tory leader predicted that the Commission would make only minor adjustments to the border. With Ulster's position therefore safeguarded, he had no issues with the other clauses in the Articles of Agreement. Certainly, Bonar Law was reading the public mood correctly, as the coalition government won widespread approval for its success in concluding the Treaty. While the final document represented a stunning volte-face for an administration that had been committed to a policy of tough coercion only six months earlier, it was viewed as a notable personal success for the prime minister. At a stroke Lloyd George appeared to have finally removed the Irish question from British politics.

In Britain the only significant opposition to the Treaty came from the Diehards, the rump of right-wing Conservatives who opposed the government on a wide range of issues. From the outset they had attacked the very notion of a conference with Sinn Féin, and they were savage in their criticism of the Treaty. Numbering around 50 MPs, the Diehards had made two determined efforts to thwart the negotiations. On 31 October they had tabled a censure motion in the Commons, and they subsequently denounced Birkenhead and Chamberlain at the Conservative Party conference in mid-November. Both of these attempts were swept aside, but further criticism of the government was expected during the debates to ratify the Treaty. The Diehards began by attacking a government that had negotiated with "murderers" before denouncing the terms of the Treaty, claiming that they were humiliating and would cause serious damage to the Empire.

In the debates, the Diehards received support from Carson who, as a new Lord of Appeal, had recently been elevated to the House of Lords. On 14 December his maiden speech in the upper chamber denounced the Treaty, which, he claimed, had been concluded by ministers "with a revolver pointed at your head". He berated the coalition government that had neither the resolve to deal with criminals in Ireland nor the "pluck" to rule over the Empire. Carson was particularly scathing in his criticism of the Conservative Party, but he reserved his harshest words for his old friend and prewar political ally, Lord Birkenhead, describing those "who will sell their friends for the purpose of conciliating their enemies" as "loathsome". Birkenhead replied in kind and an ugly scene followed when he was interrupted by Carson. In the end, however, only 47 peers voted against the government in the Lords. Carson's bitterness was a testament to his Irish Unionist past. Whatever might happen to Ulster, the Treaty confirmed that the Union was irrevocably broken.

In the Commons, an overwhelming majority of MPs supported the Treaty, with only the Diehards and the Ulster Unionists in opposition. Some of the harshest criticism came from Charles Craig, who expressed revulsion at the Boundary Commission clause and accused the government of betrayal. His approach was shared by his brother, Sir James, who also believed that the prime minister was guilty of duplicity. On 15 December, the Northern Ireland premier wrote to Chamberlain to express his anger, warning that if the Treaty clauses were not modified, the government should withdraw British troops and "allow us to fight it ourselves". Of course, the Treaty was also a major concern for southern Unionists.

They had hoped that their interests would be safeguarded and had ensured that the British delegation was aware of their views during the negotiations. Yet, with Long and Lansdowne no longer in the cabinet, they discovered that Chamberlain and Birkenhead were unwilling to jeopardise progress with Sinn Féin in defence of southern Unionist interests. Consequently, they had to content themselves with personal assurances from Griffith, who undertook to consider southern Unionist claims, particularly in regard to representation in the new state. Thus Midleton and his colleagues did not vote against the Treaty, as they sought to lobby the provisional government of the Irish Free State on possible concessions that might be included in the new Constitution.

Back in Dublin, Griffith and Collins were resigned to the fact that the Treaty would cause a split within Sinn Féin, but each was prepared to argue the document's merits in the Dáil. Meanwhile, de Valera was stunned by the delegation's failure to consult him prior to signing the document, a move that he described as an "act of disloyalty". To some observers the president appeared to be more annoyed by this personal snub than by the actual terms of the Treaty. His intention was to sack Griffith, Collins and Barton, the three cabinet members who had signed the Treaty. Accordingly, he convened a meeting of the other three ministers to ratify his decision only to be shocked by Cosgrave's refusal to support the sackings. His next move was to summon a full meeting of the cabinet at which the arguments for and against the Treaty were rehearsed. Again, de Valera was surprised by the cabinet's decision, passed by a 4 : 3 majority, to refer the Treaty to the Dáil. When the president again accused the delegates of a breach of faith in their failure to consult him, Barton responded by arguing that the real problem lay with de Valera's refusal to attend the conference. Before the Dáil could meet, de Valera sought to exert his authority by issuing a proclamation that outlined the cabinet split and stated that he

Griffith and Éamon de Valera (1882–1975), at Croke Park, 1922.

personally could not recommend acceptance of the Treaty to either the Dáil or the Irish people. Clearly, the president had erred in not attending the negotiations, but he compounded this error by his failure to provide decisive leadership from Dublin. This enabled Griffith and Collins to present him with a fait accompli, and one, to his surprise, that was acceptable to his cabinet. The mathematician had miscalculated.

The Dáil debate on the Treaty opened on 14 December 1921, and the bitter divisions within Sinn Féin were soon laid bare. De Valera hoped that the Dáil would reject the Treaty, which would allow the cabinet to table new proposals based on the external association concept. During the negotiations, the president had displayed great skill in holding the disparate Sinn Féin factions together, but he had established himself as the spokesman for the anti-Treaty element immediately after the document had been signed. The opening day of the Dáil debate was taken up by arguments over the precise instructions, or lack of them, that had been given to the Irish delegation. It was not until the secret session of 15 and 16 December that the debate focused on the central issue of national status. De Valera dominated proceedings, and he produced his alternative to the Treaty during these long and frequently acrimonious discussions. Known as "Document No 2", it was based on the concept of external association, necessitating the redrafting of all the clauses dealing with dominion status. What really concentrated the minds of the TDs was the discussion of the oath, which was Article 4 of the Treaty. Griffith argued powerfully that the existing clause was honourable:

> I ... do solemnly swear true faith and allegiance to the Constitution of the Irish Free State as by law established and that I will be faithful to H.M. George V, his heirs and successors by law, in virtue of the common citizenship of Ireland with Great Britain and her adherence to a membership of the group of nations forming the British Commonwealth of Nations.

Document No 2 made no reference to an oath, stating that "for purposes of common concern, Ireland shall be associated with the States of the British Commonwealth", though Griffith also pointed out that the term "republic" did not appear in de Valera's alternative. It was around the issue of the oath, however, that republican opposition coalesced. When he proposed the motion that the Dáil should accept the Treaty, Griffith placed great emphasis on the fact that the Irish delegation had not negotiated for a republic. He also reminded de Valera that, while they had all taken an oath to the Irish Republic, the president himself had gone on record to state that this was only an undertaking to do the best he could for Ireland. While he acknowledged that the Treaty was not the "ideal thing", he felt that it merited support as it gave Ireland equality with England. This was, of course, the basis for Griffith's old "Hungarian policy". In 1904, Griffith had produced an important pamphlet, *The Resurrection of Hungary*, in which he presented the case for an independent Ireland under a dual monarchy.

Throughout the debates, de Valera dwelt on symbolism, arguing that the oath acknowledged the king as both the "monarch of Ireland" and "the source of executive authority in Ireland". De Valera's focus on semantics perplexed many of his followers who viewed the Treaty in a less nuanced light. Initially, the discussion of Document No 2, which was still in draft form, was restricted to the private session. However, his opponents were anxious to bring these proposals into the public domain before Christmas in order to highlight the fact that de Valera's alternative was external association, not a republic. In the president's mind the difference between external association and dominion status was fundamental. Yet he argued that the British would not sanction a return to war over such a difference. To some TDs this appeared to be stretching logic. In the debates, de Valera was supported by Brugha, Stack and Childers and by most of the female deputies, including Mary MacSwiney, Kathleen Clarke, Margaret Pearse and Countess Markievicz. Probably the most effective speech in opposition to the Treaty came from Childers, who offered a detailed analysis of its defects. He concluded that the Treaty was not an honourable settlement and would confer less real freedom on Ireland than the other dominions such as Canada had. Other opponents rejected the analytical approach in favour of an emotional appeal. Austin Stack regarded "full Canadian powers" as insufficient for Ireland, and he pledged to fight in the Fenian tradition to destroy the oath of allegiance.

Collins made the most important contribution in favour of acceptance of the Treaty. He stressed that in agreeing to participate in the London conference, Ireland had compromised on the republic. Yet he was convinced that the Treaty gave Ireland freedom, "not the ultimate freedom that all nations aspire and develop to, but the freedom to achieve it." The speech resonated both inside and outside the Dáil. Behind the scenes Collins had used his influence to rally support for the Treaty among those who had fought in the War of Independence. The Supreme Council of the IRB, of which Collins was president, had endorsed the Treaty, and many IRA commanders added their support on the basis that if it was acceptable to Collins, they would give it their backing. In the Dáil, Kevin O'Higgins added his endorsement. Speaking after Childers sat down, O'Higgins acknowledged the Treaty's defects, but argued that it offered the only practical and sensible course. He was adamant that it granted "a broad measure of liberty to the Irish people", adding prophetically that the inevitable evolution of the British Commonwealth would see a natural progression towards increased freedom for all the dominions and "equality of status". O'Higgins then issued a grave warning to the Treaty's opponents that they must not vote against ratification unless they could demonstrate clearly how further concessions could be secured in practice. For him, that ruled out a return to war as it was certain to end in military disaster.

By the time the Dáil adjourned for Christmas on 22 December, all the main arguments had been aired. The Christmas break worked to the advantage of those in favour of the Treaty. As deputies returned to their constituencies, many were exposed to the people's general pro-Treaty sympathies. Indeed, a string of resolutions advocating acceptance of the Treaty were issued by a variety of public bodies, and this reflected public opinion. The press was overwhelmingly pro-Treaty, as were the Catholic bishops, and 24 county councils declared their support for the Treaty. Still, the Dáil's backing for the Treaty could not be assumed. Many of the TDs who had been nominated for the second Dáil in May 1921 at the height of the War of Independence were militant republicans.

When the Dáil reconvened on 3 January, Collins advocated a course that might limit any split in the Sinn Féin movement. He wanted those TDs opposed to the Treaty to abstain on the vote, thus upholding their principles. A provisional government could then be formed to draft a new Constitution as the Treaty had stipulated. The Constitution would derive its authority from the Irish people rather than the Crown, and this would allow the anti-Treaty TDs to take the oath, as they would not be swearing allegiance to the Crown but to the Constitution of the Irish Free State. De Valera rejected the offer, instead indicating that he would table his Document No 2, which he had revised over the Christmas recess, as an amendment to Griffith's motion that the Treaty be accepted. This threatened to prolong the tortuous process, as other amendments were likely to follow, but Griffith brought matters to a head by circulating Document No 2 to the press in its pre-Christmas format. This undermined de Valera's position but, in spite of pleas to avoid a dangerous split, he further raised the temperature with another bitter speech on 6 January. On the following day the Dáil voted to accept the Treaty by 64 votes to 57. Crucially, the seven IRB TDs all voted for the pro-Treaty side, which ensured it had a majority. De Valera then resigned as president, but he stood against Griffith in a subsequent vote. If elected, he intended to dismiss the pro-Treaty cabinet members, but he lost the presidency by 60 votes to 58. Griffith quickly selected a new cabinet, but real power rested with the provisional government that was formed on 14 January and led by Collins. It was Collins who took responsibility for the implementation of the Treaty.

The Dáil debates on the Treaty had been dominated by the question of the oath. There was very little reference to Ulster, with only Seán MacEntee, a TD for Monaghan and native of Belfast, basing his opposition to the Treaty on the claim that it perpetuated partition. Indeed, there were only very minor differences in the clauses relating to partition between the Treaty and Document

No 2. In his speech endorsing the Treaty, Lloyd George had informed the House of Commons that the agreement had given the Irish the freedom to work out their own national identity. However, it was clear from the Dáil debates that Sinn Féin was now deeply split, as the issue of the oath of allegiance had obscured such potential attractions for many TDs. In terms of numbers, the Dáil was almost evenly divided, but this did not reflect opinion in the country where there was a significant pro-Treaty majority. On the anti-Treaty side, moreover, "republicans" were divided. De Valera clearly represented a group that was ready to endorse external association, but there was another more extreme element for whom external association was not acceptable. These militants would accept nothing less than a republic, and they made this evident during the debates. Significantly, their leader, Rory O'Connor, attacked Brugha at one point, claiming that he had been contaminated by politics. For irreconcilable republicans, such as O'Connor and Liam Mellows, the fact that the Treaty had received a majority in the Dáil was irrelevant, as they believed that democracy should not be a barrier to the republic. In spite of their stance, however, it was de Valera who gave the anti-Treaty side real credibility, as he continued to enjoy enormous prestige in the broader republican movement.

The Civil War and its aftermath

One week after the Treaty was accepted by the Dáil, a meeting of largely pro-Treaty TDs in the Mansion House formally appointed a provisional government. Its primary function was to oversee the transfer of power from the British authorities that would take place over the next few months. At its first meeting, two days later on 16 January, Collins was confirmed as chairman of the provisional government, whose members included W. T. Cosgrave, Kevin O'Higgins, Eoin MacNeill and Éamonn Duggan. The agenda for this inaugural meeting was dominated by the arrangements for that afternoon's visit to Dublin Castle, where they would assume control of the various government departments. The members of the provisional government made their way from the Mansion House along Dame Street in three cars that stopped in the upper yard of the castle outside the chief secretary's office. Collins was the first to alight, and he hurried past the press and well-wishers to enter the building just after 1.30 pm. Inside, the chairman met the Viceroy, Lord Fitzalan, who delivered a brief address in which he wished the provisional government success. Collins made a very favourable impression as he introduced himself to senior civil servants and ensured that the gathering was warm and friendly.

The other provisional government members met their counterparts, and the entire proceedings were over in an hour. Dublin Castle, the seat of British power in Ireland, had been handed over to Sinn Féin in preparation for a British withdrawal. The event had been conducted with little ceremony, but a delighted Collins understood the significance of what had transpired. Behind the occasion's symbolic importance, there was a clear realisation that the Treaty had conferred considerable powers on the new state. In the background Collins had been engaging with the British on the precise details of the transfer of power. British troops were withdrawn and the RIC disbanded. However, in spite of the obvious approval of enthusiastic Dublin citizens, the provisional government faced determined opposition to the Treaty from significant sections of Sinn Féin and the Volunteers.

There was uncertainty about how to respond to such a fundamental disagreement. While some wanted to see decisive action taken against the anti-Treaty elements, others were anxious to bring the two factions together. It was clear, however, that the Dáil could not fulfil this function, as it tended to highlight the political divisions. In these circumstances the stance taken by the IRA assumed even greater importance. Both Brugha, the outgoing minister for defence, and Mulcahy, his replacement, had offered assurances that the army "would remain the Army of the Irish Republic", but it was uncertain whether the IRA could remain united or would be prepared to accept civilian authority. The IRA's GHQ, which was dominated by Collins and Mulcahy, largely supported the Treaty, but a majority of rank-and-file members, probably close to three-quarters, were opposed to the Treaty. Those in favour included units from Dublin, Longford, Clare and Donegal, while the Treaty's opponents comprised the IRA's main guerrilla forces in Munster and Connacht that had borne the brunt of the fighting during the War of Independence. In some areas, attitudes to the Treaty were determined by personal rivalry and family feuds, and this confusion was, in some ways, an extension of poorer discipline and internal wrangling that had characterised many IRA units during the truce period.

The situation was further complicated by the deteriorating security situation in the north, where reaction to the Boundary Commission proposals further inflamed sectarian tension. Indeed, Churchill had felt compelled to intervene and brought Collins and Craig together for a meeting at the Colonial Office in an effort to bring a halt to the violence in Belfast. The summit produced the first Craig–Collins pact, which was signed on 21 January 1922. Craig made a commitment to stop the persecution of the Catholic minority, while Collins agreed to end the Belfast boycott that had originally been introduced by the Dáil in August 1920 in an attempt to exert economic pressure on the north. The pact collapsed within days, as Craig told supporters that his government would only accept very minor changes to the border recommended by the Boundary Commission. A furious Collins replied with an emphatic statement, predicting that large areas of territory would be transferred to the Irish Free State. A further meeting on 2 February failed to find common ground, and this was followed by a marked escalation of the violence, resulting in 30 killings in Belfast during a one-week period in mid-February. Again, Churchill, displaying uncharacteristic patience, played a constructive role, bringing the two leaders back to London in a fresh attempt to reconcile their differences. This led to a second Craig–Collins pact on 30 March, which, at Churchill's insistence, carried the headline: "Peace is today declared". The March agreement contained more specific commitments relating to the treatment of the Catholic minority, and Collins promised to use his influence to bring a halt to the IRA's northern campaign. The two leaders also gave an undertaking to settle the border issue at a future conference without recourse to the Boundary Commission.

The second pact generated considerable optimism, but the accord again broke down as the violence in the north intensified. This prompted a renewal of the IRA campaign, and Collins and Liam Lynch worked closely together to ensure that both pro-Treaty and anti-Treaty IRA units cooperated in this latest northern offensive. Both factions were careful to conceal this collusion. Had it been uncovered, it would have led to the British government accusing the provisional government of breaching the Treaty. IRA personnel were sent across the border to assist local units, but the campaign that began in the spring of 1922 did not meet with success. The IRA, which was weak in the north, faced a formidable enemy in the Ulster Special Constabulary (USC), and the organisation's southern leaders failed to develop a coherent military strategy.

Planned joint action in the north should have had a powerful positive influence on attempts to maintain IRA unity. However, the soldiers of the republic, like their political counterparts, were obsessed with the oath of allegiance. There was also the prospect that the army might attempt to coerce the Dáil, as the Cork IRA had threatened to shoot any TD from their area who backed the Treaty. Such fears exercised the minds of those on both sides of the debate. On 11 January, anti-Treaty officers wrote to Mulcahy to request an army convention that would consider the establishment of an executive. This executive would have supreme control over the army, a development that would pose a grave danger to the provisional government. Mulcahy's instinct was to delay any such convention in the hope that the process of British troop withdrawals would cast the Treaty in a more positive light. The rapid departure of the Crown Forces during February left the anti-Treaty IRA in control over much of the country, as military barracks were occupied by local IRA units. This was particularly true in Munster, where the anti-Treaty IRA was dominant, but it was a development that the provisional government was willing to allow in order to contain the military split. Mulcahy had stalled the anti-Treaty IRA leadership for two months, but he reluctantly

Release of IRA prisoners from the Curragh, Co Kildare, 1922.

agreed to an army convention on 26 March that would meet in the Mansion House.

The greatest threat to the provisional government's strategy occurred in Limerick, where there was a serious attempt to prevent the city falling under the control of local IRA units that were solidly anti-Treaty. Limerick's strategic importance was a major concern for the provisional government, which instructed Michael Brennan's Clare-based First Western Division to occupy the city's barracks. The anti-Treaty IRA responded by moving more men into the city, and they were reinforced by personnel from Ernie O'Malley's Second Southern Division. Soon every significant building, in addition to the barracks, was occupied, and a violent confrontation appeared to be unavoidable. A clash was only averted because neither side wanted to be held accountable for opening fire on former comrades. In the end the tension was eased when a compromise was agreed, leading to the withdrawal of all troops from outside the city. This left Limerick in the hands of local anti-Treaty IRA units. The climbdown infuriated Griffith who demanded that the provisional government launch a military strike against anti-Treaty forces in the city, but he was overruled. While he was president, Griffith was not a member of the provisional government, the body which now exercised real power. As minister for defence, Mulcahy occupied a crucial position, and it was his determination to avoid a military confrontation that led to the compromise deal brokered with Liam Lynch. The reluctance of both sides to attack former comrades became a powerful feature in many parts of the country over the next few months.

In early March the provisional government tried to ban the forthcoming Army Convention, but the dissidents ignored the order and the planned convention went ahead as delegates from 52 of the 73 IRA brigades assembled in Dublin. At this point Mulcahy hoped that IRA unity might still be preserved, and he met Lynch and other anti-Treaty officers on 20 March. Lynch and Mulcahy had maintained a line of communication. The two men had great respect for each other, feelings that were undoubtedly strengthened by their shared IRB background. In effect, Mulcahy needed Lynch's support to avert an IRA split, but Lynch was not his own master within the ranks of the anti-Treaty IRA. It had become apparent that the anti-Treaty element was divided between republican pragmatists like Lynch and his fellow officers in the powerful First Southern Division, who wanted to undermine the Treaty but avoid a civil war, and the republican militants led by Rory O'Connor and Liam Mellows. They wanted to establish a military dictatorship to replace the provisional government. It was this latter group that dashed any hope that Mulcahy might have had of preserving army unity. On 22 March, O'Connor held a press conference to declare that his section of the IRA would ignore the Dáil and act as a military junta. Reconvening on 9 April, the convention elected an army executive that appointed Lynch as chief of staff. It was from this date that the press began to describe the anti-Treaty IRA as "Irregulars". However, the army executive struggled to agree a strategy that would appeal to the militants who appeared to be determined to start a civil war. In the growing confusion, the IRA executive seized control of the Four Courts in Dublin, which would become its new headquarters. Rory O'Connor and his radical faction had taken the initiative, and he now demanded an end to the provisional government.

Conventions and conflict

The occupation of the Four Courts was one of the most significant events in the slide into a civil war. In tandem with the takeover of the Four Courts, republican forces seized other buildings in the city. In a replay of Easter 1916, these were turned into defensive military positions. O'Connor and the other radicals were posing a direct challenge to the provisional government and, simultaneously, issuing an invitation to all IRA Volunteers who opposed the Treaty to follow the new executive. With tension rising, there was an obvious danger that sporadic incidents might lead to more general violence which could not be turned off. Indeed, a number of skirmishes did take place and, by early May 1922, these had resulted in the deaths of eight men. Faced with this deteriorating situation, the IRB, which had, of course, a foot in both camps, formed a six-man committee in an attempt to broker an agreement. The new body had three pro-Treaty and three anti-Treaty members, including Lynch, and they held four peace meetings. However, Lynch would not budge from his insistence that the army should remain the army of the Irish Republic and be under the authority of an independent army executive, and the negotiations ended in failure.

As the prospect of a descent into anarchy loomed, the attitude of the First Southern Division was of paramount importance. The division had 35,000 Volunteers, about one-third of the IRA's total membership, and it included the IRA's fighting elite. Six of the 16 men who formed the executive belonged to the division. These officers, Lynch, Liam Deasy, Seán Moylan, Florrie O'Donoghue, Tom Hales and Seán O'Hegarty, were anxious to restrain the militants, and a number of them were opposed to any takeover of power by the army. Without consulting their colleagues, three of these Cork officers, O'Hegarty, O'Donoghue and Hales, opened peace talks with senior figures in the provisional government. This was followed by the release of the "army officers' statement" on 1 May, which declared that civil war would be the greatest calamity in Irish history and would leave Ireland broken for centuries". The statement went on to demand the acceptance of the Treaty, which would facilitate IRA reunification, and the establishment of a joint pro-and anti-Treaty government following an uncontested general election. Although the statement was swiftly repudiated by the IRA executive, it did create some room for manoeuvre. Collins and de Valera came together at University College, Dublin, where they agreed an electoral pact on 18 May. As the army officers had stipulated, the agreement committed both pro- and anti-Treaty candidates to be nominated on a joint ticket with the subsequent formation of a coalition government.

Churchill, at the Colonial Office, was furious when he learned of the electoral pact. Previously, officials in London had accepted General Macready's judgement that the provisional government had been wise to ignore the provocation of O'Connor in seizing the Four Courts, but an electoral pact enraged Churchill who viewed it as a clear breach of the Treaty. There was an assumption that the purpose of the pact was to prevent the public having the opportunity to endorse the Treaty. On the other hand, it seems reasonable to conclude that one of Collins's objectives in agreeing the pact was to allow the election to proceed, as the army executive had made it clear on a number of occasions that it would take steps to disrupt any election. By this stage de Valera had established a new political movement, Cumann na Poblachta (League of the Republic), which effectively acted as a vehicle for the TDs who had opposed the Treaty. In public, de Valera indulged in extreme rhetoric, but he was privately working towards reconciliation with his former colleagues. This raised concerns among Collins's colleagues in the provisional government who had not been consulted about the negotiations with de Valera.

Outside the provisional government, Griffith was outraged when he became aware of the details of the pact. Such was his fury that the close relationship that had developed between Collins and Griffith in 1921 and carried the Irish delegation through the Treaty negotiations now came to an end. The electoral pact was designed to prevent a popular split on the Treaty and to preserve the peace through the formation of a unity government. Significantly, the pact made no reference to the Treaty. A national panel of Sinn Féin candidates was agreed, with the pro-Treaty faction having a slim majority to reflect the current standing in the Dáil. The establishment of a nine-man unity government would follow, comprising five pro-Treaty and four anti-Treaty ministers. Collins had been reluctant to accept so many concessions, but he was persuaded by his old IRB friend, Harry Boland, who stressed the need for unity. To some observers it now looked as if Collins might turn his back on the Treaty. When a special Sinn Féin Árd-Fheis endorsed the pact on 21 May, Collins told the delegates, "Unity at home was more important than any Treaty with the foreigner, and if unity could only be got at the expense of the Treaty – the Treaty would have to go." Of course, Collins was anxious to avoid a conflict with his former comrades, and he was hopeful that a new Constitution, which was now being drafted, would reconcile many of the republican dissidents. Yet it was also true that an uninterrupted election could not take place without the pact, as there would be widespread interference with polling, particularly in those areas under the control of the Irregulars.

Meanwhile, an angry Churchill watched from London as events unfolded. In spite of his fears, the colonial secretary had been convinced that Collins and Griffith were men of good faith who could be relied upon to implement the Treaty. Consequently, he was delighted to offer military support to the new Free State army, but Collins's paralysis in dealing with the Four Courts situation, followed by his collaboration with de Valera over the election, had altered his thinking. At the same time, Churchill was coming under increasing political pressure from the Conservatives at Westminster, who wanted the Lloyd George government to force the authorities in Dublin to take action against the republican militants. Following the announcement of the electoral pact, Collins and Griffith were summoned to London for a meeting with Churchill and Lionel Curtis, the constitutional expert who had acted as an adviser to the British delegation during the Treaty negotiations. Although Curtis pointed out that the pact was technically not a breach of the Treaty, it was evident that Churchill's trust in Collins had been shaken.

The fear that Collins had surrendered to the republican faction intensified when the two Irish leaders returned to London on 27 May with the draft Free State Constitution. There had been sufficient ambiguity in the wording of the Treaty for Collins to assume that he could tilt the Constitution in a republican direction. Accordingly, the draft he presented in London made no reference to the oath of allegiance and only a brief mention of the Crown. Not surprisingly, the British dismissed the draft Constitution claiming that it was an evasion of Dublin's responsibility under the Treaty. At a second meeting on 1 June, Lloyd George warned that the situation was now very grave, while Churchill threatened military intervention if the Irish reneged on their Treaty obligations. An enraged Collins responded by condemning the British government for its hopeless failure to protect the Catholic minority in the north, where there had been a serious escalation of sectarian violence during May. On the following day, however, Collins backed down, and a new Constitution was agreed that eased British concerns on the oath and status. Griffith and Collins also accepted that the Treaty would take precedence over the Constitution, meaning that any future amendments to the Constitution that were deemed to be inconsistent with the Treaty would be rendered null and void. In spite of these concessions, the Crown's role in the new Constitution was, as Kevin O'Higgins declared, clearly symbolic, leaving the real power in the hands of the people".

The Irish surrender on the Constitution, details of which were only made public on the morning of 16 June, the day of the election, placed a huge strain on the Collins–de Valera pact. Collins seemed to be aware of this situation and, in a Cork speech just two days before polling, he called on voters to ignore the panel and "vote for the candidates you think best". The speech, in which Collins explained, "I am not hampered now by being on a platform where there are Coalitionists", was a clear repudiation of the pact, and he was accused by republican moderates of destroying any prospect of unity. Yet, in his defence, it seems clear that Collins recognised that the pact could not survive his failure to win British approval for his "republican" Constitution. It was also true that other senior pro-Treaty figures had already jettisoned the pact during the election campaign. Prominent TDs, notably Eoin O'Duffy and Ernest Blythe, had made public their desire for voters to give their lower preference votes to other parties and independents rather than anti-Treaty Sinn Féin candidates. While there was a Sinn Féin panel of candidates, the local press had left voters in no doubt where each of these stood on the Treaty issue. Outside the panel, an array of candidates from other parties, all of whom were pro-Treaty, were on the ballot paper.

The results of the election to the Third Dáil were announced on 24 June 1922, and there was a clear majority in favour of the Treaty. Cumann na Poblachta, the anti-Treaty party, received 133,864 first-preference votes and took 36 seats. The pro-Treaty party won 239,193 votes and 58 candidates were returned as TDs. The remaining 34 seats were divided between the Labour Party with seventeen, the Farmers' Party with seven, Independents, who won six seats, and the remaining four TDs representing Trinity College. A total of 466,419 voters had backed the Treaty, while 133,864 had declared their opposition. Across the country, the anti-Treatyites won only five of the 44 Leinster seats, but they had a narrow majority in Connacht and polled reasonably well in Munster. In total they won 22 per cent of the first-preference votes. The Labour Party secured over 29 per cent of the first-preference votes and would certainly have secured more seats had they run more candidates.

In spite of such a clear victory for the pro-Treatyites, the election to the Third Dáil was not a ringing endorsement of the provisional government. Rather, it was a plea for some form of political stability from an electorate that took only a passing interest in the bitter debates over precise constitutional arrangements. The people had voted for a return to normality, but the republican militants showed little regard for the democratic process. On 18 June, before the votes had been counted, they summoned an army convention that led to a further fracturing in the ranks of the anti-Treaty IRA. The purpose of this final convention was to vote on the army unification agreement. Instead, the delegates voted on a rival resolution tabled by Tom Barry, one of the most militant officers from the First Southern Division. Barry had been one of the replacements for Hales, O'Donoghue and O'Hegarty on the army executive. He wanted to declare war on the British after giving them three days to leave the country.

Delegates voted by a very narrow majority to reject the resolution, and this prompted a walkout from the convention, led by O'Connor and Mellows. This group of republican diehards returned to the Four Courts and promptly replaced Lynch with the Belfast leader, Joe McKelvey, as chief of staff. Lynch, in turn, withdrew to the Clarence Hotel in Dublin with many of his First Southern Division officers. In his new headquarters, Lynch clung to the hope that IRA unity might yet be restored, but events took a further twist with the assassination of Sir Henry Wilson on 22 June. Wilson had been returned as a Unionist MP in a North Down by-election in February 1922 and was acting as a security adviser to the Belfast government. As such, Collins held Wilson responsible for many of the attacks carried out on the minority community in the north. On the day of his assassination, Wilson, an ardent Unionist and fierce critic of the Treaty, had unveiled a war memorial at London's Liverpool Street Station, and he was followed from the ceremony to his residence in Eaton Square. Two Volunteers, Reggie Dunne and Joseph O'Sullivan, who had lost a leg in World War I, shot Wilson as he left the taxi outside his front door. The two assailants were quickly apprehended, and both were hanged on 10 August 1922.

Neither Dunne nor O'Sullivan revealed who had ordered the attack on Wilson. A number of historians have identified Collins as the high-ranking individual who gave the order, but there is little hard evidence of this. Indeed, the chaotic nature of the operation suggests that the two men were acting on their own initiative, and the provisional government was quick to issue a condemnation of the killing. In London the Westminster government immediately pointed the finger of blame at the anti-Treaty IRA militants housed in the Four Courts. The Collins–de Valera electoral pact and the joint IRA offensive in the north had infuriated Conservative MPs, but Wilson's killing sparked a storm of outrage that was directed at Lloyd George and the Treaty.

Next day, 23 June, Macready, who had remained in command of the troops in Ireland, met the cabinet in London, where a plan was discussed for a surprise British attack on the Four Courts on Sunday, 25 June. However, Macready opted for a strategy of delay, as he feared that any such unilateral action by the army would result in a new wave of public sympathy for the republican militants. He also knew that an attack on the building would inevitably mean civilian casualties, and he may well have accepted, as did the majority of the public, O'Connor's claim that the Wilson assassination was not connected to the Four Courts garrison in any way. Macready's warning that immediate British military intervention might actually unify the IRA and suck the army into another protracted conflict in Ireland clarified the government's thinking, and Churchill was in the forefront of a determined attempt to pressurise the provisional government into taking action against the Four Courts garrison. On 26 June, speaking in the House of Commons, the colonial secretary issued what many regarded as an ultimatum to Collins. The provisional government was warned that if it failed to intervene decisively, then the British would take the required action. Churchill had given no indication of any time limit, which suggests that his belligerence might not have reflected the political reality for the Lloyd George government. In fact, Collins had been moving slowly towards acceptance of the need for action against O'Connor and the republican diehards. He knew that the deadlock would have to be broken at some stage.

The kidnapping of J. J. O'Connell, a popular pro-Treaty senior officer, by the Four Courts men, who were responding to the arrest of one of their own officers, finally tipped the balance. Collins had been very reluctant to authorise action against the republican militants, and his attempts to reach an accommodation with some of the anti-Treaty elements had exasperated both the British government and many of his own colleagues. In particular, Griffith and O'Higgins had pressed the case for military action, arguing that this would be required to establish democratic authority, but the politicians who sought legitimacy were forced to wait on Collins. In the end the chairman could only choose one course. O'Connor's defiance had the objective of provoking a British attack, but this was a course of action that Collins knew he must not allow. An ultimatum calling on the Four Courts occupants to surrender was delivered at 3.40 am on 28 June 1922, and an attack followed less than 30 minutes later.

To open the attack, the National Army had borrowed two 18-pounder artillery pieces from the British. The plan was to shell the building in 1916 style and force a surrender. However, what should have been a straightforward assault to dislodge the occupants turned into a prolonged exercise in which National Army recruits demonstrated their lack of military training. Many of them had never fired a rifle before, and even those with fighting experience struggled to use the 18-pounders loaned by the British. More worryingly, the new troops showed little enthusiasm for the conflict, and it was only through the efforts of officers such as Emmet Dalton that morale held up. News reaching London increased Churchill's frustration, and he informed Macready that it might be necessary for British gunners to take over the bombardment. Nevertheless, O'Connor and his associates had no plan other than to sit it out, meaning that the outcome was inevitable as long as the National Army troops kept up their fire. By 30 June, enough damage had been done to the building to force the surrender of the anti-Treaty occupants. O'Connor and Mellows were among those arrested, but a number of senior officers, including Ernie O'Malley, were able to evade capture in the confusion.

The fall of the Four Courts was followed over the next few days by the surrender of Irregulars occupying other key buildings along O'Connell Street. One of the last units to surrender was the group led by Brugha. After ordering his men to surrender and seeing them off from the Granville Hotel, he ran onto the street brandishing a gun. He was shot and died from his wounds later that evening. By the end of the first week of July 1922, the Irregulars were in disarray. They had left Dublin, and there was no consensus among their leaders about future tactics. The fighting in Dublin had resulted in 65 deaths, while the cost of damage to property in the city was estimated at £4 million. In finally launching an attack on the Irregulars, Collins had hoped for a rapid victory in which the fighting would be confined to Dublin. However, the attack on the Four Courts had united the different anti-Treaty elements, and they would return to the guerrilla war tactics that had proved effective in the War of Independence.

The events in Dublin saw de Valera fall in behind the Irregulars. He had condemned the attack on the Four Courts, describing O'Connor and his men as the "best and bravest of our nation", and he appealed for public support as the struggle to save the republic entered a new phase. More pertinently, the attack on the Four Courts ended Lynch's reluctance to take up arms. Although he and Liam Deasy had also been arrested, Mulcahy ordered their release in the mistaken belief that the two might dissuade their followers from taking up arms against the Free State army. However, the two men hurried south to link up with their comrades in the First Southern Division, and Lynch became commander of the Irregulars. At this point the Irregulars controlled the south and west of the country, and their relatively well-armed troops enjoyed a numerical advantage over the Free State forces. Soon this situation would be reversed, as new recruits were enrolled and a steady supply of war material arrived from Britain. By August the National Army had received nine field guns, 27,000 rifles, 250 machine-guns and 8,500 grenades. In theory, the return to guerrilla warfare by Irregular troops operating in their own localities provided them with a significant advantage, but this was balanced by the fact that many citizens in the south and west were hostile to the republican troops. In such circumstances it was apparent that if the Irregulars were to achieve a military victory, it would have to come quickly. There was not enough popular support to sustain a protracted guerrilla campaign. It was imperative, therefore, that the Irregulars should attempt to strike an early and decisive blow before the National Army inevitably became larger, better equipped and more professional.

From the outset, however, the Irregulars failed to develop a coherent military strategy, and they were further handicapped by their unwillingness to seize the initiative. Instead, they opted to defend the areas under their control before withdrawing and burning their barracks when they came under attack. This pattern was repeated in some areas of the south and west, meaning that the Irregulars abandoned control of important towns such as Clonmel, Waterford, Sligo and Castlebar. They did retain control of Cork and Limerick, but these became primary targets for the Free State army as it moved out of Dublin. The conflict quickly developed its own momentum, even though Collins disliked the prospect of further bloodshed. Indeed, he ensured that lines of communication to the Irregulars remained open in the hope that further fighting might be curtailed. Nevertheless, a recruitment campaign, conducted against a background of high unemployment, had pushed up the number of troops in the Free State army to over 14,000 by early August. Collins became commander-in-chief in order to focus on the war, leaving Cosgrave to take charge of the provisional government.

The decision was taken to launch an offensive against republican strongholds in Munster, and troops were sometimes moved by sea to avoid problems with the road and rail network. Strategically, Limerick was of crucial importance. Control of the city ensured the isolation of Michael Brennan's forces in Clare and Seán Mac Eoin's units based in Athlone, the only significant pro-Treaty strongholds outside Dublin. Yet republican forces in Limerick evacuated the city soon after the Free State troops began their attack. In mid-August Dalton's troops seized control of Cork following a daring mission in which the bulk of the National Army force landed on the south coast, having sailed from Dublin. The Irregulars in Cork put up even less resistance than the Dublin garrison, and their retreat was a hasty, confused affair that undoubtedly damaged republican morale. These early weeks of the conflict also witnessed serious skirmishing in a number of counties, and, though the Irregulars controlled large swathes of South Tipperary, Kerry, West Galway, Mayo and Sligo, their failure to hold any major urban area proved to be a major blow.

William Thomas Cosgrave (1880–1965), First President of the Irish Free State. Seen on a state visit to New York, 1928.

That August the pro-Treaty side had to cope with the loss of Arthur Griffith and Michael Collins. Griffith had been unwell for some time and died from a brain haemorrhage in a Dublin nursing home on 12 August. While the 52-year-old founder of Sinn Féin had stepped back from frontline politics in previous weeks, his passing was viewed with particular sorrow by the British, who regarded him as a mainstay of the Free State. On 22 August, Collins, who had led the procession at Griffith's funeral, was killed in an ambush at Béal na mBláth in his native County Cork. Accompanied by Emmet Dalton, he was in a motor column that had been touring Free State army positions in the county. News of his death shortly before his 32nd birthday shocked Ireland, and it sparked rumours that Collins had been in the county for a rendezvous with republican leaders. While his courage had never been in doubt, it seemed foolhardy for Collins to have been in such an Irregular stronghold without such a motive. The rumour of a possible peace meeting increased when it became known that de Valera had been in the immediate locality. It appears that he was on a mission to urge Liam Deasy to consider negotiations that would end hostilities. However, there is no real evidence that de Valera intended to meet Collins, though it was likely that the Irregulars could have expected to obtain better peace terms from Collins than from the provisional government in Dublin.

Whatever the background circumstances, the death of Collins shook the provisional government. Though he had resigned his ministry, the powerful Collins continued to dictate provisional government policy. He had been the dominant figure in both the army and the government, but Cosgrave and O'Higgins stepped into his political shoes while Mulcahy filled the breach in the army. Quickly, Mulcahy issued an address to the Free State army. He acknowledged that no other individual could match Collins's personal appeal and called for discipline as he reaffirmed the army's determination to complete the task that Collins had so reluctantly commenced.

Although the National Army had lost its commander-in-chief, the outcome of the civil war had already been determined. The failure by the Irregulars to stage an offensive when they enjoyed maximum advantage had been the decisive factor. Initially reluctant to fire on their old comrades, though this reluctance disappeared once the conflict was underway, it was evident that the militant republicans had made no preparations whatsoever for civil war. Once it began, moreover, the Irregulars made little attempt to establish any form of centralised control, a weakness that contributed to a haphazard and incoherent military campaign. Among their number were the most feared and successful fighting men in the War of Independence, but circumstances now were very different. After they had been removed from the larger urban areas, the Irregulars turned to the same style of guerrilla warfare that had proved successful in the past. However, the support of the local population was crucial to this type of campaign, and the Irregulars never enjoyed the level of public endorsement that had been evident in the struggle against the Crown Forces. Furthermore, the Irregulars were poorly financed, forcing them to commandeer food and other supplies, a practice that had a negative effect on people who were dealing with their own economic difficulties on a daily basis. On occasion, the Irregulars engaged in looting to obtain supplies, and this turned local people against them. Another surprising feature was their failure to develop an effective intelligence system, the importance of which should have been apparent to commanders with experience in the war against the British.

This catalogue of difficulties was compounded by Lynch's indecision and his inability to establish unity of command. Of course, this would have been particularly difficult to achieve with the forces at his disposal. It also proved impossible to overcome the lack of discipline that was a characteristic of many Irregular units, and it was very difficult to organise effective cooperation between neighbouring units. Communication was a persistent concern and was frequently left to the women of Cumann na mBan, but, in many cases, individual commanders generally preferred to operate with their own men in their own localities in operations that they alone had conceived. In fact, neighbouring forces were often suspicious of each other, and this was a further impediment to the development of a coherent military strategy. Yet another factor that undermined the Irregulars was the refusal of a number of able and experienced commanders to join Lynch's men. Officers such as Seán O'Hegarty and Florrie O'Donoghue chose to remain neutral even though they opposed the Treaty, and this gave the Free State army a further advantage.

The republican forces also failed to develop a clear political strategy. Many of their officers were suspicious of political leaders, and this contributed to their failure to develop a viable political alternative to their opponents, which may have helped to attract a degree of popular support. In particular, Lynch kept his distance from de Valera, whom he suspected of seeking peace terms. For Lynch, politics was a diversion from the military campaign. He was adamant that nothing must interfere with the military struggle, and he remained positive about the eventual outcome in spite of the early reverses. Nevertheless, de Valera refused to be sidelined by senior anti-Treaty officers, and he organised a meeting with Mulcahy on 6 September. However, the two men could not reach an accommodation, and the meeting appeared to end all hopes of a compromise. Mulcahy had annoyed his government colleagues by keeping them in the dark about the contact. Crucially, however, the failure of the discussions reinforced Mulcahy's determination to crush his opponents, whose aim, he insisted, was to spread chaos and anarchy. On 15 September 1922, he sought an extension of the army's powers to bring the struggle to a swift conclusion.

Accordingly, a Public Safety Bill was introduced in the Dáil on 27 September. It proposed the establishment of military courts that would be given draconian powers, including the sentence of execution for a variety of offences such as possession of arms, commandeering of property, looting and arson. Following the June election, the Third Dáil had only convened for the first time on 5 September, but the Public Safety Bill was certain to become law as de Valera's followers were boycotting the bill. Labour TDs attacked the proposals, warning that they risked turning the government into a military dictatorship. Even a number of pro-Treaty deputies were anxious about conferring such wide-ranging powers on the army. Mulcahy responded to the criticism by stressing that the army would always be subject to political control. In a further attempt to mollify the opposition, the government announced on 4 October that there would be an amnesty for all republican troops who surrendered their weapons and accepted the government's authority. Significantly, the government's action was approved by the Catholic bishops, who made their position clear in a joint pastoral on 10 October that condemned the Irregulars' actions as unjust and immoral. Thus, the Public Safety Bill came into force on 15 October, and executions took place within five weeks.

De Valera was outraged at the stance taken by the bishops. Earlier, he had persuaded his Cumann na Poblachta followers to abstain from the Dáil, as he planned to establish an alternative republican government. Of course, such a move would require the support of the Irregulars. Ernie O'Malley was keen on the idea, and it had the support of some republican prisoners, including Liam Mellows, who was advocating the need for a republican government in order to revive the Democratic Programme. Lynch remained sceptical about any such political initiative, but he relented following a meeting of his army executive on 16–17 October. A decision was taken to form a republican government under de Valera, although everyone in attendance appreciated that any such administration would exist on paper only. In abandoning Dublin, the Irregulars had already made a grave error, as they made it easy for the provisional government to present itself as the legitimate government of Ireland with little political disruption in the capital.

Erskine Childers, one of de Valera's most loyal lieutenants, was selected as minister for publicity in this shadow government. In the early months of the War of Independence he had returned to Ireland and edited the *Irish Bulletin,* which was the official organ of Dáil Éireann, before becoming director of publicity. Since mid-August he had been on the run in Cork and Kerry, using a pony and trap to transport his printing press, which he used to churn out propaganda material. As he made his way back to Dublin to meet his new colleagues in the republican government, he was arrested close to the Barton home in County Wicklow. When detained, it was discovered that he was carrying a Spanish .32 automatic pistol. The gun, which had an effective range of only four metres, had been given to him by Collins, but carrying a gun under the new legislation was a capital offence. Childers had become a hate figure in some sections of the Irish press, and it was alleged that he was one of the masterminds behind the Irregulars' campaign. Following his arrest, he was tried by a military court which found him guilty. By this stage it was clear that there was real animosity between Childers and some government ministers, particularly O'Higgins, and the court's finding did not come as a surprise. He was executed by firing squad in Beggars Bush Barracks on 24 November 1922.

One week before Childers faced the firing squad, four young men caught with firearms in their possession in Dublin were executed. Labour TDs protested loudly, and the wider public appears to have been shocked by this development. Mulcahy, however, was defiant, arguing that the army's "responsibility" was to save the country from slipping deeper into anarchy. At the end of November, Lynch responded by issuing a general order to his troops to shoot deputies who had supported the emergency legislation. Many Irregulars baulked at carrying out such a threat, but one such attack was mounted in Dublin on 7 December 1922. This resulted in the killing of Seán Hales and the wounding of Pádraic Ó Máille, who were en route to a meeting in the Dáil. Hales, the brother of Tom, a senior anti-Treaty officer, was a popular figure and his killing shocked the community.

Next day the provisional government responded by executing four prisoners – Rory O'Connor, Liam Mellows, Joseph McKelvey and Richard Barrett – one from each of Ireland's provinces. There was no attempt to try these four under the new emergency legislation, as each of them had been in prison since the capture of the Four Courts at the end of June. Rather, the executions were a reprisal for the killing of Hales. Mulcahy appears to have taken the initiative in cabinet, and he was determined to prevent any repeat assassinations of pro-Treaty deputies. O'Higgins was the last minister to give his consent. O'Connor had been best man at his wedding, but Mulcahy demanded unanimity in sanctioning such a tough response. Of course, the executions achieved the short-term objective of deterring further attacks, and the iron-fist response shook the morale of republican troops. Yet the brutal nature of the government's action marked a new departure in the civil war, and Labour TDs denounced the development in the Dáil. They only learned of the executions after they had taken place, and they used the floor of the Dáil to claim that the executions were, in effect, murders.

Following the executions, the Irregulars began to destroy property owned by their opponents. The homes of prominent government supporters were attacked and Unionist-owned property was targeted in the early months of 1923. This resulted in the burning of many of Ireland's finest country houses. Yet, as far as military effectiveness was concerned, the attack on the railway system was of more concern to the provisional government. As early as August 1922 the entire rail network in the south and west had been affected, and this led to the formation of the Railroad Protection and Maintenance Corps, which assumed responsibility for repair work. While the Railroad Corps proved very effective, many local lines in Cork and Kerry were unable to reopen until the end of the conflict. Many of the attacks on these rail routes were an attempt to block the movement of Free State troops and their supplies, but the tactic created major problems for the local population that relied on the rail network. By the end of 1922, a clear pattern of guerrilla warfare could be identified, with ambushes staged in remote rural areas. Still, Lynch was bitterly disappointed by the failure of the Irregulars to overcome the Free State army in those parts of Cork and Tipperary where the IRA had been effective during the War of Independence.

The problem for the Irregulars in such areas was twofold. Local communities in these areas, having sustained the IRA campaign in the struggle against the British, were anxious for a return to peace. Consequently, there was a lack of popular support for the Irregulars. Secondly, local particularism prohibited the kind of close cooperation between neighbouring units that would have been necessary for the conduct of a successful guerrilla-style campaign. Thus, a marked feature of the civil war was that the most active theatres were in Kerry, Galway and Mayo,

Left to Right:—
BACK ROW:—Michael Kilroy, T. Kitterick, E. Moane, J. Gibbons, J. Walsh, P. J. Cannon, P. Lambert, J. Kelly, J. Doherty, B. Malone, J. Rush, J. Rin
MIDDLE ROW:—M. Naughton, J. Hogan, J. Hearney, D. Sammon, J. Keane, J. Connolly, R. Joyce, P. McNamara, W. Malone.
FRONT ROW:—Dan Gavin, T. Heavey, J. Duffy, J. McDonagh, P. Kelly, J. Moran, J. Flaherty, B. Cryan, M. Staunton.
IN FRONT:—Dr. J. A. Madden.

The West Mayo IRA, 1921.

counties that had seen little fighting during the War of Independence. Of course, the remoteness of areas such as south Kerry, West Mayo and Connemara proved ideal terrain for guerrilla warfare. In West Mayo and West Connemara, the Irregulars were brilliantly led by Michael Kilroy. Before his capture in November 1922, Kilroy had caused major problems for the Free State army. In these poor western regions, the Irregulars enjoyed solid support from local communities. Government troops in these areas were notoriously unpopular, and there was a strong tradition of opposition to central authority. Support for the Irregulars in the poor rural areas also had a social and economic basis.

At the beginning of 1923, the Free State government stepped up its offensive and hopes were high for an early end to the conflict. The army had grown to 50,000 and, while the majority of its troops had received only the most basic training, support from the British government ensured that it was well armed. The Irregulars, by contrast, struggled to obtain arms and ammunition. In fact, they only managed to organise one significant arms shipment, when 200 German rifles and 10,000 rounds of ammunition were landed at Waterford in November 1921 before the civil war broke out. Raids for arms were routinely carried out. However, only the raids on Clonmel Barracks in February 1922 and on the *Upnor*, a British Admiralty vessel that was shipping war material from Cork to Britain during the evacuation in March 1922, yielded significant supplies. This left the Irregulars at a huge disadvantage, as they struggled to resupply the main fighting units. Defeat was inevitable, but Lynch's intransigence and his refusal to accept the hopelessness of the republican position ensured that the conflict continued into the spring of 1923.

Tom Barry had made a concerted effort to arrange a peace deal in February 1923, but Lynch refused to consider negotiations, arguing that his forces were actually gaining in strength and were in sight of victory. The capture of Liam Deasy, who acted as Lynch's deputy, on 18 January dealt a major blow to republican morale. Deasy had indicated a desire for peace, and the authorities ruthlessly exploited his changed thinking. In January alone, 34 executions had been carried out and Deasy, threatened with a death sentence, appealed to his comrades to end the conflict, arguing that this would be the correct course for the republican movement in the long term. While all the recipients of the "Deasy letter" rejected his call for peace talks, and Lynch followed with a statement sent to all officers denouncing such a move, the letter proved to be a devastating blow. Even Lynch was rattled by Deasy's action.

In view of these developments, it is somewhat surprising that the Free State army took so long to achieve victory in 1923. One obvious reason was that the troops had been hastily recruited and were frequently dispatched to the provinces with little preparation. In cabinet, O'Higgins was particularly critical of the army's performance, and he blamed Mulcahy for this state of affairs. The army was held responsible for its failure to protect civilians but, in reality, O'Higgins was taking the example of the situation in Kerry to generalise about the condition of the south and west. Of course, the civil war was more bitterly fought in Kerry than in any other Irish county. This was particularly true of parts of mid and south Kerry where ambushes on troop convoys became a regular occurrence. The Free State army occupied the large barrack towns of Listowel, Tralee, Castleisland and Killarney, but the Irregulars moved around the countryside in large flying columns, cutting communications and generally disrupting social and economic life in the county. They chose not to stage large-scale attacks, opting instead for a holding strategy that made them very difficult to dislodge. In response, the Free State troops were divided into columns that conducted large sweeps of the country in an attempt to flush out the enemy.

In January 1923, General Paddy Daly, the commander of the Dublin Guard, a crack regiment that had been created by Collins, was dispatched to the county to lead the Free State troops in a determined attempt to force a victory over the Irregulars. His men were loathed by the local population, and the Irregulars would benefit from this upsurge in popular feeling. The Dublin troops' behaviour and indiscipline frequently caused offence, and rumours quickly circulated concerning the ill-treatment, and even torture, of republican prisoners. Daly had been a member of Collins's Squad, and many of his troops were battle-hardened veterans of the War of Independence. Their reputation for ruthlessness was widely known, and, with local Irregular units matching their fanaticism, the conflict in Kerry appeared to take the form of a bloody vendetta.

While the conflict was petering out in most areas by March 1923, it erupted in Kerry in a cycle of atrocities and reprisals, though part of this had its origin in long-standing family feuds. On the night of 5 March, three officers and two soldiers were killed when a trap mine exploded at Knocknagoshel in the north of the county near Castleisland. The Irregulars later claimed that they had been targeting Lieutenant O'Connor, who was suspected of being involved in the torture of republican prisoners. General Daly was outraged by O'Connor's death, and he issued an order stating that forthwith republican prisoners should be taken from their cells and used to clear any road barricades suspected of containing trap mines. Over the next few days, 17 republican prisoners died as mines exploded while barricades were being cleared. In one incident on 6 March, nine prisoners were removed from Tralee Jail and instructed to clear a barricade at Ballyseedy. All nine men were tied together and the mine was allegedly detonated by Free State soldiers. Amazingly, one of the prisoners, a future Fianna Fáil TD, Stephen Fuller, survived the blast and managed to crawl to a safe house. He would later recall the events of that evening in a famous television interview.

On the same night as the Ballyseedy explosion, four prisoners died as they cleared an obstruction at Countess Bridge in Killarney, and a further five died when a mine exploded outside Cahirciveen. The deaths were the subject of a hastily arranged army enquiry that was chaired by Daly. It found that each of the mines had been planted by the Irregulars and firmly rejected the allegation that the prisoners had been killed as a reprisal for the Knocknagoshel attack. In the Dáil, meanwhile, Mulcahy defended the actions of the troops in Kerry, but he gave an undertaking that more careful checks would be made in future to detect the presence of explosives before prisoners were deployed to remove obstructions. Fuller, of course, offered a different view of events. As the sole survivor, he was adamant that prisoners had been taken from their cells and deliberately killed by Free State troops.

The four trap mine incidents did not end the fighting in Kerry. An Irregular attack on Cahirciveen resulted in the landing of a large body of Free State troops by sea, and, in a follow-up operation, five republicans died. A further five Irregulars who were taken prisoner were executed on 28 March. The anti-Treaty forces were being forced to find refuge in the most remote areas, but they refused to surrender and further clashes followed. Again, the details of these engagements were bitterly disputed. Free State troops surrounded Irregulars who had been hiding in a network of caves just to the north of Kerry Head. After a siege lasting several days, a number were gunned down as they tried to surrender, while others were executed following their capture.

The most significant killing, however, occurred in neighbouring County Limerick, when Lynch died in a gun battle in the Knockmealdown Mountains. Lynch had been the biggest obstacle to peace negotiations, and the republican will to sustain the struggle died with him. His successor as chief of staff, Frank Aiken, wanted to end the fighting, and de Valera intervened in early May in an attempt to secure a ceasefire on terms favourable to the republicans. When the government dismissed de Valera's proposals, Aiken issued the order to dump arms. On 24 May 1923, the date that Aiken's order was published, de Valera issued the following proclamation to republican forces:

> Soldiers of Liberty! Legion of the rearguard! The Republic can no longer be defended successfully by your arms. Further sacrifices on your part would now be in vain, and continuance of the struggle in arms unwise in the national interest. Military victory must be allowed to rest for the moment with those who have destroyed the Republic.

As the statement implied, republican forces had abandoned the conflict, but there was absolutely no guarantee that this would be the end of the struggle. There was, moreover, no recognition of the legitimacy of the Free State, and it was expected that the goal of a republic would continue to be pursued. This might well mean a resumption of armed conflict, as the Irregulars dumped, rather than surrendered their arms. The battle for the republic may have been lost, but the war would continue. That said, the Irish Civil War was over. The Free State government had enjoyed the firm support of both the press and the Catholic Church, and the people wanted peace. Only Lynch's bloody-mindedness had extended the war into 1923.

Estimates of the total casualties in the civil war vary, but a total figure of close to 2,000 deaths seems reasonable. This was extremely low by international standards. The nearest comparison to the Irish experience was Finland, where a bloody civil war in 1918 claimed over 25,000 lives out of a total population of 4,000,000. In the Finnish conflict more than 8,300 executions were carried out, dwarfing the 77 ordered by the Cosgrave-led government. Approximately 780 Free State troops had died in the fighting. While the Irish Civil War may have been a muted affair by international standards, it caused significant economic, political and psychological damage that outlived the civil war generation. On the surface the civil war was fought over different attitudes to the Treaty, particularly the question of the oath of allegiance. However, the real cause of the conflict was the split in the IRA, which Sinn Féin was unable to manage. The immediate trigger had been the pressure exerted by the British government following Wilson's assassination, but Michael Hopkinson has argued that military confrontation was inevitable once rival IRA units had taken control of military barracks following the British withdrawal at the beginning of 1922.

It was also significant that a number of republican militants were unable, or unwilling, to make the transition into politics following the 1916–21 revolutionary period. Republican dogmatists such as Rory O'Connor dismissed the voice of the people when it conflicted with their own views. They justified such action by donning the clothes of the 1916 leaders who had sacrificed themselves in the name of an Irish republic. Nothing short of a republic would satisfy these irreconcilables, and they were convinced that the 1916 leaders had provided a legitimacy for their military action. De Valera was not part of this faction, but he was on the fringes, and he gave the militants added credibility by declaring, in March 1922, that the people had no right to do wrong. Yet military rather than political factors decided the outcome of the conflict. Popular support in a few specific areas such as South Kerry, South Galway and West Mayo, which had experienced little fighting during the War of Independence, together with Lynch's stubbornness, had prolonged the conflict. However, the outcome was certain once the Irregulars failed to strike an early military blow at the beginning of hostilities when the Free State was most vulnerable.

State-building

The Free State government's preoccupation with the civil war had removed attention from the partition question. During the conflict, the most active northern IRA units had travelled south where some of them participated in the civil war. Significantly, the republican side had not made the border an issue in the civil war. Collins, on the other hand, appears to have felt a sense of personal responsibility for the sustained attacks on the Catholic minority. Between the Treaty and the start of the civil war, he had attempted to direct a joint pro- and anti-Treaty IRA offensive across the border, but this was not a success. He also supported the policy of non-recognition of the new Northern Ireland state by northern Nationalists, but the outbreak of hostilities in June 1922 consumed his entire energy. With Collins fully absorbed in his role as commander-in-chief, the provisional government formed a committee to devise a northern policy that would take account of recent events. Ernest Blythe, one of the committee's five members, tabled a memorandum on 9 August 1922 that set out a new northern strategy. Blythe, an Ulster Presbyterian and TD for Monaghan, stated his firm opposition to the use of either military coercion or economic sanctions, both of which had failed in the attempt to restore Irish unity. He thought that the policy of non-recognition should be allowed to fizzle out and sought an end to the aggressive posturing towards the new northern state. Ten days later the provisional government adopted Blythe's views and opted for a policy of conciliation towards the north. Crucially, this coincided with the death of Collins. Without his presence, the north and its problems quickly slipped down the government's list of priorities.

Clearly, the civil war had helped to entrench partition and consolidate the Unionist government's position. Cosgrave sought to improve relations with Belfast, and he argued against interference in northern affairs. His focus had been on victory in the civil war, and the view of the north as an unwelcome distraction persisted once the conflict had ended. There were more pressing problems than partition, as the Cosgrave government considered how to rebuild the country following the civil war. The conflict had postponed the establishment of the Boundary Commission, and it was with little enthusiasm or expectation that he requested its formation in July 1923. Unionist delaying tactics meant that the Commission did not begin work until November 1924. Its report, which recommended fairly minor changes to the existing border, was leaked to the *Morning Post* in November 1925, and Eoin MacNeill, the Free State representative, resigned in protest. In the confusion, the Commission was abandoned, and Cosgrave opted to sign a tripartite agreement with London and Belfast in the following month. The agreement revoked the powers of the Boundary Commission and recognised the existing border. In return, the Free State received a financial sweetener, as it was released from its liability for some of Britain's public debt.

Cosgrave's republican opponents were furious at this surrender of the north, but his ministers defended the deal and Cosgrave stated that it provided the framework for "a new era in Irish history". Of course, the deal's financial clause proved attractive to a government that faced serious economic problems. The civil war had imposed huge costs estimated at more than £50 million, which was about one-third of the Free State's national output. Facing a budget deficit and with expenditure still high after the conflict, mainly because of the large number still on the army's payroll, the government chose to follow a policy of austerity after 1923. An additional problem was the raising of taxation in the early years of the Free State, as many citizens either evaded or avoided paying taxes. Rather than borrow money to cushion its citizens, the Cosgrave government adopted the rules of contemporary financial orthodoxy and followed a course of balanced budgets. This meant taking the unpopular decision to cut public expenditure, which it did most famously in 1924 when the minister for finance, Ernest Blythe, reduced the old age pension from ten to nine shillings per week. Meanwhile, thanks to Treasury subsidies, the Belfast government was able to maintain welfare spending at British levels. The discrepancy presented Craig with one of his most powerful economic arguments in favour of partition. Ireland was also hit by an economic recession in 1923, which affected farming and rural communities badly and had some influence on the outcome of the 1923 election.

Under the terms of the Constitution accepted by the Dáil on 6 December 1923, fresh elections were to be held within a year, and Cosgrave decided on a surprise vote in August 1923. In March 1923 Cosgrave had formed Cumann na nGaedheal from his pro-Treaty supporters, and he looked forward to a comfortable majority in the election of a new Dáil that had been enlarged from 128 to 153 seats. The results, however, were a disappointment. Cumann na nGaedheal won 39 per cent of the first preference vote and 63 seats, making it the largest party. Sinn Féin took 27.6 per cent of the vote and won 44 seats. De Valera had abandoned the Cumann na Poblachta experiment, and he ran his candidates under the Sinn Féin banner, a name that was more familiar to the electorate. Labour suffered some losses, taking 15 seats, a number equalled by the Farmers' Union, while the remaining 16 seats were shared between independent candidates. Cosgrave subsequently formed the first Cumann na nGaedheal government, and he became president of the Executive Council. His ministers were Kevin O'Higgins (Home Affairs), Ernest Blythe (Finance), Joseph McGrath (Industry and Commerce), Eoin MacNeill (Education), Desmond Fitzgerald (External Affairs) and Richard Mulcahy (Defence).

Cosgrave was disappointed by the outcome, but his government enjoyed a comfortable majority in the Dáil, a situation helped by Sinn Féin's policy of abstention. The legacy of the civil war, the solid vote for Sinn Féin, which refused to recognise Dáil Éireann, and the fear of renewed violence added to the difficulty in establishing a stable government. Both Cosgrave and O'Higgins viewed the civil war as a tragic, but necessary, development if democracy was to supersede the gun in Irish politics. O'Higgins, in particular, was determined to establish the rule of law following the civil war, believing that general lawlessness and anarchy were at the root of much of the republican violence. At the end of the conflict he pushed through a Public Safety Bill, allowing the state to arrest and detain suspects without the need for a trial. These powers were widely used in the 1923–24 period, when violence, robbery, arson and other criminal activity remained a feature of Free State society. It was, of course, true that a significant minority continued to deny the legitimacy of the state.

The August election was repeatedly marred by violence, and intimidation was a marked feature of the contest. De Valera had been arrested a fortnight before polling and was only released the following July. Yet the election confirmed that both he and the republican ideal would have an enduring appeal. But if de Valera hoped to benefit from such sympathy and support, he had to extricate himself from the Sinn Féin straitjacket. In March 1926 he sought greater freedom of action at a special Sinn Féin Árd-Fheis, but his motion was narrowly defeated.

Resigning as president of Sinn Féin, de Valera declared his intention to launch a new political party, Fianna Fáil, in order to carry the fight to Cumann na nGaedheal. De Valera had cited his horror at the Boundary Commission debacle as the principal reason for the need to change political direction. The timing and circumstances surrounding the formation of his new party helped to create the impression that de Valera had rejected the Treaty because it perpetuated partition, an error that he did little to correct. Three years later, Seán Lemass, one of his most able followers, described Fianna Fáil as "a slightly constitutional party", but this was enough to ensure that normal politics was allowed to develop in the new state.

The results of the 1923 election pointed to the fact that attitudes to the Treaty would define political allegiance for at least the next generation. On the one side stood pro-Treaty Cumann na nGaedheal, led by the solid but uninspiring Cosgrave, which was intent on establishing a conservative administration that was deferential to the Catholic Church. Beyond the twenty-six counties, the Cosgrave government acknowledged the reality of partition and worked constructively in leading the evolution of the British Commonwealth, as it sought to prove the veracity of Collins's pronouncements on the Treaty. On the opposite side stood Sinn Féin and the charismatic figure of de Valera, who wanted the establishment of a united independent Ireland. The realisation that this could not be achieved from outside the Dáil prompted the formation of Fianna Fáil. Yet de Valera also recognised that some of his support in the election had come from voters who remained concerned at the level of brutality, particularly the 77 executions, which Free State ministers had resorted to in pursuit of victory in the civil war.

Beneath this obvious Treaty division, however, there was compelling evidence of a class division in Irish society. Cosgrave's party was dominant among the larger and more prosperous farmers in central and eastern Ireland, while Sinn Féin polled well among the poorer smallholders of the west where it was able to exploit the traditional resentment of authority that had been a characteristic of the civil war. Still, in spite of this geographical disparity, stability quickly returned to rural Ireland. In 1923 the Cosgrave administration passed a new Land Act that completed the Westminster government's attempts to resolve the land question. This transferred those remaining landlord holdings to the tenants. Overall, 1920s Ireland enjoyed a relatively high standard of living, certainly on a par with much of western Europe, and this helped the Cosgrave government's attempts to restore stability. An effective education system was an additional bonus. Blythe proceeded cautiously in the Department of Finance and he steadily reduced government expenditure during the 1920s. With stability the goal in post-civil war Ireland, the state-builders in Cumann na nGaedheal had the advantage of governing a relatively homogeneous Irish nation that was almost exclusively Catholic. Other new contemporary European states did not share this advantage. In this sense partition made their task more straightforward, as it ensured the exclusion of one million Ulster Protestants. Their presence would have posed serious problems for the authorities in Dublin.

In its efforts to raise revenue and demonstrate its fiscal independence from Britain, the Free State government imposed customs duties on cross-border trade on 1 April 1923, a move which the Unionist government in Belfast interpreted as partitionist. As the decision was only taken in late February, authorities on both sides of the border were given little time to make the necessary preparations, and newspapers relayed information to the public only days before the customs barriers were put in place. A long list of goods, including tea, sugar, alcohol and tobacco were now taxable, and citizens moving such goods had to report to a boundary post, where goods would be examined and duty paid. The introduction of customs controls required agreement between Dublin and Westminster to identify 16 cross-border roads that would be designated at approved crossings. Customs facilities were erected on these routes and all dutiable goods had to be transported on these roads. The imposition of customs duties inflicted economic pain on both businesses and consumers in border areas, and the rigorous enforcement of the new regulations encouraged the growth of illicit trade across the border. While smuggling became a feature of border life, particularly the movement of goods from north to south, the new regulations undoubtedly cemented the reality of partition and contributed to the growing divergence between the Irish Free State and Northern Ireland.

Not surprisingly, customs posts became a target for opponents of partition, and the first recorded attack on a facility took place as early as 4 April 1923. The Cumann na nGaedheal administration was also mindful of the lingering contempt for the democratic process among the section of society that had lost out in the civil war. Yet it was ironic that the greatest danger to the new state following the end of the conflict came not from republicans but from its own Free State army. After the cessation of hostilities, the government had to reorganise its army, which had swelled to over 50,000, of whom 3,000 were officers. Its immediate aim was to cut the army's overall strength to 20,000 men, 1,400 of whom would be officers. Financial pressure ensured that demobilisation would have to proceed quickly. Linked to this was the more complex problem of removing political influence from the force. Matters almost came to a head in July 1923, when a group of ex-IRA officers openly criticised Mulcahy, arguing, with some justification, that the minister for defence was favouring officers who had been members of the IRB. They also managed to convince O'Higgins that the IRB controlled the army. Meanwhile, another minister, Joseph McGrath, threw his weight behind the old IRA officers who, it was rumoured, were planning some kind of a coup in January 1924.

Tension had been raised by the demobilisation of 1,000 officers in December, and the crisis deepened on 6 March 1924. A group of ex-IRA officers, with General Liam Tobin, a former associate of Collins, and Colonel C.F. Dalton acting as their spokesmen, presented Cosgrave with an ultimatum. They demanded the sacking of Mulcahy and the removal of his three colleagues on the Army Council. Tobin, Dalton and the others had taken this action on the day before another list of 1,000 officers to be demobbed was due to be published. Difficulties with acceptance of authority in the army's ranks had their origins in the War of Independence, when Collins had favoured men of action who could organise raids and conduct ambushes. Many of these loose cannons had remained loyal to Collins after the Treaty and had become officers in the Free State army, but they felt constrained by the organisational structures and discipline that were necessary for a regular army.

The "army mutiny" of March 1924 presented the Cumann na nGaedheal government with a major problem. If the mutineers' demands, which included the suspension of demobilisation, were rejected, a military takeover was likely. The situation required a prompt and resolute response and, though Cosgrave hesitated, O'Higgins took decisive action. He was a committed constitutionalist who defended the principle of civilian government and barely concealed his contempt for both the old IRA officers and the IRB clique. The ringleaders of the mutiny were arrested and McGrath, their chief supporter in the government, was forced to resign. The crisis also resulted in Mulcahy's resignation. There had been considerable animosity between Mulcahy and O'Higgins, with the latter accusing the former of failing to impose strict discipline on the army. O'Higgins also harboured the suspicion that Mulcahy was not a sound democrat. However, had that had been true, Mulcahy would have used his support in the army to challenge the government. Retaining his dignity and sidestepping a personal vendetta with O'Higgins, Mulcahy tendered his resignation as minister for defence, though Cosgrave would subsequently oversee his return to cabinet in 1927 as minister for local government. Within days of his reinstatement, on 10 July, his great rival and the government's strongest personality, Kevin O'Higgins, was assassinated as he walked to mass at a church near his Blackrock home. Republicans were suspected of involvement, though de Valera was unequivocal in his condemnation of the killers. One month later the former president led his Fianna Fáil deputies into the Dáil to become the official opposition to Cosgrave's government. By 1932 Fianna Fáil was in power and de Valera found himself vindicating Collins's claim that the Treaty conferred on Ireland the freedom to achieve freedom.

Conclusion

The brief vacuum that had developed following Sinn Féin's landslide victory in the postwar general election encouraged the Irish Volunteers to fill the void. The attack on the RIC officers at Soloheadbeg would mark the beginning of a new conflict with the British that would last until the two sides agreed a truce in July 1921. The Volunteers had not prepared for such a military struggle, but it quickly acquired a momentum of its own, developing from a small number of uncoordinated and sporadic attacks on the Crown Forces over the course of 1919. With Lloyd George immersed in European and imperial affairs during this period, the British government failed to produce a coherent political or military strategy, which left it reacting to events in Ireland as the Volunteers seized the initiative. The prime minister, moreover, needed to balance Liberal calls for an imaginative approach to the Sinn Féin challenge with Conservative demands for a tough security response to meet the IRA threat. It was the Conservative voice that prevailed. Lacking political and military direction, the authorities responded to the intensification of the conflict in 1920 by deploying the quasi-military forces of Black and Tans and Auxiliaries in the misguided conviction that they must meet terror with terror. The result was predictable, yet it came as a shock to the coalition government.

In Ireland civilian support for the IRA enabled the Volunteers to increase attacks, while the publicity surrounding atrocities perpetrated by the Crown Forces in the name of the Westminster government turned public opinion in Britain against the prosecution of the War of Independence. By 1921, however, the Crown Forces had come to terms with the military challenge presented by the IRA, but the political will to complete the task and deliver some kind of victory had all but evaporated by the middle of the year. This left both sides – the republicans for primarily military reasons and the British for primarily political reasons – eager to take the opportunity afforded by a truce in July 1921.

The conflict had greatly increased the influence of a number of military-political figures within the republican movement. The most celebrated of these, Michael Collins, had ensured that the British lost the intelligence battle with the republican movement. They also lost the propaganda war and together these factors provided the Volunteers with a crucial advantage in the military struggle. Yet the guerrilla campaign that developed in 1920–21 was confined to a small number of specific geographical areas such as Dublin city, West Cork, South Tipperary, Clare and North Longford. In these localities popular support, occasionally stiffened by intimidation and, more significantly, the resourcefulness of local Volunteer commanders, ensured that an effective military campaign was conducted. In the end the IRA prolonged the conflict sufficiently to force the

British government into a change in direction in Ireland.

The truce brought de Valera and Lloyd George together for a week of peace talks that began on 14 July. Each must have recognised in the other a skilled negotiator who would squeeze the maximum advantage from whatever hand he was dealt. Little progress came from this initial engagement, though de Valera was left in no doubt that the prime minister leading a Conservative-dominated coalition government would not allow the issue of Ireland becoming a republic to be part of any future dialogue. What followed was two months of frustrating wordplay, as both men attempted to press their priorities for probable negotiations. Eventually, 11 October was agreed as the date for negotiations to begin. The aim was to reach an agreement between Sinn Féin and the British government on the outstanding issues of national status, partition, defence and finance. Crucially, de Valera was not part of the Irish negotiating team. He had a strong case for remaining in Dublin, though there was arguably a stronger one for him going to London. Though absent, de Valera wanted some degree of control, and this led to the Irish team of plenipotentiaries receiving additional instructions that created unnecessary confusion.

The intensity and duration of the negotiations took its toll on an Irish delegation that faced an energy-sapping journey each time they moved between London and Dublin. This was, of course, not an issue for the very formidable team assembled by Lloyd George. The British also enjoyed an advantage by tabling the original document on which the negotiations would proceed. The Irish, by contrast, were under-prepared. Moreover, the British delegation was united on its objectives, whereas the Irish team was divided. There was a general consensus that concessions made on the emotional issues of Crown and Empire should be contingent on the removal of the border. Certainly, partition and Craig's blunt refusal to alter his position proved a headache for Lloyd George, but the introduction of the Boundary Commission proposal allowed the prime minister to circumvent this particular obstacle. The Irish delegation should have been firmer in removing any ambiguity in Article 12, but this oversight applied equally to the Dáil cabinet when it considered the draft Treaty on 3 December.

Early in the negotiations the British had identified Griffith as the most moderate of the Irish delegates, while Collins's obvious pragmatism offered further hopes for optimism. This, in turn, led to the sub-conference process, which sidelined Childers and brought a final settlement closer. Yet, ultimately, it was Lloyd George's threat of a return to war, which may or may not have been bluff, that proved decisive. Griffith was subsequently criticised for failing to use the telephone to contact Dublin, though the recipient for such a call was hard to identify as de Valera was not in Dublin. In the end, as the Treaty debates confirmed, it was the oath, and not partition, that exercised TDs' minds. The time lag between the signing of the Treaty and the crucial Dáil vote had clearly benefited those who advocated acceptance. In that month-long interval, TDs had sufficient contact with their constituents to learn of the majority's support for the Treaty. Even with this knowledge of public opinion, the final vote was tantalisingly close.

The Treaty split exposed long-standing divisions in Irish republicanism, but this was not enough to cause a civil war. The IRA split proved crucial, and this was magnified by the haphazard rush to occupy barracks vacated by the British during February 1922. The majority of Volunteers opposed the Treaty, but Collins's influence was such that many officers joined the pro-Treaty ranks out of a sense of personal loyalty. The anti-Treaty forces, meanwhile, were split between a moderate faction headed by Lynch and other officers from the formidable First Southern Division and the group of republican militants led by O'Connor and Mellows. They undoubtedly brought civil war closer when they seized the Four Courts in April, defiantly rejecting any talk of compromise on the republic. From his actions it was clear that Lynch was anxious to preserve army unity, but O'Connor's determination to bring matters to a head left him with no room to manoeuvre. The occupation of the Four Courts had also stirred British interest, and Churchill waited impatiently for the provisional government to deal with the situation. Wilson's assassination in June was the final straw, and Collins recognised that if he further delayed action against the Four Courts occupants, then British intervention would be inevitable. He retained the hope, however, that a quick victory over this militant faction might prevent a wider conflict, but this proved impossible.

The Irregulars lost the civil war during the first few weeks, when they failed to seize the initiative and attack their weaker opponents. Soon, they faced a large, well-armed Free State army that was backed by a government prepared to take ruthless action. Lacking anything approaching a coherent military plan, the Irregulars resorted to the previous tactics of guerrilla warfare that had worked against the British. In the civil war, however, actions such as the targeting of road and rail communications only disrupted rural economic life and turned the people against the insurgents. Squeezed into more remote areas such as South Kerry by army units that had detailed knowledge of both their enemy and the terrain, defeat for the Irregulars was inevitable. With the civil war over, the Cosgrave government concentrated on state-building, a task in which it was broadly successful. The proof of this is that within a decade power would be transferred to its civil war enemies, a process that confirmed the stability of the Free State's democratic structures.

Historiography

A number of accounts have been written by participants in the War of Independence. These include Tom Barry's *Guerrilla Days in Ireland* (Dublin, 1962), Dan Breen's *My Fight for Irish Freedom* (Dublin, 1964) and the most useful, Ernie O'Malley's *On Another Man's Wound* (Dublin, 1979), which highlights the tensions between local IRA commanders and GHQ. The local commanders tended to be young, impatient and headstrong, making it difficult for headquarters to direct a more coordinated campaign against the Crown Forces.

From the British perspective, the first sustained analysis of Britain's political and military strategy was provided by Charles Townshend's *The British Campaign in Ireland 1919–1921: The Development of Political and Military Policies* (Oxford, 1975). A central theme of the book was the coalition government's failure to define British objectives in Ireland which led to a policy vacuum. In fact, Townshend is adamant that for much of the conflict the British government had no policy whatsoever and that Westminster's response to the IRA campaign was "instinctive". Conservatives in cabinet demanded the suppression of republican violence, while Liberal ministers had few constructive ideas and, consequently, tended to acquiesce in the decisions to militarise the police and engage in reprisals. While the author is critical of the government's coercion policy, he notes that it was not sustained as Westminster drifted between repression and attempts at conciliation. This leads him to conclude that the Lloyd George government adopted a policy of "mild" coercion, which was "repression too weak to root out opposition, but provocative enough to nurture it".

Townshend's *The Republic: The Fight for Irish Independence* (London, 2013) is based on recent and detailed research. He refers to sporadic incidents during 1918 to emphasise that the Volunteers had become more violent well before the War of Independence began. He comments on the tension between GHQ and Volunteer units during 1919, highlighting Florrie O'Donoghue's belief that there was resistance in GHQ "to pushing the campaign forward". In this period the attitude of the clergy was crucial. Townshend notes that Cardinal Logue disapproved of republican violence, but stresses that the lower clergy were supportive and that any condemnation of IRA action was "muted". The lack of understanding about developments in Ireland is stressed when the author notes that at the cabinet discussion on the murder of D.I. Hunt in June 1919, only one minister, the Liberal Edward Shortt, favoured an attempt "to drive a wedge between moderates and extremists". Townshend notes that the campaign of intimidation against individual RIC officers, frequently directed through written threats, reached a peak in the spring and summer of 1920. Still, Townshend argues that "the tenacious barrack defences" in early 1920 demonstrated that the RIC was not "as demoralized as many have assumed". The author points out that in rural areas, where the boycott of the RIC was applied systematically, it actually threatened the police with starvation and left them with no option but to take supplies by force.

By 1921, Townshend states, de Valera felt that "guerrilla warfare was not generating the kind of image that republican propaganda required", as he sought to extend his influence over the military campaign. The author also suggests that the level of anti-republican dissent has been underestimated, but "the sheer scale of the internal security campaign" proved effective, as the Volunteers frequently used "fear" to ensure compliance. In his conclusion, Townshend argues that General Macready's "pervasive negativity – verging on fatalism – and repeated assertions that the only possible solution must be political and not military" ensured that the army was unlikely to produce effective counter-insurgency measures. In examining the contribution made by Collins, T. Ryle Dwyer's *Michael Collins: The Man who won the War* (Dublin, 2009) suggests that morale in the RIC was never high, because even though a majority of the force was Catholic, "there was a distinct bias against promoting Catholics". The killings of senior police officers such as Smyth and Swanzy demonstrated the IRA's effectiveness, and its intelligence prowess was highlighted when Sgt William Mulhern, who had been looking for Collins in Bandon, was shot dead in June 1920. Dwyer also points out that the British, when they began to consider a truce, felt that they could deal with the "moderate" de Valera but not the "hardline" Collins.

In his local study, John O'Callaghan's *Revolutionary Limerick: The Republican Campaign for Independence in Limerick, 1913–1921* (Dublin, 2010) argues that the IRA's motivation for the execution of alleged informers "cannot be understood in isolation from the actions of the Crown forces who secured information from the local population, which included many unemployed ex-servicemen". O'Callaghan estimates that there were up to 2,000 ex-soldiers living in Limerick. He also looked at the Limerick Soviet, which was established following a general strike in the city in April 1919. However, as O'Callaghan records, the local Catholic Church was uneasy at this display of trade union power, and the strike collapsed within a fortnight with the soviet leaders frustrated by the lack of outside support. In his study of the impact of the IRA campaign in Tyrone, Fergal McCluskey's *The Irish Revolution, 1912–23: Tyrone* (Dublin, 2014) declares that activism in the county "was held back by a combination of the very real fear of loyalist reprisals, poor leadership and inadequate arms". By April 1921, McCluskey notes that the IRA faced 4,300 B Specials in Tyrone, while support was withheld by Catholic families who were opposed to the use of physical force.

Arthur Mitchell's *Revolutionary Government in Ireland: Dáil Éireann, 1919–22* (Dublin, 1995) carefully analyses the attempt by Sinn Féin to establish a "counter-state". The author relates the Dáil's early success in establishing a rival court system, financing the new administration, winning control of local government and assuming responsibility for law and order. Yet Mitchell argues that these successes did not continue in 1921, claiming that, by this point, the counter-state had lost its "vitality". He also charts the republican movement's success in terms of propaganda, describing how Sinn Féin's impressive publicity machine, which proved its influence far beyond Ireland, was run on a shoestring budget. In spite of this financial handicap, Mitchell highlights its success in shaping both Irish and international opinion. The propaganda impact is also effectively covered in Diarmaid Ferriter's *The Transformation of Ireland* (London, 2004), which illustrates the impact of the *Irish Bulletin*. It was widely available in Britain and was successful in putting the Westminster government under pressure to justify its Irish policy. In assessing the military effectiveness of the IRA, Ferriter contends that republicans came close to achieving a military draw but won a propaganda victory that gave them sufficient strength to secure negotiations in London aimed at concluding a new political settlement. He also makes the interesting point that before the conflict the RIC was more than 70 per cent Catholic, but 45 per cent of new recruits between 1916 and 1920 were Protestants. Mitchell's *Revolutionary Government in Ireland* offers some comment on the outcome of local government elections in 1920. His conclusion is that Sinn Féin's success was not as sweeping as might have been expected, particularly in urban areas. He also stresses that many of these new Sinn Féin councillors maintained lines of communication and cooperated fully with Westminster's local government board.

Some evidence of the variation in the effectiveness of the counter-state across the country is provided by Marie Coleman's *County Longford and the Irish Revolution 1910–1923* (Dublin, 2003). Frequently, the Dáil courts emerged as the result of spontaneous action by local communities, and, while they suffered from a government crackdown in 1921, they continued to function in North Longford. In many parts of the country the proceedings at these Dáil courts received detailed coverage in the local press. The financing of the counter-state is the subject of Patrick O'Sullivan Greene's *Crowdfunding the Revolution: The First Dáil Loan and the Battle for Irish Independence* (Dublin, 2020), which highlights Collins's talents as an administrator. The author stresses that the raising of the Dáil Loan was "an exceptional achievement for an alternative government setting up a counter-state in open defiance of the established and hostile British administration". Significantly, the huge numbers of subscribers to the loan "had backed the prospect of self-government on a distant, even unrealistic, promise of future repayment".

Another impressive local study is Peter Hart's *The IRA and its Enemies: Violence and Community in Cork, 1916–1923* (Oxford, 1998). It closely examines the social background of the Volunteers, concluding that many were lower middle-class young men, the majority of whom were unmarried. Hart also puts the spotlight on the sectarian nature of the IRA campaign in Cork, an argument that has been contested by a number of historians, including Meda Ryan and Andy Bielenberg. Michael Hopkinson's *The Irish War of Independence* (Dublin, 2000) confirms that the archetypal IRA volunteer was 18–25, drawn from the lower middle-class and well educated. Hart and Hopkinson conclude that less than half of the Volunteers worked on farms. More recently, Diarmaid Ferriter's *A Nation and not a Rabble: The Irish Revolution 1913–1923* (London, 2015) offers a brilliant assessment of the conflict. Up to August 1919, he claims, the IRA was largely defensive and, from that period, "the Dáil attempted to impose its authority by assuming at least some responsibility for the army's actions." Ferriter differs from other historians when he points out, using testimony to the Bureau of Military History, that relations were good between the RIC and the population prior to the War of Independence. In many areas he suggests that teachers, who exerted great influence, were particularly drawn to republicanism. In looking at the Black and Tans, the author declares that one-third of them were recruited in London, over one-third in Liverpool and Glasgow and 14 per cent in Dublin. According to Ferriter, 19 per cent of the Tans were Irish-born. In republican ranks the author states that there was "an obvious tension between the politicians and the IRA soldiers".

In developing the counter-state, Ferriter contends, Sinn Féin displayed a significant lack of concern for the most vulnerable in society. When he deals with land hunger, the author makes reference to Austin Stack who warned that agrarian agitation "could subvert patriotic opinion". By the spring of 1921, Ferriter suggests that for the IRA "it was not necessarily about winning, but about carrying on". He also highlights the tension that existed between Brugha and Mulcahy, stressing that the former objected to independent action by the Volunteers that had not been approved. This theme of personal rivalry within the republican movement is also covered by Peter Hart's *Mick: The Real Michael Collins* (New York, 2006), which argues that de Valera and Collins worked together in a supportive and "genuine partnership". This counters the view presented by Tim Pat Coogan in his detailed biographies of Collins and de Valera.

Many of the essays in the *Atlas of the Irish Revolution* shed new light on the conflict, and the extensive range of maps is particularly informative. Mary Daly's 'The First Dáil' states that the Dáil "largely ignored Ulster", with the only major debate taking place in August 1920 when Seán MacEntee raised the issue of the shipyard expulsions. The proposal to encourage the public to withdraw money from banks with headquarters in Belfast was discussed, though Griffith felt this was "practically a declaration of war on one part of their own territory". Joost Augusteijn's 'Military Conflict in the War of Independence', argues that the war "was not a consequence of careful planning or design, but a result of a mixture of coincidence, unintended outcomes and local initiatives." In discussing the autonomy of individual IRA units, he claims that the failure of both GHQ and the Dáil government to sanction attacks such as Soloheadbeg undermined their authority among many Volunteers. Indeed, IRA GHQ only officially sanctioned offensive action against the Crown Forces from 1 January 1920, even though Collins had formed the Squad in the previous August. Later, Augusteijn asserts, the killing of police and soldiers often generated a violent response from their comrades, and the result was swift revenge. Meanwhile, the IRA used coercion "to ensure compliance from the local population".

The role of the Crown Forces is examined in David Leeson's essay, 'The Royal Irish Constabulary, Black and Tans and Auxiliaries', which looks at the British theory of the conflict. For the British the violence in Ireland "was not a war, merely disorder", and, though martial law was used, the police remained on the front line throughout the conflict. After 30 years of peace, however, "the RIC was poorly prepared for the conflict". Leeson emphasises that the RIC often enjoyed a strained relationship with the Black and Tans who "were just as likely to resign as the Irishmen they had replaced". In 'Michael Collins and the Intelligence War', Michael Foy analyses the impact of Greenwood's appointment as chief secretary, describing him as a "hawk" who sought a military victory over the Volunteers. Macready then appointed General Hugh Tudor "to revitalise the police", but Greenwood and Tudor, Foy contends, were balanced by Sir John Anderson, Andy Cope and Mark Sturgis, the leading civil servants in Dublin Castle, who "worked towards a negotiated settlement with Sinn Féin." John Borgonovo's essay, '"Army Without Banners": the Irish Republican Army, 1920–21', claims that IRA recruitment was helped by World War I, which "had normalised violence across Europe". For most IRA members, Borgonovo argues, the assumption was that freedom would "bring about the social, economic and cultural transformation of the island". The author declares that GHQ's biggest failure was its inability to import arms. Meanwhile, many brigades "levied" the community, often using the established rates, a development that was not popular with property owners. Borgonovo states that "the backbone of the IRA were the shop assistants, low level clerks, civil servants and tradesmen", while men from "small farm backgrounds" were prominent in rural areas.

Pádraig Óg Ó Ruairc's essay, '"Spies and Informers Beware!": IRA executions of alleged civilian spies during the War of Independence', records that the IRA executed 196 civilians accused of spying or informing, many of whom were in Cork. Of the 78 civilians executed in Cork, 23 were Protestants, and half of the total number of "spies" were ex-servicemen. Ó Ruairc states that the "economic difficulties of ex-servicemen, coupled with their military training and previous loyal service to the British Crown, made them ideal candidates for recruitment by the British forces for the purpose of intelligence work". Niall Murray's 'Dáil Courts: A case study of Mid-Cork, 1920–22' explains that the Dáil courts dealt with debts, compensation and minor crimes such as assault, larceny, licensing, trespass and rights of way. The judges usually had strong links to Sinn Féin, and the punishment was often fines. Venues chosen for court settings included farmhouses, creameries, workhouses and even open fields. After the truce, many of the cases involved merchants and shopkeepers who were pursuing debts, but the courts closed down as the civil war began. Ian Kenneally's article, 'The Irish Bulletin', outlines the effectiveness of the journal, stressing that it pressed five main themes during the conflict. It highlighted the "disastrous polices" of the British government, exposed the violent repression instituted by the Crown Forces, demonstrated that the Dáil and its counter-state were the legitimate and effective expression of the people's will, showed national unity in the face of British aggression and defended IRA activities and its attacks on the illegal forces of occupation.

Joseph Connell's *The Terror War: The Uncomfortable Realities of the War of Independence* (Dublin, 2021) highlights the brutality of the conflict. He states that both sides used terror to intimidate the Irish population, while the strategic function of the IRA's warfare was "to defeat the British psychologically and politically – it was a war of attrition and exhaustion – but that exhaustion had to be capitalised on politically". Later, Connell adds that to succeed in the conflict, "the IRA did not need to be loved but it needed to be respected, and preferably feared as well." On the British side, Connell notes that initially Macready tolerated reprisals but did not actively encourage them, and he would later use the term "terrorism" to describe the reprisals policy. Previously, in his *Michael Collins: Dublin 1916–22* (Dublin, 2017), Connell suggests that his subject was not just concerned with war but with peace "and how to achieve it as quickly and advantageously as possible". As a "rationalist", Connell believes, Collins was "always concerned about shaping public opinion and about the political impact of violence". Collins ran an intelligence network by "making a mirror image of the British intelligence system and then improving on it". He understood, as Connell stresses, the importance of penetrating the British military and civil administration in Dublin.

Ferriter's *A Nation and not a Rabble* sums up the meetings between Lloyd George and de Valera in July 1921: "At no stage was the recognition of an Irish Republic by the British government a serious possibility, but what became crucial was the importance of symbols." This would become evident during the Treaty negotiations which followed. Lord Longford's *Peace by Ordeal* (London, 1935) provides a day-by-day account of the negotiations. Longford is sympathetic to de Valera, who refused to lead the Irish delegation, and fiercely critical of Lloyd George for what he alleges was the prime minister's "duplicity" during the negotiations. The author highlights the rapid transformation in the government's thinking in the run-up to the talks, noting that, in a matter of weeks, the cabinet went from viewing the Irish as a "murder gang" to negotiating with them as "equals". The author dwells on the serious divisions within the Irish team, which were reflected in the broader Sinn Féin movement, adding that of all the negotiators present, none attended with a more open mind than Collins. Longford also emphasises the importance of the "external association" concept. While Collins clearly grasped the essential difference between external association and dominion status, it was not a fundamental issue for him in the way that it was for de Valera. For Longford, the British team had one huge advantage over the Irish, and Lloyd George would use "the threat of war" with devastating effect at the end of the talks.

Colum Kenny's *Midnight in London: The Anglo-Irish Treaty Crisis 1921* (Dublin, 2021) offers a brilliant, brief riposte to Longford. Two points are worth noting in detail. The "personal" assurance from Griffith sent to Lloyd George on 2 November was, in fact, "an official communication", which had been discussed and amended by the Irish delegation as a whole, and "de Valera did not object to it". This was not the solo run on Griffith's part that is described by Longford. Secondly, Kenny claims that Longford's criticism of Griffith for having been duped into recognising the existing border was based on a misunderstanding. Griffith, argues Kenny, did not make secret concessions to Lloyd George on 13 November. This leads the author to conclude that the Irish were right to sign the Treaty, adding that it would have been "an irresponsible gamble for them to take a chance on the British ultimatum being a bluff". Kenny emphasises that much of the final framework was clear to both sides at the beginning of November and that the Boundary Commission concept had its origins in a Treaty of Versailles provision that was being used in 1921 on the Silesian border. The author also deals with the charge that the Irish delegation should have demanded greater transparency in the Boundary Commission clause, stating, "any ambiguity in Article 12 should have been obvious to all delegates and members of the cabinet" in the week before the Treaty was signed. In his account of the crucial Dáil cabinet meeting on 3 December, which lasted for eight hours, Kenny points out that only three decisions were taken: 1) De Valera would not go; 2) the Irish delegates were empowered to meet Craig if they wished; 3) the oath had to be amended (which it was). Barton later confirmed that Griffith repeatedly asked to have the Treaty text sent to Dublin before signing. Moreover, on the controversial claim that the Irish delegation did not use the telephone, Kenny asks pointedly "Who would they phone?" as de Valera was not in Dublin.

The British perspective on the Treaty is analysed in George Boyce's *Englishmen and Irish Troubles: British Public Opinion and the Making of Irish Policy, 1918– 1922* (London, 1972). Boyce stresses that Lloyd George's position was much weaker than Longford acknowledged, and he was clearly not a free agent in his handling of relations with Sinn Féin following the truce. Conscious of public opinion, the prime minister was careful to rally public support. This explains why he published the British offer sent to de Valera on 15 August, as it appeared to be fair and reasonable. Boyce also emphasises the great care taken by Lloyd George to bring Chamberlain and Birkenhead with him by insisting that Ireland remained in the Empire and recognised the Crown. He argues, moreover, that the Treaty was only made possible by the implementation of partition, which removed, temporarily at least, the Ulster problem, enabling Lloyd George to focus all his attention on securing a settlement with the representatives of Sinn Féin. In an assessment of the Irish tactics, Boyce judges that the plan to break off negotiations on Ulster, should this become necessary, was the correct strategy, but he adds that both factions within the Irish delegation and the Dáil cabinet then became diverted by their "Anglophobic obsession with the Crown".

A number of historians, such as Dwyer and Coogan, are fiercely critical of de Valera's actions just prior to the negotiations. In his *Michael Collins and the Treaty: His Differences with de Valera* (Dublin, 1981), *De Valera's Darkest Hour 1919–32* (Cork, 1982) and *Éamon de Valera* (Dublin, 1980), Dwyer alleges that de Valera tried to portray a moderate image in public but was more extreme in private, whereas the opposite was generally true of Collins. The author dwells on the importance of the power struggle between the two and presents de Valera as a scheming Machiavellian figure determined to destroy his chief political rival. Coogan's *De Valera: Long Fellow, Long Shadow* (London, 1993) claims that de Valera had little grasp of British political realities and did not recognise Lloyd George's precarious position. In his dealings with Lloyd George, de Valera's pride meant that he turned against compromise as it would undermine his reputation, and this influenced his decision not to join the Irish delegation. Coogan also emphasises the effort made by de Valera to ensure that history would record his actions in the most favourable light. He is adamant that de Valera was fully aware of the likely outcome of the negotiations and selected suitable "scapegoats" to make the necessary compromises. His rejection of the Treaty is described as "arrogant and destructive", and, like Parnell before him, he then set out to attract extremist support. Ferriter's *Judging Dev: A Reassessment of the Life and Legacy of Éamon de Valera* (Dublin, 2008) offers a more measured assessment, though he acknowledges that de Valera's decision not to attend the negotiations dogged him for the rest of his long political career.

On the other hand, Ferriter's *The Transformation of Ireland* observes that

Collins was "notoriously evasive" during this critical period. Alvin Jackson's *Ireland 1798–1998* (Oxford, 1999) provides a neat summary, suggesting that in his attempt to interfere with the plenipotentiaries, de Valera was "anxious to have ultimate control over the negotiation without incurring any of the unpopularity that might accrue from failure or from a problematic deal". Fitzpatrick's *The Two Irelands* (Oxford, 1998) clearly defines the problems facing the Irish at the Treaty negotiations. In unanimously agreeing to participate in negotiations, Fitzpatrick argues that the Dáil "implicitly accepted the impracticability of immediately achieving either a united Irish dominion or a southern republic". Another major problem was that republican strategists could not agree on the likelihood of renewed conflict, "or on its probable outcome, should negotiations collapse". Bew's *The Politics of Enmity 1789–2006* (Oxford, 2007) dismisses any prospect of the British reopening the war, because public opinion would have been against any such move. Consequently, Bew concludes that Lloyd George's threat of war at the end of the negotiations was not crucial to their outcome. From the "old Sinn Féin point of view", Bew claims that the Treaty was a good deal, as it achieved everything that Griffith had criticised Redmond for failing to deliver. However, he acknowledges that this was not the "agenda for which a minority had sacrificed so much – and inflicted so much".

O'Leary and Maume's *Controversial Issues in Anglo-Irish Relations , 1910–1921* (Dublin, 2004) advances an interesting interpretation of the Treaty negotiations, which highlights the central position that Ulster played during the talks. For these authors, it was Craig's refusal to consider any form of inclusion in an all-Ireland arrangement that determined the ultimate Treaty settlement. They argue that Lloyd George genuinely sought an agreement that would include Nationalists and Ulster Unionists, and it was only when he was consistently blocked by Craig that the prime minister looked for a settlement with Sinn Féin. For them, it was Craig's refusal to engage, not the divisions within Sinn Féin nor the tactical errors made by the Irish, that prevented the conclusion of a more comprehensive settlement. Nicholas Mansergh's *The Unresolved Question: The Anglo-Irish Settlement and Its Undoing 1912–72* (London, 1991) pinpoints a crucial error in the Irish negotiating strategy that had a significant bearing on the outcome. While he judges that de Valera outscored Lloyd George in both their preliminary discussions and in the correspondence that followed, the failure of the Irish to table their counter-proposals on 11 October was a huge gaffe. Only the British offer was on the table, and Mansergh declares that "the basic paper at any conference is apt to determine the parameters of subsequent discussions". On the oath, the author acknowledges that the wording was as far away from the concept of traditional allegiance as one could go, but it was the "existence" of the oath that raised objections. He also declares that Griffith's acceptance of the Boundary Commission released the British from their obligation to establish an all-Ireland parliament, as he persuaded himself that the Commission would achieve the same result.

Ronan Fanning's *Fatal Path: British Government and Irish Revolution 1910–1922* (London, 2013) emphasises the pressure facing Lloyd George and his ministers, as a failure "would trigger the end of his premiership and the collapse of his coalition government on which all the British delegates were also dependent for their political survival". However, the author stresses that the crucial debate on the cabinet's Irish policy took place before, not during, the Treaty negotiations, and the British team never deviated from dominion status for Ireland and no coercion of Ulster. Indeed, Fanning claims that during the negotiations, "Lloyd George devoted as much energy to soothing the Ulster Unionists as to negotiating with Sinn Féin's plenipotentiaries." Significantly, as Fanning points out, Lloyd George kept the difficult Balfour out of his negotiating team. In the end the author is very critical of Griffith's declaration that he would sign the Treaty whether or not Craig signed it, as it forced his colleagues to choose between disappointing him and breaking their pledge to de Valera. Finally, Maurice Cowling's *The Impact of Labour: The Beginning of Modern British Politics 1920–1924* (Cambridge, 1971) stands out as a brilliant study of contemporary high politics. Cowling demonstrates that Lloyd George "made almost total capitulation to the Conservative, if not to the Ulster position". However, the prime minister came very close to persuading the Conservative members of his cabinet to bring moral and financial pressure on Ulster to accept an all-Ireland parliament, but Bonar Law intervened to block the move. At some point between 12 and 23 November, Cowling claims, Lloyd George turned his fire on the Irish delegation, not Craig.

Michael Hopkinson's *Green against Green: The Irish Civil War* (Dublin, 1988) remains an invaluable resource for the study of the civil war. In examining its causes, Hopkinson concentrates on the IRA split, which, he claims, was the main cause of the conflict. The failure of the provisional government to control the occupation of barracks vacated by the British was of crucial importance, as only two barracks in Munster, Listowel and Skibbereen, were occupied by pro-Treaty forces. Yet the author is careful to emphasise the reluctance of even the most intransigent anti-Treaty IRA leaders such as O'Connor and Mellows to begin a civil war. In his assessment of the electoral pact before the election of the Third Dáil, the author highlights what he regards as de Valera's attempt to re-establish both Sinn Féin's position and his own leadership. However, Sinn Féin without the pro-Treaty faction was, in Hopkinson's view, already doomed. Joe Lee's *Ireland 1912–1985: Politics and Society* (Cambridge, 1989) looks at the background to the civil war in some detail, commenting that the response of O'Connor and Mellows to the June elections that endorsed the Treaty was "as contemptuous as any Black and Tan of the opinion of the mere Irish". He sums up his analysis of the causes by declaring that "the Treaty was the mere occasion, not the cause, of the war", adding that a principal cause was the basic conflict in Nationalist doctrine between "majority right and divine right". For Lee, this meant that the choice facing the Irish people was between democracy and dictatorship.

In fact, Lee subsequently revised this assessment, noting that a number of pro-Treaty TDs had voted to prevent further hostilities, not because they were fully supportive of the document before them. Indeed, Michael Laffan's *The Resurrection of Ireland: The Sinn Féin Party 1916–1923* (Cambridge, 1999) points out that a number of TDs altered their voting intentions during the Christmas break, when they were informed of their constituents' views. A key factor, as Fitzpatrick's *The Two Irelands* argues, was that the leading opponent of the Treaty was not "a great hearted if simple-minded guerrilla hero", but the Dáil's leading "tactician". While the author states that most observers were astonished by de Valera's repudiation of the Treaty, he argues that de Valera's reaction was "neither pig-headed nor irrational", as his primary objective was to maintain republican unity, and he felt that his external association formula would be acceptable to all factions. Yet Fitzpatrick concedes that the clear similarities between the Treaty and Document No. 2 only added to the bitterness of the exchanges.

In his more recent *Harry Boland's Irish Revolution* (Cork, 2003), Fitzpatrick suggests that although the leaders of both factions saw the split as a clash between "pragmatism and principle", its underlying thrust was a "disagreement as to which form of compromise was most expedient". Moreover, the author claims that in accepting the Treaty, Collins was guided as much by the thinking of the IRB Supreme Council as he was by the Dáil government. Bew's *The Politics of Enmity* is adamant that the fundamental cause of the civil war was political. He reasons that from 1916 to 1921 Sinn Féin had created "a very high-level expectancy" among its followers as to the likely outcome of the conflict. In the end, he argues, "the disappointment of the final deal was too much for many to bear".

Ferriter's *A Nation and not a Rabble* points out that prior to the Treaty split, de Valera was closer to Collins than to any other Dáil minister. In the public debate on the Treaty, he declares that "there was growing pressure from the farming community, the labour movement, business interests and the Church to accept compromise and move on." When the Supreme Council of the IRB met to discuss the Treaty in late April 1922, Lynch found himself "in a minority of one against its signature", but he made huge efforts to avert civil war and was regarded as "too moderate" by O'Connor. Agreeing with others, Ferriter declares that it was the occupation of the Four Courts by republicans in April 1922 "that had ensured civil war was likely". He adds that though Collins tried desperately to avoid civil war, he acted decisively once he recognised that there was no possibility of reaching a compromise. The author also assumes that even if de Valera had backed the Treaty a conflict was inevitable, such was the uncompromising position adopted by O'Connor and the militant faction. The argument that the Irish Civil War can be viewed as part of a broader class conflict is rebuffed in Michael Farry's *The Aftermath of Revolution: Sligo, 1921–23* (Dublin, 2000). Farry asserts that there was no social basis for civil war in Sligo and, indeed, the "men of no property" were more likely to fight for the Free State.

Bew's *Churchill and Ireland* (Oxford, 2016) states that Churchill "almost boiled over", when Collins hesitated on moving against the Four Courts occupants following Wilson's assassination. Still, Bew concludes that "his policy effectively triumphed", as he forced Collins to turn away from the idea that he could use Ulster "as a means of reconstructing the unity of Sinn Féin and to contemplate instead republican challenges to his own authority". Yet, as Bew acknowledges, it was Macready who had prevented Churchill from launching a premature British attack on republican forces in the Four Courts. However, Bew also adds that Churchill sat on his hands as he had "a certain residual trust in Collins". Subsequently, Collins and his colleagues "openly stated their debt to Churchill". Bill Kissane's *The Politics of the Civil War* (Oxford, 2005) notes that popular explanations for the split emphasise personalities, and he argues that Collins and de Valera were divided by temperament, not by ideology. For Kissane, the Civil War was "a classic succession crisis", a war for de facto control over the new state. He also points out that all the efforts to gain external recognition of an Irish republic had failed. Among the essays in the *Atlas of the Irish Revolution,* Donal Ó Drisceoil's article, 'Irish Newspapers, the Treaty and the Civil War', argues that republican attempts at "sledgehammer censorship", which was the result of vocal opposition from the mainstream Irish press, allowed the provisional government "to characterise them as lawless and dictatorial". The *Freeman's Journal* was a particular target for brutal republican attacks, while local newspapers in republican-held areas "either went out of business or continued to publish under anti-Treaty censorship". Fitzpatrick's *Harry Boland's Irish Revolution* argues that Boland was the prime mover in drawing up the electoral pact for the elections in June 1922, in which republicanism was rejected by the people. However, the author claims that by accepting a British revision of the draft constitution, which only became public on the morning of the poll, "the Provisional Government had exposed itself to the charge of deception and betrayal." This allowed the republican side to dismiss the claim that the election result had given a mandate for the Treaty.

The course of the civil war is assessed by Hopkinson's *Green against Green*. The author carefully analyses the reasons for the Irregulars' defeat, citing the lack of a coherent strategy among the various anti-Treaty units and the wide range of opinion among anti-Treaty leaders. Once the conflict began, these flaws quickly became apparent, and the failure to seize the initiative in the opening phase of the conflict, when they enjoyed a clear numerical advantage, ensured defeat for the Irregulars. In his assessment of the Free State forces, Hopkinson highlights the poor calibre of army officers, but goes on to claim that they were good enough to deal with republican troops who were largely ineffective outside their own areas. By the end of August 1922, the Irregulars had opened the guerrilla phase of their campaign, which was partially successful in more remote areas such as South Kerry and West Mayo, where there was significant popular support for the republican cause. The author notes that the executions shocked opinion in Ireland and England, but judges that they weakened republican morale and ultimately curtailed military activity.

Commenting on the geography of the conflict, Hopkinson demonstrates that it was those areas that had been quiet during the War of Independence, such as Mayo and Kerry, that saw most action in the civil war. In areas that had seen most of the fighting against Crown Forces, such as Cork and Tipperary, there was little violence, as the local population in these counties were war weary and, by 1922, wanted peace. Indeed, as Hopkinson declares, large areas of the country were really unaffected by the conflict. The author also emphasises that "general lawlessness" and "local particularism" were responsible for much of the violence during the civil war. The 77 executions are discussed in an essay by Sean Enright in *Ireland 1912: Independence, Partition, Civil War* (Dublin, 2022), which is edited by Darragh Gannon and Fearghal McGarry. Enright, a legal historian, argues that the arbitrary and brutal nature of state violence during the civil war clearly contributed to the Free State victory, but this use of terror, both official and unofficial, which began with the four executions in December 1922, "marked a pivotal moment in the abandonment of the rule of law". Ernie O'Malley's *The Singing Flame* (Dublin, 1978) offers an appraisal of "the confusion, which hampered the anti-Treaty side", by one of the key participants.

Tom Garvin's *1922: The Birth of Irish Democracy* (Dublin, 1996) places the Irish experience in its European context, demonstrating that democracy was forced on a section of Irish political opinion against the vicious background of the civil war. It was due to the success of the provisional government in 1922 that a democratic state was established along with order and stability. Garvin argues that militant republicanism always lacked popular legitimacy, and he insists that there was a good deal of popular indifference to the "entire Free State versus Republic issue". Rather, he declares, the civil war was fought over issues that "most people saw, accurately, as pointless and unreal". He also emphasises that the switch from revolutionary to politician was a difficult and painful process for many of those involved in the civil war period. Some, such as Tom Barry, made no apology for their desire to see the establishment of a military dictatorship, whereas others, notably Cosgrave and Mulcahy, both of whom he stresses were "profoundly underrated", were always willing to defer to the people's judgement. These two men, together with O'Higgins, regarded the civil war as a necessary prelude to the establishment of Irish democracy. On the opposing side, many anti-Treaty IRA leaders demonstrated a "fear and contempt" of democracy. The establishment of the Civic Guard is expertly chronicled in Eunan O'Halpin's *Defending Ireland: The Irish State and its Enemies since 1922* (Oxford, 1999). It highlights O'Duffy's strengths, which gave the organisation "a sense of purpose and direction". One reason for republican toleration of an unarmed force, he argues, was that the Guards, up to 1925, rarely interfered in republican activities.

During the civil war, O'Halpin claims, the feeling that they were defending the "popular will" was a powerful motivation for Cosgrave and his colleagues. They viewed their opponents as "misguided", but the Cosgrave government's political and military resolve shocked the anti-Treaty side, and the executions undoubtedly dented republican morale. O'Halpin's analysis of the 1924 army mutiny emphasises Mulcahy's isolation within the government from the spring of 1923 which, in turn, strengthened the position of the force's malcontents who were angered by the deep cuts to troop numbers and by the IRB's influence within the officer corps. With rumours circulating of a possible coup, the government intervened and the mutiny collapsed. O'Higgins's role in tackling the army mutiny is assessed in John McCarthy's *Kevin O'Higgins: Builder of the Irish State* (Dublin, 2006). O'Higgins was the strongest personality in the cabinet, and he was decisive in outmanoeuvring Mulcahy.

On the northern question, McCarthy stresses O'Higgins's expectation that the Boundary Commission would substantially reduce Northern Ireland territory, and he was the strongest advocate in the Cumann na nGaedheal government for the convening of the Commission. Yet by mid-1924 he had second thoughts about the Commission's approach under its British-appointed chairman. When the Boundary Commission finally moved as O'Higgins had feared, he joined the Irish delegation that signed the tripartite agreement in December 1925. In the subsequent debate, in one of his most eloquent speeches, he denounced the "irredentists" and called for peace with the Craig government. Hepburn's *Catholic Belfast and Nationalist Ireland in the Era of Joe Devlin, 1871–1934* (Oxford, 2008) emphasises Devlin's "realistic" approach to the Boundary Commission, adding that the Irish Party had never consented to any scheme that would produce "permanent partition". He also noted that Devlin and his colleagues had never agreed to the establishment of a Belfast government. Hepburn looks at Churchill's influence, following his return to the Conservative ranks, claiming that he was anxious to show that the Boundary Commission had always been intended to provide for "adjustments" to the border rather than major transfers of territory.

Finally, a number of essays in the *Atlas of the Irish Revolution* shed light on the period following the civil war. Gavin Foster's 'Locating the "Lost Legion": IRA emigration and settlement after the Civil War' states that in the first decade of post-revolutionary statehood, an estimated 220,000 people left the Free State for the United States alone, a figure that included IRA veterans and ex-prisoners "plus thousands more disillusioned anti-Treatyites". Foster notes that the defeated anti-Treaty IRA followed up its May 1923 dump-arms order with "general Order No. 22". It forbade IRA members from leaving the country without procuring travel permits from their local commanders. Men who left without permission were excluded from overseas republican groups like Clan na Gael. Even with unemployment rising in 1924, the IRA's executive refused to relax its policy, still nursing the hope of a renewed campaign against the Free State." Andy Bielenberg's article, 'Southern Irish Protestant Experiences of the Irish Revolution', confirms that most southern Protestants hoped "Ireland would remain firmly within the UK". Those "within the Irish establishment" were targeted by the revolutionaries, and the "small minority of civilians suspected (rightly or wrongly) of providing information to the Crown forces became primary IRA targets for assassination". However, Bielenberg concludes that when the revolutionary storm had passed, "Protestant farmers remained relatively over-represented among the larger farmers." However, from 1920, Protestant emigration from the twenty-six counties became a significant development. Bielenberg responds to Hart's assertion of the existence of a sectarian murder campaign in County Cork by arguing that episodes such as the violence of April 1922 were "untypical" and carried out without the authorisation of senior commanders. Such killings, notes the author, were "sporadic". He concludes his remarks on Protestant emigration by declaring that "there now at least appears to be a consensus that revolutionary violence or intimidation was of far less consequence than a host of other factors".

Joe Lee's 'The Irish Free State' argues that only with Lynch's death did it become possible for de Valera, "the nominal but powerless leader of the anti-Treaty resistance, to regain some, if still far from complete control over anti-Treaty elements." The result of the 1923 election was a shock for Cumann na nGaedheal, but "a very good one for de Valera", and, as Lee argues, the policy of abstention relieved him from having to try "to impose parliamentary discipline on potentially fissiparous followers". When the Boundary Commission's recommendations were leaked, Cosgrave hurried to London, "as any player of the game of realpolitik could have predicted", though Eoin MacNeill seemed "never to have heard of realpolitik, an unfortunate oversight for a historian". However, Lee contends that a more effective Free State representative on the Commission probably would not have made much difference.

Chapter 5
Northern Ireland and its Problems, 1920–25

The annexation and partition of territory are usually the result of war. In Ireland, however, it was a war of words that would lead to the partition of the island. There was, of course, a real fear in Ireland and Britain that Unionist opposition to the third Home Rule Bill might result in violence. This had led to the emergence of the partition concept as a workable compromise to end the political deadlock over the bill. When the postwar Westminster government returned to the Ulster question in 1919, there was a widespread assumption that some form of exclusion would be at the heart of a new settlement. The cabinet committee that considered the issue had to determine not only the area that would be partitioned but also the structures necessary to promote some form of reunion. Yet in making provision for the creation of a Belfast parliament, the Lloyd George government was, probably unwittingly, erecting a barrier to future reunification. The overwhelming priority for the new six-county state was survival. While this was accomplished, the Unionist government proved incapable of governing on behalf of all the citizens of the new Northern Ireland state.

The road to partition

The Government of Ireland Act became effective on 3 May 1921. The act made provision for the partition of Ireland by the creation of two new parliaments, one in Dublin and one in Belfast. Partition was an attempt by the British government to accommodate Nationalism and Unionism, an idea based on the exclusion of Ulster Protestants from the rest of Ireland. It was an imperfect solution. Partition first emerged as a viable concept following Asquith's introduction of the third Home Rule Bill in April 1912. In the battle against the first and second Home Rule Bills in 1886 and 1893 partition had not been suggested as a possible compromise. Then, northern and southern Unionism worked closely together to defend the Union. The concentration of numbers in north-east Ulster, which provided an electoral base for most of the Irish Unionist MPs, gave Unionism a powerful Belfast voice, but the broader Unionist movement had little difficulty in presenting a united front during the first twenty years of its existence.

The key to Unionism's ability to overcome the threat of Home Rule in the late nineteenth century was the Conservative Party's resolute defence of the Union. Many leading Conservatives had close family links with prominent figures in Irish Unionism. More significantly, they considered Home Rule a danger not just to the integrity of the United Kingdom but to the British Empire. Of course, it was also true that ambitious and populist Tories could, on occasion, exploit Ulster opposition to Home Rule for personal and purely party-political purposes. An obvious example was Lord Randolph Churchill, whose 1886 Ulster Hall speech speculated that "Ulster will fight, and Ulster will be right". Such encouragement of Orange extremism became one feature of the Conservative Party's relationship with Ulster Unionism in the period before the outbreak of war in 1914.

While Unionism welcomed passionate Tory support, Ulster Unionists, in particular, retained a nagging doubt about the Conservative Party's ultimate commitment to the Union. It was somewhat ironic that Ulster Unionist faith was tested during the long period of Tory rule around the turn of the century. In 1904 the Conservative administration briefly flirted with the idea of Irish devolution, sparking outrage among Ulster Unionists. What followed was a determined campaign to oust those individuals deemed to be responsible for this perceived threat to the Union. At the same time, changes were already underway within Unionism as the movement was transitioning from a nineteenth-century, part-time landlord party to a modern political movement. A younger cohort of more professional politicians, such as the Craigs, William Moore and J. B. Lonsdale, drawn from the ranks of the bourgeoisie, had revitalised Ulster Unionism. These professional and business Presbyterians were, crucially, more in touch with the electorate in North-East Ulster. They were eager to steer the movement in a new direction following a period of drift under the ageing leader Saunderson. He was accused of being asleep at the wheel while the Conservatives engaged in the devolution experiment. It was this group that was behind the formation of the Ulster Unionist Council (UUC) in 1905. The UUC gave Ulster Unionism a more democratic flavour, and its establishment enabled Ulster Unionists to become the driving force within Irish Unionism. The creation of the UUC was a defining event on the road to the emergence of an exclusively Ulster movement. An expanded UUC would play a leading role in directing the campaign of Ulster resistance to the third Home Rule Bill. With a strong Belfast bias, the movement provided Ulster Unionism with a new organisational framework that permitted effective grass-roots participation. Simultaneously, its formal links with the Orange Order contributed to a more militant political stance.

These developments strengthened the regional identity of Ulster Unionism. One other lesson drawn from the devolution crisis was that Unionism might not always be able to rely on unequivocal support from the Conservative Party in future struggles against Home Rule. This fostered the development of a more self-reliant style of Unionism in Ulster. Walter Long's subsequent spell as Unionist leader helped both to improve Conservative–Unionist relations and bridge the gap that had been developing between northern and southern Unionism. Edward Carson, who became Irish Unionist leader in February 1910, was also from a southern Unionist background and enjoyed a harmonious relationship with the Conservative Party. Yet under Carson's stewardship the gap between the Unionist factions in Ireland became much wider. On the other hand, relations between the Conservatives and Ulster Unionists became much closer, though this tended to expose further the regional divisions within Unionism. Desperate for an issue to unite the Conservative Party following internal strife and disastrous election performances, the Tories went for outright opposition to Asquith's Home Rule policy. The elevation of Bonar Law to the leadership in November 1911 was crucial in committing the Conservative Party to back Ulster Unionist resistance to Home Rule.

It was immediately apparent that Bonar Law's overwhelming concern was with Ulster. Carson did not share this narrow view, but he would become the leader of a more localised, partitionist and militant Ulster movement over the course of the Home Rule crisis. This had not been his intention when he assumed the mantle of leadership. Carson did not identify with the emphasis on religion at the core of Ulster Unionism, nor did he work on the basis that there were two nations in Ireland. His goal was to preserve the Union by using Ulster resistance to thwart the Liberal government's plans. Yet in launching his campaign against Home Rule, Carson created a situation in which Ulster Unionism rapidly emerged as a confident, dominant and defiant force that was quite distinct from southern Unionism. At Craigavon in September 1911, Carson addressed supporters, warning that if Home Rule became law, Unionists must take whatever steps were necessary to govern Ulster by themselves. The following month he soothed southern Unionist nerves, assuring them that they would not be abandoned. However, Carson was now set on a path that led towards partition. The Ulster domination of resistance to Home Rule was evident in mass demonstrations and propaganda events such as the signing of the Covenant. The formation of the Ulster Volunteer Force (UVF) ensured that deeper divisions would open up within Unionism. By 1913 Carson, whose judgement allowed him to see what was achievable politically, had abandoned the strategy of using Ulster to destroy Home Rule for one of saving Ulster from Home Rule. This may have been uncomfortable, but Carson was now leading the fight for partition.

Carson's initial strategy was knocked off course by the intervention of Agar-Robartes in the summer of 1912. The Liberal MP moved an amendment to the Home Rule Bill in June 1912, proposing the exclusion of the four north-eastern counties from the bill's operation. Agar-Robartes based his proposal on the premise that "Ireland consists of two nations different in sentiment, character, history and religion". Nationalists were, not surprisingly, outraged, as were southern Unionists. Carson was faced with a dilemma. If he supported the amendment, the government front bench would accuse him of abandoning all Unionists in the remaining 28 counties. Mindful of how his actions would be judged by public opinion in Britain, Carson decided that he and his fellow Unionist MPs should back the amendment. They were joined in the division lobby by their Tory sympathisers. In the end, the government stood firm and the amendment was lost by 69 votes. Carson justified his support for the exclusion proposal, arguing that it was a tactical move made with the knowledge that if it was accepted, then the Home Rule Bill would be wrecked. This ensured that his policy of using Ulster to scupper the entire Home Rule project remained intact. It also allowed him to reassure Unionists in the south and west. Indeed, Carson maintained this position when he introduced his own amendment on 1 January 1913. It proposed the exclusion of all nine Ulster counties from the bill. Again, this was presented as a wrecking amendment. Carson opened a new campaign season, having given southern Unionists a personal commitment that their interests would be safeguarded. Still, the Agar-Robartes intervention in the previous summer had introduced the partition concept to the political discourse. During the debates that followed, many Unionist MPs identified some merit in the idea of exclusion. Bonar Law declared that if Home Rule was finally enacted, then the proposal could render it "less bad", as it would, in all likelihood, prevent the eruption of violence.

As the months passed in 1913, Carson gradually shifted towards the notion of partition as a solution to the Home Rule crisis. He had clearly been moved by the events of the Covenant fortnight in September 1912, when it was confirmed that he stood at the head of a determined mass movement. The subsequent emergence of the UVF and the increasing militancy of the northern Unionists ensured that the campaign against Home Rule was almost entirely Ulster-driven. Carson was also aware of the considerable popular support for the Ulster Unionist cause in Britain, which was encouraged on a daily basis by the Tory press. To many observers, by mid-1913, partition was emerging as a reasonable compromise, and one that could prevent the possibility of violence in Ireland. At the same time, the Irish Unionist leader had become frustrated by the action, or inaction, of his fellow southern Unionists. They continued to demand assurances that they would not be overlooked in any political agreement. But, in Carson's view, they were unwilling to make the sacrifices that had characterised their opposition to Home Rule in 1886 and 1893. The shift in Carson's thinking found expression in his correspondence with Bonar Law in September 1913. He informed the Tory leader privately that he could foresee a settlement based on the exclusion of six counties. While he added some qualification about the difficulties of his own position in such an arrangement, this was the position that Carson stuck to as the Ulster crisis continued to unfold. The Liberal government was made aware of Carson's thinking through contact between Bonar Law and Churchill. He, along with Lloyd George, had been in favour of special treatment for Ulster when the cabinet first considered the impending Home Rule Bill in February 1912.

When Asquith met Bonar Law in October 1913 for the first of three secret meetings, the prime minister discussed Ulster exclusion. This gave the opposition a clear indication that the government was giving serious consideration to partition. It was also apparent that there was uncertainty about the precise area that might be excluded. As the crisis now entered its crucial phase, Redmond came under strong pressure to concede the principle of exclusion. He finally relented in March 1914 and reluctantly accepted Lloyd George's county option proposals. This marked a significant milestone on the road to partition. Thereafter, it was apparent that any solution to the Home Rule controversy would be based on the principle of partition, leaving only the questions of area and time to be resolved. This was clearly illustrated at the Buckingham Palace Conference. While there was no agreement on the area to be excluded, some form of partition now appeared as the only workable compromise if the government pressed forward with Home Rule.

However, the outbreak of war with Germany took the spotlight off Ulster. By September 1914 Home Rule was on the statute book, but Ulster's future was left undecided. Redmond's Irish Volunteers and Carson's Ulster Volunteers joined the British Army in significant numbers, eager to demonstrate loyalty to the Empire and hopeful of influencing any postwar Irish settlement. Nevertheless, events transpired in a manner that clearly worked to the advantage of the Ulster Unionists. First, the war weakened the Liberals and they never regained their prewar strength. By May 1915, a coalition government had been formed. The presence of Bonar Law and Carson in the cabinet ensured that Ulster interests would be safeguarded. Sound Nationalist reasoning had led Redmond to decline Asquith's offer of a cabinet seat. He thus lost the chance of exerting influence on the Westminster administration. The war also exacerbated the Irish Parliamentary Party's (IPP) problems and presented the Irish Republican Brotherhood (IRB) with the stage for a rebellion.

One consequence of the Easter Rising was the reinforcement of the partitionist mindset. In his search for a political breakthrough in the immediate aftermath of the rising, Lloyd George persuaded both Redmond and Carson to accept the six-county exclusion, albeit on contradictory terms. While the Lloyd George scheme was not implemented, it did mark another important milestone on the road to partition. Carson had to overcome the hostility of Unionists in Cavan, Monaghan and Donegal, many of whom had signed the Covenant but were now abandoned in a sectarian headcount. Redmond, in his greater need for a settlement, had gone further in surrendering, even temporarily, Nationalist Tyrone and Fermanagh, infuriating IPP supporters in those counties. With both Unionism and Nationalism having earlier accepted the principle of partition, the area to be excluded was taking a more definite shape. In the end, southern Unionists, who were more afraid of partition than Home Rule, used their waning influence at Westminster to block the peace plan. Lloyd George was content to leave the next attempt at navigating a route towards Home Rule to the Irish themselves. The Irish Convention revealed the depth of Nationalist and southern Unionist opposition to partition. The Ulster Unionists, confident that they had secured their own territory, refused to consider, in spite of occasional prodding by Westminster, any concessions towards Irish Nationalism. This ensured that the Irish Convention ended in stalemate.

Sinn Féin's triumph over constitutional Nationalism also had implications for partition. Indeed, the emerging movement had made political capital by repeatedly attacking Redmond's readiness to embrace partition. In 1917–18 de Valera argued that the IPP had been misguided in its efforts to appease Unionism, implying that Ulster might have to be coerced into acceptance of an all-Ireland legislative body. Though he would subsequently moderate his views on the north, the rise of Sinn Féin undoubtedly stiffened the resolve of Ulster Unionists to keep their distance from Dublin. They were, moreover, angry at Sinn Féin's opposition to the war and fiercely critical of the role played by the Catholic Church in the anti-conscription campaign, citing this as evidence that the Catholic hierarchy would interfere constantly in the political affairs of any new Dublin legislature. It was apparent that the gap between Unionism and Nationalism had widened since 1914, when Ireland looked to be on the brink of civil war. With no likelihood of a consensus emerging between the Ulster Unionists and Sinn Féin, the response of the coalition government would be decisive.

In the quarter of a century before the war, the Irish question had been one of the key issues dividing the two main parties at Westminster. Then the all-consuming nature of the war effort wedded the parties together, and they shared a common interest in keeping potentially difficult Irish affairs off the political agenda. Significantly, when intervention was unavoidable, particularly after the Easter Rising, it was Conservative thinking that dominated the coalition government's approach. While both main parties had grown tired of Irish political quarrelling, the Conservative commitment to Ulster Unionism was still evident. This meant that the exclusion of Ulster from any future Irish political settlement was assured. For most of the Westminster actors, however, Churchill's "dreary steeples" speech reflected their disillusionment with Irish politics. Although the face of Europe had been radically altered by the war, Churchill concluded that "the integrity of their quarrel remained unaltered". The postwar Lloyd George government would have to address this issue.

The Government of Ireland Act

Of course, the priority for the British government in 1919 was the Peace Conference, and Lloyd George and Bonar Law spent much of their time in Paris deciding Germany's fate. Still, the threat to peace in Ireland emanating from the Irish Volunteers forced Westminster to consider the state of the country. One cabinet minister, however, had retained an abiding interest in Irish affairs. Walter Long was First Lord of the Admiralty, but his background, experience and confident pronouncements on political and military developments in Ireland qualified him as the cabinet's Irish expert, a role for which there was no competition. Indeed, colleagues were usually relieved to defer to Long's expertise in Irish matters. From the opening shots in the War of Independence, Long urged the adoption of a tough security response. He argued that the government would only be in a position to consider a political settlement when order had been re-established through coercion. Yet the terms of the 1914 Home Rule Act, which had to be revisited by government officials anxious to acquaint themselves with potential outcomes, stated that it would come into effect when the last of the European peace treaties was signed. This necessitated an earlier engagement with Ireland than most of the cabinet would have desired. In its manifesto for the 1918 election, the coalition government stated that it had an open mind on any future Irish settlement, though it did add two provisos. One was that Ireland must remain within the Empire; the other was that "the six counties of Ulster" could not be forced into an all-Ireland parliament against their will. Indeed, Ulster's position had been further strengthened by the outcome of the recent election. Following a redistribution of seats giving more representation to urban areas, Unionists won control of 22 of Ulster's 37 constituencies. This added weight to their demand for the permanent exclusion of the six-county area. Carson's switch to the Duncairn constituency in Belfast marked a final symbolic split with southern Unionism. He had, hitherto, represented Trinity College Dublin since July 1892.

The government eventually broached the Irish question when a cabinet committee was appointed on 7 October 1919 to draft a fourth Home Rule

Bill. Not surprisingly, Long was selected to chair this five-man Irish Situation Committee, as it was formally known. Long's appointment should have reassured Ulster Unionists, as his negative view of Irish Nationalism had remained unaltered for over 20 years, though Carson was unimpressed. The committee's first meeting on 15 October concluded that the new bill should make provision for a northern and southern parliament together with a "Common Council" that would deal with matters pertaining to both areas. Throughout its subsequent deliberations, the Long committee operated within these general parameters. In its first report to cabinet on 4 November, the committee recommended that special treatment for Ulster should be at the core of the new settlement. Questions over area, time and the precise constitutional arrangements would be open for discussion. The report also stated that the committee had considered an all-Ireland parliament with certain safeguards for Ulster, but this was rejected as unworkable. It also dismissed the county option concept as a method of determining any area to be excluded. Long had consistently opposed plebiscites which, it was feared, would be a catalyst for inter-community violence. What was clear, therefore, was that partition would be the basis for a settlement but that the route to future reunification should be kept open.

To this end, and indeed for the sake of convenience, the Long committee expressed its preference for a nine-county Ulster, in which the two communities would be more evenly balanced. The cabinet assembled on 11 November, one year on from the armistice, to consider Long's report. A good deal of the discussion focused on the situation in the south. Tory ministers were concerned that Sinn Féin might use the proposed southern parliament as a stage to declare an independent republic. With violence in parts of the south on the increase, some members of the cabinet were anxious that their actions could be construed as a surrender to terror. Indeed, Birkenhead only gave his approval for the concept of two new parliaments because he was confident that Sinn Féin would reject what American and Dominion opinion would regard as a reasonable offer. Long, meanwhile, proceeded on the basis that law and order would have to be restored in advance of any political offer, and he continued to agitate for a tougher security approach by the Crown Forces.

Conservative ministers also worked on the assumption that Ulster Unionists would oppose the creation of a Belfast parliament, believing that they would favour direct rule from Westminster. The cabinet, in general, wanted an end to direct rule, as it was anxious to extricate itself, as far as possible, from Irish affairs. Ministers were also anxious to distance themselves from any charge that partition was nothing more than a device to allow the continuation of British rule in Ulster. Here they received unexpected assistance from Craig who, by late 1919, had effectively replaced Carson as the principal spokesman for Ulster

Unionism. In mid-November the cabinet learned, to Long's surprise, that Craig was sympathetic to the concept of a "Home Rule" parliament in Belfast, adding that his clear preference was for a six-county unit. The new convert to devolution felt that powers should be transferred at an early date, and this caused the Long committee to expedite its discussions.

A second report on 17 November emphasised the desirability of pressing ahead with legislation as soon as possible. Two further reports followed in quick succession. One dealt with financial considerations, the other with potential arrangements for the transfer of powers. These issues were brought before the cabinet at two meetings on 3 and 10 December. The tenor of the discussions indicated that nearly every minister viewed partition as a temporary expedient. Again, there was a clear preference for the partitioned area to consist of the historic nine-county province, a cut that would be more easily defended against criticism both from within and from outside the Westminster parliament. It would also prove more temporary. There was, however, one powerful dissenting voice. Balfour supported Craig's desire for a six-county bloc, though he argued that the excluded area should not have its own Belfast parliament. Moreover, Irish unity was clearly not his long-term objective, as he hoped that partition would be permanent.

When he updated the House of Commons on the Long committee's progress on 22 December, the prime minister revealed his government's latest Irish strategy. He stated that his ultimate objective was to create a devolved all-Ireland parliament under Westminster's authority. Lloyd George was deliberately vague on the area to be excluded. *The Times*, in its report of the proceedings, declared itself in favour of a nine-county bloc, arguing that "the ancient province of Ulster should remain a unit in any scheme of Irish self-government". In justifying its position, the article claimed that "the existence of a strong Nationalist minority in Ulster would not merely be a guarantee of the protection of the rights and interests of that minority, and of certain harmony of development between the two Irish States, but that it would also prove a powerful force working in the direction of union". During December the cabinet edged towards approval of a nine-county split, though nothing definite was agreed at this stage. The larger Catholic population in the nine-county area was regarded as an advantage in clearing the path to future reunification, and the coalition government assumed that partition on this basis would be viewed more favourably by international opinion.

While the bill was being drafted, Craig worked tirelessly to have the proposed excluded area limited to six counties. Unionists in the north-east were adamant that their control over a nine-county Ulster would be precarious, and the argument that the higher Catholic birth rate would jeopardise their position was routinely made. As a junior minister in the Westminster government, Craig enjoyed easy access to the Long committee. He had been a member of Lloyd George's wartime coalition administration but had resigned in solidarity with Carson in January 1918. When Lloyd George formed his postwar government, Craig was again appointed to government as parliamentary secretary of the ministry of pensions. Later, from April 1920, he would serve alongside Long in the Admiralty. Carson had refused office, leaving Craig, the more authentic voice of Ulster Unionism, in a key position. By February 1920 the bill had been carefully revised, though the fundamental issue of the area to be partitioned had yet to be resolved. Another outstanding issue was the possible transfer of customs and excise powers either to each of the two parliaments or on the occasion of their union. When the Irish Situation Committee considered this financial issue on 17 February, Bonar Law, at Lloyd George's request, was in the chair, but there was no consensus on a way forward. On the crucial question of area, Long relayed Craig's plea for a six-county bloc, but the committee, still concerned about the need for future reunification, returned to its original recommendation for a nine-county Ulster parliament. The decision infuriated Ulster Unionists, who also took exception to the committee's support for an all-Ireland judiciary.

When the committee met on the following day, its members unanimously agreed to drop the idea of a single judiciary. Long next met the Ulster Unionist leaders who reaffirmed their desire for a six-county bloc in which they would enjoy a significant majority. A meeting of the full cabinet on 24 February heard an appeal by Long before agreeing to ignore the committee's recommendations by opting for a six-county parliament. Balfour had taken the lead in cabinet, and a hastily redrafted Government of Ireland Bill had its first reading the next day. On second reading in the Commons, it was carried by 348 to 94 votes, with the Ulster Unionists abstaining in the division. Only Joe Devlin raised effective objections to the bill, claiming that it would condemn Ulster Catholics to the status of a permanent minority in a ridiculous six-county statelet. An illuminating contribution in the parliamentary debate was made by Charles Craig, James's brother and the MP for South Antrim. On 29 March 1920 he insisted that Ulster Unionists would have preferred the continuation of direct rule from Westminster. He also acknowledged that a Belfast parliament would offer clear advantages for Unionism, telling MPs "once a parliament is set up and working well ... we feel that we would then be in a position of absolute security". In Craig's view, a Belfast parliament would be a buffer against the designs of Irish Nationalism and act as a bulwark against a future, hostile Westminster government that might favour reunification. The one threat to Unionism in the legislation was the Council of Ireland, the device that had been intended to act as a bridge to an all-Ireland political structure.

Craig's success in establishing a six-county unit was tempered by the growing divisions within Unionism. Unionists in Cavan, Monaghan and Donegal had been abandoned, and their plight dogged the UUC. At its crunch meeting on 10 March 1920, these "border" Unionists reminded delegates of commitments made under the auspices of the 1912 Covenant. They clashed with the leadership in a repeat of the bitter exchanges of June 1916, when Lloyd George's peace plan was adopted. There were approximately 70,000 Unionists in the three border counties living alongside some 260,000 Nationalists. Significantly, no Unionist candidate had been returned in any constituency in Cavan, Monaghan or Donegal in the recent general election. This would, in all likelihood, have changed in any election to a nine-county Belfast parliament, which would use the proportional representation (PR) system. The leadership warned that Unionism could expect to have only a narrow majority in a nine-county parliament and they would be faced with the very real prospect of defeat in the longer term.

Nevertheless, Unionists from the three-county area pleaded with the UUC to abide by the spirit of the Covenant. They moved a resolution proposing the expansion of the six-county area defined in the Government of Ireland Bill. Although their amendment was defeated, many of the delegates from the six-county area were acutely embarrassed by the proceedings. This was not the end of the matter, as a further meeting of the UUC was scheduled for 27 May to ratify the decision. In the meantime, the excluded Unionists intensified their struggle. In April, they produced a pamphlet entitled *No Partition of Ulster*. It set out the historical, geographic and economic case for a nine-county parliament and argued that the creation of a six-county parliament would send the wrong message and play into the hands of the enemies of Unionism. In a detailed analysis of the numbers, the pamphlet suggested that the fact that they were in a clear minority could not be sufficient grounds for their exclusion. The same held true for Tyrone, Fermanagh and Derry city, each of which had a clear Nationalist majority, while in South Armagh and South Down Unionists were in a minority. Moreover, North Monaghan and East Donegal had much clearer concentrations of Unionists than a number of areas within the six-county bloc. Still, Unionist leaders dismissed these arguments as they stood by their earlier decision. At the meeting on 27 May, only 80 of the 390 UUC delegates backed the nine-county option.

During the summer of 1920, violence erupted in the north, and this hardened the Unionist approach. Meanwhile, Lloyd George was belatedly turning his mind to the developing War of Independence and considering the implications for the impending legislation. The Government of Ireland Bill was delayed in the hope that order might be restored in the south. There was speculation that the bill could be altered to give the south dominion Home Rule, but the government, with

Long predictably defiant, rejected the idea of making concessions to Sinn Féin. Towards the end of 1920, it was clear that the bill would have to be implemented. However, in the prevailing circumstances, it would only apply to the new state of Northern Ireland, where it appeared likely that the Unionists would be handed a permanent majority. The government had surrendered tamely to Unionist pressure for partition to proceed on a six-county basis, but a fundamental concern for the government was that it would rely on the Ulster Unionists to make the bill work. Realising the government's predicament, the price of Craig's cooperation was a six-county bloc. There was also a lack of conviction in the government's desire to see Ireland reunited at some date in the near future.

While it was evident that a majority of ministers wanted the Government of Ireland Bill to facilitate ultimate unity, this was more of an aspiration than a firm commitment. Indeed, Charles Craig had warned MPs that Ulster Unionists did not view partition as a temporary feature. They also planned to ignore the Council of Ireland, which was to be drawn from representatives of the Belfast and Dublin parliaments. It would have fairly modest powers, though it was anticipated that these could be widened with the full support of northern and southern representatives. In effect, therefore, the Ulster Unionists would have a veto over the operation of the Council of Ireland. The scheme to consider matters of common concern such as transport and fishing afforded equal representation for Ulster Unionists on the council, but cooperation was unlikely. Austen Chamberlain perceptively noted that reunification could not be imposed by a Westminster government but would only come about through agreement between north and south. However, the British government could have done more to facilitate future reunification. A nine-county parliament and a Council of Ireland with real powers might have gone some way to achieving this. Of course, this was not Lloyd George's main priority. He was anxious to end Westminster involvement in Ulster affairs. It was the influence of Ulster Unionists, together with the government's dependence on them to work the new legislation, that determined the outcome.

While a number of southern Unionists launched a vehement attack on the bill in the House of Lords, it made its way through parliament with only minor alterations and received royal assent on 23 December 1920. In a self-congratulatory speech the previous evening, Lloyd George informed the Commons that he had been faced with a hugely complex problem in Ireland. Only by embracing both Home Rule and partition was his government able to resolve this difficulty. The new legislation included a number of clauses designed to limit the powers of the devolved parliaments. Section 5 of the act prevented either parliament from passing laws that interfered with religious liberty or equality. In theory, this would stop the Belfast parliament enacting legislation that would disadvantage the Catholic minority. As a further safety net, Section 75 of the act decreed that in all cases the regional parliaments would be subordinate to Westminster. This meant that any law passed by the Belfast parliament could be annulled by Westminster instructing the governor, the king's representative, to withhold royal assent. More restrictions applied to the range of services over which the regional parliaments could exercise control. The financial constraints imposed on the devolved administrations were particularly severe.

The act took effect from 3 May 1921, and elections for both parliaments were scheduled three weeks later. In the south Sinn Féin, as expected, refused to recognise the new assembly. Instead, the election was used to return the Second Dáil with 124 Sinn Féin TDs elected without a contest. The remaining four seats were allocated to Trinity College. In the north a full-blooded election campaign resulted in the return of 40 Unionist MPs, with the remaining 12 MPs split evenly between Devlin's Nationalists and Sinn Féin. The Unionists had surprised themselves with the scale of their victory. Craig, who had formally taken over from Carson as Unionist leader in February, had the task of selecting the first Northern Ireland cabinet. All of the ministers had been prominent in the prewar struggle against Home Rule: Hugh McDowell Pollock (finance) Sir Richard Dawson Bates (home affairs), John Miller Andrews (labour), Lord Londonderry (education) and Edward Archdale (agriculture and commerce).

Sir Richard Dawson Bates (1876–1949). ©National Portrait Gallery, London

The challenges facing the Northern Ireland government, 1921–25

The rapid establishment of a separate administration including the requisite bureaucratic paraphernalia marked a significant achievement for Ulster Unionism. Craig, the new prime minister, understood that the creation of the institutions and the day-to-day functioning of an administration would give the new state strong roots. It would also convey the impression of an air of permanence around partition. As far as possible, the Ulster Unionists had sought to create a clear separation of the powers transferred from the old Irish executive. The objective was to ensure that the new Northern Ireland state was virtually independent from the rest of Ireland. The key administrative role was played by Sir Ernest Clark. In September 1920, Craig had secured Clark's services from Dublin Castle and, in Basil Brooke's description, Clark became "midwife to the new Province of Ulster". Clark remarked that he started with just "a table and chair and act of Parliament", but his administrative ability oversaw the establishment of government departments and a civil service.

In the summer of 1921, the Unionist government was benefiting from the assistance of nearly 20 administrative experts from Whitehall. Delayed by the prolonged negotiations between Lloyd George and Sinn Féin, the final transfer of services took place before the close of 1921. A total of 300 volunteers were moved from Dublin to fill new civil service posts in Belfast. This success in establishing a functioning administration gave the Unionist leadership a much-needed boost, as they faced significant threats from a number of quarters. The Anglo-Irish Treaty was, on the surface, an all-Ireland agreement. It provided for the operation of a Boundary Commission, should the Belfast parliament, as expected, exercise its right to opt out of an all-Ireland assembly. With some doubt hanging over the future of Northern Ireland, the solid foundation work in establishing the new state apparatus proved to be significant.

When the new parliament was opened by George V on 22 June 1921, there was much optimism about a bright future in a state that would seek to ensure fair treatment for all its citizens. Yet it quickly became clear that the new state would struggle to deal with long-standing divisions in Ulster society. Before partition had been implemented, sectarian violence that began in Derry in May 1920 spread quickly to Belfast with disastrous consequences. "The Troubles", as this period became known, lasted for two years until June 1922. The Unionist government's response to the violence greatly exacerbated tension between the two communities. Before the eruption of the fighting in Derry, violence from the War of Independence had occasionally spilled over into the six-county area, heightening tension between the two communities. The outcome of the local elections, which took place in the city in January 1920, also fuelled Unionist anger. For the first time Derry had a Nationalist mayor, and this led to increased tension. On 15 May a gun battle took place between the RIC and local units of the IRA. The violence intensified over the next few weeks and was notable for the involvement of UVF members who were allowed to attack Catholic areas with little interference from the police. By the time calm was restored, there had been more than 20 deaths.

The violence soon spread to Belfast, where an inflammatory speech by Carson at the city's Twelfth demonstration undoubtedly stoked Unionist anger. The Unionist leader warned the government that if it could not protect Ulster from the republican threat, then "we will take the matter into our own hands. We will reorganise". Carson's rhetoric had spread fear among the city's Catholic community. This was compounded by the shooting of Colonel G. F. Smyth, the Royal Irish Constabulary (RIC) divisional commander, in Munster on 17 July. Smyth had been implicated in Tomás MacCurtain's murder in March, and his routine condemnation of Sinn Féin made him a target for the IRA in County Cork. However, Smyth was a popular figure in his native Banbridge, and his funeral on 21 July was a prelude to serious attacks on the town's small Catholic population. Smyth's assassination, together with the refusal of southern rail workers to transport the body back to Banbridge, also sparked violence in Belfast, where Carson's Twelfth speech was still being absorbed. It was the Catholic workforce in the shipyard that felt the full force of loyalist mobs. That evening, which was the first day back at work after the July holidays, trains carrying Protestant shipyard workers were attacked close to the predominantly Catholic Short Strand area of the city. By the following day, 22 July, trouble had spread to other places of work such as Mackie's and the Sirocco works. In total, about 10,000 Catholic workers had been driven from their employment, and Catholic-owned businesses, particularly in the east of the city, were attacked.

An uneasy calm was restored, but this was shattered by the shooting of district inspector Swanzy in Lisburn on 22 August 1920. Swanzy had previously been named at the inquest into MacCurtain's killing. He was shot dead by an IRA unit as he left a church service in the company of his sister. Serious trouble erupted in the town immediately after the shooting. Catholic homes and businesses were targeted, and many of the town's Catholic population fled to Dundalk. This upsurge in violence led to a revival of the UVF. The UUC had taken a decision at the end of June to revive the force, but Protestant vigilante groups had already been organised in a number of areas in response to the growing disorder. The most prominent of these was the group in Fermanagh under Brooke's leadership. Based on his Colebrooke estate, Brooke, who had served as an officer in World War I, formed "Fermanagh vigilance" before the end of April 1920. Brooke would go on to become prime minister of Northern Ireland in 1943, and he wanted his local force to be recognised by the Westminster government as special constables. This prompted other Unionist leaders to support growing calls to have a revived UVF reconstituted as a special constabulary that could provide assistance for the police. The violence in the summer of 1920 strengthened this demand. Craig also believed that the establishment of such an official force could curb growing loyalist sectarian attacks, which were clearly damaging the Unionist cause at Westminster.

Naturally, the authorities in London were hesitant about the creation of an official armed force that would be almost exclusively Protestant and would be responsible for upholding the rule of law. However, a precedent had been set in the south where the Tans and Auxiliaries were operational by the autumn of 1920. The government surrendered to Unionist pressure, and the formation of the Ulster Special Constabulary (USC) was announced on 22 October 1920. Again, in a repeat of the deployment of the Black and Tans and Auxiliaries, the British government failed to consider fully the implications of such a decision. The USC was divided into three classes. The "A" Specials were full-time, paid constables who could be dispatched to any trouble spot to provide support for the RIC. The "B" Specials were part-time constables who received an allowance and operated in their own localities. The "C" Specials were an unpaid reserve of usually older men who could be called upon in an emergency. By the close of 1920, 3,500 A Specials and 16,000 B Specials had been enrolled in the USC. As anticipated, the bulk of these recruits were ex-UVF men who would prove effective when operating in their own areas. Indeed, the USC enjoyed considerable success in combating the IRA. Still, its sectarian character, and the fact that some of its members undoubtedly engaged in attacks on Catholics, easily outweighed whatever benefits the force may have delivered on the security front.

While Ulster was largely free from the effects of the War of Independence, violence became a recurring theme during the winter of 1920–21. In April 1921 there was a fresh wave of killings in Belfast, and the IRA increased its attacks in border areas. At the British government's request, Craig made an astonishing personal attempt to reach an agreement with de Valera. On 5 May he travelled to Dublin at the height of the violence in the south, and he was taken to a secret location to meet the Sinn Féin president. The "peace faction" in Dublin Castle led by Andy Cope had been active in laying the ground for reconciliation with the republican movement and believed that a face-to-face meeting between Craig and de Valera might be useful. Reaction to news of the meeting in the British press was positive. The chief secretary, Hamar Greenwood, gushed that it was the "most hopeful thing in 750 years". The timescale was indeed appropriate, as Craig later recalled that after half an hour in the meeting de Valera had got as far as Brian Boru. In Craig's report he continued in this vein. The two men parted amicably, but no progress had been made. De Valera had been dumbfounded by Craig's obvious devotion to the Empire and the Union, recording that the Ulster leader "spoke of the Union as if it were a mystical thing".

However, the most significant consequence of the tête-à-tête was the cool response from Craig's colleagues once news of the meeting was in the public domain. Of course, the election campaign was underway in the north and tensions were running high. One prominent figure, Samuel McGuffin, the MP for Shankhill and candidate for North Belfast in the forthcoming Northern Ireland parliament election, denounced the visit on the evening of Craig's return to Belfast. As a new leader who had only been in post for three months, this was an early test of Craig's capabilities. His response was swift. On 6 May he summoned all of the Unionist election candidates to a meeting in the Old Town Hall. He assured them that there would be no further concessions after the Government of Ireland Act, adding that going forward the Council of Ireland would be the forum for any future contact between north and south. Yet he also stuck by his claim that the meeting with de Valera had been a success, as Sinn Féin was now fully aware of the Unionist position.

However, the Unionist leader would soon be reminded of the threat to his position. Northern Ireland's interests were subordinated to the greater need of Anglo-Irish relations, when the Lloyd George government and Sinn Féin agreed to a truce as a prelude to negotiations. Unsurprisingly, the partition question was reopened during these negotiations, as the Irish delegation sought to exploit what it regarded as the British government's greatest weakness. Westminster was not due to transfer security and policing powers to the Northern Ireland government until 22 November 1921, and a decision was taken to reduce the security presence following the signing of the truce on 11 July. This involved the immobilisation of the USC and the withdrawal of the army from peace-keeping duties. Craig's new government, which had not been consulted on the decision to immobilise the USC, was furious. It was already under pressure before the upsurge in violence between July and September when loyalist vigilantes began taking law and order into their own hands. Craig pointed the finger of blame at the Westminster government, which had suspended the USC, claiming that the force acted as a safety valve for Protestant aggression. Furthermore, Unionists were enraged by the sight of the IRA regrouping and openly drilling in the north under the protection of the truce. They demanded that the suspension of the USC should be lifted. By the end of September, the Westminster government had relented, though it stipulated that the B Specials should be confined to protection duties in Protestant areas, leaving the regular police responsible for patrolling Catholic districts.

During the week in late November when security powers were transferred to Belfast, more than 30 lives were lost in bitter sectarian clashes, including seven who were killed in trams which had been targeted by IRA bombs. Further violence in December brought the number killed in Belfast over the course of 1921 to more than 100. The IRA was attacking the new state, while Craig was failing in his struggle to keep a lid on Protestant violence. His answer to both problems was to strengthen the USC, and the force began recruiting additional

In June 1921, the IRA blew up this train near Newry. It was conveying King George V's horses and officers from Belfast to Dublin for the Holyhead boat, after the opening of the Northern Ireland Parliament.

personnel before the end of 1921. The difficulty of sourcing extra revenue to fund an expanded USC was conveniently overlooked. The violence intensified during the first six months of 1922, claiming the lives of 236 people, with Catholic losses outnumbering Protestants by two to one. Attempts by Craig – this time in conjunction with Michael Collins – to defuse the tension failed, as the pacts of January and March quickly collapsed.

This new wave of violence had its origins in the "Monaghan footballers" affair. On 14 January Dan Hogan, a Clones railway clerk and brother of Michael, the Tipperary footballer shot dead in Croke Park on Bloody Sunday, was arrested by USC members in Dromore, County Tyrone. Hogan was part of a Monaghan football team that was en route to Derry city where a challenge match was due to take place. However, a search by the Specials uncovered documents detailing a plan to secure the release of three republican prisoners awaiting execution in Derry Jail. When a number of the players were placed under arrest, the IRA, acting on orders issued by Eoin O'Duffy, kidnapped over 40 prominent Unionists in Tyrone and Fermanagh on 7–8 February. They were quickly transported across the border and held as hostages pending the release of the Monaghan footballers. The IRA operation spread panic among Protestants living close to the border. A few days later on Saturday, 11 February 1922, a party of 19 A Specials were dispatched to Enniskillen from their training base at Newtownards. The rail route chosen for the journey meant that the 19 Specials, all of whom wore uniforms, would have to change trains at Clones in County Monaghan. When the local IRA unit was informed of their presence at Clones station, they rushed to the scene and a gun battle ensued in which four Specials died. Tension on the border was eased by the decision to reprieve the Derry prisoners, while Westminster put pressure on the Craig government to order the release of the Monaghan footballers. Collins, in turn, made the necessary arrangements for the staged release of the kidnapped loyalists.

An uneasy peace returned to the border area, but the Clones affair had ignited a wave of sectarian clashes in Belfast. In a three-day period, 13–15 February, a total of 31 were killed in this violence, with Catholics again suffering disproportionately. A further 60 lives were lost in the city during March. These included four members of the McMahon family and their lodger, who were gunned down in their Antrim Road home on 23 March. The McMahons were part of a well-known business family in Belfast and, though friendly with Joe Devlin, had no involvement in politics. It was immediately claimed that a rogue element in the Belfast police had been involved in the atrocity. The event received wide coverage in the British press. It had been the aim of the perpetrators to spread terror in the city's Catholic community. The Craig government, particularly Bates, the minister of home affairs, was fiercely criticised for a lack of impartiality when it came to law and order. In the following week a bomb was thrown into a Protestant home, killing the male occupant and his two young sons. In London, meanwhile, Churchill was becoming increasingly frustrated by the Belfast government's failure to bring the violence to an end. He brought Craig and Collins together again at the end of March, when they agreed a second pact. Collins had been quick to seize upon the McMahon murders, as he sought to bring pressure to bear on Craig's administration with the aim of securing greater protection for the Catholic minority. In the previous month Sir Henry Wilson had been appointed as security adviser to the Northern Ireland government. Collins held him responsible for the increased persecution of northern Catholics, though he had little evidence for the claim.

The Unionist government's response to this spate of violence was to rush through the Civil Authorities (Special Powers) Act which became law on 7 April 1922. While it was viewed as emergency legislation that would run for one year, it was set to become permanent. The Special Powers Act was a draconian piece of legislation that gave extensive powers of arrest and detention to the Royal Ulster Constabulary (RUC), which was formed on 5 April 1922. The act also allowed special courts to hand out a variety of punishments, including flogging and the death sentence, though the authorities initially hesitated in applying the full force of the new legislation. Clearly the act was controversial, and serious objections were raised in London and Dublin. Yet it was equally clear that the authorities at Westminster were relieved to evade responsibility for Ulster's problems, preferring to leave contentious issues such as security to the new administration in Belfast. Here, Craig played a crucial role. Many of the key players at Westminster viewed him as the one Unionist statesman. Craig was able to offer reassurance in his frequent visits to London, arguing that special measures were required to overcome the grave difficulties facing his government. While the Unionist premier was an effective ambassador for his government in London, his calm leadership was frequently missed in Belfast where important decisions were left to hardliners such as Bates.

A new burst of violence in May 1922 saw the government make extensive use of the wide powers contained in the Special Powers Act. On 22 May W. J. Twaddell, a Belfast Unionist MP in the new Northern Ireland parliament, was shot dead in the city centre. The Craig government responded by introducing internment, and the USC arrested 200 Catholics that evening. Those detained were held in appalling conditions on the *Argenta,* a prison ship moored in Belfast Lough. The internment strategy overseen by Bates defied logic. Of the 66 people killed in May, two-thirds of the victims were Catholics, but only Catholics were targeted in the arrests. Moreover, between May 1922 and Christmas 1924, when internment was suspended, the vast majority of those brought before the special courts were Catholics. This failure to tackle Protestant violence undermined the new state's legitimacy in the eyes of the minority community.

The prewar arming of the Ulster Volunteers ensured that loyalists had easy access to weapons. The most notorious of these loyalist paramilitary groups was the Ulster Protestant Association (UPA). The UPA had its origins in the rabidly sectarian Belfast Protestant Association, and it was active in the city from the autumn of 1920. Although the government had access to intelligence about UPA operations, it was slow to act against this violent organisation. The authorities justified this strategy by arguing that their priority was to deal with the republican threat, as the very survival of the state depended on defeating the IRA. Indeed, the security forces did take belated action against the UPA when the IRA threat subsided. Following a number of key arrests, the UPA was wound up in February 1923. Undoubtedly, a more timely response to the UPA threat would have prevented considerable loss of life. A further factor complicating the new state's response to Protestant violence was the apparent collusion between loyalist paramilitaries and the security forces. In Belfast, one rogue police element operating from the Shankill Road was implicated in a number of serious attacks on Catholics, including the McMahon murders. Many of these attacks were prompted by the killing of police officers in the city. There is also little doubt that reprisals were conducted by the Special Constabulary outside Belfast. Therefore, while the USC may have played a pivotal role in the defeat of the IRA during The Troubles, its actions served to widen community divisions in the new state.

When complaints were made to the British government about the Unionist administration's discrimination, its only official response was to dispatch Sir Stephen Tallents, Lord Fitzalan's private secretary, to Belfast at the end of June. His brief was to conduct a one-man investigation into the reasons for the collapse of the second Craig–Collins pact and report his findings to Churchill. While Tallents was critical of Bates, he blamed the IRA for most of the violence in the north and generally overlooked the sectarian attacks carried out by loyalist mobs. On his advice the government rejected the need for a wider judicial inquiry into the violence. This outcome delighted both Craig and the British ministers who were anxious to stay out of Ulster affairs.

In fact, the Unionist government had faced a serious threat at the end of May, when IRA columns entered the north and seized control of the Belleek-Pettigo triangle, an area of approximately 30 square miles close to the Fermanagh-Donegal border. Collins, angered by the Belfast government's failure to protect the Catholic minority, had some involvement in the planning of a joint IRA northern offensive. This had the twin objectives of attempting to maintain IRA unity following the army split and adding to Craig's difficulties in the north. The IRA invasion quickly spread panic among Unionists living in the border area. With Lloyd George's government keen to avoid direct military involvement as civil war looked inevitable in the south, Churchill seized the initiative by sending troops to the area with orders to dislodge the IRA and secure the border. This was quickly accomplished as artillery was used on the occupying forces. Thereafter, there were isolated incidents along the border, but the outbreak of the civil war at the end of June lifted the pressure on the northern security forces. It also eased Craig's political difficulties. Belfast continued to experience occasional bursts of violence, but an uneasy peace descended in the summer of 1922.

The Northern Ireland state had survived, but the cost of survival had been high. The Unionist government concentrated its security strategy in combating IRA attacks. Consequently, Protestant violence went unchecked. In the two years of The Troubles, 428 lives were lost, the majority of them Catholic, but the government hesitated to deploy the full rigour of the law to curb Protestant violence. Significantly, the sectarian nature of some of the IRA's operations during the northern campaign led to urgent demands from grass-roots Unionists for a much more assertive security policy. While the IRA campaign primarily targeted the Crown Forces, it also engaged in sectarian reprisal attacks. In one of the most infamous incidents in the entire revolutionary period, a group of Volunteers under the command of Frank Aiken crossed the border on 17 June 1922 and carried out a series of arson attacks on isolated Protestant farms near Newry. Six Protestant civilians were shot dead during the operation. These killings at Altnaveigh were followed by a USC reprisal in the following week, when three Catholics were killed in Cushendall, County Antrim. Almost immediately, however, IRA activity in the north ceased with the outbreak of the civil war. The final killing in The Troubles took place on 5 October when a Catholic died at the hands of the UPA.

In addition to the security problem, the new state was plagued by serious financial difficulties during its formative years. Not surprisingly, security costs placed a heavy financial burden on the new administration. This was compounded by the financial limitations and constraints that had been imposed under the provisions of the Government of Ireland Act. Under the legislation, Northern Ireland was liable for an annual "imperial contribution", which was calculated against the cost of imperial services. However, it was set at such a high level, initially close to £8 million per annum, that it threatened to bankrupt the province. Craig's government made repeated requests for a reduction in the imperial contribution, but there was little sympathy from the Treasury in London. At the same time, the province was experiencing serious economic difficulties related to the general postwar slump. Unemployment in Northern Ireland had been increasing since the spring of 1920, with the key employers in the shipbuilding, engineering and textile industries laying off workers as demand fell sharply. With unemployment approaching 100,000, the new Unionist administration committed itself to a "step-by-step" policy, meaning that it would keep pace with Britain in the provision of major cash social services. Yet the province's relative poverty in comparison to other parts of the United Kingdom created immediate financial difficulties for the Belfast government, particularly in relation to unemployment insurance.

Craig and his colleagues had pledged to maintain Northern Ireland's unemployment benefits at the British level, but this proved disastrous for a small country experiencing such a high level of unemployment. Towards the end of 1923, Hugh McDowell Pollock, the minister of finance, was forced to admit that Northern Ireland's unemployment fund was insolvent. The Unionist cabinet pleaded with Westminster for a complete revision of the financial relationship between Belfast and London, but the Treasury dismissed the case. Instead, it was suggested that the Northern Ireland authorities should reduce unemployment benefits to a more affordable level, but Unionist ministers viewed this as politically dangerous. Any lowering of the unemployment payment would undermine support for the Unionist government among the Protestant working class. It was 1925 before the Belfast administration enjoyed any financial respite. Under the terms of the Colwyn Award, the British government agreed that domestic expenditure on Northern Ireland services, such as welfare payments, rather than the imperial contribution, would be the first charge on the province's income. This brought some form of financial stability for the remainder of the 1920s, though severe problems returned in the great economic recession of the early 1930s.

In November 1921 the Belfast government assumed responsibility for law and order. It relied on the USC as its primary peace-keeping force. Of course, when violence intensified in the first half of 1922, the cost of security spiralled. Craig urged the British government to meet the additional financial cost, but Treasury officials argued that as law and order was a devolved responsibility, the Belfast administration must find the money to finance the USC. In the end, despite Treasury hostility, the Westminster government agreed to provide the necessary financial support for the Special Constabulary. Craig had played a key role in persuading the authorities in London to treat Northern Ireland generously. Westminster missed an opportunity to make additional financial support for the new Unionist administration contingent on evidence that sensitive issues relating to the minority were handled more fairly. Still, Craig was able to argue that some of the financial problems faced by his government were outside Unionist control. In January 1921 the Dáil gave its formal backing to the "Belfast boycott", an embargo on Ulster goods that had earlier been imposed by Sinn Féin local councils. The boycott was retaliation for the expulsion of Catholic shipyard workers in July 1920. The Dáil hoped that the use of such economic pressure would force Unionists to end discrimination against the minority community in the north. The boycott certainly damaged the Northern Ireland economy, as exports to the south collapsed. Craig attempted to negotiate an end to the boycott in the two Craig–Collins pacts of early 1922, but nothing was achieved. Moreover, Catholic workers were not reinstated to their positions of employment in the shipyards or the large engineering concerns. One unintended consequence of the Belfast Boycott was that it widened the economic gap between north and south and tended to reinforce partition.

Again, the civil war greatly reduced pressure on the Unionist government, as it sought to come to terms with the minority community's strategy of non-recognition of the new state. All shades of Nationalism had been bitterly opposed to partition, and both Sinn Féin and the old Irish Parliamentary Party representatives refused to take their seats in the new parliament. Nationalist disaffection further increased, as the Unionist government's policy in the areas of law and order and the administration of justice was characterised by discrimination. Clearly, the use of internment and the Special Powers Act, together with the role played by the Special Constabulary, deepened divisions and strengthened the Catholic minority's determination to withhold their allegiance to the new state. When the

RUC assumed responsibility for policing on 1 June 1922, there was some hope that it would quickly acquire the reputation of an impartial force and gain the confidence of the Nationalist community. The intention was to build the RUC to an establishment of 3,000, one-third of whom would be Catholics. In the recruitment process preference was given to ex-RIC officers, but the new force failed to attract Catholics in sufficient numbers.

The issue of policing became a recurring problem for the Northern Ireland government in its relations with the Nationalist minority. Certainly, the minority's non-recognition policy proved an embarrassment for the Unionist administration. Parliament, with only Unionist MPs in the chamber, had an unreal atmosphere, but it was at local council level that the situation became more serious. In January and June 1920, a combination of Nationalists and Sinn Féiners had won a majority on Derry Corporation and both Tyrone and Fermanagh county councils. When partition was implemented, these local government bodies refused to recognise the new Unionist government, instead giving their allegiance to Dáil Éireann. The Unionist cabinet was furious and was determined to bring about change. Consequently, the Local Government Bill was rushed through the Northern Ireland parliament in the summer of 1922. Its headline feature was the abolition of PR in local government elections. The intention was to use the majoritarian voting system and, crucially, the redrawing of local government electoral boundaries to give the Unionist party an advantage in future local government elections.

Nationalists in the north were outraged by these new proposals. Collins intervened on their behalf, warning Westminster that the changes would not only discriminate against northern Catholics but also impose a severe strain on Anglo-Irish relations. The 1922 Local Government Bill passed all stages in the Belfast parliament by 5 July, but royal assent was delayed until 11 September. The authorities at Westminster had sought to use the interim period to exert pressure on the Belfast administration in an attempt to force the devolved government to withdraw the measure. The Lloyd George government was clearly concerned about the implications of these controversial changes, and the cabinet was embarrassed by the development. Craig understood Westminster's reservations, but he shared his government's determination to insist on the changes. When Craig discovered that the British government was instructing the governor to withhold royal assent, he threatened to resign and call an election on the local government issue. The prospect of a new constitutional crisis with the Ulster problem again taking centre stage at Westminster filled the coalition government with a sense of gloom, and a decision to authorise royal assent to the Local Government Bill was finally taken with some relief.

The way in which the crisis over the bill unfolded had an important bearing on the future relationship between London and Belfast. The Government of Ireland Act had, of course, confirmed Westminster's supremacy, but the government in London experienced problems in reining in the Unionist administration in Belfast. Still, Westminster had chosen the easy option. Clearly, it did not want to become embroiled in Northern Ireland affairs and was more than happy to leave controversial issues to the Unionist government. Financial pressure could have been used to greater effect, but, significantly, Westminster was dependent on the Unionists to work the Government of Ireland Act. It was likely, moreover, that had Craig resigned, his place would have been taken by a more extreme figure. While the Westminster authorities may have harboured reservations about Craig, they believed that the Unionist premier offered the best hope for political stability in the north, and this would enable London to keep Northern Ireland at arm's length.

The 1922 Northern Ireland Local Government Act achieved what Unionists required with local government electoral areas being redrawn to maximise the Unionist vote. This was gerrymandering, and the practice enabled Unionists to regain control of Tyrone and Fermanagh county councils and, more controversially, Derry city council. Naturally, this left the Unionist administration open to further charges of discrimination, though Craig's government made some effort to act impartially in other areas. The 1923 Education Act set out to create non-denominational schools under local control. The first minister of education, Lord Londonderry, had never shared the narrow sectarian views of some of his colleagues, and he was determined to rid Northern Ireland schools of clerical control. Initially, he faced a major problem with Catholic teachers in Catholic schools who refused to recognise the authority of his department. Their stance was supported by the provisional government in Dublin, which took over the payment of these Catholic teachers' salaries from the beginning of 1922. For a ten-month period until October 1922, nearly 800 teachers in 270 Northern Ireland schools refused to accept salaries from the Northern Ireland government and were paid by the ministry of finance in Dublin. However, the cost of this action, running at £18,000 per month, was putting an intolerable strain on the provisional government's stretched finances, and it was decided to stop the payments at the end of October.

Thereafter, Londonderry's focus was on preparations for his forthcoming bill. The groundwork for the bill had been completed by a committee under the chairmanship of Robert Lynn, a Unionist MP and editor of the *Northern Whig*, that had begun work in September 1921 to examine education service in the new state. While the committee claimed to take account of Catholic views on education, no Catholic agreed to serve on the committee. The Catholic hierarchy was furious at the content of the 1923 Londonderry bill and the bishops demanded a return to clerical control. Clerical criticism of the measure, which wanted all children educated together irrespective of their religion, also came from the three main Protestant churches. The Protestant church leaders enlisted the help of the Orange Order, as they pressed Londonderry for a return to clerical influence in the state schools. Protestant opposition was meticulously organised, and Craig agreed to surrender to Protestant demands. The resulting 1925 Education Act overturned Londonderry's plans for non-denominational education, and the minister resigned in January 1926. Following further pressure from both Protestant and Catholic church leaders, a further Education Act in 1930 established a dual education system that both religious groups had sought.

Craig held the premiership until his death in November 1940. His capitulation to pressure from the Protestant churches and the Orange Order in 1925 had already become a feature of his leadership. He had called a Northern Ireland general election in April 1925, when Unionist voters were asked to focus on the border question. The Boundary Commission had finally convened in November 1924, and the three commissioners were due to begin gathering evidence when they toured the frontier in the spring of 1925. Craig was determined to demonstrate that the electorate stood fully behind his government's pledge not to surrender any part of the six-county area. To ensure that this would happen, Craig needed to restore Protestant unity, and this required him to bow to populist pressure on the education issue. Of course, making defence of the border the defining issue in any election played to Unionist strengths, and Craig's "Not an Inch" slogan was popular with his supporters.

Indeed, the Unionist government had already demonstrated its defiance of the Boundary Commission. Craig had refused to nominate a commissioner to represent Northern Ireland. This forced Westminster to amend the Treaty and appoint J. R. Fisher, a former newspaper editor and prominent Unionist, to represent the Belfast government. Although the border had been untouched for four years, the Unionists viewed the Boundary Commission as a serious threat and Craig described it as "the root of all evil". The frontier weaved its way along a 280-mile stretch using county boundaries that had never been designed for such a purpose. This created a number of anomalies along the border that were, not surprisingly, highlighted by opponents of partition. Perhaps the greatest anomaly was an area on the Fermanagh–Monaghan border known as the "Drummully Salient". This was a parcel of land extending about four miles (six kilometres) north to south, and, two miles (three kilometres) at its widest point, west to east. The salient was entirely in County Monaghan but was almost completely surrounded by County Fermanagh. Only a very narrow neck of land, approximately 100 yards across, linked the salient to the rest of County Monaghan, and it could only be accessed by road or rail from Northern Ireland.

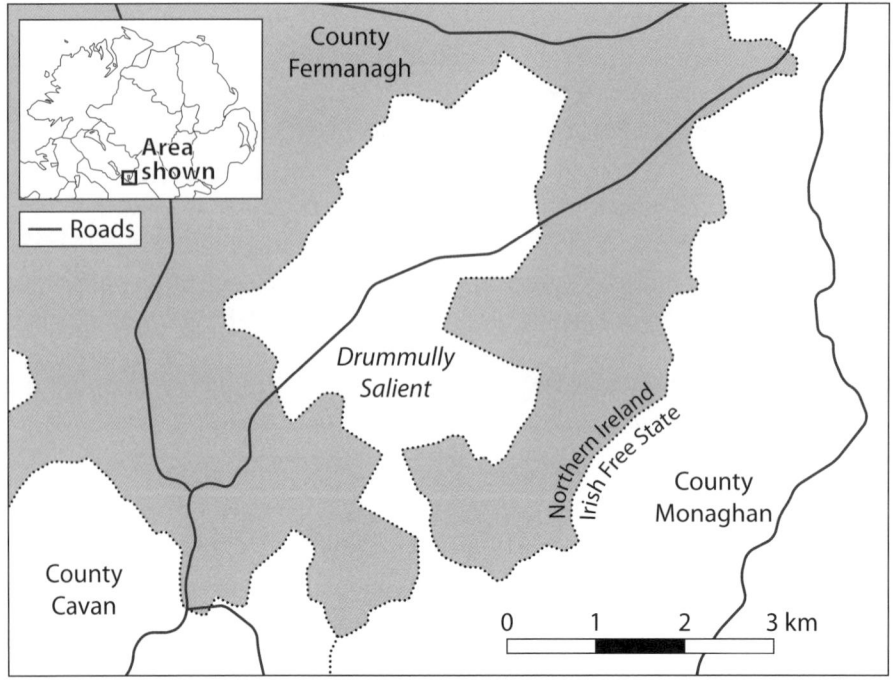

The Drummully Salient.

Drummully featured prominently in the Boundary Commission's deliberations. Its Protestant inhabitants, led by a local Church of Ireland clergyman, presented a persuasive case for the transfer of the salient to Northern Ireland. Indeed, there were a number of other areas in North Monaghan and East Donegal where local Protestant communities met with the Commission to argue their case for inclusion in Northern Ireland. Craig was fully aware of the plight of border Unionists living in the Irish Free State. Since the establishment of the Northern Ireland state, the Unionist premier had been bombarded with correspondence from "loyalists" in such areas reminding him of their predicament.

Undoubtedly, Craig felt a greater sense of responsibility than any of his cabinet colleagues for these communities. However, his real concern was that the Boundary Commission would recommend the transfer of significant areas of Northern Ireland to the Irish Free State. Fermanagh, Tyrone and Derry city had, as the 1920 local government elections confirmed, clear Nationalist majorities. Nationalists in the north were optimistic that the Boundary Commission would endorse a major boundary revision, but the Unionist government had received secret information from Fisher, indicating that the Commission was only considering the transfer of border townlands. Of course, when the Boundary Commission completed its work, its final report was leaked to the *Morning Post* on 7 November 1925. Nationalists were outraged, and MacNeill, the Irish Free

State representative, resigned in protest, but the Cosgrave government had no contingency plan in place. Yet the Boundary Commission's report, had it been implemented, would have led to significant change. First, the border would have been shortened by 50 miles, as 183,290 acres would have been transferred to the Free State, with 49,242 acres going to Northern Ireland. In terms of population, some 31,000 people (including 28,000 Catholics) were to be transferred to the Free State, with 7,600 (including 4,830 Protestants) moving in the opposite direction. Most of the territory to be transferred to the Irish Free State was on the Fermanagh border and in South Armagh. However, it was the four-mile-wide strip that would become part of Northern Ireland that placed the Cosgrave government in a very embarrassing position. Following hurried negotiations, the tripartite agreement was signed on 3 December 1925. It confirmed the existing border, and Craig presented the agreement as a triumph for his government.

The Northern Ireland state had survived internal and external challenges, and Craig predicted a new era of stability. Still, Catholic disaffection with the new state remained strong. Indeed, many of the policies pursued by the Unionist government that were deemed necessary for its survival had contributed to this sense of alienation. Craig's instinct was to foster reconciliation, but he frequently took the easy option and allowed Bates and other hardliners in his government to institutionalise Unionist supremacy. Thus, the changes to local government, the lack of impartiality in policing and justice, and the systemic discrimination in areas such as employment combined to intensify Catholic opposition to the new state. Towards the end of the 1920s, Joe Devlin, the Ulster Nationalist leader, moved tentatively towards greater participation in the institutions of the state. Devlin and Craig shared a mutual respect, but he received little by way of encouragement from other Unionists. By 1929, Unionists had also taken steps to abolish PR in Northern Ireland parliamentary elections. Ulster Unionists were intent on suffocating political alternatives, preferring to keep alive the old sectarian division in politics in which, of course, their numerical advantage would ensure continued success at the ballot box. The challenge to create a more normal society was a daunting one given the circumstances, but it was a challenge that was never taken up.

Conclusion

Partition was a device used by the British government to placate Ulster Unionists who had demonstrated conclusively that they would not accept Dublin rule. The concept had entered the public discourse in 1912 with the failed attempt by Agar-Robartes to amend the third Home Rule Bill by excluding four counties from its operation. When the Liberal cabinet subsequently ruled out the coercion of these Ulster Unionists, partition became a likely compromise. It was, of course, a compromise that was acceptable to Bonar Law and a Conservative Party that had enthusiastically backed the Ulster Unionist militarist campaign against Home Rule. The idea of partition was also accepted, albeit reluctantly and only on a limited and temporary basis, by Redmond and an IPP that had looked to the Liberal government to stand firm on all-Ireland Home Rule. Ironically, the leader who was most identified with partition was the southern Unionist, Edward Carson. He displayed fleeting concern about the fate of Unionists in the south and west.

By 1913, however, having abandoned the policy of using Ulster to destroy Home Rule, Carson had decided that the exclusion of six counties from Dublin rule would represent the best outcome for Unionism. Like Bonar Law, with whom he enjoyed a close relationship, Carson recognised that public opinion in Britain disliked Home Rule, and he exploited this to the benefit of Ulster Unionists. The outbreak of the war postponed the Home Rule problem, but important parameters had been established. The Easter Rising strengthened these parameters and further entrenched partition. It also allowed Ulster Unionists to justify their earlier warnings about the obvious dangers in subjecting themselves to Dublin rule. Indeed, Sinn Féin was later unable to produce a workable alternative to partition. De Valera was no more successful than Redmond in preventing the establishment of two states in Ireland.

After the war the Conservative-dominated coalition government was obliged to return to the Ulster problem. The one enthusiast in the cabinet, Walter Long, headed a committee charged with drafting a fourth Home Rule Bill. From the outset Long proceeded on the basis that there should be two parliaments in Ireland. This was a significant departure from previous partition proposals, as "Ulster" would now have its own Home Rule parliament. Strangely, Long firmly believed that a Belfast parliament would "enormously minimise the partition issue". Long favoured a nine-county bloc, as it would provide the basis for earlier reunification, and he included a Council of Ireland forum in his bill to smooth the path to unity. By 1920 Craig was the leading Unionist voice, and he fronted a determined campaign to have a six-county Northern Ireland. Long, who had been stunned by Craig's support for a devolved northern parliament, acceded to his wishes. A Northern Ireland state comprising six counties was formed.

Craig had grasped the importance of quickly establishing the necessary bureaucratic structures to give the new state an air of permanence. As prime minister, he faced some serious challenges, not least an IRA campaign to destroy the new state. Northern Ireland survived this threat, and the outbreak of the Irish Civil War at the end of June 1922 came as a relief to the new Unionist administration. By that point, however, Craig's government had gone too far down the road of repression. Unionist ministers were subsequently unable to escape from their bunker mentality. They failed to begin the process of reconciliation with the Catholic minority, and this ensured that the new state was plagued by political instability. The other, more surprising, problem that dogged the Unionist government was its often-difficult relationship with Westminster. Yet this had been a long-standing feature since the beginning of the twentieth century. Ulster Unionists combined loyalty to the Crown and Empire with distrust of Westminster governments, both Liberal and Conservative.

Historiography

Laffan's *The Partition of Ireland* (Dundalk, 1983) begins by declaring that in 1911 all Irishmen "would have been amazed" if they could have foreseen partition. Looking at its causes, he identifies the reaction of a "few British and Irish politicians to the impact of developments as varied as the threat of civil war in 1914, the reality of rebellion in 1916, the effects of the world war, and a fundamental change in the political balance of power in both Britain and Nationalist Ireland". Laffan stresses that British politicians did not view Ulster as a priority in the immediate aftermath of the war, and he highlights the fact that the Conservative Party exhibited greatly reduced enthusiasm for the Ulster cause in the postwar period. David Fitzpatrick's *The Two Irelands* (Oxford, 1998) emphasises the crucial influence of Bonar Law. In 1912 Bonar Law claimed that there were two nations in Ireland and what separated the two peoples in Ireland was "'far deeper' than what separated Britain and Ireland". Fitzpatrick notes, moreover, that Bonar Law believed that if separate treatment for Nationalists was justified, then Ulster Unionists were equally entitled to such self-determination. But Fitzpatrick questions this argument, as he contends that the acceptance of partition by Ulster Unionists only confirmed that "their primary concern was with the consolidation of Protestant power, rather than the defence of liberty throughout the United Kingdom". Alvin Jackson's *Home Rule* (London, 2003) dwells on the significance of Ulster Unionist support for the amendment moved by Agar-Robartes in 1912. This, he argues, marked a shift in Unionist thinking, but clear evidence of this change only emerged in September 1913, when Carson adopted partition as a means of resolving the Home Rule crisis. This meant, of course, that he had to abandon his southern Unionist friends, though Jackson states that, by this stage, his frustration with his southern Unionist colleagues had turned to contempt. Subsequently, Carson was an enthusiastic advocate of the Lloyd George 1916 scheme, informing the UUC that it would provide a permanent Protestant majority in the six-county area.

Thomas Hennessey's *Dividing Ireland: World War I and Partition* (London, 1998) argues that Ireland would have been partitioned in some form even without the intervention of World War I. Yet he claims that the war created a feeling of "psychological partition" that could not have been envisaged before the war. English's *Irish Freedom* (London, 2006) highlights the view expressed by David Trimble in the late 1990s, which contends that partition was "inevitable", as it was the only response to "the social reality of two Irish nations". Fitzpatrick's *The Two Irelands* explains that republicans generally followed the path taken by Redmond and the constitutionalists towards acceptance of some form of partition on "the optimistic assumption" that it would only be temporary. Kendle's *Walter*

Long, Ireland and the Union (Dublin, 1992) illustrates its subject's full support for the maintenance of the Union, in addition to Long's strong preference for a nine-county unit, when his committee first met. By February 1920, however, he suddenly recognised that his bill would only be successful if it made provision for a six-county bloc, though, as Kendle declares, he was "naturally reluctant to open the door for a permanent partition".

Laffan's *The Partition of Ireland* (Dundalk, 1983) also considers the debate over the area of the two new states, commenting that similar decisions were being taken in contemporary Europe. Laffan contends that this created a dilemma for the Long committee, because plebiscites were the accepted methods of deciding such issues, but Long was firmly opposed to this type of referendum. This, notes Laffan, left political leaders at Westminster open to the accusation that they were ignoring the principle of self-determination. Jackson's *Home Rule* confirms that Long and his colleagues were "emphatic" that the Government of Ireland Bill should include structural mechanisms for the encouragement of Irish unity. Although the partition of Ireland had already been conceded, Jackson claims that the Long committee was more anxious about "the survival of Ireland within a redefined Union" than it was about Ulster Unionist concerns. Craig's influence on the Long committee is highlighted in O'Leary and Maume's *Controversial Issues in Anglo-Irish Relations* (Dublin, 2004), which describes the crucial role that he played in convincing ministers to shape the 1920 bill in the interests of Ulster Unionism. Indeed, as the authors illustrate, he was also responsible for ensuring that the Council of Ireland would have little impact and that safeguards for the minority would not infringe on the new administration's powers.

Nicholas Mansergh's *The Unresolved Question: The Anglo-Irish Settlement and Its Undoing 1912–72* (London, 1991) argues that during the cabinet discussions on the forthcoming bill in December 1919, "the general trend of cabinet opinion" wanted to see a single all-Ireland parliament in the future. However, he claims that once it was agreed to create a separate parliament for the north, the most likely outcome was a six-county Northern Ireland state, because such a move would require full Unionist cooperation. Consequently, the cabinet had to drop its preference for a nine-county unit that would have facilitated reunification. John McColgan's *British Policy and the Irish Administration 1920–22* (London, 1983) stresses that administrative partition was already in place by the time that the Government of Ireland Act took effect. McColgan also expresses surprise at how the British government maintained the "pretence" that the 1920 bill would pave the way to unity, when it was clear that the Unionists would boycott the Council of Ireland. Bryan Follis's *A State under Siege: The Establishment of Northern Ireland, 1920–1925* (Oxford, 1995) claims that the key purpose of the Government of Ireland Act was to allow the British government to disengage from the Ulster problem. At the same time, the author notes, the Ulster Unionist leadership quickly recognised the importance of putting the necessary bureaucratic infrastructure in place to give the new state a strong foundation.

Ronan Fanning's *Fatal Path: British Government and Irish Revolution 1910–1922* (London, 2013) returns to the significance of Long's appointment as chair of the Irish Situation Committee, arguing that "Long's chairmanship of the committee fireproofed Lloyd George's premiership against the flames of Tory revolt in Ireland". The choice of Phillip Kerr to serve as secretary was also important, as Fanning stresses that Kerr was close to the prime minister. While the committee imposed partition, Fanning notes that it left its ending to the Irish. Indeed, in Fanning's words, the committee repeatedly emphasised the advantages of disengagement. While the ultimate aim of government policy was a united Ireland, Fanning declares that this had to be achieved without offending the Protestants of Ulster. When the violence erupted in the north during the summer of 1920, Craig seized the initiative by demanding that "Ulster" no longer be governed from Dublin Castle.

Charles Townshend's *The Partition* (London, 2021) notes that Long was "amazed by the fervour" of Craig's conversion to Home Rule. Yet the author also states that the cabinet was "against keeping the six counties an integral part of the UK, since it might well make eventual unity less likely, and indeed give the impression that partition was the aim of British policy". Townshend also claims that the cabinet "took fright" and altered the area to a six-county unit. Ministers apparently feared that Dawson Bates, the UUC secretary and a prominent hardliner, might "engineer an agitation" in Ulster that would force the government's hand. In the prime minister's Commons speech on 22 December, when he justified support for partition, Townshend notes that Lloyd George quoted Fr O'Flanagan's 1916 essay on the two Irish nations. Interestingly, Townshend demonstrates how far out of touch Long was with Ulster Unionist thinking. When he visited Ulster in January 1920, Long was "stunned" to learn that Unionists wanted only six counties.

The challenges facing the Unionist government and its actions in the formative years are succinctly summarised in Brian Barton's essay, 'Northern Ireland, 1920–25', which appears in Jacqueline Hill's (ed) *A New History of Ireland VII* (Oxford, 2003). Barton shows how southern attitudes to the new state "reinforced the Unionist sense of siege, largely determined security policy within the six counties, and exacerbated Nationalist hostility towards the new government". Barton also emphasises the negative role played by Dawson Bates who "took advantage" of Craig's frequent absences in London during the first half of 1922 to subvert the security provisions agreed under the Craig–Collins pacts. In Barton's view his action contributed significantly to the failure of the pacts. In his explanation of the Unionist government's hesitant response to the more peaceful climate after 1922, Barton suggests that a change in the cabinet's thinking was "hampered by uncertainty, inertia, or simply because it was inconvenient". By the autumn of 1922, "the conditions of the siege had receded", but, as Barton points out, "the policies of the Northern Ireland government remained uncharacteristically defensive and unresponsive to their changing context". The author concludes that this was "predictable", as the main priority for the new government was "to maintain Unionist loyalty and unity".

The early performance of the new state is criticised in Patrick Buckland's *The Factory of Grievances: Devolved Government in Northern Ireland 1921–39* (Dublin, 1979). Buckland accepts that the new state faced violent internal and external opposition, but he is, nevertheless, critical of the Unionist administration's actions. This criticism involves a careful analysis of the Unionist government's approach in a number of areas, including security, justice, representation, education and finance. The author also points the finger of blame at Westminster governments which were extremely reluctant to intervene in these formative years. A more nuanced interpretation of these early years is provided by Paul Bew's *The Politics of Enmity 1789–2006* (Oxford, 2007), which suggests that Craig was flexible on the border issue in 1922. Responding to his Unionist critics following the first Craig–Collins pact, Bew describes how Craig informed rank-and-file Unionists that it was his duty to lead, not to follow. The Unionist premier, in Bew's opinion, was also seriously concerned about the fate of southern Protestants. While he advised them to acknowledge the Free State government as "the least-unpleasant available option", Bew argues that he also signalled that the north should convey "a possible long-term willingness to come in with the South, in order to protect that community from republican onslaught". In looking at the fallout from the Boundary Commission, Bew notes that Cosgrave rushed to London to demand the four-county solution "agreed" in the Treaty but was confronted by an unsympathetic Baldwin government.

Diarmaid Ferriter's *The Border: The Legacy of a Century of Anglo-Irish Politics* (London, 2019) concurs with Fanning's view that "Ulstercentricity" was paramount during the cabinet discussions on partition in 1919. In his analysis of the British government's approach, Ferriter states that the keenness of both Liberals and Conservatives to get the Ulster issue out of British politics suggests that there was little love for Ulster Unionism among the political establishment at Westminster. He also declares that the Northern Ireland state quickly became "an expensive nuisance". While British politicians are routinely criticised for introducing partition, Ferriter emphasises that "partition was born with the assistance of Irish midwives … Unionist and Nationalist". The author also declares that while Sinn Féin insisted on local plebiscites to amend the border during the Treaty negotiations, its delegates still recognised partition. Subsequently, he argues that Collins's pacts with Craig gave Northern Ireland a certain legitimacy. Cormac Moore's *Birth of the Border: The Impact of Partition in Ireland* (Dublin, 2019) demonstrates that the Belfast boycott, which was implemented after the shipyard expulsions but enforced in earnest from 1921, was "an unmitigated disaster". It generated anti-northern feeling in the south, and the Dáil ignored Ernest Blythe's warning that "it would destroy for ever the possibility of any union".

In his examination of sectarian violence in Belfast, Moore argues that the announcement of the truce ending the War of Independence was the catalyst for even greater trouble, as Unionists viewed it as a reward for the IRA's murderous campaign. The violence in July 1921 saw Specials firing indiscriminately into Catholic areas as they drove through city streets in armoured vehicles. Moore records that the truce led to the demobilisation of 20,000 Specials, but they were quickly replaced by Protestant vigilante groups. Later, Moore claims that the belief that the transfer of large areas of territory from the north to the south would leave an "unviable rump" was deeply flawed. The author states that Northern Ireland could easily have coped without Tyrone and Fermanagh. He suggests, moreover, that the more the Boundary Commission favoured the Nationalist cause, the less chance there was of the smaller Nationalist community that remained pressing successfully for reunification.

When the Commission finally met, Moore asserts that, unlike similar commissions in Europe which always had an independent chair, the Irish version had Justice Feetham, a British-born South African judge with very conservative political views. What the Boundary Commission did create was much greater Unionist unity, a development that Craig was quick to exploit. During the Treaty negotiations, Moore declares, the Irish delegates did not know how to use the fact that government services were not due to be transferred to Belfast until 22 November 1921. While they were withheld, partition appeared to be negotiable, but the Sinn Féin delegation had its focus on a boundary commission. Finally, Moore points out that Ernest Clark, the first head of the Northern Ireland civil service, attempted to steer the Belfast government towards impartiality in its dealings with the Nationalist minority, but he adds that Clark himself had little understanding of the fundamental Catholic opposition to the existence of the new state.

Alan Parkinson's *A Difficult Birth: The Early Years of Northern Ireland 1920–25* (Dublin, 2020) offers a comprehensive treatment of the challenges facing the new state. On the loyalist side in Belfast, Parkinson states that lower skilled workers, "the rivet boys", were the main protagonists in the violence, and this group was hit by rising unemployment from May 1920. The author is critical of the Unionist leadership for its failure to intervene in the shipyard expulsions on 21 July 1920. In the city, the very high number of Catholic-owned spirit-groceries in the east of the city were particular targets. Parkinson chronicles the actions taken by Rev John Redmond, the Church of Ireland minister at Ballymacarrett, to restore calm by organising vigilante groups during this period when police resources were stretched. In the author's view the clergyman "undoubtedly made a significant contribution to defusing the passions of local Protestants", though the success of Redmond's "peace pickets" in the summer of 1920 persuaded the authorities of the value of a new force that could assist the police. When Craig came under pressure from grass-roots loyalists for a more assertive security response both in Belfast and along the "border", he put the case to the Westminster government. Parkinson claims that Westminster's swift response was not a "sop to Unionism", but a matter of pragmatism for a government that was reluctant to maintain a high military presence in Ulster. Later, the author notes that the Special Constabulary was viewed as the equivalent of the Black and Tans by many northern Nationalists. Parkinson regards the IRA's campaign in the north as "counter-productive".

Attacks on the police and Specials and operations against Protestant civilians both in their homes and on their journeys to and from work provoked "revenge counter-attacks by corrupt police officers and loyalist gunmen and bombers". Those involved in the UPA, Parkinson estimates, were responsible for approximately 350 Catholic deaths, but he suggests that "the start of the Irish Civil War and the impact of the Special Powers legislation, specifically James Craig's introduction of internment, culminated in the speedy elimination of sectarian killings". In the Northern Ireland parliament, meanwhile, Devlin's followers abstained. Therefore, the only real opposition came from a "small but voluble group of die-hard Unionist MPs who periodically took James Craig to task over his administration's perceived softness on security". Agreeing with others, Parkinson quotes Follis in stating that "Ulster Unionists secured the survival of Northern Ireland at the expense of deepened divisions" between the two communities in the north.

Townshend's *The Partition* argues that the distinction between constitutional Nationalists and republicans, which was "sharper in 1920 than perhaps ever before", was lost on Ulster loyalists. As they reacted to the security threat in the summer of 1920 by reorganising the UVF, Macready, the military commander in Ireland, predicted that such a move would lead to civil war, and he threatened to resign if the UVF was officially recognised. Townshend's book places the violence in the north in a wider Irish context and considers the impact of Westminster thinking. He claims that reaction to the "Lisburn inferno" following Swanzy's assassination overcame Macready's objection to "arming the Protestants", though he adds that the creation of the USC "had an air of inevitability". The author emphasises the real threat felt by Ulster Unionists when they learned of the

Boundary Commission provision in the Treaty. By late 1921 Townshend points out that British responses to northern government requests "became gradually less obliging, and a note of actual hostility appeared at the end of the year". Craig was also furious at what he saw as the anti-Ulster campaign in the British press, and Townshend notes that news of the Boundary Commission "sent a shiver of dismay through the north".

In assessing Sir Henry Wilson's appointment as the north's security adviser in March 1922, Townshend stresses that Wilson had a very low opinion of the northern government, especially Dawson Bates. He believed that the army rather than the police should assume responsibility for security, but the outbreak of the civil war relieved the pressure on Craig. In analysing the impact of the Boundary Commission, Townshend is critical of MacNeill's appointment, noting that he was badly briefed on the border issue. Yet it was Feetham's appointment as chairman that proved crucial to the outcome. In his conclusion, the author claims that the adjustments to the border "however short they might fall from Nationalist hopes" were not trivial. They would have shortened the border by over 50 miles and met the wishes of some border inhabitants.

The impact of partition on border communities is covered by Peter Leary's *Unapproved Routes: Histories of the Irish Border 1922–1972* (Oxford, 2016). Leary opens by stressing that the new line of demarcation imposed in 1921 had little connection to prevailing economic and geographic circumstances. The author also draws attention to the many anomalies created by the new border. Leary argues that the imposition of customs controls in April 1923 ensured that partition was further entrenched before the Boundary Commission was convened. In effect, this greatly reduced cross-border trade and was a significant blow for towns on either side of the border such as Newtownbutler and Clones. The tensions within northern Nationalism are described in Hepburn's *Catholic Belfast and Nationalist Ireland*. There was a marked difference between the attitude of west and east Ulster Nationalists to the formation of the Northern Ireland state. Belfast Nationalists, "could see no prospect of saving themselves through the Boundary Commission", and they were convinced that Dublin had no interest in their plight.

Once the boundary issue was resolved, Devlin, who held out little hope for a major revision through the Boundary Commission, intended to enter the Northern Ireland parliament and end what he called "permanent disenfranchisement". The Catholic clergy were supportive, but west Ulster Nationalists continued to pin their hopes on the Commission. Adrian Grant's *Derry: The Irish Revolution, 1912–23* (Dublin, 2018) highlights the importance of local government elections in 1920. Nationalists believed that if they could take control of local government in areas such as Derry city, "then they could more forcefully argue against partition in general, but also make a case for Nationalist-held council areas to come under the jurisdiction of the southern parliament". Later, Grant chronicles the extraordinary response by the authorities to the violence in Derry in the summer of 1920. By the end of the year there were over 5,000 members of the Crown Forces stationed in Derry. He concludes that with "a population of less than 50,000 and an IRA membership of no more than a few hundred, and even fewer active members, Derry was not a place where open revolt was likely".

Conclusion

On Saturday, 5 December 1925, a letter signed by the heads of the three Protestant churches appeared in the *Belfast News-Letter*. It outlined arrangements for making the following Sunday "an occasion of thanksgiving to Almighty God" to celebrate the successful outcome of the London negotiations. In an interview with the newspaper on the same day, Craig was keen to emphasise the positive and friendly atmosphere in which the negotiations had been conducted: "Representatives of the Irish Free State and Northern Ireland had met each other without an atom of ill-will on either side, all determined to do their part in bringing about an agreement which should obliterate any sad memories of the past, and leave the way open for better things in the future." Unionists in Ulster, with the church leaders to the fore, congratulated themselves in standing firm against internal and external pressure designed to undermine the Northern Ireland state. From this position of apparent strength and stability, however, the Unionist government failed to develop institutions and structures that would engage a bitterly disaffected minority community. Craig was not a bigot, and there was a genuine respect between himself and Cosgrave. However, he proved unwilling or unable to step outside the narrow sectarian parameters within which Ulster Unionism had operated for the previous two decades. In any crisis the first instinct of Craig and his ministers was to seek to mollify right-wing critics of their government. Consequently, suspicion and mistrust intensified following the confirmation of the partition settlement in 1925.

At the beginning of the century, no political leader advocated the division of Ireland. When faced with the prospect of Home Rule in 1911, Carson's declared intention was to use Ulster resistance to destroy the entire devolution scheme. When this proved unachievable, Unionists quickly switched to the fallback position of Ulster separation, preparations for which had begun in 1905 with the formation of the Ulster Unionist Council (UUC). Carson led this populist campaign, which proved sufficiently menacing to force the Liberal government's hand whilst taking care not to antagonise voters in Britain. Redmond and his senior colleagues were slow to recognise Unionist intentions. Once they did, however, they were accommodating enough to accept that the principle of exclusion should form the basis of any compromise to break the Home Rule deadlock.

Therefore, when Home Rule was put on the statute book in September 1914, all of the parties realised that partition would be part of any future devolved settlement. That still left the excluded area to be defined. Unionist demands for the exclusion of Ulster, already strong, intensified after the Easter Rising. The rebellion and, more particularly, the British response put Ireland on the path to separation from the United Kingdom. Constitutional Nationalism was being slowly asphyxiated by the war, and the rising allowed a more radical strain of Nationalism to take centre stage. By the beginning of 1917 it was clear that Sinn Féin would fill the void, and the movement demonstrated its political reach at the 1918 general election. The War of Independence that followed further discredited British rule. Irish fury at the reprisals conducted by the Black and Tans and Auxiliaries was matched by international condemnation of British policy in Ireland. Eventually, public opinion in Britain cajoled Lloyd George into dealing with Sinn Féin's demands.

However, by the time negotiations on an Irish settlement began, the Northern Ireland state was a reality. Craig had used his influence in London to press the case for a constitutional arrangement that was favourable to Ulster Unionism. The Council of Ireland posed some threat, but its operation would require Craig's consent. The coalition government was prepared to facilitate future reunification, but it would not actively encourage, never mind pressurise, Ulster Unionists to move against their will. By 1925 four successive governments had demonstrated their determination to keep their distance from Ulster affairs. Yet Craig had been nervous about the outcome of the Treaty negotiations. He had never been willing to place his full trust in any British government. Moreover, he was fully aware that the Sinn Féin delegates would seek to exploit the unpopularity of partition to strengthen their demands for concessions on Crown and Empire. The Treaty, of course, made provision for a Boundary Commission to review the existing border.

After the Irish Civil War, Nationalists in the north and south clung to the hope that the Boundary Commission would recommend the removal of large chunks of territory from Northern Ireland. This did not materialise. In truth, it quickly became evident during the Treaty negotiations that the Sinn Féin leadership viewed the removal of partition as a negotiating strategy and not as an end in itself. It was, therefore, a combination of the Irish pursuit of sovereignty and the British desire for disengagement that soothed Unionist concerns about the border.

Of course, the campaign for partition and the subsequent determination to defend the border had created an irrevocable split within Irish Unionism. This appeared to play on Craig's conscience, but it was of no consequence to rank-and-file Unionists in the six counties. Craig did not share Carson's concern about the impact that loyalist violence would have on public opinion in Britain. For the Unionist premier, the overwhelming priority was to defeat IRA violence, as it represented the greatest threat to the Northern Ireland state. His government's failure to reach out to Nationalists when the violence abated in 1922 was a missed opportunity for the new state. The outbreak of civil war had lifted the pressure on the Belfast administration, though Craig assumed that both sides in the republican split wanted to undermine the "Unionist" state and end partition.

In the end the conflict consolidated partition, with the Unionist government more than happy to take a watching brief. Thereafter, Craig had turned up the rhetoric by declaring that his government would defy any attempt by the Boundary Commission to transfer even small parcels of land to the Irish Free State. However, his attitude changed considerably following the signing of the tripartite agreement in 1925. The Unionist leader even indicated that there might come a point when the Free State could persuade Ulster Unionists of the merits of unity. Unfortunately, however, he and Cosgrave appeared content to co-exist rather than cooperate.

CONCLUSION

Indexes

Index of People

References to images are in italic

Agar-Robartes, Thomas 69, 275, 299–300, 302
Aiken, Frank 247, 293
Aitken, Sir Max 81
Amery, Leo 87
Anderson, Sir John 202, 261
Andrews, John Miller 284
Archdale, Edward 284
Armour, Rev J.B. 66
Ashe, Thomas 132, 145–7, *147*, 168
Asquith, Herbert *20*, 20–1, 34–5, 42–4, 46, 50–2, 55, 59, 67–70, 76–7, 79–85, 88–90, 93–6, 98, 101, 104–7, 110–11, 118, 135–6, 138–40, 199, 274, 276

Baldwin, Stanley 305
Balfour, Arthur 25, 28, 30, 40–2, 44–5, 55–6, 60–2, 69–71, 106, 118, 139–40, 168, 266, 280–1
Balfour, Gerald 14, 16–17
Barrett, Richard 243
Barrie, Hugh 150, 170
Barry, Kevin 186
Barry, Tom 188, 195–6, 203, 235, 245, 257, 269–70
Barton, Robert 208, 213–20, 223
Bates, Sir Richard Dawson *284*, 284, 290–2, 299, 304, 308
Benedict XV, Pope 213
Bernard, Archbishop John 152
Birkenhead, Lord (F.E. Smith) 70, 72, 77, 135, 139, 209–10, *211*, 212, 215, 217, 219, 222–3, 264

Birrell, Augustine 17–18, 39, 67–8, 79, 83–4, 95, 97–9, 101, 105, 126–7, 133, 140, 161
Blythe, Ernest 127, *173*, 234, 248–51, 306
Boland, Harry 180, 206, 233, 268
Bonar Law, Andrew *60*, 60–2, 65–71, 74, 76, 79–83, 87–9, 93–6, 99, 102–3, 105, 110–11, 118, 139–40, 166–8, 178–9, 199, 211, 215–16, 221, 266, 274–6, 278, 281, 300, 302
Bowen-Colthurst, Captain J.C. 135
Breen, Dan 173, 257
Brennan, Michael 230, 238
Brooke, Basil 285–6
Broy, Éamon 177
Brugha, Cathal 147, 156, *173*, 180–2, 205, 207, 209, 214, 217–18, 225, 227–8, 237, 260
Bryce, James 17

Campbell-Bannerman, Sir Henry 17, 38, 50
Carson, Sir Edward 1, *33*, 33–5, 44–7, 54, 58–61, 65–74, 77–81, 83, 85–9, 92–5, 98–100, 103–7, 110–11, 118–19, 137, 140, 149, 159, 162, 164–8, 170, 222, 274–9, 281, 284, 286, 300, 302, 310–12
Casement, Sir Roger 91, 128, 135–6
Ceannt, Eamonn 122, 124, 134
Cecil, Lord Hugh 72
Cecil, Lord Robert 139
Chamberlain, Austen 56, 60–1, 118, 139, 209–11, *210*, 213, 215, 219, 223, 264, 283
Chamberlain, Joseph 25, 41
Chartres, John 217
Childers, Erskine *91*, 91–2, 194, 204, 208,

314

212–20, 225, 242, 255
Childers, Margaret *92*
Christensen, Alder 128
Churchill, Lord Randolph 35, 273
Churchill, Winston 59–60, 65–8, 70, 75, 79–81, 87–9, 95, 98, 100–1, 105–6, 189, 199, 210, *211*, 215, 228–9, 232–4, 236–7, 256, 268, 270, 276, 278, 292
Clancy, Peadar 187–8
Clark, Sir Ernest 285, 306
Clark, George 150
Clarke, James 197
Clarke, Kathleen 225
Clarke, Tom 120–4, 126, *121*, 133, 162, 164–5
Clune, Conor 187–8
Cohalan, Bishop Daniel 201
Colbert, Con 134
Collins, Michael 143–4, 146–7, *147*, 156, *173*, 177, 180–2, 187, 197, 202, *207*, 207–8, 212–20, 223–9, 232–40, 242, 245, 248–9, 251, 253–6, 258–65, 267–8, 289–90, 292, 294–5, 304–6
Connolly, James 116–17, *124*, 124–6, 130–1, 134, 159, 164
Connolly, Sean 195–6
Cooper, Bryan 34–5
Cope, Alfred "Andy" 202–3, 261, 287
Corkey, Rev William 64
Cosgrave, W.T. 146, 156, *173*, 180, 192, 206, 223, 227, *239*, 240, 249–50, 253, 270–1, 305
Craig, Charles 26–7, 53, 222, 273, 281, 283
Craig, Sir James 53, *58*, 58–9, 63, 71–2, 80, 85, 93, 104–5, 111, 204, 215–16, 218, 222, 228, 249, 255, 265, 273, 279–301, 303–8, 310–12
Crawford, Fred 63, 86–7, 89–90, 107
Crewe, Lord 138
Crozier, Auxiliary commander 198

Dalton, Colonel C.F. 253
Dalton, Emmet 237, 239
Daly, Edward 131, 133
Daly, General Paddy 245–6
D'Arcy, Bishop Frederick 100
Davitt, Michael, Jr 143
de Valera, Éamon 131, 134, 145–9, 153–6, 158, 168–70, *173*, 179–81, 197, 200–9, 212–18, *223*, 223–7, 232–4, 236–7, 239, 241–2, 247–8, 250–1, 253, 255, 258, 260, 262–8, 271, 277, 287–8, 300

Deakin, James 122
Deasy, Liam 232, 237–9, 245
Derby, Lord 202
Devlin, Joe *21*, 21, 49, 66, 68, 78, 84–5, 96, 97–8, 138, 150–1, 153, 158, 167–9, 270, 290, 299, 307–8
Devoy, John 128
Dicey, A.V. 76, 97
Dickson, Thomas 135
Dillon, John 4, *8*, 8–9, 11–13, 17, 23, 40, 49–50, 52, 78, 82, 84, 94, 98, 111, 114–15, 127, 134–5, 137, 145, 153–5, 158, 160, 162, 166, 168–9
Dolan, Charles 18, 49
Donnelly, Patrick 153
Duggan, Éamonn 208, 218–19, 227
Duke, H.E. 136
Dunne, Reggie 235–6
Dunraven, Lord 12, 16, 27, 29

Edward VII, King 5, 7, 21, 43
Elgar, Edward 76
Emmet, Robert 123
Erne, Earl of 72

Farren, Thomas 116
Feetham, Richard 306, 308
Figgis, Darrell 91
Finegan, Bishop Patrick 196, 201
Fisher, J.R. 297
Fitzalan, Lord 227, 292
Fitzgerald, Desmond 250
Fitzgerald, Michael 186
French, Field Marshal Sir John (Lord French) 89, 156, 176
Fuller, Stephen 246

Gallagher, Frank 194
Garvin, J.L. 221
Gavan Duffy, George 208, 213–16, 218–19
George V, King 21, 43, 59, 77–81, 85, 93, 102, 105–6, 200, 202, 213, 285
Gifford (Plunkett), Grace 134
Gilhooly, Lawrence 142
Gilmartin, Archbishop Thomas 201
Ginnell, Laurence 14, 48, *173*
Gladstone, William 1, 3, 37–8
Glendinning, R.G. 25–6
Gonne, Maud 5, 49
Gough, Brigadier-General Hubert 88–9
Gough, Brigadier-General J.E. 106

315

Greenwood, Hamar 188–9, 191–2, 198–9, 210, 261, 287
Grey, Sir Edward (Viscount Grey) 51, 105, 109, 200
Griffith, Arthur 5–8, *5*, 18, 48–9, 133, 143, 146–8, 156, *173*, 179–80, 204–5, 207–9, 212–20, *223*, 223–6, 230, 233–4, 236, 239, 255, 260, 263, 265–6
Gwynn, Stephen 98, 166

Hales, Seán 242–3
Hales, Tom 232, 242
Hamill, Bernard 116
Harbison, T.J.H. 153
Harrington, Timothy 7, 10
Healy, Frank 142
Healy, Tim 4, 9, 11–12, 20, 49, 108
Heuston, Sean 134
Hewart, Gordon 210
Hobson, Bulmer 121–2, 128–9
Hogan, Dan 289
Hogan, Michael 187
Hogan, Seán 175
Hogg, David 78
Hunt, Michael 175, 257
Hurley, Charlie 195
Hyde, Douglas 86, 120

Johnson, Thomas 157, 179
Jones, Tom 210, 215–16, 219

Kavanagh, James 177
Kent, Thomas 134
Kerr, Philip 304
Kidston, Jane 61
Kilroy, Michael 244
Kipling, Rudyard 76, 87
Kitchener, Lord 111, 163

Lansdowne, Lord 56, 62, 76–7, 81, 93, 96, 138–41, 160, 167
Latimer, William 195
Lemass, Seán 251
Lindsay, Mrs 197
Lloyd George, David 32, 67–8, 70, 75, 77, 79, 82–4, 93–5, 98, 105–6, 136–41, 143, 149, 151, 153–60, 166–7, 172, 178–9, 189–90, 199, 202–6, 209–17, *210*, 219–22, 227, 234, 236, 254–5, 257, 262–6, 276–8, 280–3, 285, 302, 304, 311
Logue, Cardinal Michael 153, 158, 201–2, 257

Londonderry, Lady 61
Londonderry, Lord 28, 284, 296
Long, Walter 16–17, *17*, 28–33, 41–2, 54, 61–2, 69, 138–41, 160, 167, 178–9, 190, 274, 278–81, 283, 300, 303
Lonsdale, J.B. 27, 33, 40, 53, 273
Loreburn, Lord 79, 98
Lowther, James 93
Lynch, Diarmuid 147
Lynch, Liam 176, 229, 231–2, 235, 237–8, 240, 242, 244–5, 247–8, 256, 267
Lynch, Patrick 146
Lynn, Robert 296

MacBride, Major John 134
McCann, Alexander and Agnes 64
McCartan, Patrick 153, 155
McCullough, Denis 121–2, 129
MacCurtain, Tomás 142, 182–3, 185, 286
MacDermott, Sean 120–4, 126, 129, 134, 164
MacDonagh, Thomas 121–4, 129, 131, 133, 164
MacDonnell, Sir Antony 16, 26, 28, 30, 40, 42
MacDonnell, Patrick 174
MacEntee, Seán 226, 260
Mac Eoin, Seán 238
McGinley, Pat *92*
McGrath, Joseph 206, 250, 252–3
McGuffin, Samuel 288
McGuinness, Joe 144–5, 168–9
MacIntyre, Patrick 135
McKean, Rev Dr William 73
McKee, Dick 187–8
McKelvey, Joe 235, 243
McMahon family, Belfast 290–1
MacNamara, Patrick 177
MacNeill, Eoin 86, 112–14, 118–19, 122, 129, 132, 164, *173*, 180, 227, 249–50, 271, 298–9, 308
Macpherson, Ian 178, 182
Macready, General Neville 189, 191, 198–9, 202–3, 232, 236–7, 258, 261–2, 268, 307
MacSwiney, Mary 225
MacSwiney, Terence *173*, 185–6
MacVeigh, Jeremiah 138
Mahon, General Sir Bryan 111
Mallin, Michael 125, 131, 134
Markievicz, Countess Constance 131, *132*, 134, 156, 180, 225
Maxwell, Major-General Sir John 133, 135–6,

140, 165–6
Meehan, F.E. 18
Mellows, Liam 127, 132, 227, 231, 235, 237, 242–3, 256, 266
Mernin, Lily 177
Midleton, Lord 138–9, 149, 152, 203, 223
Milner, Lord 87
Milroy, Seán 153
Moneypenny, W.F. 65
Moore, Maurice, Colonel 113
Moore, William 25–8, 40, 53, 273
Moran, D.P. 118
Moylan, Seán 232
Mulcahy, Richard 169, 182, 197, 207, 228–31, 237–8, 240–3, 245–6, 250, 252–3, 260, 270
Mulhern, William 258
Murphy, Joseph 186
Murray of Elibank, Lord 77

Nathan, Sir Matthew 126–8, 133
Neligan, David 177
Nugent, T.D. 116

O'Brien, Constable James 131
O'Brien, William 4, 10–13, 22, 27, 46, 49, 142
O'Connell, J.J. 236
O'Connell, James 174
O'Connor, Lieutenant 246
O'Connor, Rory 147, 227, 231, 235–7, 243, 248, 256, 266, 268
O'Connor, T.P. 78, 81, 84, 96, 97
O'Donnell, Bishop Patrick 151
O'Donoghue, Florrie 232, 241
O'Donovan Rossa, Jeremiah 123
O'Duffy, Eoin 234, 270, 289
O'Dwyer, Bishop Edward 135
O'Flanagan, Fr Michael 143, 169, *173*, 304
O'Hanrahan, Michael 134
O'Hegarty, Diarmuid 147
O'Hegarty, Seán 232, 241
O'Higgins, Kevin 192, 225–7, 234, 236, 240, 242–3, 245, 250, 252–3, 270
O'Kelly, J.J. 143
O'Kelly, Seán T. 179–80
O'Leary, D.L. 142
Ó Máille, Pádraic 242
O'Malley, Ernie 230, 237, 242, 257, 269
O'Rahilly, The 122, 129
O'Shea, Katharine 3
O'Shea, William 3

O'Sullivan, Joseph 235–6

Paget, Lieutenant-General Sir Arthur 88–9
Parnell, Charles Stewart 1–4, 6, 9, 14, 51
Pearse, Margaret 225
Pearse, Patrick 119–24, *120*, 126, 129–31, 134, 164
Pearse, Willie 134
Pirrie, Lord 66
Plunkett, Count George 143–4, 146, 156, 168, 170, *173*, 180
Plunkett, Grace (*née* Gifford) 134
Plunkett, Horace 150
Plunkett, Joseph 121–4, 129, 133–4, 164
Pollock, Hugh MacDowell 284, 293

Redmond, John 4–5, *5*, 9, 11–13, 15, 17–18, 20–2, 34, 42–4, 46, 49–52, 60, 62, 66, 68, 70, 77–9, 81–6, 91–6, 97–8, 103–5, 109–13, 115–16, 118–19, 121, 127, 137–8, 140–1, 149–51, 153, 159, 161–3, 166–7, 170, 276–7, 302, 311
Redmond, Rev John 307
Redmond, William 154, 158
Redmond, Willie 145, 149
Richardson, Lieutenant-General Sir George 75
Roberts of Kandahar, Lord 75
Robinson, Séamus 173
Rosebery, Lord 38
Russell, T.W. 24–6
Ryan, Monsignor Arthur 174

Salisbury, Lord 25, 72
Saunderson, Colonel Edward 24–9, 31, 53, 273
Seely, Colonel J.E.B. 88–9, 106
Selborne, Lord 139–40
Sexton, Thomas 9
Sheehy-Skeffington, Francis 135, 165
Sheehy-Skeffington, Hanna *135*
Shephard, Gordon *92*
Shipsey, Dr 142
Shortt, Edward 257
Sinclair, Thomas 27, 71–2
Sixsmith, Rev A.E. 100
Sloan, Thomas 25–6
Smith, F.E. *see* Birkenhead, Lord
Smith, Harry 177
Smyth, Colonel G.F. 258, 286
Smuts, Jan 200, 203, 205

Spring-Rice, Sir Cecil 136–7
Spring-Rice, Mary 92
Stack, Austin 193, 204–5, 207, 214, 225, 260
Stamfordham, Lord 106
Stopford Green, Alice 91
Strickland, General Edward 189
Strickland, General Sir Peter 196
Sturgis, Mark 202, 261
Swanzy, Oswald 258, 286, 207, 286, 307
Sweetman, Roger 201

Tallents, Stephen 292
Tobin, General Liam 253
Tone, Wolfe 123
Treacy, Seán 173
Trimble, David 302
Trimble, William Copeland 72
Tudor, Major-General Hugh 189, 198, 261
Twaddell, W.J. 291

Victoria, Queen 5

Walsh, Archbishop William 145
Whitby, P.J. 116
Willoughby de Broke, Lord 72, 76
Wilson, Major-General Sir Henry 88, 154, 235, 247, 256, 290, 308
Wilson, Woodrow 180
Worthington-Evans, Laming 210
Wyndham, George 7, 14, 16, 26–8, 30, 39–41, 53, 55

Index of Historians

Adams, R.J.Q. 102
Augusteijn, Joost 260–1

Barry, Tom 257
Bartlett, Tom 100
Barton, Brian 161, 164, 304–5
Bew, Paul 48, 50, 55, 100–1, 107–8, 162–3, 169, 265, 268, 305
Biagini, Eugenio 56
Bielenberg, Andy 260, 271
Blake, Robert 102–3
Borgonovo, John 261
Bowman, John 169
Bowman, Timothy 99–100, 162
Boyce, George 52, 264
Breen, Dan 257
Buckland, Patrick 53, 305
Bull, Philip 48

Callanan, Frank 49, 53
Campbell, Fergus 48
Coleman, Marie 168, 259
Connell, Joseph 262
Coogan, Tim Pat 260, 264
Cowling, Maurice 266
Crowley, John 53

Daly, Mary 260
Dangerfield, George 101
Doherty, Erica 97
Doherty, Gabriel 97
Dooley, Chris 98, 167–8, 170
Dutton, David 55–6, 103
Dwyer, T. Ryle 258, 264

English, Richard 107, 302
Enright, Sean 269
Evans, Stephen 55

Fanning, Ronan 50–1, 105–6, 166, 170–1, 266, 304
Farry, Michael 268
Ferriter, Diarmaid 100, 106, 174, 259–60, 262, 264–5, 267–8, 305–6
Fitzpatrick, David 168–9, 265, 267–8, 302
Follis, Bryan 303–4, 307
Foster, Gavin 271
Foster, Roy 51, 106, 163, 165
Foy, Michael 161, 164, 261

INDEX

Gailey, Andrew 55
Gannon, Darragh 269
Garvin, Tom 164, 269–70
Grant, Adrian 308–9
Gwynn, Denis 97, 163

Hart, Peter 259–60, 271
Hennessey, Thomas 302
Hepburn, A.C. 49, 167, 169, 270, 308
Hill, Jacqueline 304
Hopkinson, Michael 247–8, 260, 266, 268–9
Hoppen, Theo 55
Hyde, H. Montgomery 54

Jackson, Alvin 51–3, 100, 102–5, 107, 161–2, 166, 169–70, 265–6, 302–3
Jalland, Patricia 101–2
Jenkins, Roy 102

Kendle, John 54, 302–3
Kenneally, Ian 262
Kenny, Colum 263
Kirkpatrick, Laurence 97
Kissane, Bill 268

Laffan, Michael 164, 167–70, 267, 302–3
Leary, Peter 308
Lee, Joe 106, 163, 165, 266–7, 271
Lewis, Geoffrey 54, 99, 165, 167, 170
Longford, Lord 262–3
Lyons, Leland 51, 166

McAtasney, Gerard 165
McCarthy, John 270
McCluskey, Fergal 162, 165, 258
McColgan, John 303–4
McConnel, James 50, 53
McDowell, R.B. 170
McGarry, Fearghal 161, 164–6, 269
McGee, Owen 48–9
McNeill, Ronald 55, 99–100, 162
Mansergh, Martin 98
Mansergh, Nicholas 103, 163, 265–6, 303
Maume, Patrick 49, 108, 163–4, 166, 265, 303
Meleady, Dermot 50, 52
Mitchell, Arthur 258–9
Moore, Cormac 306
Murphy, Mike 53
Murray, Niall 262

O'Callaghan, John 258
Ó Drisceoil, Donal 53, 268
O'Halpin, Eunan 270
O'Leary, Cornelius 108, 265, 303
O'Malley, Ernie 257, 269
Ó Ruairc, Pádraig Óg 261–2
O'Sullivan, Patrick 259

Parkinson, Alan 98–9, 306–7
Paseta, Senia 48
Peatling, G.K. 56
Phoenix, Eamon 167, 169

Ryan, Meda 260

Scholes, Andrew 100
Shannon, Catherine 56
Smith, Jeremy 56, 103

Townshend, Charles 97, 161, 164–5, 170–1, 257–8, 304, 307–8
Travers, Pauric 170

Valiulis, Maryann 169

Walker, Graham 53–4
Wheatley, Michael 107–8, 163

General Index

References to images are in italic

A Specials *see* Ulster Special Constabulary
abstentionism 6 *see also* Sinn Féin
Act of Union (1800) 37
agrarian agitation 2, 10, 12, 14–15, 23, 37, 107, 156–7, 260
agriculture 15, 63, 117, 157 *see also* tenant farmers
All-for-Ireland League (AFIL) 13, 20, 22, 46, 49, 142
An t-Óglach 174
Ancient Order of Hibernians (AOH) 23, 49, 51, 65, 71, 78, 107–8, 153
Anglo-Irish Treaty *220*, 227–8, 255–6, 263, 285, 305, 308, 311
    aftermath 221–53
    British proposals: 203–6, 212;
        counter-proposals 212
    Dáil debates on 224–6
    draft 217
    negotiations: 212–21, 262–5, 306; delegations 207–12
    pro- and anti- factions 226–39, 241–3, 246, 248, 250–1, 256, 266–71
Antrim, County 60, 137
Archer-Shee trial 34–5
Argenta 291
Armagh, County 60, 137, 282, 299
Army Act (1689) 87
Army (Annual) Bill 87
Army Convention *see* Irish Republican Army
Asgard 91–2, *92*
Ashbourne, County Meath 132
Ashtown, County Dublin 176
Athenry, County Galway 132
Athlone, County Westmeath 238
Aud 127–9
Auxiliaries 187–9, 191, 194, 198, 254, 287, 311

B Specials *see* Ulster Special Constabulary
Bachelors Walk killings 92, 94, 110, 163
Balbriggan, County Dublin 185, 190, 199
Ballyseedy, County Kerry 246
Banbridge, County Down 286
Béal na mBláth, County Cork 239
Belfast 23, 26, 34, 66, 71–5, 85, 87, 100, 228–9, 273, 285–8, 290–2, 307–8
    industries 63–4, 99, 107

shipyards 286, 307
Belfast boycott 228, 294, 306
Belfast conference (1904) 27–8
Belfast News-Letter 27, 42, 310
Belfast parliament *see* Northern Ireland parliament
Belfast Protestant Association 26, 291
Belgium 110, 161
Black and Tans 183–5, *184*, 189, 191, 194, 198, 203, 254, 260–1, 287, 311
blood sacrifice ideology 123–6, 129, 141, 162–4
Bloody Sunday 187–8, 190
Boer War 5, 11, 40, 49, 63
Boland's Mill 131
border, Irish *see* Northern Ireland
Boundary Commission 215–16, 219, 222, 228–9, 249, 251, 255, 263, 266, 270–1, 285, 297–9, 305–6, 308, 311–12
boycotting 11, 14, 32 *see also* Belfast boycott
British Army 87–8, 95, 132, 141, 154, 165, 191, 276 *see also* conscription crisis; Crown Forces
    36th (Ulster) Division 111, 113, 141, 164
    Irish Divisions (10th, 16th) 113, 116
    recruitment 111, 113, 115–17, 159, 162;
    opposition to 116–17, *117*, 125;
    see also conscription crisis
British Commonwealth 205, 214–15, 217, 224–5, 251
British Covenant 87
British Empire 4, 24, 41, 63, 112, 161, 179, 200, 203–6, 212, 219, 278
British League for the Support of Ulster and the Union 76, 87
Buckingham Palace Conference 93–5, 98, 140, 276
Budget Protest League 32
by-elections 18, 25–6, 78, 98–9, 106, 116, 142–5, 149, 153–4, 156, 162, 168–9

Cahirciveen, County Kerry 246
Carsonism 119, 121, 126
Castle document 129
Castlebar, County Mayo 238
Castledawson incident 71
Castleisland, County Kerry 245
Catholic Church 9, 18, 64–5, 107, 155, 170, 247, 251–2, 258, 277, 296–7, 308
clergy 48, 65, 97, 134, 138, 143, 145, 153,

167–8, 182, 193, 196, 201, 225, 241, 257, 308
Catholics 55, 71, 178, 259, 280, 286, 289–94, 299, 306
Cavan, County 60, 95, 277, 282
Church of England 200
Church of Ireland 1, 24, 97–8, 100
    clergy 100, 298, 307
    General Synod 64–5
Civic Guard 270
Civil Authorities (Special Powers) Act (1922) 290–1, 294, 307
civil war *see* Finnish Civil War; Irish Civil War
Clan na Gael 271
Clare, County 14, 157, 168, 175, 190, 238, 254
Clones, County Monaghan 290
Clonmel, County Tipperary 238
coalition governments (British) 109, 118, 140–1, 154, 166, 168, 172, 178, 221–2, 257, 266, 276–8
Cobh, County Cork 176 *see also* Queenstown
Collins–de Valera pact 232–3, 235
Colwyn Award 293–4
Congested Districts Board 29
Connacht 10–11, 228, 235
conscription crisis 109, 118, 141, 154–7, *155*, 160, 161, 168, 170, 277
Conservative Party 1, 5, 9, 13, 17, 23–5, 29, 33, 37–8, 41–2, 44–7, 51, 55–6, 98, 102–3, 141, 178, 215, 221, 233, 254, 257, 266, 273–4, 277–9, 302
    Diehards 214, 222
    and the Ulster crisis 57, 59, 62–3, 67, 69, 71, 76, 80–4, 96
Constitution *see* Irish Free State
constitutional conference (1910) 21, 43–5
constitutional crisis (1910) 21, 32, 34, 43, 51, 59, 101, 103
Cork, County 20, 22, 176, 183, 190, 195–6, 243, 254, 259–60, 269, 271
Cork city 182–3, 188–9, 238–9
Council of Ireland 281, 283, 288, 300, 303, 311
courts-martial 133, 186, 191, 198
Covenant *see* Ulster Covenant
Craig–Collins pacts 228–9, 304, 306
Craigavon demonstration (1911) 58–60, 274
Crossbarry, County Cork 196
Crown Forces 174–7, 181, 184, 187–8, 190, 194–201, 229, 240, 254, 257–8, 261–2, 269, 271, 279, 292, 309
Cumann na mBan 131, 143, 156, 240
Cumann na nGaedheal 5, 117, 250–2, 270–1
Cumann na Poblachta 232, 234–5, 241–2, 250
Curragh incident 88–9, 95, 105–6
Curtis, Lionel 233
Custom House, Dublin 197
customs duties, cross-border 252, 281, 308

Dáil courts 193, 201, 258–9, 262
Dáil Éireann 179, 258–9
    see also Anglo-Irish Treaty
    oath of allegiance 181–2
    sessions: First Dáil *173*, 173, 179–80, 260; Second Dáil 180–1, 284; Third Dáil 181, 235
    suppression 181
Dáil Loan 181, 259
Declaration of Independence 179
Democratic Programme 179–81, 242
Department of Agriculture 157
Derry, County 60, 85, 137–8
Derry city 282, 285, 298, 308–9
Derry City by-elections: (1913) 78, 99; (1914) 116
Derry Corporation elections (1920) 295
devolution scheme 16–18, 27–8, 30, 35, 37–41, 47, 53, 55–6, 273, 280, 310
Document No. 2 224–7, 267
dominion status 200, 204–5, 211–13, 217, 263
Donegal, County 60, 95, 277, 282
Down, County 60, 137, 282
Dripsey, County Cork 197
Drummully Salient 297–8, *298*
Dublin 116–17, 196, 239, 254
    by-elections: College Green (1915) 116; Dublin Harbour (1915) 116
    Volunteers 113–14
Dublin Castle 7, 29, 114, 126–7, 176, 192, 201–2, 227–8, 287
Dublin Corporation 4–5, 7–8
Dublin Guard 245–6
Dublin Lockout 125
Dublin Metropolitan Police (DMP) 92, 175
    G branch 177
Dunmanway, County Cork 189

East Cavan by-election (1918) 156
East Clare by-election (1917) 145–6, 149, 168–9
East Down by-election 25

East Tyrone by-election (1918) 153, 169
Easter Rising 109, 129–32, *130*, 159–60,
    164–6, 276–7, 300, 311
    aftermath: 132–6; Lloyd George
        negotiations 136–42, 152, 160,
        166, 169, 277
    arrests 131, 133, 135–6, 160, 165
    causes 117–26
    executions 133–4, 137, 159–60, 169,
        171
    planning 126–9
    Proclamation 121, 123–4, 126, 130,
        134, 179
economic warfare 184
education 39, 251, 296–7 *see also* universities
Education Acts (1923, 1925) (Northern
    Ireland) 296–7
elections *see* by-elections; general elections;
    local government elections
electoral reform 2, 158
emigration 63, 118, 271
Enniscorthy, County Wexford 132
Eucharistic Congress (London, 1908) 51
external association 205, 208–9, 212, 217–18,
    224, 263

Farmers' Party 235
federalism 44–5, 67
Fenianism 6, 53, 112, 121–3, 162, 164–6, 225
Fermanagh, County 82, 94, 137–8, 277, 282,
    286, 298–9, 306
Fermanagh County Council 296
    elections (1920) 295
Fermoy, County Cork 176
Fianna Fáil 251, 253
First World War *see* World War I
Four Courts 131
    occupation 231–3, 235–7, 243, 256,
        267–8
Free State *see* Irish Free State
Free State Army *see* National Army
Freeman's Journal 7, 9, 12, 18, 158, 268
Frongoch camp 133, 143, 146

Gaelic Athletic Association (GAA) 156
Gaelic League 51, 86, 119–20, 123, 143, 156,
    164, 181
Gaelic revival 123
Galway, County 10, 14, 239, 243–4, 248
Galway East by-election (1914) 116

general elections
    1885: 1
    1895: 9
    1906: 13, 26, 29–30, 39, 41–2, 49, 56
    1910: (January) 20–1, 32–4, 42–3, 46,
        50, 52, 57; (December) 35–7,
        44, 46
    1918: 109, 158, 179, 181, 254, 278
    1921: 284, 288
    1922: 234–5, 266–8
    1923: 250–1, 271
    1925 (Northern Ireland): 297
General Post Office (GPO) 130–1
general strike (1918) 155
German plot 156
gerrymandering 296
Government of Ireland Bill/Act (1920) 190–1,
    199, 272, 281–3, 288, 293, 296, 303–4
graziers 10, 14, 48, 193
guerrilla warfare 182, 190, 197, 237–40, 254,
    256, 258, 269
Guinness 116
gun-running
    Irish Volunteers: Howth 91–2; Tralee
        128
    Irregulars: Waterford 244
    UVF: 86–7, 107; Larne 89–91, *90*,
        105–6

Home Rule 1–5, 8–9, 13, 21–4, 31, 34–5,
    37–8, 42–6, 50–6, 59–62, 69–70, 78–80,
    85, 93–4, 96, 111–12, 114, 117–18, 137,
    149–53, 190–1
    exclusion proposals 137–41, 149, 159,
        300
    federal ("Home Rule All Round")
        44–5, 67
    opposition to: 4, 23–4, 27, 30–1, 34–5,
        37, 46–7, 55–6, 70, 76, 97, 109,
        119, 273–6; economic 106–7;
        rallies 58–60, 66–7, 70, 72–4,
        77–8, 98, 106–7; religious 64–5,
        107; *see also* propaganda; Ulster
        crisis
    rallies 98
    and threat of civil war 70, 77–8, 81–4,
        91, 97, 102
Home Rule Act (1914) 94–5, 163, 276, 278,
    311 *see also* Government of Ireland Act
Home Rule Bills
    first (1886) 3, 5, 38, 64, 272

second (1883) 5, 38, 57, 64, 272
third (1912): 12, *45*, 46–7, 59–60, 66–71, 101, 111–12, 119, 272–3; Agar-Robartes amendment 69, 97–8, 101–2, 105, 275, 299–300, 302; amending bill 93, 95; Carson amendment 74–5, 275; committee stage 74; exclusion proposal 67, 70–1, 82–6, 93–4, 96, 97, 101–7, 275–6; passed 94–5; third reading 76; *see also* Government of Ireland Act; Ulster crisis
fourth (1919) 278–81, 300
Home Rule crisis *see* Ulster crisis
Home Rule rally, Belfast 66
Home Rule within Home Rule 79, 83–4
House of Commons 1–3, 17, 24, 34, 39, 41, 67, 74, 85, 94, 97, 109, 111, 170, 186, 194, 199, 214, 280
House of Lords 3, 15, 17, 20–1, 24, 32, 34, 38–9, 42–4, 50, 59, 61, 87, 93, 96, 103, 140, 200, 283 *see also* constitutional crisis
Howth gun-running 91–2
Hungarian policy 225
hunger strikes 146, 185

imperial contribution 293–4
Independence, War of *see* War of Independence
Independent Orange Order 25–6
informers 187, 194, 196–7, 258, 261
intelligence, military 187, 195, 198, 202, 240, 254, 258, 262, 291
internment
    post-Easter rising 133, 136, 142–3, 171
    Northern Ireland 291, 294, 307
    War of Independence 201
Irregulars *see* Irish Republican Army
Irish-Americans 2, 137, 149, 180 *see also* United States of America
Irish Bulletin 194, 242, 259, 262
Irish Citizen Army (ICA) 125, 127, 131, 133
Irish Civil War 227–52, 256, 262, 266–70, 292, 294, 300, 307–8, 311–12
    executions 241–3, 245, 247, 251, 269–70
Irish Convention 149–53, 160, 170, 277
Irish Council Bill (1907) 17–18, 31–2, 39, 42, 51

Irish Divisions *see* British Army
Irish Film Company 181
Irish Free State 152, 217, 220, 229, 247–8, 256, 305
    Constitution 233–4, 250, 268
Irish Freedom 121, 126
Irish Independent 145
Irish language, revival 23, 120
Irish Nation League 138, 143–4, 167
Irish National League 2–3, 10
Irish Parliamentary Party (IPP) 1–5, 7–8, 11–15, 17–18, 23, 33, 38–9, 43, 46, 48–53, 55, 107, 270, 277, 294 *see also* propaganda
    and the conscription crisis 154–5, 170
    decline 107–8, 109, 115–16, 118, 276
    post-Easter Rising 134, 137–8, 140–2, 144–6, 148, 153, 157–8, 160, 166, 169
    election campaign (1910) 20–2
    and the Irish Convention 150, 152–3
    National Convention (1909) 13
    Parnellite split 3
    reunification 11–12
    and the Ulster crisis 64, 77–9, 85, 91, 95–6
Irish question 1, 22, 31, 37–47, 73, 140, 179, 222, 277–8
Irish Republican Army (IRA) 225, 260, 287 *see also* propaganda
    army conventions 229–31, 235
    executions by 196–7, 261
    executive 231–2, 235, 271
    First Southern Division 232, 235, 238, 256
    flying columns 188, 190, 194–6, 198, 201–3
    General Headquarters (GHQ) 203, 228, 257, 261
    Irregulars (anti-Treaty) 229–31, 233, 235–48, 256, 266, 268–71
    northern campaign 229, 292, 300, 307
    in Northern Ireland 285–7, 289–92, 312
    pro-Treaty 229, 232, 248
    split 231, 247, 256, 266–8
    and the War of Independence 172–3, 183, 186–91, 193–9, 201, 254–5
    West Mayo *244*
Irish Republican Brotherhood (IRB) 86, 112–14, 117, 119–22, 128, 143, 146,

182, 209, 217–19, 226, 232, 252, 270, 276
    Military Council 122–30, 159, 164
    Supreme Council 114, 121–2, 164, 217–18, 225, 267
Irish Situation Committee (Long committee) 279–81, 303–4
Irish Tory Party 1
Irish Unionist Alliance (IUA) 29–31, 152
Irish Unionist Party 1, 16, 24–6, 30–5
Irish Universities Act (1908) 18
Irish Volunteers 86, 86, 91, 108, 110–15, 119, 121, 124, 127, 142–8, 156–7, 159, 161–2, 171, 254, 276, 278 see also Irish Republican Army (IRA)
    banning of 156, 181
    convention (1917) 146–8
    General Headquarters (GHQ) 173, 182
    and the War of Independence 172–4, 177–8, 182
Irregulars see Irish Republican Army

Jacob's biscuit factory 131
Joint Committee of Unionist Associations 31–2

Kerry, County 239, 243–6, 248, 256, 269
Kilkenny by-election (1917) 146, 169
Killarney, County Kerry 245–6
Kilmichael ambush 188, 190
King's County (Offaly) by-elections: (1914) 116; (1918) 155
Knocklong, County Limerick 184
Knocknagoshel, County Kerry 246

Labour Party 22, 46, 116, 150, 157, 179, 186, 192, 199, 235, 241, 243
Land Acts 23
    1896: 25
    1903 (Wyndham Act): 7, 12, 14–16, 39–40, 48
    1909: 39
    1923: 251
land agitation see agrarian agitation
Land Conference (1902) 7, 12, 16
Land League 2, 10, 175, 193
land purchase 14, 23–5, 37, 39–40
land question 4, 10, 24–5, 115
land reform 15, 115
Land War 48
landlordism 2–4, 12–13, 16, 23–8, 40, 48, 53,
    62, 115, 124, 193, 251, 273
Larne gun-running 89–91, 105–6
Leader, The 118
Leinster 11, 235
Leitrim, County 107, 195
Lewes Jail 144–5
Liberal Party 1, 3, 5, 17, 19, 22, 32–3, 37–9, 41–3, 46, 49–51, 53–4, 56
    and coalition government 118, 178, 257, 276
    and the Ulster crisis 57, 60, 62, 69, 71, 78, 81–4, 95–6, 101, 104
Liberty Hall 125
Liberty League 144
Limerick, County 190, 247
Limerick city 230, 238, 258
Limerick Soviet 258
Listowel, County Kerry 245
local government 4, 18, 39, 192, 197, 259, 295–6, 299
Local Government Act (1922) (Northern Ireland) 295–6
local government elections
    1899: 48
    1920: 191–2, 259, 285, 295, 298, 308–9
Londonderry see Derry
Long committee see Irish Situation Committee
Longford, County 107, 168, 254, 259
Loreburn letter 79, 98
Louth North by-election (1916) 116
loyalists 27, 35, 61, 99, 258, 286–8, 291–2, 298, 306–7, 312

Mansion House Conference (1918) 154–5
martial law
    Easter Rising 133, 136, 160, 165
    War of Independence 198–200, 202, 261
Mayo, County 2, 10–11, 157, 239, 243–4, 248, 269
McCann case 64, 107
Meath, County 14
Methodists 97–8
Military Service Bill (1918) 154
Monaghan, County 60, 95, 277, 282
Monaghan footballers affair 289–90
Mountjoy Prison 146, 180, *186*, 186, 219
Morning Post 139, 199, 249, 298
Munster 11, 120, 158, 181, 183, 194, 197, 228–9, 235, 238, 266

National Army (Free State Army) 233,
    237–41, 243–5, 256, 269
    demobilisation 252–3
    mutiny 253, 270
National Council 7–8
National University of Ireland 18–19, 39
National Volunteer 113
National Volunteers 112–13, 115, 119, 162
Nationalism 1–2, 4, 6–8, 13, 22–3, 36–7,
    40, 43, 46, 55, 60, 68 *see also* Ulster
    Nationalism
    constitutional 4–5, 8–9, 49, 109, 115,
        118–20, 136, 141, 145, 149–51,
        153, 159, 169, 170, 191, 275, 277,
        302, 307, 311
    cultural 51–2
    divisions in 117
    economic 6
    and the Irish Convention 150–1
    militant 119–21, 148–50, 169
    and the Ulster crisis 90, 95, 97, 96, 107
Ne Temere decree 64, 107
North Fermanagh by-election 25
North Leitrim by-election (1908) 18
North Roscommon by-election (1917) 143,
    168–9
Northern Ireland 204, 212–13, 215, 272–301,
    302–9, 310–12
    border 282, 287, 289–90, 292–3, 297–9,
        305–8, 311–12 *see also* Boundary
        Commission; customs duties,
        cross-border
    composition: four counties 95, 107,
        299–300, 305; nine counties
        279–83, 300, 303; six counties
        82, 94–5, 137, 140, 149, 160, 215,
        272, 276–8, 280–3, 285, 297, 300,
        302–4
    industries 293 *see also* Belfast
Northern Ireland government 248–9, 252,
    284–99, 304–5
Northern Ireland parliament 200, 203, 272,
    279–85, 288, 291, 295, 299–300, 303,
    307–8
Northern Whig 64, 296

oath of allegiance (to the Crown) 111,
    218–19, 224–5, 226–7, 229, 234, 247,
    255, 263
Observer 221

obstructionism (parliamentary) 2
Offaly *see* King's County
old age pension 19, 42, 50, 249
Orange Order 1, 24, 54, 57, 70, 75, 273, 297
    see also Independent Orange Order

Pall Mall Gazette 43
Paris Peace Conference 158, 172, 179–80, 278
Parliament Bill/Act (1911) 59, 61, 68, 70–1,
    93, 98
partition 57, 77, 80, 85, 97, 100, 103, 105, 108,
    137–40, 152–3, 166, 169, 190, 204, 211,
    226, 248–9, 251, 255, 264, 272, 275–7,
    279, 295, 299–300, 302–4
    area 272, 276–7, 279–83, 311
    settlement (1925) 249, 270, 299, 310,
        312
passive resistance 11, 156
peace faction 202, 287
Peace with Ireland Council 199–200
People's Budget (1909) 42, 50
Plan of Campaign 3, 10
Poor Law Union 94
Presbyterian General Assembly 64–5
Presbyterians 24, 37, 53–4, 66, 97–8, 273
Proclamation (of the Republic) *see* Easter
    Rising
propaganda
    anti-Home Rule 31–2, 63–5, 73, 90,
        99, 107
    anti-IPP 5–7, 48
    anti-war 116
    IRA 182–3, 194
    IRB 123, 198
    republican 180, 242, 254, 258–9
    Sinn Féin 156, 174, 191, 194, 197, 259
    Unionist 32, 63–5, 73, 90, 99, 107, 141,
        274
proportional representation (PR) 191–2, 282
protectionism 6, 41
Protestant clergy 64–5, 97–8
Protestant churches 64–5, 297, 310
Protestants 24, 55, 60, 63–5, 71, 74, 81, 97,
    178, 252, 259, 261, 271, 272, 288–91,
    298–9, 305
provisional government (Dublin) 130, 180,
    223, 226–7, 230–1, 235–6, 240, 243,
    256, 266, 268–9
provisional government (Ulster), planned
    58–60, 77, 80, 85–8

325

Public Safety Bills/Acts
   1922: 241
   1923: 250

Queenstown, County Cork 127–8 *see also* Cobh

Railroad Protection and Maintenance Corps 243
Ranch War 14–15, 32, 48, 54
Reading Jail 142–3, 146
recession 250, 294
republican courts 192–3
republican police 193
Restoration of Order in Ireland Act (ROIA) (1920) 191
Roscommon, County 10, 14, 107
Rosscarbery, County Cork 196
Royal Irish Constabulary (RIC) 48, 99, 107, 126–7, 132, 156, 170, 285–7
   and the War of Independence 172–8, 181–5, 187, 189, 193, 196, 203, 254, 257–61
   boycott of 175, 178, 181, 183, 255
   disbandment 228
   intelligence 176–7
   in Northern Ireland 285
Royal Ulster Constabulary 290, 295
royal visits, to Ireland 5, 7, 48

St Enda's school 123, 129
St Stephen's Green 131
Saorstát Éireann *see* Irish Free State
Scotsman 185
Scottish National Covenant (1638) 72
sectarianism 26–7, 49, 54, 56, 65, 71, 93, 107, 228, 234, 260, 271, 277, 285–93, 296, 299, 306–7, 310
Selton Hill, County Leitrim *195*, 195
separatism 5, 8, 46, 51, 53, 109, 114, 116–20, 135–6, 142–4, 146–9, 157, 160, 161, 165, 168, 174, 178–81
Sinn Féin 8, 18, 46, 48–9, 114, 116–17, 133, 138, 142–50, 153–4, 157, 160, 161, 167–8, 170–1, 179–80, 190–1, 194, 216, 254, 258–60, 264, 277, 279, 305–6, 311
   see also propaganda; republican courts
   abstention policy 6, 142, 154, 160, 168, 190, 250, 271
   and the Anglo-Irish Treaty 221, 223–4, 226–8, 233, 263

Ard-Fheiseanna: (1917) 148, 169; (1922) 233; (1926) 250–1
   arrests 156
   banning of 156, 181
   clubs 144, 157
   and the conscription crisis 154–6
   constitution 148
   Executive 148
   and general elections: (1918) 158, 179–80; (1923) 250–1
   land-grabbing 157
   and local elections 192
Sinn Féin Volunteers 114–15
Sligo, County 107, 157, 239, 268
Sligo town 238
Soloheadbeg, County Tipperary 173–5, 254, 261
South Africa 112 *see also* Boer War
South Antrim by-election 25
South Armagh by-election (1918) 153–4, 169
South Longford by-election (1917) 144–5, 168–9
southern Unionism 24, 54, 60, 62–3, 74, 80, 96, 97, 100, 104–5, 138–41, 149–53, 222–3, 275, 277, 283
Special Powers Act *see* Civil Authorities (Special Powers) Act
spies *see* informers
Squad, the 177–8, 187, 261
Suspensory (Home Rule) Act (1914) 95, 111
Swinford revolt 12–13

tariff reform 6, 29, 31, 41–2, 59, 62–3, 96, 103
taxation *19*, 19–20, 32, 63, 150, 216, 249
tenant farmers 1–2, 7, 12, 14–15, 22–5, 37, 48, 115
Thurles, County Tipperary 175–6, 182
Times, The 65, 79, 185, 191, 194, 199–200, 212, 280
Tipperary, County 174, 190, 192, 239, 254, 269
Tipperary North by-election (1915) 116
Tipperary Star 176
Trades Union Congress 199–200
Tralee, County Kerry 128, 245
Transport Union 125
Trim, County Meath 184, 190
Trinity College Dublin 18
Troubles, the (1920–22) 285–92, 304, 306–7, 309

two nations argument 65, 70, 81, 97, 169, 274–5, 302
Tyrone, County 82, 94, 137–8, 165, 258, 277, 282, 298, 306
Tyrone County Council 296
    elections (1920) 295

Ulster 60, 67–8, 72, 78, 81, 98, 137, 287
Ulster Covenant 72–6, *73*, 95, 97, 99–100, 137, 274, 282
Ulster crisis (Home Rule crisis) 57–96, 97–108, 159, 274, 302
    context 58–65
Ulster Day 72–5, 98, 100
Ulster Declaration 74
Ulster Division (36th) *see* British Army
Ulster Farmers' and Labourers' Union and Compulsory Purchase Assocation 25
Ulster Liberal Association 65–6
Ulster Nationalism 78, 138, 167, 248, 306, 308
Ulster Protestant Association (UPA) 291, 293, 307
Ulster question 57, 99, 101, 204–5, 211, 221, 272
Ulster Special Constabulary (USC) 229, 287–9, 292–4, 306–7
    A Specials 287, 290
    B Specials 258, 287–8
    C Specials 287
Ulster Unionism *19*, 24–8, 30–2, 37, 40–1, *45*, 47, 49, 53, 55–6, 57, 61, 63, 67–8, 80, 97–101, 107, 119, 149–51, 151–3, 160, 162, 170, 215–16, 221–2, 272–4, 277–8, 280–5, 299–301, 302–5, 307, 310–12
Ulster Unionist Council (UUC) 27–8, 31–2, 41, 47, 53–4, 57, 66, 75, 77, 86, 137, 149, 273, 282, 286, 302, 304, 310–11
Ulster Unionist Party 28
Ulster Volunteer Force (UVF) 75–7, 80, 86–91, 94–5, 99–100, 105, 110–11, 162, 164, 274, 276, 286, 291, 307
unemployment 116–17, 161, 271, 293, 306
Union Defence League 31
Unionism 2, 4, 14, 17, 23–37, 40, 44, 46, 53–4, 57, 62, 95–6, 107, 192, 312 *see also* Irish Unionist Party; propaganda; southern Unionism; Ulster Unionism
Unionist Clubs 57–8, 98
Unionist Committee 152
United Irish League (UIL) 4, 10–16, 18, 22–3, 48–9, 51, 107, 115, 157

United States of America 41, 128, 136–8, 143, 149, 154, 180–1, 271 *see also* Irish-Americans
universities 18–19, 27, 39, 42, 54
University College Dublin 19
Upnor 244

Versailles, Treaty of 263

War of Independence 172–203, 253–4, 260–2, 278, 282, 285, 311
    escalation 194–9
    moves towards peace 200–3
    truce 171, 203, 254–5, 288, 306
War Office 88–9, 111, 113, 115, 117–18, 163
Waterford by-election (1918) 154
Waterford city 238
West Cork by-election (1916) 142
Westmeath, County 14, 107
Westminster 1–2, 5–6, 8–9, 11–12, 15–18, 20, 26–7, 31–3, 37, 39, 42–4, 46, 56, 57, 59, 77, 96, 102, 104, 108, 109, 118, 136–9, 145, 150, 154, 160, 166, 185, 200, 236, 251–2, 257, 259, 272, 277–81, 283–4, 288, 290–1, 295–7, 301, 303, 305, 307 *see also* House of Commons; House of Lords
Wicklow West by-election (1914) 116
Woodenbridge, County Wicklow (Redmond speech) 112–13, 118, 122, 141, 159, 161
Workers' Republic 117, 126
World War I 95, 109–15, 117, 126, 141, 154, 158–9, 161, 170–1, 276–7, 302
Wyndham Act *see* Land Acts: 1903